Business Information
A Systems Approach

Third Edition

Professor M. J. S. Harry

Senior Visiting Fellow
University of Bradford Management Centre

FINANCIAL TIMES
Prentice Hall

An imprint of Pearson Education

Harlow, England · London · New York · Reading, Massachusetts · San Francisco · Toronto · Don Mills, Ontario · Sydney
Tokyo · Singapore · Hong Kong · Seoul · Taipei · Cape Town · Madrid · Mexico City · Amsterdam · Munich · Paris · Milan

Pearson Education Limited

Edinburgh Gate
Harlow
Essex CM20 2JE
England

and Associated Companies around the world

Visit us on the World Wide Web at:
www.pearsoneduc.com

First edition published in Great Britain as *Information Systems in Business*
under the Pitman Publishing imprint in 1994
Second edition 1997
Third edition 2001

ISBN 0 273 64670 2

British Library Cataloguing-in-Publication Data
A catalogue record for this book can be obtained from the British Library.

Library of Congress Cataloging-in Publication Data
A catalog record for this book can be obtained from the Library of Congress.

10 9 8 7 6 5 4 3 2 1
06 05 04 03 02 01

Typeset by 30
Printed and bound in Malaysia

bs

Business Information
A Systems Approach

WITHDRAWN

We work with leading authors to develop the strongest educational materials in business and information technology, bringing cutting-edge thinking and best learning practice to a global market.

Under a range of well-known imprints, including Financial Times Prentice Hall, we craft high quality print and electronic publications which help readers to understand and apply their content, whether studying or at work.

To find out more about the complete range of our publishing please visit us on the World Wide Web at:
www.pearsoneduc.com

Contents

9 Implementing and maintaining information systems   320

Preface

'Go broke: own a horse.' So said a sticker in the back of a very expensive car I saw in the very expensive Mayfair district of London. It seemed like a pretty accurate comment, since most of us have to make do with a mass-produced car for transport, while the rich own and ride horses. Not always true? Well, I suppose not; but it makes a point. The 'modern' is not always the rich future, and the 'old' is not always the poor past. I suspect that there will be more redundant software engineering degrees in ten years' time than there will be farriers out of work.

I have a book on my bookshelf that covers the subject of 'strategy' as applied to information systems. It is by a perfectly respectable author from a well-known business school. The book is only six years old, yet it contains not a single reference to the Internet or the World Wide Web. So much for strategy in this rapidly changing world of information and communications technology, which some people see as a revolution equivalent to the one that replaced the horse with the car, the plane and the space rocket.

I'm not trying to be clever. I don't claim to have any special insight into what's going to happen to e-commerce, e-business or any of the rest of it; but I do know two things. First, we are going to be surprised. It will be the things that strategy can't anticipate that will be the most significant. Second, *labels* and other external appearances rapidly go out of fashion and are forgotten.

In such a situation, it is especially important that we focus on *concepts* and *frameworks* for an understanding that will outlive particular language, technology or applications. Thus 'computers' may disappear, but systems for gathering, processing, storing and communicating information will still be needed. Few people in ten years' time may know what a LAN was, but networks will still be operating. The way managers work in terms of where, when and how may be quite different, but they will still manage.

I think that the best tools with which we can equip ourselves to deal with such a world are ones that can be applied to new situations. We are at a time when boundaries are becoming conceptual rather than geographical, products are becoming weightless and intangible, reproduction is becoming virtually costless, and communities are flexible and global. That is why I believe that *systems concepts* are more relevant now than they were when this book was first published.

Now it's time to climb down off my high horse and get back into a car. Last week I met a very successful manager whose company is jogging along perfectly happily using its old COBOL software. So I've tried not to get too carried away. Mainline, traditional material is still to be found in Chapters 6, 8 and 9 for the horse-shoe farriers of the information world.

Also, I thought it would be fun to keep the spelling of connexion.

A *Tutor's Guide* is available free of charge to lecturers adopting this book and is also on the website *http://www.booksites.net/harry* (see p. xii).

Mike Harry
www.mikeharry.com

Hard:

When you can measure what you are speaking about, and express it in numbers, you know something about it. When you cannot measure it, when you cannot express it in numbers, your knowledge is of a meagre and unsatisfactory kind.

LORD KELVIN

Soft:

There's nothing I hate more than nothing;
Nothing keeps me up at night.
I toss and turn over nothing:
Nothing can cause a great big fight.

EDIE BRICKELL AND THE NEW BOHEMIANS

Uncertain:

All the business of war, and indeed all the business of life, is to endeavour to find out what you don't know from what you do; that's what I called 'guessing what was at the other side of the hill'.

ARTHUR WELLESLEY, DUKE OF WELLINGTON

A Companion Web Site accompanies
  Business Information

Visit the Companion Web Site at http://www.booksites.net/harry
to find valuable teaching and learning material.

● *Tutor's Guide*
● Link to the author's website
● Links to other relevant websites and institutions

CHAPTER 1

The approach and structure of this book

1.1 INTRODUCTION

I'll begin with a story that is untrue. The great scientist Isaac Newton was sitting under an apple tree. One of the apples fell off the tree and hit him on the head. As a result of this minor trauma, Newton is supposed to have wondered why apples fall downwards. The end result was his discovery of the laws of gravity.

The story may not be true, but the bit about the apples is. Every apple I've ever seen or heard about goes downwards, not upwards or horizontally, when it falls from a tree.

I find students to be different from apples. Student behaviour is not automatically predictable like apple behaviour. If I'm right in thinking that, then there can't be laws of learning and teaching like there are laws of gravity.

My experience as a trained teacher is more homely. I find that different students, at different times, in different subjects, with different teachers, benefit from different approaches. As a result, I've tried in this book to avoid the fiction of 'best practice' and instead have opted for various forms of 'it could be pretty good practice'.

Website support

It is my intention to support this book with a website, and I have acquired the web address *www.mikeharry.com*. I hope to be able to make overhead transparencies, lecture notes, case updates and other teaching and learning material available free to bona fide students and lecturers. My subsequent comments about the teaching and learning approach of this book should be seen in relation to this intention.

1.2 WHO THIS BOOK IS FOR

This is intended to be a teaching book and is designed for you, the reader, who wants to *learn* about information systems applied to the operation of businesses and organizations.

I have emphasized the two words teaching and learning because I think they will help to explain:

- the style I have used when writing this book;
- the detailed structure of the book in terms of the variety of components to be found in each chapter.

The way I have dealt with both of these features comes from what I have learned from my own experience of teaching and thinking about the subject of information, systems and business; working with learners. To understand this background, I need to explain that some of the features of this book are different because I am trying to overcome certain unfriendly and negative trends that I think have come into teaching, learning and the books used to support them.

I have tried to be positive, and to avoid two distortions that can interfere with the main messages of any book teaching systems thinking, with its emphasis on holism. The distortions I am trying to avoid can be explained in terms of two stereotypes, which you may already have come across as a learner.

The first distortion focuses on the teaching process. I will call this the *hard stereotype*. Teachers, lecture rooms, teaching materials and assessment all cost money. Any institution that aims to make the teaching process more economic can apply the Henry Ford principle of economies of scale and mass production. Thus large-scale lecture theatres maximize student-to-staff ratios. Standard syllabi and fixed lecture schemes deskill teaching and maximize staff interchangeability. Standard presentation materials and student handouts cut library and materials costs. Mechanical assessment procedures like multiple-choice questions streamline examinations and testing. I suppose I could parody this approach by saying, 'So just be quiet and listen to what you are told: it may be coming up in the exam.'

Many of my readers have probably experienced that kind of teaching. It used to be mainly found in subject areas such as quantitative methods for business or statistics. These days I find that anything from marketing to HRM is sometimes taught this way. Successful students learn to regurgitate: they have been successfully taught, but have learned very little.

The second distortion represents a reaction to this heavy prescriptive emphasis. I will call this the *soft stereotype*. The impersonal large lecture is replaced by small seminar discussion groups. Students are encouraged set their own agenda to the point that the teacher will sit and say nothing until somebody is so agonized by the silence that they feel obliged to blurt out some platitude. The reading material for such a course is very 'open', which means nothing is given and everything is possible. The assessment is likely to take a very unstructured format like an embarrassing role play, keeping a diary or some kind of project, preferably of a personal nature.

I expect that this kind of learning is also familiar to many of my readers. It can result in the development of a very high level of learning in terms of self-analysis, group political skills and guessing what the lecturer really wants you to say. It can also be very attractive to institutions that wish to pass off lack of management and poor teaching in the guise of 'student-centred learning'. Under this regime, students learn a lot about themselves and their teachers, but are taught very little about anything else.

At their best, however, both structured teaching and open learning are not like these stereotypes and can form vital ingredients of the teaching–learning partnership. There are times when students have the right to recieve direction from a teacher and clear answers to questions. But having had that direction and having been given those answers, students who have really learned something will be able to go on and use what they have learned by setting their own objectives and developing their own methods. They recognize that using something can often result in what is used being modified, added to, and eventually replaced.

Both the writing style and the structure of this book are based on the assumption that it is for those who want to be taught and to learn. If I am trying to teach the subject of business information with a systems approach, then I need to present facts and answer questions in a structured framework while avoiding the rigidity of the hard stereotype. If you want to learn, I have to open up discussion of issues and show potential diversity while avoiding the universal 'definite maybe' of the soft stereotype.

Since this is a teaching–learning book, the writing style will be different from books that aim to be catalogues of facts or academic dissertations. As you have seen already, I often use the style of 'I think', 'you may find' or 'we discussed', rather than 'in the author's opinion', 'it may be found' or 'as was discussed'. This is because my aim is to develop a teaching–learning partnership rather than record for posterity what I think I know about the subject. For the same reason, I frequently use personal examples or illustrations with a strong human element rather than impersonal catalogues of events.

The intimacy of the style does not, however, mean that this is an elementary book. Systems thinking has a strong conceptual foundation. Therefore although the way this book is written tries to avoid unnecessary difficulties, what it covers in terms of subject matter can often be quite advanced. You shouldn't be surprised if some parts look quite difficult the first time around. I have found that there is no substitute for *time* and *thought* for understanding *concepts*.

A final point before we finish this section. Out of the 800 or so words I have written so far, several have been put into *italics*. My purpose when doing this is not just to emphasize the flow of words as we would use them when speaking, but to identify concepts or themes that will be taken up and discussed further in the book. So even the emphasis on simple words like *what* and *how* above is already leading us into some important systems concepts which will be taken up later.

1.3 WHAT SUBJECTS ARE COVERED

Old names and new meanings

When we get into a train we go into a 'carriage'. The reason it is called a carriage is because people up to the early nineteenth century used to travel in carriages pulled by horses. After Richard Trevithick invented the steam engine and railways were created, the engine was regarded as an 'iron horse' and the things it pulled were sufficiently similar to the old way of transporting people to be called 'carriages'.

Using old names to describe new things in this way can help us relate the new to the old. It also has the disadvantage that the new way can be limited by the old ideas. Unlike a horse, an 'iron horse' in the form of a modern electric locomotive can run equally well backwards and forwards. If we had kept thinking about the horse concept, we would never have progressed to the idea of having power units at both ends of trains that could both push and pull, running forwards or backwards.

Information and communications technology-based information systems went through a similar change in the last years of the twentieth century to the one transport systems went through in the middle years of the nineteenth. Old words are still being used to describe new ways of doing things in order to help people make the adjustment to the changes. Besides being helpful, however, these ways of describing things can prevent us realizing the important changes that are taking place and their practical implications.

To understand what subjects are covered in this book, we need first to understand how the words *information*, *systems* and *business* of the title are commonly used. We can then give some indication of how the whole book will develop and build on these uses.

Information and information systems

The term 'information system' is commonly taken to imply an information technology system that gathers data and produces the information the user requires. In this context, the term information is used to describe what the system either records via a keyboard, processes using software, sends over the Internet, prints out on paper, shows on a screen, or stores on a computer disk. We are not going deliberately to redefine 'information' and 'information system' in this book in some new, smart fashion that throws away this view and, with it, the learning and experience of the past. Much of what has developed with the big advances in information and communications technology can be built on rather than thrown away.

What we will see, however, is that the more common uses of information and information system are particular examples of how these concepts have been applied. What they could be is something much wider, and something with much wider practical implications.

Business

Similarly, the use of the word business, particularly following world political developments at the end of the 1980s, is narrower than the concept it originally implied. The frequent use of the word to imply operations principally concerned with money and motivated by profit represents a reduction of its meaning. In this book, the words business and organization will be often put together to show a resistance to this process. The word business in the title of this book is intended to mean the wider senses of 'task', 'duty', 'serious work' or 'what we are about', which can still be found in a good dictionary. When we talk of *business* information, we recognize that commercial business is just one particular example of the wider subject of purposeful activity. A modern innovation like electronic commerce covers much more than just selling on the Internet, as we shall see in Chapter 3.

Subject areas for information, systems and business

If we look at the large number of existing books whose titles contain the words information, system and business, we find three common types of emphasis or subject area:

1 Books considering businesses or organizations as systems, like Beer (1985) or the excellent Schoderbeck *et al.* (1990), but not studying information systems in particular detail. These use the principles of systems thinking, which have been applied across a whole range of subjects, to take a systems view of businesses and their management. This represents a change from older views, where a business is thought of primarily in terms of departments and organization charts, and management is thought of as the name of a class of employees and what they do. A *systems approach* looks behind the names and labels for how things are done to see what is going on in a business.

2 Books covering the subject of information systems applied to management and business, such as Laudon and Laudon (2000). These interpret the terms information and information system in the mainly information and communications technology-

based sense discussed above, and do a thorough job relating such a view of an information system to a mainly conventional, organizational view of management. What they do not do to any great extent is to see businesses or organizations as systems.

3 Books focusing on the analysis, design and development of either the broad range of management systems, like Wilson (1990), or information systems in particular, like Hoffer *et al.* (1998). Such books have a strong emphasis on methodology.

In this book we shall be covering all three of these subject areas, but not by merely joining them together. I shall use a systems view from the first subject area above to establish the concept of a business as a system and the role of management as a component of that system. The second subject area is then covered by placing information and the information system as integral components of the management system, so they are viewed in business and management terms. The third area of systems development methodology then studies systems development methods in terms of how they serve the needs of a business as a system, rather than as a predefined set of techniques. The overall unity of the three subject areas therefore comes from the key concept of a system, and in Chapter 3 I shall develop a particular systems model for applying the concept.

1.4   HOW THE CONTENTS ARE ORGANIZED

The organization of the chapters

The organization of the chapters in this book is intended to reflect the view of its subject content laid out in Section 1.3. The structure of the individual chapters is intended to work with the view of teaching/learning argued in Section 1.2.

Let us begin with the effect of the subject of the book on the organization of the chapters. This book aims to present and develop the subject of information systems in a *local* and *global* business context, using a systems view to bring the subject components of management in businesses, information systems, communication and networks together with systems analysis, design and development.

Any attempt to develop a subject in this way is unlikely to succeed unless we have some understanding of the key words that describe it. For us these words are *information*, *system* and *business*. Presenting and developing the subject of information systems in business will therefore require an explanation and understanding of the concepts of information and system, followed by study of their application to business. The chapters of this book are therefore grouped to reflect the sequence of *concepts* (Chapters 2 to 6), followed by applications (Chapters 7 to 9).

We also saw in Section 1.3 that concepts associated with a particular technology can take on new applied forms as that technology is developed. When this happens, there is a danger that the new development becomes restricted by the older thinking. Since information is closely bound up with recent developments in information and communications technology, we need to ensure that our understanding of this key concept does not become confined to a particular technological view. Chapter 2 is therefore designed to open up the concepts related to information, to show some of the variety of forms it can take, and to prepare for the detailed treatment in Chapters 3 to 6.

Concepts

The sequence of Chapters 3 to 6 then follows our aim of placing information systems in a business context using a systems approach. In Chapter 3 we establish the fundamentals of systems thinking and use these to build a systems view of businesses and their management. The role of information as a component of management is developed using the concept of *control* in Chapter 4.

Once we understand the role of information systems in management, we are ready to say more about the nature of the product it delivers to management: namely information itself. Hence Chapter 5 covers the important concepts relating to information. In these days of networked organizations and a networked globe, communication adds an important dimension to information.

In Chapter 5 the coverage of the key concepts of information will have explained the role of data as the building blocks we use to construct information. To understand the concepts behind the application of this principle to data processing, databases and database management, Chapter 6 therefore covers the data concepts relevant to these applications.

Our view of the subject of information systems in business not only leads to a sequence of concepts followed by applications, it is also reflected in the sequence of individual chapters. We set the systems context for business and information systems first in Chapters 3 and 4, before looking in detail at information and communication in Chapter 5. Similarly, we wait until we have some understanding of information as a whole before looking at the concepts behind the detailed data from which it is constructed. As we shall see in Chapter 3, this view – which seeks to understand individual components in relation to their role in a greater whole – is an important aspect of systems thinking.

Applications

The same systems principle governs the sequence of the two applications chapters. We look first in Chapter 7 at what information systems have to do when applied to businesses. Once we know what they must do, we are in a position to consider what methods we might use for their development and implementation. Hence Chapters 8 and 9 look at systems development methodology.

The structure of the individual chapters

The organization of the chapters is based on the sequence of concepts before applications, and setting the whole picture before looking at the details. Such an approach, as we shall see in Chapter 3, can be described as top down. For understanding and learning about a subject, however, there is also a need for a bottom-up approach. When using this, we start with a particular example as a first step towards understanding wider principles.

The structure of the chapters recognizes the need for both approaches. We will now see the roles they are intended to play in the teaching/learning process.

The lead-in case

The purpose of the lead-in case is to introduce the subject of the chapter in a way that shows some of the issues and questions that have to be sorted out for us to learn about the subject.

Some of the cases deal with large-scale events concerning companies or even whole nations. Others are quite intimate and personal. Some are about things that actually happened, while others are fictitious but true to life in that they are based on my own experience. What all the cases have in common is that they illustrate situations that actually happen, so the first section of every case is entitled 'What happened'.

The style of the cases may seem less formal than those you are used to. This is deliberate, and reflects what they are trying to achieve. The essential point is to be able to read through a case and take in a feel for the atmosphere and the issues. The cases are not designed to be sources of detailed facts or technical points. Material of that type is found in the cases in the appendices, which I will deal with below.

While it may be very relaxing and easy just to read through a case and 'take in a feel for the atmosphere', if the all the cases stopped at this point we would be left in a soft stereotype position of wondering what we were trying to achieve. Each case therefore includes a section that looks back at what happened and gives a viewpoint, comment or interpretation of the events. Once we have got past Chapter 3 and have begun to build some basic systems concepts, this second section of the case will take up what was covered in previous chapters as a basis for comment. Thus, for example, the case in Chapter 6 is interpreted from an information systems viewpoint and takes up aspects of systems thinking and information systems covered in Chapters 3 to 5.

Once you have read a case and seen some comment on it, I think you will be ready to move from a broad, unstructured consideration of the case to a clear statement of the issues. Each case finishes with a section entitled 'The issues', which spells out in a more formal, serious way what the case was designed to introduce.

The issues raised, learning opportunities and objectives

The result of the lead-in case should be that you are beginning to understand what sorts of questions need to be answered by the main subject content of the chapter. The 'learning objectives' spell out the subject material that must be understood if we are to answer these questions. I have frequently prefaced objectives with the phrase 'to understand', because I believe that this is the real test of learning. Understanding implies that we not only know a fact or know how to do something, we also know how one fact fits in with another or when it makes sense to use a skill that we have acquired.

I know that there is a currently fashionable school of thought that understanding cannot be directly observed and therefore cannot be an objective. Such a view confuses whats and hows. The objectives of this book spell out what you should hope to learn from the chapters. How you show that you have acquired this understanding will be through everything from successfully answering review questions to producing a successful dissertation.

The subject content

This is the main part of every chapter, which aims to deliver the subject material set up by the learning objectives. I have already explained why the writing style is the way it is and the significance of the use of italics. In addition, four other features need to be explained:

1 The text is interspersed with RQs or review questions. Their aim is to encourage you to pause after some important point has been made in the script and check to see if you have understood what has been said. You may feel that this interrupts your flow of reading; if so, ignore them and come back later. I've assumed from my own

experience that pausing to check is a good idea because it prevents me from kidding myself that I've understood something. Consequently, the narrative following an RQ sometimes builds on the answers to it, which are found at the end of the chapter.

2 Examples of principles in the text may refer to any of the lead-in cases you have studied so far, or to the ones in the appendices. If, like me, you are someone who does not read a book starting at page one and going through it a page at a time, you will need to check the names of the various cases so that you know what is being referred to.

3 The text contains many diagrams. In Chapter 3 we shall learn about systems diagrams, but the diagrams in this book cover other kinds of diagrams too. The diagrams include some explanation of what they show, but they are just one part of the whole presentation of the book, so do consider them in relation to what is said about them in the text.

4 The subject content of the text is divided into sections and subsections, which are numbered in relation to the chapter in which they occur. Thus the subject content of Chapter 3 is divided into sections 3.1, 3.2, ... , etc.; and a section like 3.1 is divided into 3.1.1, 3.1.2, ... , etc. To avoid complexity, I call all sections and subsections 'sections' for short.

Boxes

Chapters 2 to 9 contain various *boxes*. These are mainly extracts from very recent articles in the *Financial Times*. My decision to include these comes from my experience of teaching concepts. Just as nourishment from food takes physical digestion and time, so concepts require a mental digestion period. Most students find the process much easier, however, if they can relate concepts to actual examples and experience. In the text I often use quite simple ideas to relate things to personal experience. This approach is user friendly, but there is a danger that the link with the hard world of business will be missed if not enough factual material is included. So in this edition I have included the boxes to reinforce the message that concepts do relate to the real world.

Key words

Every subject has its own specialist vocabulary. The purpose of the key words section at the end of each chapter is designed to give you an opportunity to test that you have acquired the vocabulary you need to feel easy with its subject matter. Key words also act as a list of the important facts or concepts you should have learned.

Seminar agendas, exam topics and project/dissertation subjects

This section is intended to indicate how you can develop your learning in two different ways:

1 By suggesting how an issue or subject area that has come up in the text can be pursued in more depth.
2 By suggesting new 'by-product' or 'spin-off' subjects that are not part of the main chapter subject but could be developed from it.

Since this section is intended to open up further thinking rather than consolidate what has been covered, the suggestions are often very broad. Remember, however, that making the aims of a dissertation too broad is a common student fault. I remember when I was a young lecturer about to supervise my first dissertation, I asked my head of department for advice on how to start. He said, 'You make an appointment for the student to come and see you. When he comes in the door, and before he can say anything, you tell him it's too broad.' My subsequent experience suggests that this is not as absurd as it sounds.

If you are thinking of a dissertation topic, it might be worth having an open seminar on suggestions with a tutor, your peer group or a business contact at an early stage, but be prepared to narrow down to a specific issue or application from the general area considered.

References, bibliography and the Web

Books can be included in references and bibliographies for a range of very different reasons:

- as an authority or original book on the subject referred to
- as the source of a quotation
- as an illustration or example of some particular style or school of thought
- as further or alternative reading on something already well covered in the text
- as a reference book
- as a book to avoid
- to show that that the person compiling the bibliography (or their assistant) has done their homework

and so on.

It is therefore important to check why a book is in the bibliography and not assume that this constitutes either a reading list, a list of endorsements or a recommendation to buy. When a book is referred to in the text, I normally explain why this is, and I often make comments on its style and difficulty. Many of the books I recommend are ones I own myself. I have avoided indiscriminate listing of large numbers of books on the same subject, but I do refer to some very different types of book where I want to show the potential range of a subject.

However, in this era of the Web, I think that the days of the old academic bibliography are numbered. A simple search on, say, 'soft systems methodology' will bring much more up-to-date information than a stuffy bibliography. So if my bibliographies look mainly like *historical* sources, that is what I suspect future bibliographies will become.

Appendices

The lead-in cases are mainly designed to be readable introductions to the issues and subject matter of the individual chapters. It is also useful to have cases that can be referred to for examples and issues on the whole subject range. I have therefore included some additional short cases in the appendices for this purpose. Besides making these cases suitable for illustrating a range of subject content, I have also deliberately chosen very different kinds of organization in an attempt to mainatin a wide view of the term *business*.

In addition to the extra cases, I have used appendices for factual material that would block the flow of the main text.

The appendices are also designed to provide you with additional material for discussion and comparison throughout the book. You may find them useful seminar material for just about all the subjects that arise.

For all these reasons, it is worth reading the appendices at an early stage in your studies so that you become familiar with them.

Teaching/learning suggestions

In the previous section we explained the teaching/learning material that is to be found in all the main chapters of this book. Besides this specific material, there are a number of general suggestions that you may apply throughout your reading:

1 Before reading the issues section of the lead-in cases, you could try to identify what you think the issues are. If you find that an issue you thought was present has not been picked up by me, it would be worth seeing if it is covered in the main body of the chapter. If it isn't, perhaps you've discovered a useful seminar agenda or dissertation topic.

2 When discussing the learning objectives, I made the point that you as an individual learner are being guided on what you should understand. Those who test you will be concerned with how this understanding can be shown. If you are studying for a specific course with a syllabus or some other official course documentation, it will be worth checking whether it has 'learning outcomes' or a similar statement of assessment policy. It is also worth investigating whether past assessments such as exams or test papers take any notice of these, since lecturers and teachers don't always follow the official line.

3 The RQs in the subject content usually refer to one particular lead-in case or a case in the appendices. Relating the RQs to other cases in the book or to your own experience can be equally useful. Don't be too quick to downgrade your own experience if you are not in conventional employment. If you are involved in the business of working at home, looking for a job or bringing up children these are all potential sources of experience to which you can relate. As a student at a college or university, you are involved in the business of producing educated and qualified people. One of the main themes of this book, which distinguishes the whats and the hows, should continue to open up the idea that 'the word business in the title of this book is intended to mean the wider senses of "task", "duty", "serious work", or "what we are about".'

4 The key words provide an agenda for testing and revision. The real test of whether you understand something is to explain it to someone else. Get an intelligent critical person to ask you to explain to them what the key words mean. If they understand your explanation, the chances are that you understand the word yourself.

References/bibliography

Beer, S. (1985). *Diagnosing the System*. Wiley, Chichester.

Harry, M.J.S. (1990). *Information and Management Systems*. Pitman Publishing, London.

Hoffer, J.A., George, J.F. and Valacich, J.S. (1998). *Modern Systems Analysis and Design*. Addison-Wesley, Reading, MA.

Laudon, K.C. and Laudon, J.P. (2000). *Management Information Systems*. Prentice-Hall, Upper Saddle River, NJ.

Schoderbeck, P.P., Schoderbeck, C.G. and Kefalas, A.G. (1990). *Management Systems*. Business Publications, Homewood, IL.

Wilson, B. (1990). *Systems Concepts, Methodologies and Applications*. Wiley, New York.

CHAPTER 2

Information and management

'Something so stupid, it could only be thought up by a really intelligent person': the sad story of the Child Support Agency

What happened

When Mrs Margaret Thatcher was Prime Minister of the UK, her traditional moral beliefs had led her to state that 'there was no such thing as society' and that 'individuals should be assumed to be responsible for their actions'. In the late 1980s, she became alarmed to find that not only was there an increasingly high level of marriage breakdown in the UK, but also that in 80 per cent of cases, mothers with children got no financial support from the absent father.

Mrs Thatcher's assertive style soon addressed the problem. It was time for absent fathers to be responsible for their actions and for a large cost burden to be lifted from society. A selection of government ministers and their supporting Civil Service departments were given the task of producing a system that would ensure that absent fathers took financial responsibility for the children that they had helped to produce. If anyone had the feeling that this might be difficult, one of those involved pointed out that the word 'impossible' was 'not part of Mrs Thatcher's vocabulary'.

Under the UK system, the various tasks of government are divided among ministries and departments. Examples of this division are finance, foreign policy, transport, health etc. Each ministry or department is led by an elected politician, supported by a branch of the Civil Service, the name given to the UK's administrative bureaucracy. The leading Civil Servant of each branch usually has the title of Permanent Secretary.

The two main candidates for the unattractive job of producing the system required by Mrs Thatcher were the Treasury, with its experience of finance and collecting taxes from reluctant payers; and the Department of Social Security, with its experience of financially supporting the poor and underprivileged with government payments.

In the subsequent internal Civil Service battle, the argument was not so much about who should take responsibility for the new system, but rather, who should not. No one wanted to take on what looked like a very unattractive task. Considered in that way, the Department of Social Security was the loser, because it got the job of implementing the system that Margaret Thatcher wanted.

Those concerned with setting up the new system realized that at least they might not have to start from nothing. In the USA, the State of Wisconsin already had a Support Collections Trust Fund that identified absent fathers and was empowered to ensure that money was taken directly out of their pay and given to the mother of their children. The UK minister and some of his Civil Service staff went to study the American organization and decided to implement something similar in the UK, which was called the Child Support Agency or CSA.

However, those concerned with the system in the USA issued a warning to their British visitors: it was important that the system should be a means of directly *supporting* the mother and child of the absent father, *not* a means of saving government money.

Once back in the UK, the politics began and the American warning was ignored. The Treasury, pursuing its legitimate function as the protector of public money, pressed for changes to the American system. Instead of all the money collected from the absent father going to the mother and child as an additional aid, it would be used to help compensate the government for the social security pay-outs it made. An important result of this decision was that a mother's financial motivation to give the CSA information about absent fathers was greatly reduced.

The zeal of the Treasury went further. Instead of this system being introduced for new cases of marriage breakdown, previous financial arrangements between separated couples were to be reassessed. Thus, even couples who had agreed financial arrangement for their children before separation were to have them assessed again. Fathers who had made amicable financial agreements were therefore often pursued for still more money, while irresponsible fathers who had disappeared without payment were often able to remain untraced.

As to the system of assessment itself, there was the design problem of how you assess what an absent father ought to or could pay. One solution might be to choose a simple formula, like an extra percentage on his tax rate. Another solution might be to assess every father's individual financial position in detail.

The more complex, second of these alternatives was chosen. The assessment form consisted of over 100 pages. Perhaps not surprisingly, both those who filled in the forms and those who interpreted them had problems. As far as the CSA was concerned, this complex assessment procedure had to be implemented by newly recruited staff. They had to use an information technology system for which the bought-in software had originally been designed for Florida, but was then given in-house modifications.

Margaret Thatcher was not a person to tolerate slipping deadlines, so the CSA started in April 1993, even though not all of its procedures and systems were fully in order. The Chief Executive of the CSA, Ros Hepplewhite, seemed to fit her job exactly. She had experience of children's charity work and was herself the child of a mother who had been deserted by a father who paid little financial support. In a video promotion aimed at the staff of the CSA, she described the Agency as 'a service for up to 2 million people'. She frankly admitted many of the difficulties that the CSA faced, but was enthusiastic to employ teamwork, face the challenge and make the Agency work.

Despite the planning, effort and commitment, it took less than a year for the CSA to be the subject of angry demonstrations and severe controversy. There was even a suicide, in which the dead man left a note blaming his ills on the pressure he felt that he had experienced from the CSA. Despite her enthusiasm, Ros Hepplewhite did not remain in the job for very long: she was replaced as Chief Executive by a career civil servant. By early January 2000, a Labour Secretary of State was promising reform of the CSA since it was '90 per cent processing information and only 10 per cent ensuring payment'.

As to the CSA itself, one critical observer remarked that it was 'something so stupid, it could only be thought up by a really intelligent person'. We shall now consider whether such a criticism is appropriate.

The issues raised

Management issues

It is very easy to see that much went terribly wrong with the CSA. It is also very easy to ignore the simple fact that the overall approach to setting it up was *rational, conventional management*. Consider what happened:

1 Margaret Thatcher, as the Prime (=first) Minister, determined a strategy that was to be applied in the area of Social Security.
2 The Head of Social Security, Permanent Secretary Sir Michael Partridge, was given the job of administrating the conversion of that strategy into an operational plan for the CSA.
3 As Chief Executive of the CSA, Ros Hepplewhite had the task of implementing and managing the operations of the CSA in line with its plan.
4 The employees of the CSA sat at computers and at the end of telephones and carried out its operations.

This so-called top-down view of management is one you will find in most main-line textbooks. Thus Hannagan (1998) states, 'While the strategic plan sets the expected, proposed and desired direction and the objectives to be achieved, this has to be translated into activity which can be implemented and controlled.' Then going down the so-called management hierarchy, we find that 'Operational managers have to develop plans at the appropriate level in order to produce the actions required on a day-to-day basis to implement the strategic plan.'

If we ask what we should learn from what happened, it seems hard to criticize the management principles that were followed. They closely resemble those in the textbooks. The highest executive is concerned with strategy, and the lowest operator is concerned with carrying out day-to-day tasks. Anything that went wrong seems to have come from individual mistakes or unforeseen events, rather than the conventional management structure and process. Perhaps if the new system had been phased in more slowly, or the operators given more training, or the payment assessment rules been more simple, things might have been different. We need to consider if the alternatives were as simple as that, or whether the rational, conventional, top-down view of management itself is flawed.

Information systems issues

It wasn't just the management structure and processes that played their part in the story. What about the development of the information system? Was there anything unusual about the way this was done? Look into the history of information systems development, and you will find that it is littered with examples of delays, overspends and failures (we shall refer to several of these in this book); but was the CSA all that different? If we look at its approach to information systems development, the main stages seemed to have been:

1 Looking at what part the information system would play in the planned operations of the CSA in terms of meeting the requirements of gathering, processing and outputting information.
2 Considering what kind of system, particularly in terms of its software capabilities, could meet these needs.
3 Deciding which aspects of the system to import and which to develop in-house.
4 Producing a schedule for systems development and implementation.

Hardly high-powered intellectual stuff, but it looks like a respectable version of a sensible approach that many main-line textbooks continue to advocate. (Note that this is the second time I've used the phrase 'main-line'.) Thus Turban *et al.* (1999) see the main stages of what they call 'IT Planning' as:

1 Strategic IT planning.
2 Information requirements analysis.
3 Resource allocation.
4 Project planning.

Strategic IT planning is concerned with relating the IT plan to the overall organizational plan. In the CSA case, once its developers decided the plan for creating the CSA, they fitted the plan for creating the information system inside it. They didn't jump into an IT system before they'd gone to the US and planned the CSA itself.

Information requirements analysis aims to identify broad, organizational information requirements and to consider the kind of hardware and software systems that could provide such information. The CSA spent some time looking at existing systems and software, as well as considering the *resource allocation* that had to produce plans for developing the hardware, software and data communications needed to meet the requirements analysis. Thus it decided on the allocation of facilities, personnel and finances. A notable example of this was the decision to use new staff rather than trained existing ones.

Project planning involves the production schedules and resource requirements for the detailed components of the IT plan. An important instance of this with the CSA was in the planning and resourcing of the software development. Is this where the Civil Service got it wrong, in terms of its management approach? Returning to our authoritative Turban *et al.* (1999) reference, its review of approaches to systems software development states that this can be some combination of:

1 *In-house* development by the organization itself.
2 *Outsourced* development by an outside specialist.
3 *Purchased* systems software from a supplier.

How should manages decide what combination of these is appropriate to their situation? Further reading reveals that:

- *Outsourcing* may be best for large and complex systems where the risk of failure can be high: a 'leave it to the experts' philosophy.
- *In-house* development may be preferable if the organizational needs are very individual or security is involved: a 'we know best what we want and we want to keep it in the family' approach.

If we return to the CSA, I believe our case shows that many of the civil servants involved in setting up the information system for the CSA were aware of these considerations and took account of them. They could not have read our reference, which was published in 1999, but the considerations are much older than that text. The principle of balancing the advantages of producing a product yourself, against obtaining it from outside specialists, was understood long before we had computers. It is called the 'make or buy' decision, and managers in the CSA team would have been aware of it. The considerations behind a make or buy decision are these:

- *Making* a product yourself meant that you had better control of what you actually wanted, rather than what your supplier believed or decided you did.
- *Buying* a product from a supplier meant that you could benefit from the experience of a specialist, rather than reinventing the wheel.

Those responsible for the development and implementation of the information system for the CSA recognized that software already existed to do a similar job to the one they wanted. Where the properties of that software were appropriate, they adopted them; where the properties was not appropriate, they modified them in-house. There may have been mistakes, but we cannot say the management were unaware of the major principles behind what was done, or that there was no attempt to apply them.

Opportunities for learning

I know several people who didn't like Margaret Thatcher and her Conservative government. I suspect I know even more who don't like politicians and are critical of civil servants. My researching in the media and on the Web also tells me that there are still many people who feel very aggressive about the CSA. But can the sad story of the CSA be *exclusively* explained by assuming that people were lazy, incompetent or vindictive? I don't think so.

Human beings have often been lazy, incompetent or vindictive, but that hasn't stopped them from doing many good and clever things as well. I would like to suggest that much of what went wrong with the CSA wasn't unique to that organization. I would suggest further that similar mistakes have been made, and continue to be made, in many other organizations that may seem very different from the CSA. Wherever they occur, I think that these mistakes come from three false assumptions:

1 False assumptions about the nature of organizations and what management does in them.
2 False assumptions that what managers can hope to do only depends on how hard-working, clever or well-motivated they are.
3 False assumptions about what information is, or is not, and about the role of information systems in management.

I believe that these false assumptions are the basis for many of the unsuccessful management methods we find mixed in with otherwise sensible approaches to management thinking about information, management and business.

In this book we shall look at an alternative *systems* approach which does not make such assumptions.

We are now ready to form some broad aims as a starting point for our study.

Strategic learning aims for this book

The learning aims for this book are to establish:

1 What management can actually hope to do and achieve in our age of globalized information, and what it cannot ever hope to do.

2 What information systems can do to support management.

3 A cohesive framework of information concepts and methods that are relevant to implementing information systems.

4 Co-ordination of all these aims through the use of systems (i.e. *systemic*) thinking.

Learning objectives

The learning objectives for this chapter are to answer the questions:

1 What is *management*: what does it do and what does it not do?

2 What is *information*: what roles does it play in management?

2.1 WHAT IS MANAGEMENT?

2.1.1 Definitions

The word *management* is used in different ways. Two common ones are:

1 A general name for the people who do the managing, as in such phrases as 'I complained to the management'.

2 A description of what the people who do the managing do, as in such phrases as 'the management of the marketing operation'.

In this section we will use *management* to mean what the people who do the managing do; and *the management* or *managers* as a name for anyone who does the managing.

2.1.2 Management structures

You don't have to look far in many books on management before you come across a diagram like Figure 2.1. It tells you that both management and managers can be classified in terms of labels telling us what they do. Thus, a financial manager manages finance and a production manager manages production.

This kind of classification we shall call a *horizontal* division of management, because what the various managers do is at the same level of authority within the organization, but within different sections of the whole management process. Thus the finance director of a company is just as much a director as a marketing director. They are both at the same *level*, called 'director', within their company, but they do different things.

Just as common within many books on management is Figure 2.2. It tells you that both management and managers can be classified in terms of their different *levels*. There is a strong suggestion in diagrams like this that the higher the level a manager is, the more important and powerful they are. 'High-level' managers have more

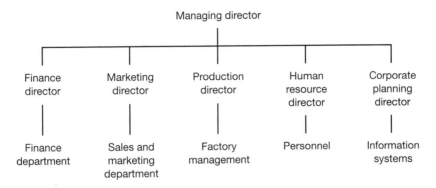

Figure 2.1 Divisions of management by horizontal function
Managers labelled in terms of their departmental membership.

expensive company cars, need to be more far-sighted in their decision making and have much more effect on the organization than those at 'lower' levels.

This kind of classification we shall call a *vertical* division of management, because what the managers do is supposed to relate directly to their level of authority within the organization. Thus directors are higher than managers, managers are higher than supervisors, and operators seem to have to do what they are told.

We shall now look at these two ways of dividing up management and see why they are not a sufficient way of answering the question 'What is management?'

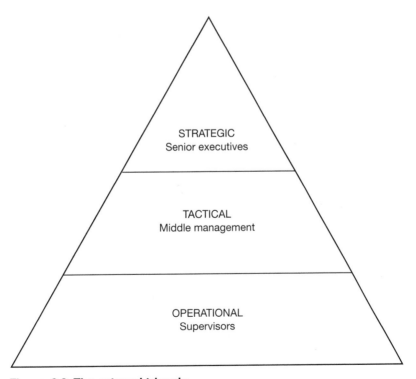

Figure 2.2 The external triangle
The author's academic enemy no. 1. It falsely implies that each 'level' of management is exclusively involved with its own 'level' of information. In real life things are much more complex.

Horizontal division of management

Figure 2.1 shows management divided into five functions. It happens to follow the names and numbers of divisions to be found in one of our previous references, Hannagan (1998). If we looked in some other respectable textbook we could find other names and numbers of divisions. The fact that we find a variety of ways of dividing up management is not the issue I would like to explore. It isn't surprising that if different organizations operate in different ways, their organization charts should also look different. Instead, I would like to look at the idea of division itself, whatever particular form it happens to take.

First, consider a small two-person business like MX Marketing in Appendix 3. Who is the finance director or the corporate planning director? Is it Ben or his wife Anne? In a business with only two people, it is impossible to fill five directorship positions in any formal way unless someone does more than one job. What happens in small organizations like this is that people fulfil a range of functions. When it comes to finance, for example, Ben and his wife both sign company cheques and work together on the annual accounts.

So is horizontal division of management only a reality in large organizations with organization charts like Figure 2.1? I would say that it isn't even real there. Consider the finance director of a large company like Carry-Out Cupboards. Do they just concern themselves with managing finance? Can you imagine a successful finance director who was so completely devoid of human relations skills that they couldn't get the co-operation of their finance team, so ignorant of the company's products that they couldn't understand how the budget was being allocated, and so unaware of the market that they didn't understand what made a good sales target? Or how about a marketing director who couldn't keep to their budget because they were totally innumerate? Perhaps there are such people, but I don't think we would call them successful managers.

The reality is that *all* managers *legitimately* use a much wider horizontal range of skills, and fulfil a much wider horizontal range of management functions, than is shown on the organization chart. One way that textbooks try to show this is by recognizing that there will be also networks of people on what is called a functional basis. Thus members of marketing and finance at Carry-Out Cupboards might form a committee to assess the costs of a new advertising campaign. In practice, some companies deliberately develop matrix structures to facilitate these communication networks, as in Figure 2.3. However, even a matrix structure still retains the concept of horizontal division by thinking in terms of finance managers, marketing managers etc. It still isn't able to represent fully the fact that a complete picture of management needs to *look behind the labels* used to describe things, and we still need a framework of concepts and methods that will enable us to deal with the complexity that is management.

Vertical division of management

Just as the horizontal division of management looks like a simplification of what managers actually do, so do the vertical divisions of Figure 2.2. To understand why, let's look at the where its words and ideas come from. If we do this, we can see that they come from the context of war and a military view of hierarchy and strategy.

	London HQ	Brussels	Taiwan
Finance	Susan Smith	Sean Barker	Morag Tang
Marketing	Karl Heinz	James O'Connel	Joan Jacobs
Production	Anna Cloutis	Mike Carter	Ann Patel
Human resources	Vacant	Kel Pot	Aksent Fabillo
Corporate planning	Tufton Beamish		

Figure 2.3 Matrix structures in management

Managers shown as having two dimensions to their position: a functional position, like finance, and a project or team position, like Brussels.

Many early management gurus, like Urwick (1943), saw this business of management very much in military terms. Thus the word *strategy* comes from the ancient Greek for the leader of an army, or a general; and the word *tactics* from a word meaning a lieutenant or officer. These words bring with them an accompanying assumption that the higher few strategically lead the lower many, via the tactical supervision of the middle ranks. We see in Figure 2.2 that the triangle is narrowest at its highest point, meaning a small number of top people involved in strategy; and widest at its lowest, meaning large numbers of people involved in operations. Just as strategy is for generals, tactics for officers and doing the fighting for ordinary soldiers, so Figure 2.2 links strategy with such descriptions as 'senior executives', tactics with 'middle management' and 'operators' with doing the work itself.

In an information age this is easily shown to be nonsense, even if it were ever true. Consider this simple case. An international business conference is being held at a university. There are delegates from all over the world. During one of the conference sessions, a presenter causes a scandal by departing from his subject and treating his hearers to an offensive, racist diatribe. Most of his hearers walk out and some stay to make a noisy protest. In less than 24 hours, the scandal caused is loudly featured in the local and national media. When confronted with this situation, does the vice-chancellor of the university concerned refuse to get involved, on the basis that his job is 'strategic' and this local difficulty is a firefighting, tactical or operational issue? I think not. In practice, what happens on such occasions is that the highest levels of the management hierarchy intervene and take command. In this case, a press conference is called at which a bevy of 'senior executives', supposedly concerned with strategy, appear before press and television in an attempt to take control of day-to-day operations.

The example is fictitious, but is regularly reflected in the life of public and private organizations and businesses. The work of senior executives, like the work of the middle management below them, is actually a complex mix of decision making, not the simple vertical division of management that Figure 2.2 tries to tell us.

The real problem with the picture presented by Figure 2.2 is that it confuses the logical and the physical, or the 'whats' and the 'hows' of the management hierarchy. It is *what* a manager, or any other person, does that determines whether they are involved in strategy, not *how* they are described by their job title. In real life, a middle manager may attend a meeting that formulates strategy or a top executive may get involved in day-to-day operations. When the middle manager helps formulate strategy, they are part of a larger strategic *system*. When the senior executive contributes to daily operational matters, they are just one part of the operational system. At some other time their roles could be different. What managers *legitimately* do is much more complex than the simple vertical divisions of Figure 2.2.

Box 2.1

What/which is information?

Date: 29/01/00
Name of Game: Football
Location: Grimsby, UK
Result: Grimsby Town 1, Crewe Alexandra 1.
'Result' is defined in terms of 'goals scored'.

The upper part of this Box looks like conventional information, but what about the lower part? A bit of a mess? Complex? Ambiguous? Yes, but the *whole* picture of the football match is much *richer* than just cold statistics. As we shall see throughout this book, information is much more than data. If you'd like to jump ahead and learn more, try Figure 9.4 and its associated reading.

What we have discovered about the limitations of a simple vertical division of management reinforces the conclusion we came to when considering horizontal divisions:

- We need to look behind the labels used to describe things.
- We need a framework of concepts and methods that will enable us to deal with complexity.

The instrument that we shall use to deal with these needs is called *systems thinking*, and in Chapter 3 we shall introduce this conceptual core material to our studies in this book.

2.2 WHAT IS INFORMATION?

2.2.1 The importance of the question

The title of this section is another broad question, but it is one we need to answer if we are to make sense of the business management use of information. Since any view of what constitutes an information *system* will also depend on the view taken of information, our exploration of the question 'What is information?' will also affect our views on the further question, 'What is an information system?'

When we asked the question 'What is management' in the previous section, we found that we needed some framework or set of concepts that would make sense of all the different aspects of management we might come across. We saw that some of the existing ways of describing management weren't always adequate, and I suggested that a *systems* view could overcome these inadequacies. Our approach to the question 'What is information?' will follow a similar path to the one we used when exploring 'What is management?' First, we will look at some different ways in which we could answer the question, and then we will see how the limitations of these various answers might be overcome.

2.2.2 Opening up views of information

The CSA case may have seemed a fairly clear choice for introducing the subject of information and information systems. After all, wasn't it a system to gather and process information about absent fathers, so that further information could be produced about how much they should pay to their abandoned families? As we shall now explore, the information involved in the management of the *whole* CSA project was much more *rich* than that.

The concept of *richness* of information is one we shall develop further in this book, but we can begin by making it mean the *fullness* or *wide-ranging* nature that information can take. While some of the forms we find in a rich view of information are not always relevant to business, we shall see that the subject of business information is much wider than is often found in conventional coverage of information systems. We shall now consider some possible answers to the question 'What is information?'

Structural views of information

If we consider most examples of something we call information, we shall find that it is likely to be made up of parts or components, which are put together in a particular structure. Thus information about an absent father held by the CSA would include such details as his name and address, plus data about his earnings, outgoings and other commitments. All of what we have referred to as 'details' or 'data' would consist of words and numbers like 'Father's name: John Smith, Address: 23 Foxthorn Paddock, Torcross, Northumberland. Gross annual income £17 534'.

In this example, the information is essentially constructed by putting together characters in a particular sequence or structure to form words, or individual figures to form numbers or values. These, in turn, can be arranged into a structure that forms sentences, records or some greater whole. If we take such a structural view of information, then we see it as data, like characters, figures or words organized in a particular way to form information.

This simple example illustrates a major, practically applied concept of information forming the basis of data and database management systems, which we shall explore further in Chapter 6. If information is seen as data assembled into a particular structure, then designing a database to support an information system raises the issue of what sort of structure should be used.

It is also worth noting that this view of information is not confined to structures of words and numbers. Data about the occurrence and colour of pixels on a computer screen can be brought together in an overall structure to form the information conveyed by a diagram or a picture. In this media age of web videos, there is a big difference between one collection of coloured ingredients that would make a picture of a commercial product on a web page, and the same coloured ingredients rearranged to make a beautiful but abstract design.

Processing views of information

A structural view of information leads naturally to a complementary processing view. We saw above that a structural view sees information as 'made up of parts or components that are put together in a particular structure'. To understand how this leads to a process view, we should look at the phrase 'put together'.

Anything that exists in a particular structural arrangement must have been put together in that way as a result of some process. If we look at the geometrical structure of bricks in a wall or the more sophisticated and subtle construction of our own bodies, they are the way they are because some process such as bricklaying or biological growth has gathered the components and assembled them together in a particular sequence to create that structure.

If we see information as a structure of data components, various processes will have be carried out to construct both the individual components and then the whole. One component of the whole with its own particular structure is 'Gross annual income'. To create this component and add it to the whole, some process like collecting monthly salary slips, totalling up income and recording this on a document must take place. For the result of this process to be successful, all those involved need to share a common view of what the output from the process will look like in terms of its own structure and how it fits into the structure of the whole.

Without this common view, the sequence of operations needed to process the information can become confused, and the resulting output garbled. The experience of those who had to fill in the original 100+ pages of the early CSA form knew about this to the point that some of them were reduced to tears. I know from my own experience that understanding the answer to even a simple question like 'What is your name?' is not as obvious as it seems. Many cultures, e.g. Magyar or Chinese, put the surname first; and some British surnames (like mine) sound like first names anyway. Thus the structural arrangement of the forename and surname components that make up the information 'Father's name' determines how the process of assembling those components is carried out. Just one simple slip of juxtapositioning a forename with a surname can result in the loss of all the other components in the wider structure that determines whether the information ever gets further than a useless document. Is this trivial? Yes, but it is the cause of many so-called computer errors that continue to frustrate many of us.

Hence the structural view of information, which regards it as a particular logical arrangement or structure of data components, implies a complementary process view, which sees information almost as some form of substance that is gathered up, transmitted, transformed, assembled and recorded. This process view might see an information system as a kind of information 'factory' that produces a product called information from raw materials called data.

The complementary nature of the structure and process views of information will be developed further in several parts of this book. In Chapter 4 we shall see how a control process view helps us put information systems into a management context. In Chapter 6 we shall look in depth at the way data structures can be accessed and processed as well as defined, and the practical implications for database management. In Chapter 8 we shall see how complementary structure and process views of information affect the nature of methods used for information systems development.

Information as communication

We often talk of things like books, documents or filing cabinets as 'containing' information. This idea of information being inside something is misleading, however. At the beginning of the classic cult book *The Hitch Hiker's Guide to the Galaxy*, (Adams, 1979), vital information about the forthcoming demolition of planet Earth has been available 'on display in the bottom of a locked filing cabinet stuck in a disused lavatory with a sign on the door saying *Beware of the Leopard*'. Not surprisingly, the person who needed this information felt he had not been properly informed. If information is going to have any real use at all, it is not sufficient for it to be contained in something or recorded somewhere. We have to be aware of its existence, and we have to be able to access it or have it transmitted so that we can receive it. Information is not information until it has been communicated and understood.

Notice the addition of the word *understood* to the concept of communication. Just seeing or hearing something does not make it information. It is possible to listen to a whole conversation in a language we do not understand and receive no information at all. Similarly, a complete electronic circuit diagram for a piece of equipment contains a lot of information, but only for someone who understands circuit diagrams. We can therefore identify one view of information saying that information is essentially the communication of understanding. In Chapter 5 we shall develop this view further and explore the concept of a *shared symbol set* as an essential of an information system that enables understanding.

Before leaving this view of information, we can discover another important aspect of it by referring to the CSA case. People don't just communicate information by words, pictures or symbols. Tone of voice, so-called body language and other aspects of general behaviour can all communicate information too. When one of those involved in setting up the CSA stated that the word 'impossible' was 'not part of Mrs Thatcher's vocabulary', they were 'reading the signs', 'taking the hint', or some other phrase we use to indicate that communication of information between human beings is more than speech and writing.

Information as an organized body of knowledge

The importance of *understanding* in relation to information can lead us to the broad consideration of what we can know, and how we can know it. The study of such questions is the concern of what is called *epistemology*.

These two sorts of ways of answering questions have been talked and argued over for centuries. For those of us who are not expecting to pass a philosophy degree, it is sufficient to realize there are two complementary ways for us to increase our knowledge of something. We often call the study of what things are, and what we know about them, to be some form of science, a word that comes from the Latin word *scientia*, meaning knowledge. Names for many particular sciences often end in 'ology', comes from a Greek word indicating a branch of knowledge or study. Given the way that the English language includes so many words derived from Greek and Latin, it is not surprising to find two words that cover the science of answering questions and knowing about things:

- Epistemology – from the Greek *episteme* = knowledge, which is the study of what we know and how can we know it.
- Methodology - from the Greek *meta* = along and *odos* = a way, which is the study of method or the ways of doing things.

Thus an answer to a question that explains things in terms of *rational relationships* or the structure of our knowledge is likely to be *epistemological*. An answer based on a method of experimental testing or some other process of *finding out* will be methodological in emphasis.

There is, however, one particular way of viewing what we know that is widely used in relation to communication and understanding. If we consider an important ingredient of both our own understanding and our ability to communicate it to others, we find that we frequently use ordering and classification of information to help us relate things and build on our experience. The ability to make sense of things through ordering and classification comes from our being able to set procedures or define rules.

Particular examples of such organization of information can cover a wide range. There are formal, universal classification systems like those used by botanists to classify plants, or by mathematicians to define functions. Such information is usually set in the wider context of science and human knowledge. In business and management, less grandiose and universal ways of organizing information can still be of great practical importance. Being able to classify customers in markets or products on the basis of manufacturing methods can be important information for a business, without necessarily having any great universal significance. The success of the UK postcode system is especially due to the fact that it enables companies to classify markets, creditworthiness, insurance risk and many other aspects of business knowledge.

As individuals, we also use informal, personal ways of grouping things according to our tastes and interests. If someone says that they do not like spicy food, we might guess that they would not like some Indian dishes, but we couldn't be sure. My mother's apple pie always had cloves in it: is that 'spicy'? We might feel that classification of this kind is not as rigorous or scientific as the kind done by mathematicians or biologists, but if we consider very practical issues like the user-friendliness of computer software, is classifying tastes in software so different from classifying tastes in food?

In subsequent chapters of this book we shall find that viewing information in terms of classifying and ordering is relevant to ways of constructing databases in Chapter 6 and object-oriented approaches to systems development in Chapter 9. We shall also say more about this view in Chapter 5.

Information as clarification and the reduction of uncertainty

Many situations that we would describe as uncertain or confused are those where information is either lacking or is wrong. If you have ever been stuck at an airport or on a train, waiting for an explanation for a delay, you will probably understand how lack of information equates with uncertainty. The less information, the greater the uncertainty.

The reverse also seems to apply in the way we use the word information and words related to it, like being 'well informed'. Being well informed implies not just that we know something, but also that we know how to deal with things: that we are in control.

In the CSA case, most of those involved would have appreciated the concept of information as a reducer of uncertainty. Many mothers who did not have enough information to fill in the 100+ page form felt less than certain. Where absent fathers were able to avoid providing some or all information, they reduced any certainty that the CSA or the mothers of their children would receive any payment.

In Chapter 5 we shall look further into the relationship between information and certainty to see that information need not be viewed in terms of the absolute distinction of knowing or not knowing. The concept of *entropy* will help us develop a view of how informative particular information can be. We shall prepare for this in Chapter 4 by distinguishing uncertainty, which comes from lack of information, from uncertainty, which comes from differences in opinion.

Information as possession and power

Being well informed, which we have just discussed, leads on to 'being in the know', one of many popular phrases implying that the possession of information means possession of power. The arch Nazi propagandist Joseph Goebbels is reputed to have said that whoever ran the information also ran the show. If we consider examples of the concept that possession of information gives power, we can see that different forms of information are often referred to, and that the power also takes different forms.

An absent father who possessed information about himself that the CSA did not, had the power to avoid most or all of his potential payments to his children. Once the CSA possessed information about an absent father, it had greater power to enforce payment.

When we come to formalizing the role of information and information systems in businesses and organizations in Chapter 7, we shall produce a model to relate different forms of information to different levels of possession and power. For the moment, it is worth considering that power could come from many different forms of information, such as:

● Facts and figures: knowing how much an absent father had earned.
● What someone was trying to do: the CSA's targets for recovering money.
● How something was done: the workings of the CSA's computer software.

- Policy: the CSA's decision to investigate earlier settlements.
- Beliefs and personal motivation: Margaret Thatcher's views of society.

Whatever the form of the information and the power that it brings, the fact that it does bring power can make it a desirable commodity or resource. As such, information takes on a value and can be something that is traded, exchanged and hoarded. Many of the currently fashionable attempts at 'open government' or 'the right to know' reflect the belief that since information gives power, in a democracy it should be shared. Whether it is sensible to expect the possessors of information to give it up willingly depends on your view of human nature. Although not a complete cynic, I am cautious enough to believe that voluntary sharing of power cannot always be relied on and that the practical design of information systems will need to recognize this.

In Chapter 7 we shall see how a systems view of businesses and organizations enables us to look past how a particular business or organization works to the role of the information system within it. From this we can get a clearer view of what forms of power are present.

In Chapter 8 we shall see that technical development of information systems that does not take account of wider issues of power and politics is unlikely to succeed. We shall therefore consider how systems development methods can take account of these wider, non-technical issues.

Information as interest

People often love to talk and exchange information. One of the vivid memories I have of my early childhood in a small Cornish community was of people talking. My mother, her two sisters, one of her brothers and my grandparents, all squeezed into the little kitchen of a terraced house and discussing everything from who had had which baby to what was right or wrong with the government.

Exchange of information for reasons of interest and entertainment takes place in most societies, including those within businesses and organizations. Indeed, in organizations where I have worked, knowing where people informally congregated and conversed seemed to be one of the most important pieces of information a manager could have. Often the kind of information acquired in such situations gives power in the way described above, but at other times it is less specific and less threatening. Listening to people talk, finding out their interests and their attitudes, can lead to an understanding that facilitates relationships and working together. It is not hard to see that such information can be relevant to management and business, and that it cannot always be dismissed as gossip and time wasting.

However, it is hard to imagine information like this being processed by the computer system along with the monthly payroll. We shall therefore need some way of deciding what consideration should be given to such information in a book about information systems in business; and if so, how it can be related to the other forms of information we have discussed.

Information as intuition

There is a story of an Englishman who went to live permanently in the Gaelic-speaking Western Isles of Scotland. Wishing to fit in socially, he taught himself Gaelic from a book. One day, two local people observed him going past. 'Ah', said one, 'there goes the Englishman who speaks the Gaelic.' 'Aye', said the other, 'he speaks it, but he doesn't know it.'

When I was told this story by a Gaelic speaker, I recalled how the great jazz trumpeter Louis Armstrong once remarked that if you had to ask what jazz was, you would never know the answer.

Both of these examples from different cultures illustrate a kind of information that appears to crop up in business too, but is often the subject of controversy. Despite the high level of education and professionalism of those involved in initiating and setting up the CSA, one of them subsequently remarked, as we saw in the case, that it was 'something so stupid, it could only be thought up by a really intelligent person'.

Another possible role for intuition is in relation to sympathetic listeners, confessors and counsellors, who often seem to understand in a way that can't be defined in a logical, formal way. This sort of information comes into business when we consider questions of product design and people's tastes, or in the application of sympathetic and supportive leadership.

While most people recognize this view of information, there is often controversy about its value, its role in any information system, or even the fact of its existence. The contrast between the quotations from Eddie Brickell and Lord Kelvin at the beginning of this book highlights the main issue. From Lord Kelvin we learn of the danger of accepting the existence of things that cannot be defined and detected through observation and measurement. Like the emperor's new clothes in Hans Anderson, they can be a complete confidence trick. But we also know that the word 'nothing' can hide powerful human forces. It may not be possible to computerize this kind of information, but its real business effects can be dramatic.

Did many of the CSA's failures come from a lack of feel for the people who were to be affected? Many of the so-called absent fathers were people who had gained a lot of experience of the often bitter legal conflict that can follow a separation or divorce. Perhaps the assumptions that the CSA made about its potential victims or opponents, as many of the fathers continue to describe themselves, showed a lack of intuition.

2.2.3 Answering questions

So far we have opened up the question 'What is information?', after we had first explored the question 'What is management?' Our analysis has shown that a wide range of answers is possible. If I were now to say that choosing between this wide range of possible answers will depend on how we interpret the question, I suspect that many of my readers would throw me into the wastebin marked 'old 1960s relativists'. But I think that we need to be careful. We now live in a networked, multimedia world where television interviews of those who have power motives, such as politicians, contain carefully choreographed questions designed to make sure that the answers fit the questioner's objectives. That tells us that we should look carefully at the form of questions and understand what they imply. The 'Information as power' section above is relevant here.

If interpreting questions is important, I'd like to propose that two important ways in which the question can be interpreted are in terms of whether we approach the question from a 'thinking' or *conceptual* viewpoint, or from a 'doing' or *application* viewpoint.

To understand this distinction further, we will take an apparently simple example before turning to the subject of information itself. Consider the question: 'What is blue?' A straight answer would be that it is a colour, but that in itself doesn't tell us too much. We might know more if we were told that it is the colour of the sky, a darker colour than yellow, and more often the favourite colour of men than of women.

If these answers look more informative but still rather mixed, we could call in a scientist to give us a definition. A scientist might say that blue is the description we give to a particular form of light, that all light is a form of electromagnetic radiation, and that differences we call colours represent radiations of different wavelengths. If we look at the rainbow, the red end of the spectrum of colours is formed by radiation with a longer wavelength, and the blue end by radiation with a shorter wavelength. Thus the colour blue can be defined as light of a particular wavelength.

If we look at these various answers to our simple question, we can see that they tell us two different sorts of things about the colour blue. Answers like 'it is a darker colour than yellow' or even just 'it is a colour' put it into place in relation to other things we know. If we know what we mean by the idea of a colour or the concept of light and dark colours, these sorts of answers help us fit the colour blue into our existing knowledge. Generally, we fit new things into our existing knowledge by identifying their characteristics, distinguishing them from other things, and classifying them in relation to other things in terms of these similarities and differences. This sort of answer considers that what we know can be explained in terms of rational relationships or the structure of our knowledge.

But what do we mean by 'similarities' and 'differences'? Answering this question leads into the second sort of answer that can be made to questions like 'What is blue?' The answers 'more often the favourite colour of men than of women' or 'light of a particular wavelength' imply the idea of experimental testing or what process we have to go through to establish or confirm our knowledge. They imply that interviewing people or measuring the wavelength of electromagnetic radiation is the way we can establish our knowledge of what 'blue' is.

When answering the question 'What is information?' in this book, we shall use both approaches. Sometimes we will try to understand what information is by looking at the characteristics of different kinds of information, and comparing how they differ as well as what they have in common. The result of answering the question in this way will be to focus on what information is and how it fits into the overall structure of our knowledge. In these situations the approach will be mainly epistemological.

At other times we shall be answering the question 'What is information?' by studying what it does or the process. In these situations the approach will be methodological.

I have said that we will use both of these approaches and that they are complementary. This is not completely fair. You will notice a clear bias as we go through this book towards a methodological approach. My bias comes from a belief that it is very hard in a practical subject like business to separate completely what something is from what it does. Therefore, although we will often answer the question 'What is information?' in an epistemological way, the structure of our knowledge, in terms of comparisons and classification, will depend ultimately on our experience of what the information does and what it is used for. Since this latter view is essentially methodological, I confess a methodological bias.

2.3 INFORMATION, MANAGEMENT AND SYSTEMS

2.3.1 Information and management

So far, we have a selection of possible answers to the question 'What is information?' As Figure 2.4 shows, these different views of information often overlap and can be related to each other. We have also considered the different ways in which we might choose an answer.

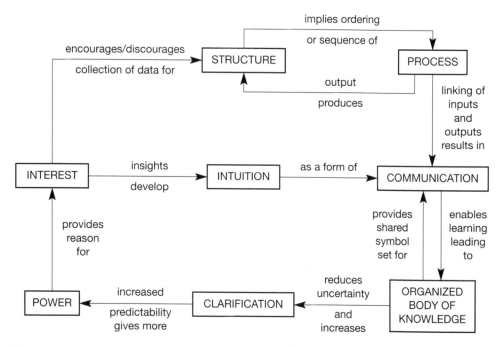

Figure 2.4 Some possible relationships between different types of information
This diagram does pretend to cover all possible views of information and exclusively to define their inter-relationship, but it should open up the concept of the richness of information

If we are to make sense of information in all its richness, we need a criterion or yardstick that will enable us to recognize when a particular answer to our question 'What is information?' is acceptable. This would mean that there could be many answers to the question, but all of these answers would share some common property. This method of defining things is one I used in my previous book (Harry, 1990) and is one I will explain in detail in Chapter 3. For the moment we can note that it is a way of avoiding both the open-ended vagary of soft stereotype learning and over-simplification that does not recognize the richness of information as a concept.

The approach I shall use to assess answers to the question 'What is information?' will be to start by considering its relevance to management. Deciding what information is will therefore come from looking at its role and function in businesses and organizations. This shows my bias towards a methodological approach, as in the previous section.

The results of this approach may sometimes give a different view of both information and information systems from the one you might find in books bearing titles containing the words 'management information system'. The rich view of information we opened up in the previous section includes such factors as power, interest and intuition as well as structure, process and communication. The last three are views similar to those found in most books on management information systems that regard an information system as being not too far away from a computer system. It is harder to imagine information as power, interest or intuition if it is machine based.

However, if we are going to study business information rather than 'some business information' or 'computerizable information systems in business', we need some way of looking at information as a whole. To do this we need a model that will enable us to understand how all the different forms of information play their roles and interact as part of the whole business or organization, whether or not they are processed by a computer or stored on a database.

Even from a computer-biased view of information systems, there are beginning to be good reasons for taking this wider view. As information technology has advanced, forms of information that were once thought not to be relevant to computer systems are now being machine processed. Within the last decade, for example, a personnel database has moved on from only storing information about people in the form of words and numbers. Now, not only can a picture of the person be included, but advances in video disk technology mean we can add moving pictures and sound. Quite subtle information about people's character and behaviour can now be captured, stored and transmitted by such technology. So perhaps information as power, interest and intuition is not as separate from the computerized information system as we might have thought.

Whatever the advances in technology, however, information in a management context will involve a mix of human and machine-based contributions. Having a model that covers and relates them both will not only give us the whole view, but will make sure that we identify important issues of the connexion between them. Designing a successful interaction between human activity and computer systems will be essential if the whole is not to fail.

2.3.2 Information systems

In Section 2.1 we concluded that systems thinking would be the key to understanding the complexity of management. If our understanding of information is to depend on understanding its role in management, with its human as well as information technology components, we will also need to look carefully at what we mean by system when used in the term information system. Again, we will do this more fully in Chapter 3, but for the moment we can see that information system has to mean much more than information technology, if we are to cover the richness of information we have explored in this chapter. Answers to the question 'What is information?' can then come from understanding the concept of a system and the particular relationship between management and information systems.

As a start to introducing what we mean by an information system, I would like to introduce three important themes that will recur throughout this book:

1 *An information system is more than a collection of information technology equipment.* Despite the fact that computer manufacturers often describe a computer system plus its supporting equipment as an 'information system', we shall find that real information systems only work if there are other vital components actively present, especially human beings and all they bring with them. Unlike the machines, human beings do not work tirelessly and obediently; nor is their behaviour always logical, consistent or predictable, like that of a machine. As components of an information system, human beings bring qualities to it that go beyond the calculated data processing of a machine. Any view that the CSA information system merely consisted of the computers and software that calculated payments would be very misleading. Where either father or mother did not co-operate with the system by providing data, or the human designers had failed to produce a workable formula, not much

successful processing took place. Any view of information in the context of real information systems will therefore need to take account of a much wider range of components that are essential to its success than the technology.

2 *An information system is not something detached and isolated with an existence and objectives all its own.* Badly designed or implemented computerized information systems may sometimes give this impression, but the title of this book was chosen to send the message that business information has to be studied in the wider business systems context. At the CSA, many of the problems arose because it was not always consistent with or relevant to the *messy* way that people, prejudices and politics actually work in real life. It was called The Child Support Agency not because that is what it did, but because the wider political context required a name that would sell it to the voters and its 'victims'. As we consider the wide range of activities that can be involved in business management, so our view of the range of information that may be relevant will also be widened. This will include a consideration of the *soft* and *messy* issues with which information systems have to live.

3 *The distinction of 'whats' and 'hows' is an important one for understanding information systems.* We have already come across this concept of *looking behind the labels* when considering 'What is management?' Focusing on who does something, or how or where they do it can often distract us from what is actually being done. We saw that financial managers, for example, don't just manage finance. Similarly in the information context, we could be distracted by the fact that a document is headed 'Child Support' from realizing that it is really about 'money extraction'.

Identifying these three future themes is just a beginning to our exploration of what information is and its role in the context of information systems in business.

Seminar agendas, exam topics and project/dissertation subjects

1 Take a recent, high-profile, political issue that has dominated the media. Note which senior politicians or business executives have been involved in statements to the press, television etc. Is it possible to classify the issue(s) exclusively in terms of the hierarchical triangle of Figure 2.2? How far are the various people involved fulfilling a function exclusively connected to one level of the hierarchy in Figure 2.2? What other functions are they fulfilling?

2 In this chapter I frequently refer to the linguistic source of the meaning of words like method or science. Does all information depend on language? Is, say, 'Je suis un homme' the same information as 'I am a man'? Is the concept of information as something that is manifested equivalently in various hows, like languages, real or useful?

3 Investigate the uses of the term information by computer hardware manufacturers in their sales literature. Do these equate the term information system with a computer hardware or networked systems?

4 In Chapter 1, I emphasized that the concepts in this book are as relevant to bringing up a family or being a student as they are to running a commercial organization. Take some of the possible answers to 'What is information?' in this chapter and consider how they might apply to a football club, play group or student union.

5 Look at a textbook that may be recommended for one of your courses in the human aspects of management, and that apparently has nothing to do with information systems.

The closer it comes to the context of the soft stereotype of Chapter 1, the better. Then consider information in the human systems context. Try out an exercise like that in Pegler *et al*. (1986), which invites you to explore the telephone directory of your organization or the location of people's offices to discover who is who. How might the results of such an exercise be seen in terms of the answers proposed in Section 2.2?

6 Refer to question 4, if you don't like question 5.

7 Where do staff meet in your organization?

8 Consult Janis and Mann (1977). Does information reduce risk?

9 Consider a successful attempt to bridge human and computer use of information, like Microsoft Windows. Compare this with the role of information in communicating a popular product to the customer in the fast-food retailing industry. Is there any connexion between the use of the word 'menu' in these different applications?

References/bibliography

Adams, D. (1979). *The Hitch Hiker's Guide to the Galaxy*. Pan Books, London.

Flew, A. (1983). *A Dictionary of Philosophy*. Pan Books, London.

Galliers, R. (1987). *Information Analysis: Selected Readings*. Addison-Wesley, London.

Hannagan, T. (1998). *Management: Concepts and Practices*. Financial Times Pitman Publishing, London.

Harry, M.J.S. (1990). *Information and Management Systems*. Pitman Publishing London.

Janis, I. and Mann, L. (1977). *Decision Making: A Psychological Analysis of Conflict, Choice, and Commitment*. Free Press, New York.

Lacey, A.R. (1986). *A Dictionary of Philosophy*. Routledge, London.

Pedler, M., Burgoyne, J. and Boydell, T. (1986). *A Manager's Guide to Self-Development*. McGraw-Hill, Maidenhead.

Turban, E., McLean, E. and Wetherbe J. (1999). *Information Technology for Management*. Wiley, New York.

Urmson, J.O. (1991). *The Concise Encyclopaedia of Western Philosophy and Philosophers*. Routledge, London.

Urwick, L.F. (1943). *The Elements of Administration*. Harper & Row, New York.

CHAPTER 3

Individual, organizational and global systems

'Big bangs or bursting bubbles?': the e-commerce explosion

What happened

On Friday, 12 November 1999 the *Financial Times* (FT), a major UK and European financial newspaper, brought out its latest edition. It didn't appear to be that unusual. There were 22 pages of the paper itself, 28 pages of information about companies and markets, and an eight-page supplement on 'Private Banking'. Pretty standard stuff, and all on the famous pink FT newsprint. Yet I wonder how many people who were interested in business realized just how much the contents of this ordinary 1999 edition differed from what the same newspaper would have contained only three years before?

The difference wasn't in the format or the styling; the FT looked much the same as usual. What was different, however, was some of its content. Here are just four examples from that 12 November 1999 edition:

- 'NEC, the Japanese electronics conglomerate, yesterday announced an alliance with Hewlett-Packard and Oracle to develop business platforms and solutions for the Internet.'
- 'Ebookers shares leap on New York debut – shares in ebookers.com, the UK online travel agency, initially soared 100 per cent in their market debut on Nasdaq yesterday – another example of the market's obsession with Internet stocks.'
- 'Christie's rethinks Internet policy – Christie's International, the international auction house, is to launch a redesign of its Internet strategy that will eventually create an online bidding venue for every one of the company's auctions.'
- 'Professor Kevin Keasey, Director of the International Institute of Banking, says investment in new technology is needed if the city of Leeds is to be wired into the new digital age.'

I won't go any further with my analysis. Sufficient to say, there were nearly 100 references to digital networks, Internet trading and other topics directly linked to the subject of *electronic commerce*. The stories covered banking, printing, farm produce, school supplies, chemicals, industrial and building equipment.

Electronic commerce, usually called e-commerce or EC, seemed to come from nowhere at the end of the 1990s and then to become something that has dominated the media and business education ever since. Unfortunately, the more some vivid change in our lives is talked about, the less clear it can be. So we will begin by asking what we mean by the term 'electronic commerce'. An academic way of answering that question could be a definition. Here's one:

'Electronic commerce is any form of business or administrative transaction or information exchange that is executed using information and communications technology (ICT).'

But definitions tend to be logical and abstract. To be more practical and understandable, we shall look in more detail at some of the main types of electronic commerce, using business examples.

RQ 3.1 Look again at the four examples from the *Financial Times* of 12 November 1999, quoted above. In terms of who is buying and who is selling, what differences can you see between them?

Box 3.1

The richness of a networked world

Tony Jackson

It is received wisdom these days that the digital revolution changes everything, companies and industries, we are told, are shifting before our eyes. No business model will survive intact. Everything is up for grabs.

Then again, the people pushing this line hardest are those with most to gain, such as software companies and consulting firms. So a book by two partners from the Boston Consulting Group should be approached with due caution.

All the same, *Blown to Bits* commands attention. First, it is an attempt to fit the whole phenomenon into an intellectual framework. Second, it does not over-hype. It has the temerity to suggest that some industries might not be greatly affected after all.

The book's basic thesis was set out by the authors in the *Harvard Business Review* two years ago, and is here usefully expanded. It begins with the economics of information versus the

economics of things. Take that well-worn example, the bookshop.

Books are expensive and slow to shift, so the economics of things argue you should stock as few as possible. The economics of information suggest the opposite. The more you display, the more you sell.

The old-style bookshop is therefore a compromise. In the digital revolution, that compromise is resolved. Information on books is displayed online, while the books themselves are stored in warehouses.

The handler of information, such as Amazon, obviously stands to profit from this. But so too may the warehouser and distributor. The point is that both information and things can be better managed apart. And the bigger the original compromise, the greater the value which can be released.

In the mail-order business, by contrast, the economics of things and of information are separate

already. In the grocery trade, too, physical products, can be stored well enough in out-of-town super-stores. The compromise is much smaller to begin with. An online grocer such as Peapod has a market value less than a tenth of Amazon's.

So, to the second argument. This involves what the authors call richness versus reach. Reach is what you get when you advertise to millions on television. Richness is when a salesman sits down for an hour with an individual client.

In old-style business, the two conflict. The more you have of one, the less of the other. This is a line along which businesses position themselves. Take clothing. At one end is the bespoke tailor, at the other the catalogue retailer. Chains such as Marks and Spencer are somewhere in between.

In the digital revolution, the authors argue, this trade-off is shifted or even abolished. A networked world offers not only reach but, increasingly, richness as well.

In the old world, a car maker such as Toyota would prefer richness to reach in choosing its component suppliers. Rather than shop around, it would take a few chosen suppliers into close partnership. What it lost in cheap deals it would make up in reliability and lower inventories.

Compare the Automotive Network Exchange (ANX), a so-called extranet set up by the big three Detroit car makers involving some 5000 suppliers worldwide. In essence this is a global auction. Buyers post their requirements, and suppliers instantly respond.

Obviously, this is a huge extension of reach. But, it is claimed, there is richness too. Enough information can be exchanged to ensure quality and delivery. The old trade-off is losing its force.

As the authors admit, these are special cases. Amazon has done splendidly in bookselling, but the millions of titles it offers were already listed in the book trade's catalogues. It could therefore achieve instant critical mass.

Similarly with ANX. Detroit's big three form a quasi-monopoly of US car manufacture. If they agree on a standard, it becomes universal.

The final part of the argument relates to corporate structure. In the old world, we are told, activities that depended on richness – on communication, control, trust and so forth – belonged within the company.

Those depending on reach, by contrast, were assigned to the market. Thus, the boundary of the corporation was itself a point on the trade-off between richness and reach.

In a networked world, that trade-off vanishes as well. Internally, the company hierarchy gives way to a kind of structural soup, in which *ad hoc* teams form and dissolve. Externally, companies form shifting alliances.

The model for the future corporation is thus Silicon Valley: a community in which no-one can tell the difference between competitors and allies, and where workers mean everything and corporate boundaries nothing. Applied to most industries, this may be baloney. It is thought-provoking baloney, just the same.

Source: Financial Times, 18 October 1999. Reprinted with permission.

See Evans, P. and Wurster, T.S. (2000). *Blown to Bits: How the New Economics of Information Transforms Strategy.* Harvard Business School Press, Boston, MA.

Comment

What is really important about this book is not whether we agree with the detailed conclusions of either the authors or the reviewer. Instead, it is the fact that issues of 'richness', 'communication', 'control', 'boundary', 'hierarchy' and 'trade-off' in a 'networked world' are supposedly leading to 'a shifting', 'whole phenomenon' and differentiating the 'economics of information versus the economics of things'. If we are to decide what implications this 'networked world' has for business and organizations, we need to have a framework that will help us understand what 'richness', 'communication', 'control' etc. actually mean.

Business-to-business (B2B) electronic commerce

How does a business selling to another business differ from a single business selling to a final consumer? One answer is that many businesses form part of a *supply chain* or *supply line*. When this happens, the customer is not just the last one in the chain, like the people who buy furniture kits from Carry-Out Cupboards in Appendix 1. Instead, a retailer such as Carry-Out Cupboards itself forms the last part of a supply chain that ends with the retail selling. At each of the stages along this chain, buying and selling transactions take place, with one business as a supplier and the other as a customer. Thus Carry-Out Cupboards is itself a customer of those who supply its packaging material or its metal fittings, and the company that supplies the packaging material is a customer of a paper and cardboard manufacturer. Finally, it goes back to a company in somewhere like Sweden that is replenishing trees for paper manufacture in 40 years' time. Figure 3.1 shows a general form of this relationship.

Supply chains like this, with their complementary information flows, are not new. Over 2000 years ago, Phoenician traders voyaged from North Africa to an obscure region called the Tin Islands to buy tin from the natives of those islands. They then shipped it back to the Mediterranean and sold it to those who manufactured products made from tin. These were in turn purchased by retailers, who then sold them to the peoples of Northern Africa and Southern Europe. (The Tin Islands are now called Britain, and I suspect that my Cornish ancestors helped sell the tin.)

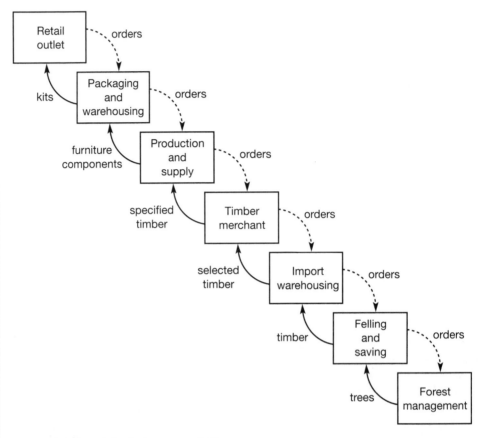

Figure 3.1 A supply chain or supply line
As we explore in Appendix 1, independent and unco-ordinated actions by the individual components of the chain can lead to instability. *Supply chain management* attempts to co-ordinate the whole with the use of information systems.

The information flows involved in such chain transactions have always contained details like what has been ordered, how many are required, or when they should be delivered. The way that most businesses did this at the end of the twentieth century wasn't much different from the Phoenician traders. Information was carried either as a physical record like a document or stored in the brain of the person carrying it. Examples might be an invoice in the post, or 'when you get to the Tin Islands, tell them we want enough tin to fill the ship'. What is different about today's supply chain information flows is their *speed, weightlessness, ubiquity, connexion* and *reproducibility*, which comes from the exploitation of information and communications technology (ICT).

- *Speed,* not only refers to the fact that electronic information flows at about a quarter of a million kilometres per second, it also relates to the rate at which data can be electronically *processed.*

- Electronic information can be considered *weightless* when it takes a form that is intangible and does not create mass. Thus when the hard disk on a computer is completely 'filled' with information, it weighs no more than when it is empty. The same is not true of a traditional filing cabinet. As to information flows, the space around us is more packed with them than ever before, but we don't notice them because they take the form of weightless radiation. If all the information flowing around us were on paper documents, we'd be buried by them.
- The *ubiquity* or 'everywhereness' of information comes from the fact that connexion to the Internet and other networks is possible anywhere in the world. If there is no telephone line, a computer can work through a mobile. If there is no local mobile telephone mast, we can connect through a satellite dish.
- The ease with which information can be *reproduced* or copied at essentially zero cost means that the same information can be made to appear virtually simultaneously anywhere.

A major enabler of B2B electronic commerce through the use of ICT has been *electronic data interchange* or EDI. This was first used by ocean, motor, air and rail carriers nearly two decades before electronic commerce even started to dominate the business headlines. EDI employs standard electronic message formats, called transaction sets, to replace conventional business documents like invitations to tender, purchase orders, delivery notes and invoices. Such transaction sets allow the exchange of business information between a supplier's computer system and a customer's computer system without the need to produce paper documents. The weightlessness of electronic business information in this form can bring the advantages of:

- speed of transmission: electronic signals are faster than physical delivery;
- virtually costless reproduction: electronic data can be rapidly and easily copied without paper mountains;
- accuracy: the reduction of the need to *transcribe* information from one medium to another reduces the opportunities for error, when for example rekeying data into a system.

EDI has been particularly attractive to organizations that are both locked into a supply chain and able to afford the required ICT systems. Hence the use of EDI has spread from transport to other areas of business that can benefit from its advantages. Examples now include manufacturing, warehousing and retailing, public utilities, banking and insurance.

Not all B2B electronic commerce uses EDI, but it is an important example of how *connexions* and *communication*, in supply chains or elsewhere, need their own shared ways of viewing the information that they exchange. When Evans and Wurster (2000) make the point that information is the glue that holds the structure of business together, they are neither using an original way of describing it nor making a new point; but they are saying something that continues to be central to understanding networked information systems. I am sure that the Phoenician tin traders understood their own equivalent of Evans and Wurster's 'When two companies build a long term relationship, they establish channels for the rich communication of information. These channels may be personal acquaintances among executives or sales and purchasing staff, mutual understandings that are implicit or written.'

What is new is the way in which the speed, weightlessness, ubiquity, connexion and reproducibility of modern electronic communication of information flows enable the supply chain to be *managed*. Once the Phoenician tin trader set out for Britain with his instructions about what to buy, that was it. Barring a very fast following boat from North Africa that could catch him up, the ordering process was fixed with a long delay or *lag*. By the time he got back to his home port, he could be delivering a supply of tin that reflected a demand that was months, if not a year, out of date. Contemporary organizations connected into a supply chain, and supported by networked electronic communication, can react to changes within minutes. Appendix 1 looks further into the issues of delays and lags in supply chains.

Business-to-consumer (B2C) electronic commerce

Less than two years ago, I was in a UK university bookshop. Like many other UK citizens, I had grown used to the fact that any book from the US would cost the same price in UK pounds as it did in US dollars. Given that the US dollar was worth two-thirds of the UK pound at the time, I considered that the UK price was too high. I got on to the Internet and ordered the book from Amazon, who was then a dominant Internet bookseller. The net result (sorry about the 'net' pun) was that I got the book at 60 per cent of its local UK price, including delivery.

That is just one personal example of the exciting, frightening, stimulating or annoying way in which worldwide electronic communication is transforming business. It illustrates the effect of electronic commerce on business relationships and loyalties, or *affiliation*. Even the briefest reference to current sources of business information, like the *Financial Times*, will reveal examples telling the same story. Shopping is no longer something you do at certain hours of the day at convenient *physical locations*. The Internet is open 24 hours, anywhere in the world where you can connect.

Consumer-to-consumer (C2C) electronic commerce

Is electronic commerce just business? Our previous example of Christie's, an international auction house that is connecting individuals who have something to sell with individuals who may want to buy, is not unique. The early pioneers of electronic commerce, like Amazon, also introduced Internet auctions for much more humble and personal items. As I write this in the last days of year 1999, news reports include a spokesman from another auction house, Sotheby's. He warns that there are too many Internet auction facilities and that at least 50 per cent will fail. However, I don't think we should see such predictions as the main issue. The advent of the Internet means that *anyone* who is connected to it can develop *commerce* with anyone else is also connected.

Consumer-to-business (C2B)

The liberation of the consumer hasn't just been a liberation from the business supplier in regard to what they need in terms of goods supplied. The way that consumers themselves behave as customers of business has also been changed by the Internet and electronic commerce.

A colleague of mine had an idea for a new book. His publisher was unimpressed. There appeared to be no market for the book proposed. My colleague set up a web page with all the details of his proposed book, complete with a web page access counter and a questionnaire for potential users. In less than two months he had enough evidence from the access figures and responding e-mails to convince his publisher that there was a market. A human being was able to sell his services to a business using the Internet.

Non-business EC

If we accept that the word commerce can mean social intercourse as well as financial transactions, we can go on to explore the concept that electronic commerce is something even bigger than global electronic commercial business. The Internet hasn't just blown to bits the commercial relationships of Evans and Wurster (2000). *People, politics, societies, cultures* and *convictions* are now a major feature of electronic commerce.

Beyond money transactions, the Internet reveals:

- education
- politics and pressure groups
- government
- personal and social relationships
- art
- religion

and many other non-commercial uses as subjects for electronic commerce.

Box 3.2

Electronic government

Government.direct was the name given by the UK government in 1999 to its strategy for the electronic delivery of central government services. The government issued a consultation document, called a Green Paper, with its proposals. It also suitably placed a downloadable copy of this document on the www.open.gov.uk official government website.

As in many other countries, people in the UK interact with government daily, whether they are applying for a driving licence, filling in government forms or paying taxes.

Government.direct envisages a time when people will no longer have to queue up, fill out paper forms and send off cheques for government licence; instead, they will be able to link directly into government through their television sets or from kiosks in post offices, libraries and shopping centres.

Pensioners, for example, could check their income tax at the rural post office. Parents in the urban high street could compare performance of local schools. Citizens could use one electronic form to tell several departments about a change of employment status.

Government.direct will also lighten the burden of government on the small businessperson and it will help those seeking work to sift through job vacancies. Services will be more accessible, more convenient, easier to use, quicker in response and less costly to the taxpayer. This will make dealing with government as easy as the supermarket laser checkout or the bank cash machine. If the take-up of electronic services follows the pattern of that for cash machines, then five years from now, 25 per cent of simple government transactions with the public could be electronic.

Comment

Tony Blair, UK Prime Minister, received many criticisms about proposals like these in April 2000, when Barclays Bank announced that it was closing many of its rural branches in the UK and said that the Post Office would take up the business of ensuring that people could still get cash from their government payments or their own bank accounts.

Poor people tend to be those who receive money payments from the UK government, and they also tend to be the people who don't have bank accounts or access to the Internet.

Anxieties like these are well founded in terms of what the problem could be. People who desperately need government financial support can be easily frightened into believing that some traditional method, like having a local bank or post office, is the only how, the only way it can happen.

Are there other ways? I suspect there may be, but the first stage in developing any new system is to look behind the labels. Ensuring that people can get cash payments is one objective, retaining banks and post offices is something else. We shall look further at this in Chapters 8 and 9.

Again, these are not new: a Phoenician tin trader would have recognized and have been involved in all of them. As we found with commercial electronic business, however, it is speed, weightlessness, ubiquity, connexion and reproducibility that make the difference. Only one student can have a particular book out of the university library at a time, but thousands can see the same web page. Two football fans living on opposite sides of the world can electronically swap opinions and pictures over the Net as easily as two in the same town. Political alliances and action can be simultaneously organized over wide areas and populations in a way that is not possible by phone calls and post.

Whatever we may think about the complex aspects of electronic commerce that we have explored so far, for good or evil, they represent a major area of concern for business.

The issues raised

Describing complexity

We don't have to read far into the mountain of material about electronic commerce and the Internet to realize that we are involved in a complex subject area. People who write about it try to simplify the overall picture by explaining how the *whole* is made up of various parts or *components*. This approach would show how the Internet is made up of computers, service providers, telephone lines etc. Another way of trying to simplify is to put things into categories or classes. Thus electronic commerce can be split up into B2B, B2C etc., as we saw above.

However, do these ways of explaining complexity always work? My computer is only part of the Internet when I've got it *connected*. I can also use it as a stand-alone machine. Likewise, my telephone line does other things besides giving me Internet access. If we look at explanations of electronic commerce based on classification, they too can be blurred or *messy*. If I purchase some software over the Web for my private use, that's apparently B2C. If I purchase the same software in the same way from the same supplier, but for my business use, that's apparently B2B. What's the difference?

What we discover when we look at complex *systems*, like electronic commerce on the Internet, is that names and labels can be misleading. *What* something is can be very different from how it is labelled or described.

Recognizing value judgements

A second issue is hidden behind the words 'bangs or bursting' in the title. Many of the enthusiastic and assertive presentations of electronic commerce and global information strategy that we can find in books, the media and on the Internet itself present electronic commerce as something positive. They feed us with a message implying that information and communications technology are 'good'. In our examples above, the NEC alliance with Hewlett-Packard and Oracle is going to develop 'solutions'. The city of Leeds needs to be 'new', not old-fashioned or out of date. Ebookers shares 'leap', which suggests a dynamic image of success.

We can also find another message in material about electronic commerce. This doubts whether electronic commerce and global information are necessarily beneficial at all. In my example of business-to-consumer electronic commerce I showed the advantages of purchasing a book over the Internet. I could also have said that the fact that I made that particular choice has future job implications for the people employed at that university bookshop. It could also affect me as an author. Why have books at all? Why not let readers download their own copy and cut out the delivery charges?

When we look at the way systems are described, we find that the descriptions carry *views* or *values* with them. Besides needing a way of describing complexity, we also need to recognize *what kind of*, or *whose* description of it we are getting.

Opportunities for learning

The two issues of describing complexity and recognizing value judgements are not new to us: we came across them in Chapter 2. They weren't specifically mentioned, but we did establish, for example, that classification and labels like 'strategic' or 'financial' were often an oversimplification of both what management really did and what information was used. We also discovered that words carry loaded meanings with them, as in the way the CSA was named to include the persuasive phrase 'Child Support'.

The lead-in case for this chapter may have moved away from an intimate and emotionally charged subject like deserted mothers and children to a global and impersonal survey of electronic commerce, but we have come across new versions of the same issues. A mother, father and child relationship may seem much smaller than an inter-organizational supply chain; but which of these examples is the less complex? I suspect that there are many managers who would rather sort out a supply chain problem than interfere in a family row. I also know that the language of corporate public relations or political battles can be as vicious as that of an aggrieved father objecting to excessive financial demands from the CSA.

The important lesson is that issues of complexity and value judgements do not relate to physical size, financial importance, number of people, or any other single simple measure. Instead, these issues start to appear when we see something as more than one uniform thing. The Child Support Agency wasn't just about money for children: it was about political machinations, lost tempers, complicated calculations, computer software and many other things. Electronic commerce isn't just about ordering a book over the Internet: it's about lost jobs, financial fortunes, cultural changes, training people in new skills and many things we have yet to realize. Both the Child Support Agency and electronic commerce lead-in cases are about systems. If we expect to go further with understanding them, and most other complex and value-loaded characteristics of our management world, we need to begin with the key word *system* itself.

Learning objectives

The learning objectives for this chapter are to:

1 Identify and understand the range of concepts that may be associated with the term 'system'.

2 Establish a framework for these concepts that can be used for understanding complex business contexts, particularly the role and nature of information and management systems in business.

3 Characterize systems behaviour in the context of this framework.

4 Introduce selected methods and techniques for use in the analysis, definition and development of systems.

3.1 DESCRIBING AND DEFINING SYSTEMS

3.1.1 Using the word 'system'

I expect that you have often heard the word system used to mean a way of doing something. The way that the Child Support Agency tried to process claims for maintenance could be described as a system. The way that my first book order over the Internet was processed by those Amazon B2C electronic commerce pioneers could also be described as a system. How often have you heard someone say 'what you need is a system' when they are criticizing disorder or chaos and suggesting an ordered or systematic approach? We might therefore expect a system to be essentially an *organized process* or procedure.

In this book we won't say that such a description is totally wrong; instead, we shall see that systems involve more than just organization and process. We shall be going further and show that when we talk about a system we will need to cover a wide range of areas, such as dynamics, order, membership, relationship, ideas and beliefs, psychology, complexity, uncertainty and decision.

3.1.2 Defining the word 'system'

Why use definitions?

Defining what we mean by the word *system* would appear to be essential in a book that claims to use 'a systems approach' and repeats the word hundreds of times. In fact, I am not going to produce a set of words to form a conventional definition at all. Instead, I will propose a different approach to helping us understand what we mean by a system. Instead of looking for a precise verbal definition that excludes all others, we will try to find some common ground among those who use it and build up an understanding of the term *system* as we go along. I believe that there are three good reasons for this:

1 There is no universally accepted definition of the term system.
2 The concept of a single *verbal* definition is alien to a systems approach and systems thinking.
3 Starting explanations with a definition of a concept is usually a bad way of teaching something.

Let's expand on these points in more detail.

Definitions of the term 'system'

The word *system* is used widely in everyday speech, as well as in a broad range of subjects such as physics, engineering, biology, economics and sociology. We shall find that many other words to do with systems thinking, as well as the word system itself, are also used in popular situations.

Box 3.3

Dangerous definitions

When the first nuclear bomb exploded over Hiroshima in 1945, it did so because the amount of the metal uranium$_{235}$ it contained had reached a *critical mass*. In other words, it had become *unstable* and *burst apart*. Look at the use of the term 'critical mass' in the media, and I suspect that you will find it being used to mean a *minimal survival* size: the opposite to the original meaning of the term.

The term *zero-sum game* refers to a game theory concept where any gain by one player is exactly matched by an equivalent loss by another player. The net result is *zero*, because for every winner there is a loser. Look at the use of the term 'zero-sum game' in the media, and I suspect that you will find it being used to mean that everyone loses: a *negative*, not zero, sum game.

Then there's *positive feedback*. As we shall see in Chapter 4, that's something that anyone interested in stability would avoid like the plague. But the popular use implies that it's a welcome, constructive thing.

When technical or specialist language is taken into popular use, its meaning is frequently changed. Systems language is no exception, so we need to check how authors use their words.

This is where we have a problem as students in a *business* context. Whatever precise definitions of technical terms can be produced by academics, the way that words are used in the *messy* world of business application will often blur what is written in books and journals. In this book we will not feign our way out of this issue by saying 'there are no right answers'. Instead, we will recognize that words are used in different ways, by different people, at different times and in different contexts. If this is true, then it is more useful to build up an understanding of a term that helps make things work, rather than trying to claim some final truth.

From this starting point, we will concentrate on attempts to define system in the areas of management and business, and then see what general understanding comes out of them. A good, early reference for selected readings in this context are the succeeding editions of Beishon and Peters (1972, 1976 and 1981). I suspect that these are still to be found in many academic libraries because many of the issues they raise remain relevant.

Coming more up to date, Schoderbeck *et al.* (1990) propose a definition that they think is 'a verbal and operational one which, though nonmathematical, is quite precise and as inclusive as that of the exact sciences':

> *A set of objects together with relationships between the objects and their attributes related to each other and to their environment so as to form a whole.*

However, if we look back to Beishon and Peters (1972, p. 12), we find the same definition described as 'widely quoted' but criticized as failing to recognize the 'subjective aspect' of systems. These authors then go on to define a system as an *assembly of parts* where:

1 the parts or *components* are *connected* together in an *organized* way;
2 the parts or components are *affected* by being in the system and are *changed* by leaving it;
3 the assembly *does something*;
4 the assembly has been *identified by a person* as being of *special interest*.

Item 4 of this definition attempts to cover the main reason the authors of the second of these definitions were unhappy about the first: the issue of the 'subjective aspect'. Beishon and Peters are emphasizing the point that what a system is seen to be depends on whose view we are taking and why they are interested.

We shall be considering the effects of this issue in much more detail both later in this chapter and throughout the book. In the fields of management, organizations and business, where human beings and their 'subjective aspects' are always present, any attempt to say what we mean by a management, organizational or business system must take account of them.

Alternatives to specific definitions

We can therefore find that the term system is used in a very wide range of subjects, and that what is seen as a system can vary according to who is using the term. In these circumstances, I think the chances of success for a very specific definition of the term are very limited.

Apart from this practical reason for being unlikely to find a single acceptable definition, there is another reason we might be against it in principle. Perhaps the success of systems thinking in being so widely applied has come from its flexibility and avoidance of a definition straitjacket. The fact that a physicist, an engineer, a biologist, an economist and a sociologist can all use the term system is one of the strengths that comes from its diversity. Indeed, we shall see that this diversity is part of systems thinking itself. If this is the case, then we would wish actively to avoid a single definition as being 'alien', as we said above.

If we take this position, however, we need to provide an alternative to a specific definition. I think the best alternative is to use what I called 'confining' in Harry (1990) when considering the term management. Since I wrote that book, I have heard this alternative approach better described as 'extensive definition'. Whatever word we use, the alternative is to consider the common properties that a range or family of uses would share, rather than defining the term itself.

Thus for the remainder of this chapter we shall look in more detail at the shared range of properties that characterize the different uses of the term system in the fields of management, organization and business. We shall find that when we do this, the meanings of the terms information and information system can then be understood in this context.

Before we do this, however, it remains for me to justify the assertion that starting with a ready-made or acquired definition of a concept can sometimes be bad educational practice, and to say why I believe it to be so in our case.

Definitions and the learning process

Although we shall be considering a range of theoretical material in this book and emphasizing the role of concepts, our ultimate goals are concerned with information systems in business, i.e. practically applied. When we consider the practical application of information system concepts, we shall find that the process of application has two important characteristics:

1 Definitions need to follow our understanding and experience, not precede them. Definitions play the role of concisely summing up the results of our experience and helping us form a model of our understanding. Thus if a statistician defines an arithmetic mean as $\Sigma x/n$, anyone with even limited experience of statistics would find it trivial to understand, but to someone with no mathematical experience it would be mysterious gobbledy-gook. (Indeed, I think that this is a common reason for mathematicians not getting their message across. They will insist on beginning with definitions for reasons of 'purity'.)

2 When we come to the practical activity of defining particular information systems and their properties, we shall find that we have to go through a discovery, learning or heuristic process before we can form a definition. We shall find that much of the actual 'problem' is that what forms a definition is not what follows, but what precedes it. This will be an important part of systems development in Chapter 8.

All of the preceding arguments in this section therefore lead us to consider the common properties that a large range of uses of the term system would share, and we cover these in the next section.

3.2 SYSTEMS CONCEPTS

3.2.1 Components

The concept

We began this chapter by exploring systems based on information and communications technology (ICT) applied to electronic commerce. One of the early examples of such systems that many of us first used was when buying books or CDs over the Internet. I suspect that few of us would have seen the mouse button, that we clicked when placing the order as a system. What about the mouse itself, or our computer? The answer to questions like these is likely to depend on who you ask. For someone who designs pointing devices for computers, a mouse isn't just a plastic shape with a couple of buttons: it is a system for translating small hand and finger movements into changes on the computer screen. A great deal of complex thought about ergonomics, electronics and human psychology has gone into designing the humble mouse. Yet to the materials scientist, even a plain mouse button is made up of a complex collection of chemical structures that have been formulated and synthesized to give the material the right strength and other properties.

When we come to the computer as a whole, with its mouse, keyboard, processor etc., I suspect that most PC users would describe our computer as a system. However, at the level of global electronic commerce, an economist or an accountant would probably see a single PC as just one tiny part of a system.

The clue to what unites these different views is the use of phrases like 'part of' and 'made up of'. If we consider something that someone calls a system, we shall find that it is seen as containing at least two, and usually many more, parts or *components*. What constitutes a component will depend on the *level* that the interested person is looking at. The economist who looks at the global level of electronic commerce is likely to see individual customers with their PCs as the smallest component in the system. The materials scientist choosing what the mouse should be made of is likely to be thinking about what molecular components will make up the material. Note how the different views of what constitutes a component reflect the 'has been identified by a person as being of special interest' aspect of understanding systems that we introduced above.

When we consider different kinds of component, however, we find that they can be classified according to their properties. Our electronic commerce examples can take us further with this. Phrases like 'buying and selling transactions' indicate that money and goods change hands between buyer and seller. Similarly, when news reports talk of shares that 'soared 100 per cent in their market debut', someone is charging a price and someone else is paying it. We can therefore see money, goods and shares as components of the systems described. However, goods like CDs or motor parts have different properties from money or shares. It is hard to believe that large sacks of £1 coins or $10 notes were winging their way between buyer and seller in the various commercial transactions that we described. Money in fact changed hands simply because buyer and seller agreed that it should. The transfer of the money is regarded as having happened once a sales agreement has resulted in certain figures being recorded or amended in their bank accounts. In these days of EDI, bank transfers and direct debit, exchanging physical money in the form of cash is no longer the only way of payment, but the money exchanged is very real nevertheless.

We can therefore take the concept of a system as being made up of components a stage further and recognize that these components may be *concrete* or *abstract*. *Concrete* components have a physical existence, like a coin or note, and can be detected by at least one of our senses. *Abstract* components are mental concepts and are not physically detectable. We used the term *weightless* earlier to describe forms of information that flow as electronic signals rather than paper documents. We can now see that weightlessness is another way of describing components that are abstract.

RQ 3.2	Is it possible to see one of the cupboards produced by Carry-Out Cupboards as anything other than a system of concrete components?

This leaves us with one other important issue that we need to understand about systems components. What if I asked whether the saving I made on my Internet book purchase, described above, was a lot of money? Comparing this to the amount of money involved in global electronic commerce on the day I bought that book, we might have been tempted to say that the money I saved was very little indeed. Yet we could also consider that on that same day, the money I saved on the book could have cured someone's blindness or even saved their life in poorer parts of the world. From this viewpoint, the money I saved was hardly 'very little indeed'.

We therefore need to understand something more about the components of a system, beyond describing them as concrete or abstract. We should also consider whether their properties are *hard* or *soft*. A property that can be defined, measured or assessed in some way that does not depend on someone's personal sense of value is called *hard*. If we have to count how many £1 coins there are in a purse, to measure their diameters or to weigh them, we know that the answers we get can be checked to see if they are correct. If two people count or measure the same thing and their results are not the same, they would agree that both of the answers couldn't be right. They would not consider the number of coins or their measurable properties as just a matter of opinion.

Soft properties are different. If one person thinks a certain sum of money is 'very little indeed' and another person thinks it is not, there is no agreed objective test to prove one of them right and the other wrong. Questions that depend on *personal values*, *opinions*, *tastes* or *ethics* cannot be resolved by counting, measurement or some kind of proof. They depend on who you are and what you think is important in life. Such values are often described as making up your *Weltanschauung* or *world view*. We shall have more to say about this later in this chapter when we explore *conceptualism*, and again in Chapter 8 when we consider how personal values are built into systems. For the moment, we note that the components of a system can have soft properties.

Box 3.4

Cracking the code for a caring image

Alison Maitland

Are businesses doing enough to protect their reputations?

The number of leading companies claiming to have ethics programmes has grown significantly in the past three years. But many still do not understand how to translate their statement of principles into effective behaviour, says a study published today.

The study, by Arthur Andersen and London Business School, finds 78 per cent of companies have a code of conduct, compared with 57 per cent three years ago. Three in five say they give business ethics high priority, against one in five giving it low priority.

The increased attention being paid to the issue is remarkable given the competition for resources from such issues as the millennium bug, the euro and cost-cutting, says the report. However, it points out that values statements and codes of conduct are usually not enough on their own.

'A committed investment by the chief executive to developing a corporate culture that values ethical behaviour is essential to success,' says John Quelch, Dean of London Business School.

The study, described by its authors as exploratory, is based on 78 survey responses from FTSE 350 companies and non-quoted companies of equivalent size. It says the participating companies are likely to be those most active in the field of business ethics.

The three most common reasons for pursuing ethics programmes were to protect and improve corporate reputation, to adhere to corporate governance guidelines, and to respond to 'increased emphasis on values'.

The survey reveals gaps in ethics programmes. The percentage of companies training employees in ethics has doubled in the past three years but is only 40 per cent. Of these, only 61 per cent train all staff. Employees are not usually involved in drawing up codes of conduct. Nearly half of companies with codes

do not make them publicly available on request – while a minority market them on websites.

Many companies are missing opportunities and risking a backlash, says the report. Excluding some employees can foster a 'them and us' culture. Restricting involvement in codes of conduct can encourage cynicism.

A particular concern raised by the survey is that employees and managers are perceived to have low awareness of business ethics risks, especially in companies that do not have codes or training, or do not make them available to all.

'It is as important that the driver of a delivery vehicle subscribes to the policy at least as much as his or her manager, because it is the driver who interfaces directly, with the public,' says Peter Newman, a partner in Arthur Andersen's risk consulting practice.

Source: Financial Times, 7 December 1999. Reprinted with permission.

Comment

Any idea that soft properties are just some 'touchy-feely' aspect of systems, with little practical importance, is refuted by the issues raised in this article. Awareness of business ethics and the politicization of the market means that soft properties can have hard financial effects. Attempts to confine concepts of business to hard components like money ignore the fact that there is no business and there are no markets that do not contain those sources of soft components called human beings. Far from being some kind of academic luxury, taking account of soft components is part of being practical and realistic.

You may come across some writers talking about fuzzy properties in this context. This term should be treated with caution. We need to distinguish between two different meanings sometimes given to it:

1 The first meaning can be illustrated by looking further at a monetary example. Suppose we were asked to say how much money would be involved in global electronic commerce during the next decade. The answer to such a question would be fuzzy, in the sense that we could not be certain about the actual amount of money until we reached the year 2010. We might say now that we thought it would exceed $100 billion. However, whatever our uncertainty, it will can be eventually resolved by recording the

actual data of global electronic commerce in the years 2000–9. The total of the figures recorded will not be determined by personal values, opinions, tastes or ethics. Even if we cannot get agreement over the amount of money, this disagreement will come from disputes about the records or the correctness of the calculations, not from the possibility of legitimate differences of opinion about what we mean by $100 billion. This kind of fuzziness that comes from uncertainty about hard properties we call *hard uncertainty*.

2 A second use of the term fuzzy coincides with the meaning of *soft* that we considered above. Where something is an issue of legitimate dispute coming from differences of personal values, opinions, tastes or ethics, it is fuzzy in the sense of having several possible answers; some of which may differ more than others.

In this book we will avoid using the term fuzzy just because there is this ambiguity about it. However, we will come across it in Chapter 5 when we mention fuzzy logic. This is a term that does have a clear meaning, but is used mainly outside the subjects covered in this book.

RQ 3.3	What hard and soft properties might a customer of Carry-Out Cupboards see in one of their products?

The practical implications of the concept

So far we have discussed the concept of a system having components and the properties of those components, but why should this be important for understanding business and information systems? The full answers to these questions will come when we consider the application of systems theory in the remaining chapters. For the moment, we can establish some important points.

First, the distinction between *concrete* and *abstract* components is important because information and data are themselves abstract concepts. In today's world of rapidly changing information and communications technology (ICT), failure to make this distinction can mean that our management thinking will fail to take advantage of important changes in the business technology environment. A major example of this is *software*. Until recently, purchasing software meant buying disks. In the 1980s it was 5.25 inch disks, in the 1990s it went from 3.5 inch disks to CDs, now much software is downloaded from the Internet. *What* we buy when we buy software is a set of *logical* or *abstract information*; the fact that *how* we buy it is one or other kind of medium is secondary. Thinking that software is a disk or a telephone connexion can lead to some muddled business decisions, such as investing in old-fashioned floppies rather than in the copyright of the software.

Well-intended graphical-user interfaces don't always help with our understanding. The picture you see in Windows, for example, when you extract a 'document' from a 'folder' is an image of something *concrete*, which is dangerously misleading. You don't take the so-called document 'out' of the folder at all. It is still there to be extracted as a *copy* an infinite number of times. The *abstract* or *weightlessness* of information in modern ICT systems means that its reproduction is virtually costless, in contrast to a *concrete* product like a CD, which costs money to manufacture.

We shall see other examples of the importance of the distinction between concrete and abstract components later, for example when we look at the design and use of databases in Chapter 5 or information systems development in Chapter 8. Meanwhile, as we first saw in Chapter 1, we shall frequently refer to the distinction between *whats* (*abstract, logical or weightless*) and *hows* (*physical* or *concrete*) in the information and other systems contexts.

A second important point for the practical implications of the concept of systems components comes from the distinction we made between *hard* and *soft* properties. It is important because it enables us to distinguish different kinds of information. We shall explore these differences in more detail in Chapter 4, but for the moment we can show two reasons that it is important from a practical viewpoint:

1 Since *hard* properties, like a bank balance, can be defined and assessed, it makes it easier to design routine, computerizable procedures to calculate and process them. Dealing with *soft* properties cannot be left to machines, because the *world view* or *Weltanschauung* of the people involved has to be taken account of. The soft properties of information systems require us to look carefully at the ways in which the information system should interact with the wider, human aspects of the management system of which it is a component.

2 The different nature of the *problems* that come from hard and soft properties of systems can mean that different *methods* or *approaches* are needed to deal with them when developing information systems. We shall study this in detail in Chapter 8.

Box 3.5

ECB hurdle to electronic money

Peter Norman, Tony Barber and James Mackintosh

European Union finance ministers yesterday postponed a decision to regulate institutions issuing electronic money, following last minute objections from the European Central Bank.

Sauli Niinisto, Finnish finance minister, said yesterday's meeting of EU finance ministers took the proposal off its agenda after Otmar Issing, an ECB board member, urged more discussion when he met finance ministers from the EU's single currency area on Sunday.

Mr Issing's intervention followed a letter from Wim Duisenberg, ECB president, to the Finnish EU presidency in which he voiced concern over plans which would exempt issuers of electronic money from some banking supervision if they did not offer other banking services. The ECB feared that, as electronic money grew in popularity, it would escape the close scrutiny of conventional banking activities and could eventually weaken monetary policy.

Electronic money is used by consumers in the form of electronic 'purses' where monetary value is stored on a chip card or computer memory for the purchase of goods and services on the Internet.

Large card-based projects are led by banks and so are unlikely to be worried about demands for full banking regulation. But small Internet-only operations could be forced to link with banks or apply for banking licences, which are not easy to qualify for.

The directive due for a decision yesterday was intended to promote the growth of e-commerce and looked set for approval. It will now be debated further.

The ECB's doubts about the Commission's proposals stem from its desire to ensure that all electronic money is subject to the central bank's regulatory framework. 'There must not be loopholes in the monetary control,' said the ECB's vice-president, Christian Noyer, in Basle yesterday.

The central bank is also concerned that expanded use of electronic money should not jeopardise its ability to control inflation, partly through influencing money supply growth in the eurozone.

At yesterday's meeting the ministers decided on rules for the introduction of euro notes and coins in 2002 and new proposals for debt relief for poor countries.

On the euro they agreed:

- to do everything possible to ensure cash transactions in euros will be the norm after the first two weeks of January 2002;
- the period in which national currencies and notes and coins would circulate in parallel would be limited to between four weeks and two months from 1 January 2002;
- to supply banks, retail and cash transport companies with notes and coins shortly before January 2002.

The ministers also said EU should provide 1bn euros (£641m) to help ease the debt burden of big indebted countries linked to the EU as members of African, Caribbean Pacific group of countries.

Source: Financial Times, 9 November 1999.
Reprinted with permission.

▶

Comment

Just as we saw that soft properties are no less important or realistic than hard ones, so this report shows that abstract components are no less real than those that are concrete. Here the EU is trying to manage the interaction of abstract money, which can be weightlessly transferred as a set of electronic signals from card to computer over a network, and concrete notes and coins, whose existence is easily known about.

Issues of security and other forms of control require a view of financial systems that can cover their complexity and intangibility. Concepts are not just academic playthings.

3.2.2 Connexion

The concept

Having identified that a system is a collection of components, we need to go further. We could, for example, describe an electronic data interchange (EDI) system as a collection of:

- *concrete* components like computers or lines carrying data
- *abstract* components such as legal agreements or orders
- *hard* properties of components like amounts of money transferred
- *soft* properties of components like the credit limit allowed to a customer.

For EDI to work as a system as in Figure 3.1, however, the components would need to be *connected*. One way in which *connexion* can be made is by making *concrete* or *physical* connexions with such things as optical cables between the various concrete components, like the computers. However, successful connexion into a system needs more than this. We have already seen above that: 'EDI employs standard electronic message formats, called transaction sets, to replace conventional business documents like invitations to tender, purchase orders, delivery notes and invoices'. This reference to 'standard' implies that there have to be defined *abstract* or *logical* properties for the components of the system for make connexion possible.

Connexion is therefore an essential property of a system, but it may be an *abstract* or *logical* connexion that will be physically manifested in the way components relate and interact with each other, not just through concrete physical links.

RQ 3.4 Are all of the connexions between the concrete components of a cupboard physical or spatial?

The practical implications of the concept

The particular importance of this concept for information systems comes from the implications of *logically* connecting *abstract* components. As we saw in the previous section, information and data are themselves abstract concepts that may be physically manifested in different ways. If we are designing or implementing an information system, we need to decide or know how information and data can be, or are, connected together. Thus in a business like Carry-Out Cupboards there will be a connexion between the number of various products in stock and the entries in the stock record, as in Figure 3.2. The stock record itself will consist of data that is *logically* connected because it makes up information about the particular stock item, and *physically* connected by being printed on the same document. It is important to notice in this example that *what* should be in the stock record has to be decided first, before we can decide *how* to record the details in terms of medium and layout. In Chapters 6 and 9, where we study *data modelling*, we shall look in detail at defining the logical connexions between data and information components of systems, as the necessary prelude to deciding how they should be physically recorded.

STOCK RECORD		
PART NO. DN 3480	DESCRIPTION CALABRIA 35	UNIT DESCRIPTION PACK
REORDER LEVEL 50	MINIMUM LEVEL 10	ORDER QUANTITY 50
LEAD TIME 4	STANDARD PRICE 205.00	IN STOCK 47
ALLOCATED 10	FREE 37	ON ORDER 50

Figure 3.2 A print-out of a stock record
How this information is presented needs to be distinguished from *what* it shows.

Connexion is therefore much more than physical linkage in most modern systems. So where a firm like Carry-Out Cupboards is connected to ICT systems like a supply chain, or to other organizations through the Internet, a major aspect of connexion is the defining information about *membership*, *standards* or *protocol*. I suspect that many of us have had vivid experience of this essential need as the result of frustrating experiences when failing to connect to the Internet. How many people in the late 1990s decided that it was time for them to be connected to the Internet, only to find that buying a computer, modem and software was not enough? Just one fault in setting up the software could result in hours of aggravation. My own son, who worked on a help-line at that time, was the recipient of much anger and verbal abuse from new users who thought that connexion was just about fixing bits of information technology equipment together.

Having explained the importance of connexion as a systems property, we have come close to introducing two other closely related concepts. In referring to how components are *related* and the way that they *interact*, we need to introduce the concepts of *structure* and *process*. The two concepts are complementary, so we will consider them in the next two sections.

3.2.3 Structure

The concept

We have seen that the components of any system have to be connected, and that these connexions may be *concrete/physical* or *abstract/logical*. While for a single PC there may be only one way of connecting components like the keyboard or the mouse, there are several ways in which a particular PC system could be connected to a wider system like the Internet or to an EDI system. As systems become more complex, there will be an increasing number of alternative ways of connecting the components, each of which can still lead to a working system. Furthermore, the way in which they are connected will affect the way in which the overall system operates.

When we talk of the 'the way in which they are connected', we are referring to the *fixed relationships* between the components of the system. We call this overall scheme of fixed relationships the *structure* of a system.

Although connexions can be concrete or abstract, the structure of a system is an *abstract* or *logical concept*. If we take the Internet as an example, it includes *concrete* connexions like telephone wire and *abstract* connexions like protocols; but overall it is the *logical* set of relationships behind these connexions that is important. Thus if I move the telephone extension to another part of my house, so that I access the Internet from a different room, I don't alter the structure of the wider Internet system of which my PC is a part. I could replace my PC with a palm-top computer integrated with a mobile phone. This would enable me to access my e-mail or the Web from a hotel room far away from home. However, despite the large change in what things looked like and where they were, the essential relationship between me and the Internet would be unchanged. *How* the structure of the system looks may be different, but *what* the structure is remains fixed. If, however, I replaced my PC system with a large computer that enabled me to set up as an Internet service provider, my *relationship* to or my *role* in the Internet would be different. Here the change would be structural, even though I and my computer system stayed in the same place.

One very common and important information and management systems structure is the *network*. If we look at the design of a whole range of networks, the essential point is what relationships they provide between their various components. Internal networks like an organizational intranet have to ensure that users have access to the software and data they need as members of that organization; while external networks, like those supporting EDI, will have to ensure that the orders and payments go from the right source to the right destination.

Not all aspects of systems structure relate to large or widespread components like networks. At a fundamental level such as that of single documents or computer screens, as in Figure 3.2, structural properties are important. Consider how individual entries like 'Lead Time 4' or 'In Stock 47' could be rearranged in many ways on the sheet, yet this would appear to make no difference to the overall information given by the stock record. However, if we rearranged the previous components to read 'Lead Time 47' and 'In Stock 4' the overall information given by the stock record would be very different. Hence the way that we logically structure *data* is the essential property that determines what overall *information* it records or transmits. We shall say more about this later in this section.

What is important for both abstract and concrete connexions, therefore, is that certain details of the logical form of the connexion between components *cannot* be altered without giving the connected whole very different properties, so that it ceases to be what it was and becomes something different. This applies to all our various Internet, EDI, electronic commerce or simple stock control document examples; and indeed, to all systems.

The practical implications of the concept

Many important organizational, management and communication systems that pre-dated information and communications technology were essentially *concrete*. Such systems as road, rail or telephone networks tended to be things that could be seen, touched and pictured. Tarmac, steel rails or cables have manifested these systems over the landscape in ways of which it is hard for us to be unaware.

Recent business, information and communication systems are different. Where, for example, is the Internet? No concrete record of the place where I live, such as a series of physical camera snapshots taken over the last two decades, would show that my village has computer-based information and communications technology systems that:

- process the business accounts of an organization 150 kilometres to the south
- give tutorial support to students in Moscow
- accept satellite data to manage 1000 hectares of agricultural land
- transmit water-management data to assist in the management of potential flooding of three major towns.

These are specific examples, but I am sure that whether you are reading this book in Egypt, North Dakota, Portugal, Kenya, Singapore or India you can find your own equivalents. The important structures that we can now detect in information systems, whether for good or ill, are less *concrete*, *tangible* and *visible*; and are increasingly *abstract*, *untouchable* and *invisible*. If our aim is to create and manage information systems in support of business, we need to look beyond the information and communications technology, to see what structural relationships are needed to give the system the properties we desire. This means that *concepts* in our minds are not just an intellectual exercise, but essential tools to be used in the design and management of information systems.

We also need to recognize, however, that the concept of structure is not just important for large-scale information systems like those based on the Internet. Our comment on Figure 3.2 that 'the way that we logically structure *data* is the essential property that determines what overall *information* it records or transmits' refers to the importance of structure as a concept at the lowest systems levels. Thus in our description of EDI in the lead-in case at the start of this chapter, we saw that 'EDI employs standard electronic message formats, called transaction sets, to replace conventional business documents like invitations to tender, purchase orders, delivery notes and invoices'. That phrase 'standard electronic message formats' is referring to the *logical*, *abstract* structure of the data that will electronically represent the information about a stock movement, product sale etc., regardless of what *concrete* form it could also take as a document or printout. The concept of information as a *data structure* is one that we will explore further in this chapter, and is central to the subject of *data modelling* and database applications that we shall study in Chapter 5.

3.2.4 Heirarchy

Having established what we mean by *structure* and shown why it is important, there is one particular form of structure that helps us to understand just about any system. This structure we call the *hierarchy* of a system. Figure 3.3 shows the concepts and language used to describe systems hierarchy. A system may consist of two or more *subsystems* and a subsystem will consist of two or more *elements*. Thus elements are components of subsystems and subsystems are components of systems. Although we have shown three levels of hierarchy in Figure 3.3, sometimes we may have simple systems with no

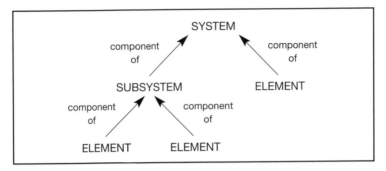

Figure 3.3 Describing systems and their components
Just as a system may have subsystems as its components, so a subsystem may be regarded as a system with subsystems as components of itself. A systems hierarchy may therefore have many more than three levels shown.

subsystems and just elements as their components. We can also have systems with many *hierarchical levels* in which subsystems have their own subsystems as components.

Our hierarchical view of any system will vary according to our *world view, purpose* or *set of values*. For example, to an information technology specialist who is concerned with designing EDI to support a supply chain, the number and the function of the various terminals on the network will be important. Hence, although the overall information system may be a large one that supports the whole supply chain, it is still relevant for the specialist to consider details down as far as individual PCs or data-entry devices. However, we could take another example like the proposed alliance between NEC, Hewlett-Packard and Oracle in the lead-in case for this chapter. Here the aim was to develop business platforms and solutions for the Internet between large organizational systems. The lowest level of interest in this case is likely to be the main classes of information technology involved, rather than the details of individual machines or equipment.

When we read *any* description, or see *any* diagram, which says that it is of *the* (whatever name) *system*, we should remember that an element will be the lowest-level component of interest. Deciding on this level, is a *management* decision based on *world view, purpose* or *set of values*, not a given technical fact.

RQ 3.5 How might this principle apply to perceptions of a cupboard to a sales manager and a production manager at Carry-Out Cupboards?

A final important point about the use of hierarchy as a *systems* concept. If we refer back to Box 3.3, we can see that the popular use of words can differ from, or even be the opposite to, their specialist use. *Hierarchy* is just such a term. As a systems concept it refers to *levels of aggregation*, for example when two or more components make a system. In popular use it is different: hierarchy is used to describe an organizational level or position. Thus in an army, a general is considered 'higher up' the command hierarchy than a private soldier. In a business organization, a managing director is considered 'higher up' the management hierarchy than a machine operator. From a systems viewpoint, and if we are concerned with a *practical* view of business management, such models of hierarchy are misleading. Just as generals are impotent without soldiers, so soldiers without unifying leadership are a discussion club. It is the coming together or *aggregation* of the components that makes for something *higher* in the systems sense. Thus a general *plus* the soldiers makes for something higher called an army.

I have developed the military example in order to link back to Chapter 2 where we first encountered it. As we saw there, when discussing *vertical divisions of management* in Section 2.1, levels or positions within an organization are only a limited guide to *what* managers actually do. In Section 3.2.7, we shall go further and see that a systems view of hierarchy as levels of aggregation helps explain essential properties of systems that traditional hierarchy does not.

Finally, it is worth noting that other views of hierarchy are used in the field of information systems. We shall cover these under the subject of object-orientation in Chapter 9.

The practical implications of the concept

The two connected concepts of structure and hierarchy lead to a whole range of related practical implications for the understanding, design and implementation of information systems in business and organizations. Some of these practical implications will become clearer as we consider the concepts of *holism* and *emergent property* in Section 3.2.7, and *control* in Chapter 4. These, in turn, will form the basis of the practical information systems development material of Chapters 7 to 9. However, there are two important practical implications that we can cover immediately:

1 Understanding the hierarchical structure of management systems will be the key to understanding *what* managers do, and hence the role of information systems as a component supporting management systems. Figure 3.4 summarizes this relationship, which we will develop further throughout this chapter and on through the book.
2 Understanding the role of data as a component of information will be the key to constructing information from its data components, and understanding the role of data processing as a component of information systems. This will be particularly important when we consider data and databases in Chapter 6.

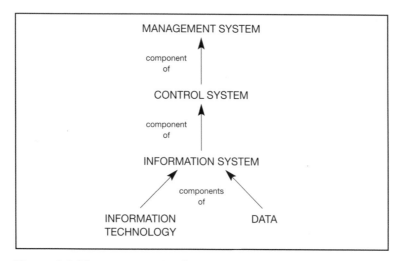

Figure 3.4 The components of a management system
Seen as a system, management is viewed in terms of what its components are, not how any particular management organization may be arranged.

The use of the term 'understanding' may not sound like a practical implication for the concept. However, the purpose of business information is to support *management* in *business*. If we have a false view of *what* businesses are or *what* managers do, we are unlikely to decide correctly *what* information an information system ought to deliver to provide such support. I've used the word 'what' three times in order to reaffirm the message we first put out in Chapter 2, that we *look behind the labels*.

Generally, deciding *what* a system should be is the essential prelude to detailing *how* it should be implemented. A whole range of practical topics such as information systems development or database management require such understanding and decision making as part of their implementation process.

3.2.5 Process and interaction

The concepts

A connected structure on its own does not make a system. The complex set of connexions of components that make up an inter-organizational supply chain do not form a working system just because they are connected into a network. Imagine an organization that is part of such a supply chain. What also has to happen after it is connected? As we saw in the lead-in case, at each of the stages along this chain buying and selling transactions take place, with flows of goods in response to information flows about what has been ordered, stock levels etc.

For us to describe something as a system, therefore, connected *components* have to *interact* so that the system *does something*. We also can see that the interaction of components within the system takes the form of one component's output being another component's input. For example, a purchase by a customer is a sale by a supplier; or a payment by customer is a receipt for a supplier. The term process is used to describe the concept of 'does something' or the dynamic properties of the system.

An important aspect of the concept of process is that any process *transforms inputs* into *outputs*. This may seem a trivial point at first, but we should look at it more closely. The concept of *transformation* means that any output is not something separate from the input, but rather the input *emerging* in a different form.

If we consider a system that carries out a physical process using concrete components like in the case of Carry-Out Cupboards, the concept of a transformation process is fairly easy to understand. Inputs such as bonded chipboard, cupboard fittings and packaging are transformed by the assembly and packing process into complete kits.

RQ 3.6   What transformation processes might be carried out by an EDI system?

We have already seen that a system, its components, their connexion and the system's structure may be *concrete* or *abstract*. So also *transformation processes* may effect *concrete* or *abstract* transformations. Abstract transformations are often referred to as *logical* transformations, because they concern the way we think about the differences between the inputs and outputs, rather than any physical change.

Abstract transformation processes aren't just relevant to large organizational systems, as in the use of EDI by supply chain management. The simple stock record of Figure 3.2 would look essentially the same for both large- and small-scale stock control systems. The data items stating 'Free 37' and 'Allocated 100' refer to how many of the cupboards have been allocated to a particular retail outlet and are free for future use. If we were to go to the warehouse and look at the 137 stock items, we would not see any *physical* difference between them; but here is an example of where concepts are not just academic nit picking. If we were to assume that the lack of *physical* or concrete differences meant that there was no difference between 'Free' and 'Allocated' stock, we could allocate the same cupboard, to several different retail outlets at the same time. For any cupboard, therefore, the transformation from one *logical* or *abstract* state to the another may not involve any physical change in the cupboards themselves, but it represents important *information* about the cupboards.

Similarly, a student who graduates may look physically the same before the graduation moment as after, but I suspect that most of us knew what a big *transformation* in our *logical* or *abstract* education and employment state took place at our graduation.

The practical implications of the concept

We have now established that another important property of a system is that its components have to interact so that the system does something. We shall further see that for an information system this means processing input data, or previously processed information, to produce output information we need to manage our organization or business.

The transformation processes carried out by an information system may involve a wide range of operations such as:

- recording
- communicating
- calculating
- updating
- sorting
- merging.

These transformation processes may also be done in many different physical ways. Thus our stock record in Figure 3.2 shows the amount of a particular item in stock. This amount can be calculated by subtracting any stock that has gone out since we last updated the record, and adding any new deliveries. The output of this data processing is placed in the stock record. Notice that I have just described what the process of updating the stock record involves, i.e. the *abstract* or *logical* process. If we consider *how* it could be done, we then identify the concrete or physical ways in which the process could be carried out. We might update the stock record by manual calculation and record the result on a paper sheet looking like Figure 3.2. We might computerize the process, as in EDI, so that the calculation and recording are done electronically.

We shall therefore find that we need to distinguish clearly between what an information system process does, and how it is or can be done. When we come to study information systems development in Chapters 8 and 9, we shall find that making this distinction enables us to improve existing systems and develop new ones by separating what is essential from what is a matter of choice.

3.2.6 Holism, emergent properties and behaviour

The concepts

'A mother holding her child is a group of two human bodies, a human body is a collection of cells, cells are entirely made up of molecules, molecules are arrangements of atoms; so a mother holding her child is just an atomic arrangement.' While such a statement might be a good way of starting a discussion or spoiling a social occasion with an argument, few people that I know would find such a statement acceptable or satisfactory.

The problem is not that the statement is untrue, but that it is incomplete. When we see a mother holding her child we do not see atoms, atoms cannot be seen in any case. But the fact that we do not talk of mother and child in terms of atoms does not mean that the image of the mother and child is an illusion. The mother and child may feel a strong emotional relationship, but the fact that molecules do not have emotional relationships does not make these emotions a fiction. The child will be growing day by day through the reproduction of its cells, but the fact that atoms or molecules do not reproduce themselves does not mean that the child will weigh the same in two years' time.

What we do find in our mother and child example is something that occurs across the whole range of our experience. We find that we can understand, interpret and talk about *wholes* in a way that does not necessarily work with their individual parts. When we consider collections of atoms and molecules making up cells, the whole cell has properties, like reproductive ability, that the atoms and molecules do not. Similarly, if we bring together a whole collection of cells in the form of a human being, then we can identify properties, like colour or emotion, that just don't make sense when applied to an individual atom or cell respectively.

The concept that a *whole is more than the sum of its parts* is called *holism*. The properties that make sense in terms of the whole but not in terms of separate individual parts we call *emergent properties*.

We were already implying these concepts previously when considered that 'components have to interact so that a system does something' and that its overall nature will depend on the particular way the components were connected, as well as which components are involved. When we did this, we implied that *a system itself is a holistic concept*. The need to see a *whole*, which we call a *system*, implies that the whole has *emergent properties* that motivate us to consider it as more than just several separate components.

For example, there could be a wide range of properties that we might require to emerge from the workings of B2B electronic commerce. One important property would be the security of financial transactions. However, this can only come about as a result of inter-organizational co-operation. Security is a property of the whole system. A transaction record that is only secure for part of the time is not a secure transaction, or a supply chain in which only some of the links are secure is an insecure supply chain. If we wish to establish or promote these properties, we need to regard the system as a whole. Thus security *emerges* as a *property* when individually secure electronic transactions are brought together with individually secure warehouses and transport, with some form of overall secure control. It is only at the level of all the different components interacting as part of a greater system that concepts like security, reliability or indeed commerce itself have any meaning.

The twin concepts of *holism* and *emergent property* also enable us to understand the concept of *systems hierarchy* (Figure 3.3) in more depth. Just as the need to recognize *emergent properties* leads us to see a collection of components as *a greater whole* called a *system*; so within the system itself we might wish to identify groups of components, or *subsystems*, that exhibit certain emergent properties that interest us.

In our mother and child example, we saw that certain *levels of aggregation* of components show properties not shown by the components themselves. Thus cells reproduce, but their component molecules do not. Or again, a single human being has emotions but the cells making up the human being do not. Similarly in a business example, neither human resources, production facilities, finance nor material procurement on their own constitute a manufacturing business. Bring all these components together, however, and we have a manufacturing business. To get an emergent property called B2B electronic commerce, two businesses then have to come together as customer and supplier, with all the necessary electronic and other connexions.

When we choose to see a system as a hierarchy, and the particular hierarchy that we choose to see, will reflect our *world view*, *purpose* or *set of values*, in terms of what emergent properties we think important and therefore what levels of aggregation we wish to distinguish. We could see the whole system of electronic commerce as made up of subsystem components like B2B, B2C etc. These subsystems could then be seen as having components like supplier and customer. However, this view reflects our purpose of understanding a picture of electronic commerce, regardless of where it might happen to be operating. If we were, say, a *Financial Times* reporter trying to report on the success of electronic commerce in different parts of the world, we might want to classify businesses in terms of geographical location. In this case, our hierarchy would look different. We might want to break down the global system into major economic subsystems like the US and the European Union, and into components like states and regions.

So far we have not mentioned our third concept, *behaviour*. We have already identified *process* as an important systems concept because every system 'does something'. Thus the bringing together of buyers and sellers of shares in an Internet trading system can result in share dealing. We can link the concept of process with that of emergent property when we refer to something that is done by a whole system, like dealing, commerce or co-operation, as in our various examples above. Thus 'dealing' is seen as a 'property' that 'emerges' from a system like Internet trading. Where emergent properties like these are explicitly *dynamic* and involve a *change in the state of the system over time*, we refer to the pattern of changes as *behaviour*. In our Internet trading examples, the state of the system would include data on such things as the number of trading accounts, the shares held by the various dealers, the price of shares or amounts of money owed. Over time, all of this data will change as a result of the interaction of the various components.

Although the term behaviour is normally confined to clearly dynamic emergent properties of a system, we can note that all emergent properties are dynamic in some sense. An emergent property like systems security may seem static as long as nobody breaks into the system. After all, the whole idea of security is to prevent undesired changes. However, we only know a system is secure because it dynamically repels attempts at unauthorized change. In this book we will avoid being over-correct and use the term behaviour for overtly dynamic emergent properties.

RQ 3.7 How might the concepts *emergent property* and *hierarchy* be interpreted in terms of the simple stock record of Figure 3.2 and its relationship to the context of Carry-Out Cupboards described in Appendix 1?

The practical implications of the concepts

The concepts of holism and emergent property will recur frequently in this book as we seek to understand the role and application of information systems in businesses and organizations. Meanwhile, there are three important practical implications that come from the concepts:

1 Understanding the hierarchical structure of a management system (Figure 3.4) is necessary if we are to understand what management does. Only when we know

what management does can we decide what kind of information the information system should supply in support of management, and what form it should take. If we now recognize that it is our view of the emergent properties that defines the systems hierarchy, then identifying the required emergent properties of a system will be the necessary first step to developing it. Most of the practical systems development methods of Chapters 8 and 9 are based on this conceptual view.

2 The concept of holism in relation to the hierarchical view of Figure 3.4 implies that a management system will have other components beyond the control system shown. As we saw above, there will almost inevitably be a human component that will bring soft issues with it to the whole management system. When we develop an information system, it will be just one component that has to go with technical, financial and other hard components to make up the desired emergent properties. We shall therefore need practical ways of co-ordinating information systems development with clarification and management of soft systems issues. Chapter 8 will cover these practical ways under the subject of soft systems methodology.

3 *Information itself is an emergent property.* When discussing structure and hierarchy, we established that certain details of the logical form of the connexion between components cannot be altered without giving the connected whole very different properties. The 'properties' we have just referred to are the *emergent properties* of the particular *whole* with which we are concerned. This 'whole' could refer to a raft of information flowing along a supply chain, or to the contents of a simple component, like a stock record. In both examples we can identify data as a component of the information, and state that the overall meaning of the information will depend on the construction of this information from its data components. In this context, information is the emergent property that comes from processing data so that it is transformed into a structured whole that we call information. Chapters 4 and 5 will cover the properties of information and data in this relationship.

Box 3.6

Broadcasters try to box in borderless TV

Edward Alden

It took less than two weeks for William Craig to make some powerful enemies. Since launching the world's first website offering a broad range of free, real-time television over the Internet, Mr Craig has been threatened with lawsuits by an alphabet soup of the world's mightiest broadcasting corporations – including ABC, NBC, and even the BBC.

The object of their anger is not, in itself, that impressive. The website iCraveTV.com is produced from an unmarked suite of offices in a nondescript suburb north of Toronto, and offers live broadcasts from 17 different networks – 10 Canadian and seven American. The signals are pulled from the airwaves via large antennae, converted to digital signals and retransmitted across the Internet.

While legally available only to Canadian residents, the site is easily accessed from anywhere in the world simply by typing in a Canadian telephone area code. Viewers receive a tiny screen on their computer offering grainy, broken images that are perfectly adequate for soap operas but not up to football games or high-speed car chases.

But in the world of the Internet, the future matters more than the present. Television executives, fearing the rapidly approaching day when broadband access will permit high-quality video images to be transmitted to most Internet users, have branded Mr Craig a pirate.

'This programming is all copyrighted and being transmitted without the owners' consent,' says Tom Davidson, a lawyer for WKBW-TV in Buffalo, an ABC affiliate that is one of the stations used by iCraveTV. 'And it is readily available to anyone around the world.'

The company has been threatened with injunctions and massive fines not only by the broadcasters but also by the producers of television programming. These include the National Football League, which owns the rights to US football games for which broadcasters are currently paying more than $1bn per year.

But the television and programming giants may have more of a fight on their hands than they imagine. Mr Craig, a 46-year-old veteran of the Canadian and US cable industries, and formerly a senior policy analyst with Canada's television regulatory agency, has a good grounding in broadcasting and cross-border copyright.

Under Canadian law, he says, the airwaves are a public good, and anyone is free to retransmit those signals without the permission of the broadcaster. It is just that nobody ever thought of doing it on the Internet before. The claim is not as outlandish as it seems. The huge Canadian and US cable television industries were initially built by stealing broadcasters' signals and retransmitting them over cable lines to subscribers outside the broadcast area.

After long battles, a legal regime eventually arose in both countries that allowed cable companies, and later direct-to-home satellite providers, to use those signals provided they compensated the programmers by paying into general funds divided among the copyright owners.

Matthew Fraser, a professor of communications at Ryerson University in Toronto, says iCraveTV is doing 'exactly what the cable industry was doing 55 or 30 years ago, and the cable industry attracted exactly the same outrage from the broadcasters'. In an unusual move for a country fond of regulation, Canada decided this year it would not regulate the Internet. When the broadcasters complained to Ottawa about iCraveTV, they were reminded that they had hitherto been strong supporters of keeping government out of the Internet.

That has encouraged others to ponder whether they should follow the lead of iCraveTV. Among them is Mark Cuban, president of Broadcast.com, an Internet company bought this year for $5.7bn in stock by the Internet portal Yahoo! Mr Cuban said this month that Canada has a much more favourable environment than the US for Internet video. Broadcast.com's radio programming is vast, but its television offerings, constrained by US copyright law, are meagre compared with those of iCraveTV.

Despite such rumblings, the broadcast industry's response to iCraveTV seems vastly out of proportion to the threat. Its revenue potential, based on web banner advertising, is probably minimal.

While some people may choose to keep an eye on a favourite programme while working at the computer, the same product may in future be available in better quality on television sets in many more places. Unless he can negotiate for private rights to cable programming, Mr Craig will also be limited to re-transmitting the network broadcasts.

Jeremy Schwartz, analyst with Forrester, the US research group, says the Internet's real threat to television will come from its scope and interactive capacity to offer users programming they cannot get from networks or cable companies. 'To just take TV content and dump it on the web is to miss the whole point and potential of Internet media,' he says.

Source: Financial Times, 18 December 1999. Reprinted with permission.

Comment

Here we see how information and communications technology-based information systems require a concept of boundary that goes beyond geography and lines on the map. Note that the abstract concept of boundaries does not deny their existence, it merely alters the form that they take. When the article title talks of trying to 'box in', it points to what the new form of boundary will be. It is abstract concepts like legal agreements or shared con-nexion protocols (see Chapter 5) that will replace physical location as the determiner of being 'in' or 'out'.

Note also the wise comment, 'To just take TV content and dump it on the web is to miss the whole point and potential of Internet media'. New components of the Internet, as a system, mean that it has new emergent properties not possessed by one-way TV communication.

3.2.7 Environment, boundary and identity

The concepts

We have now got as far as seeing a system as a whole, with its internal structure and processes, and its overall emergent properties. This enables us to talk of a system in a way that implies that we can also:

- *identify* a particular system as something *separate* from other things;
- state what *is*, and what is *not*, a component or a *property* of a system.

Identifying a system by making statements about it involves using the concepts of structure, process and emergent property that we have already developed. Making statements about what a system is not requires the two further concepts of *boundary* and *environment*.

We can illustrate these two concepts by referring to our lead-in case. We can decide whether NEC, Hewlett-Packard, Oracle or any other organization is part of a business alliance by seeing whether it is logically connected by legal agreement and whether it participates in some interactive process like B2B electronic commerce. If any organization decided to leave the alliance system, we would say that it was then 'outside' the alliance. Yet for an organization to 'leave' and to be 'outside' has nothing to do with physical movement. Despite this, we often use words with physical or concrete associations to describe conceptual or logical changes. Hence the term systems *boundary* refers to our *conceptual* dividing line between that set of conditions that defines membership of a system and other conditions that do not. Perhaps we come near to this in everyday life when we describe bad behaviour as being 'beyond an acceptable limit' or 'outside' the law.

Once we have the concept of an identifiable system *separated* from what is not that system by a conceptual *boundary*, we need to consider what may be 'outside' that system. If we do this we can distinguish two different things:

1 Some things may not be members of a system, but we do not see them as being totally disconnected and irrelevant. Thus as far as the NEC–Hewlett Packard–Oracle alliance goes, Microsoft and many other ICT organizations may not be part of that system. However, what these other organizations do is likely to *affect* the alliance in many ways.
2 Other things may not only be outside a system, but also completely irrelevant to it. Thus what goes on in my garden, or in the distant galaxies of the universe, is neither part of the NEC–Hewlett-Packard–Oracle alliance, nor does it affect it.

Things that are outside the system but have relevance to it and interact with it, we call *components* of the system's *environment*. We also conceive this environment as a whole that has more effect on the system than the system does on the environment. Thus, whatever the strengths of Microsoft or other ICT organizations individually, the whole world ICT economy of which they are part has much more effect on the NEC–Hewlett-Packard–Oracle alliance than the other way around. We could put this concept differently and say that a system has little *control* over its environment, but an environment can be a major *disturbance* to the system.

> **RQ 3.8** Are we defining the term environment here to mean something different from its use in the context of conservation and 'green' issues?

Systems that have an environment that disturbs them are called *open* systems. Systems that can be considered as essentially isolated, with no significant disturbance from outside their boundaries, are called *closed* systems. In a practical subject like business, it is difficult to imagine a business system that is independent of economics, the market, social attitudes, the law or any of the other common components of a business environment. In this book, therefore, we shall take the word *system* to refer to an *open system*. As we shall introduce in the next section, and develop in Chapter 4, it is the existence of a disturbing environment that is the main reason that business needs information.

Box 3.7

Linux

In 1991, Linus Torvalds, a Finnish computer science student, acquired a personal computer that ran on the Microsoft DOS operating system, the dominant PC operating system at that time. He was dissatisfied with DOS and thought about a better alternative. He explored an operating system called Minix, which was a version of Unix, but found that it had limitations.

Minix required a licence, which was restrictive and he felt stifled improvement. As a result of his experience, he decided to write a new operating system that would take better advantage of his hardware. He wanted to 'write a better Minix than Minix'.

A code was released under a GNU Public Licence, which meant that anyone could use and improve Linux however they liked, as long as they made their contributions available to the rest of the world.

This meant that anyone who wanted a new feature for Linux, or had an idea for a possible improvement, could try it out for themselves. They could request help, or work by themselves, or organize a project, so long as they made their changes or developments available.

Linux supporters (try searching for 'linux' on the Web) claim that this has led to a snowballing effect, because as Linux becomes more useful, it can also became more interesting to new programmers and therefore more useful. (See positive feedback in Chapter 4.)

Comment

I believe the issues raised from this Internet example show what separates rational, reductionist *thinking from* systems *thinking*. Rationalism *can easily make both of two cases:*

1 *Bill Gates has the money, so Microsoft will easily counteract the attempts by a Finnish computer science student to affect its Windows operating systems.*
2 *Linux is so much more sensible, and in tune with today's global information world, that Bill Gates' days are numbered.*

Systems thinking *presents some other views:*

1 *Will developments in information and communications technology mean that both Bill Gates and Linux will be forgotten by history?*
2 *What are the new possibilities for complex, constructive interactions between Linux and the Microsoft empire?*
3 *What do our Martian leaders say I should believe? (I'm assuming that they've just landed.) That is, there are no formulas that enable us to predict the unpredictable. Strategy has its limitations because all systems have environments that disturb them and over which they have limited control. How we cope with this is covered in Chapter 4.*

Recognizing the role of the environment also enables us to develop our understanding of systems *behaviour*. Although there may be as many different forms of behaviour as there are different systems, there is one general property that all systems share. For any system to exist, and continue existing, it must have the property of *homeostasis*.

We have already seen that all systems *do something*; that is, they carry out various processes and are dynamic. Thus Carry-Out Cupboards may sell products, hold stocks, receive payments, communicate information and so on. We can now see that such overall *dynamic* behaviour comes ultimately as a response to environmental disturbances such as demands from the market, the state of the economy or the availability of resources. Whatever dynamic behaviour the system executes, however, it must take some form that does not result in disconnexion or break-up if the system is to continue to exist. Thus the revenue from the sales of Carry-Out Cupboards may go up and down, its product range may change in response to demand, it may increase or decrease its labour force, it may change its facilities and their locations; but in the end, these changes must be ones that Carry-Out Cupboards as a system can accommodate.

A system's ability to respond and adapt to environmental disturbance without being destroyed is called *homeostasis*. By definition, a system that does not have this property soon ceases to exist, hence all enduring systems have the property of homeostasis.

The practical implications of the concepts

The practical implications of the concepts of boundary and environment can be understood in terms of Figure 3.4:

1 As managers, we need an information system because it is an essential component of a control system, which is in turn an essential component of a management system. As we shall see in Chapter 4, this need for a control system arises from the fact that all management systems have an *environment* that is a source of *disturbances*. These disturbances cannot be fully predicted or prevented, but they have to be allowed for and responded to if management is to achieve its goals. It is the control system that enables the management system to do this, and an information system is an essential component of any control system. Developing and maintaining an information system that supports the goals of a business or organizational system therefore requires a clear identification of that system's environment and its disturbances.

2 Even where a need to identify a business or organizational system's environment has been recognized, the systems *boundary* must be correctly defined. If the concept of a business or organizational system's boundary fails to include all its components, then we miss the opportunity of minimizing uncertainty and maximizing control. As we shall see in the next two chapters, information systems reduce *uncertainty* and support control. If, however, the concept of the boundary is set so that components of the environment are wrongly seen as components of the system, then we wastefully attempt to control the uncontrollable.

Point 1 shows that an information system has a vital role in ensuring that the business or organizational system of which it is a part has homeostasis. In Chapter 4 we shall open up a related concept: that of a system's *viability*, as in Beer (1985). For the moment, we can say that if any system is to survive the disturbances of its environment, or to be *viable*, the role of its information system is irreplaceable. If this is true, then the ability to understand the role of information systems, and to manage their specification and implementation, is essential for business managers.

Common examples of failing to understand point 2 are those that fail to recognize the role of human components both inside and outside the system. Quite elaborate technical expertise is frequently used to develop, implement and operate information systems, while the human component is either ignored or wrongly treated as if it were no different. The CSA lead-in case to Chapter 2 was a classic example of this.

3.2.8 Conceptualism

Conceptualism

Throughout this chapter we have established a set of properties that would be possessed by anything we would call a system, and we have called these *concepts*. If we take a *conceptualist* view of systems and their properties, then we are claiming that what a system is seen to be, and what properties it is considered to have, depends on the *world view*, *purpose* or *set of values* we have when forming our concept of the system.

We can find examples of this around us in everyday life. My house has an electrical system, a water system, a computer system and a telephone system. All these are concrete and fairly easily identified, but there are important systems that are not so obvious. Ours is an old house with a complex biological system of spiders, summer flies, woodworm, small mites, the cat and occasional mice. There is also the human activity system of myself, my wife and our children and friends when they visit. It would hardly make sense to talk of 'the' system in this context without knowing whose viewpoint we were taking. So if a man turns up and says he has come to 'check the system', we need to know that he is a telephone engineer before we can know what system he is talking about.

With systems that have more soft and abstract components in their make-up than the telephone system, the issue of whose system becomes stronger. I guess most telephone engineers would agree what 'the' system was in our house, but if we considered my business system it would be more complex. The fact that my wife and I use a networked computer system, a van and a car, etc., both professionally and privately, means that defining their role in my business system for tax purposes is much more complex than identifying what constitutes our simple telephone system.

Since most businesses, organizations and inter-organizational systems can be seen as having significant soft and abstract components, any attempt to understand the relationships of Figure 3.4 as a prelude to information systems development and implementation must recognize that a system is:

1 *A concept.*
2 *Someone's* concept that reflects their *world view, purpose* or *set of the values.*

The practical implications of the concept

Having established that any approach to developing and using systems that claims to be practical must take account of the essential principle of conceptualism, it is very important not to interpret this principle as some kind of woolly relativism.

Conceptualism does not claim that all systems are 'equally valid' or that 'there are no right answers'. Instead, it emphasizes that terms like 'valid' or 'right' imply a standard or yardstick against which the systems can be measured. We have seen that conceptualism means that what a system is seen to be, and what properties it is considered to have, depends on whose view or concept of the system we are taking. Therefore, any practical attempt to develop and implement a 'valid' or the 'right' system must include some means of systems specification or definition as part of its methodology.

One common type of information systems development problem will illustrate this principle. Case histories of practical problems in organizations and businesses associated with the supposed failure of computer systems are numerous. I expect that there will be one in the news when you are reading this. What so often is blamed on the computer in fact turns out to be a failure of the management system to have a clear idea or agreement as to what the computerized information system should achieve. The common reason for subsequent failure is that hard, technical approaches are then applied to computerize existing ignorance and disagreement.

The lead-in case on the CSA in Chapter 2 was an example of this. I find it hard to believe that the mess of the CSA stemmed from the fact that we did not possess enough knowledge of computer hardware and the software programming ability to create a successful system. I am quite sure that all the tasks that such a system would have had to carry out would be versions of ones that have already been successfully computerized. The problem with the CSA was trying to satisfy the complex and conflicting needs of fathers, mothers, children, civil servants, politicians, the British government and many others with legitimate and often powerful interests in what the eventual system should deliver. These problems have little to do with information technology *per se*, and very much to do with the conceptual relationships between the various systems shown in Figure 3.4. 'Absent fathers' isn't a computer systems problem, but it is an information and *management* systems problem.

As we progress through this book towards Chapters 8 and 9, we shall look at the implications of applying systems principles to the practical tasks of *information systems* development. When we do so, we shall find that the essential importance of deciding *whose* and therefore *what* system we are concerned with is never far away in any practical application.

3.3 DESCRIBING, MODELLING AND DIAGRAMMING SYSTEMS

3.3.1 Systems description

Section 3.2 has given us a set of concepts that enable us to talk about and describe systems. The next logical topic would be to study how we could bring all these concepts together and describe a system as a complete whole. However, our final point on the *conceptual* nature of systems means that we should first realize that any such description will reflect a particular *world view* or *Weltanschauung* held by whoever's description we're getting. In the corporate, global context of many business applications of information systems, sorting out whose world view we're getting, or ought to be getting, can itself be *the* main problem.

Given the potential magnitude of the task of describing, modelling and diagramming systems in a practical context, we shall devote most of Chapters 8 and 9 to the subject. Meanwhile, we shall consider some simple foundations.

One simple account of what is involved in producing a systems description was pioneered by Mayon-White and Morris (1982). They saw it as a six-stage process:

1 Awareness.
2 Commitment.
3 Detection.
4 Separation.
5 Selection.
6 Description.

Taking *awareness* as the first stage recognizes that every system is someone's concept. In our case, that 'someone' is one or more people who wish to use a systems approach to management. What was it that made them conscious of a particular situation and start thinking that a systems view of it might be relevant? We have already established that *complexity* in a situation can be a good indication that a systems view is relevant, but what is likely to make us aware of the complex situation in the first place? In Chapter 8 we shall see that two common reasons are:

- shortcomings or *failure* in the existing system as a result of environmental disturbance;
- awareness of change in the environment and a desire for *innovation*.

However, in a *management* context, merely being aware is not enough. If we are to sort out some failure, or push on with an innovation, we need a reason or *commitment* that will make the process of systems description worthwhile. Whatever the details of any commitment, it has to be based on at least the assumptions that:

- we have some choice of actions
- chosen actions can make things better.

The belief that our actions can make things better is an essential tenet of management. We shall explore this belief further in Chapter 4. For the moment, we note that it is called *meliorism*, and that without such a belief, why waste time trying to manage?

We have now reached the stage where, as managers, we would like to create a *systems* description of a situation that we would like to manage. At the detection stage we consider what, if any, sorts of system may be seen in the situation. What *conceptions* are possible?

If the situation we seek to address as managers looks worthy of a systems approach, particularly because of its complexity, it is very likely that we will need to distinguish, or make a *separation*, of the different conceptions. Having done this, we need to make a *selection* from these conceptions of the one that seems most in line with the commitment and *world view* that we established earlier in the method.

We should now have an initial concept of the system for which we need a description. What should we put into such a description? Mayon-White and Morris (1982) suggest a list of:

- components of the system
- components of the environment
- inputs and outputs
- state variables of the system
- structural relationship between the systems components
- relationships between the state variables

all of which link to our study of systems concepts in Section 3.2.

What comes out of this list is the material for a systems *model*; that is, a way of representing our concept of the system in relation to our management *commitment*. The issues implied by the use of the word *commitment* are not just academic niggling. Instead, they are part of a major message of this book that we shall see coming out of Chapter 4:

> *Every information system is the implementation of a policy: if management does not determine this policy, it will be determined elsewhere.*

Given this *critical* comment, we can meanwhile note that the approach we have covered is just one from a rich history of systems thinking. Also in those formative times, Ulrich (1983) produced a set of *critical systems heuristics*: questions that push the derivation of a systems description towards a recognition of whose system we might be describing and from *what* world view or Weltanschauung it came.

3.3.2 **Types of models**

We have already seen in our development of systems language that where a term has both a systemic and an everyday meaning, we need to check any distinction between them. Model, however, is a term that means much the same in everyday life as it does in systems language. The main difference is that the systemic use of the term covers a wider range.

A model is a way of representing something. The thing represented may exist in real life or it may be a concept in the mind of the person making the model. Models can be created using different approaches:

- We can make a physical representation of something by using the same properties for the model as those possessed by what is being modelled. Usually the only difference between the model and the thing being modelled is a change of scale. Such models look like the thing they represent but are just a different size. These are the sort of models that planners or engineers often use to represent a new shopping centre or a new aircraft. They are often called *iconic* models, from the Greek word *eikon*, meaning an image.
- We can represent the properties of the original thing being modelled by substituting different ones to represent those in the model. Thus one property, like temperature, can be represented in a model by another property, like length in the mercury column of a thermometer or colour shades on a weather map. Such models are called *analogue* models.
- We can represent the properties of the original thing by using symbols in the model. This is what a mathematician does when describing the behaviour of something using algebra and equations. Such models are called *symbolic*. The most important examples of symbolic models as far as information systems are concerned are those we create when we produce diagrams to represent some properties of a system.

RQ 3.9 Are so-called icons, which are used by graphical user interfaces like Microsoft Windows, iconic models?

Given that diagrams are a form of model, it is worth considering why models, including diagrams, are used. We have already used several diagrams in this book so far, and this, like just about any other book you may find with the word 'system' in its title, contains many more. In the next few sections we will see why diagrams always seem to go with systems and how they are used. This should prepare us for their frequent use in this book and in the analysis, definition and development of systems.

3.3.3 **Why models and diagrams are used**

Models

We shall begin by generally considering why models, including diagrams, are used. We shall then go on to consider specific reasons for using diagrams in the context of information systems analysis, definition and development.

Understanding the use of models becomes clearer if we note that they are a substitute or stand-in for the thing they represent. We would wish to use a substitute in this way when any of the following apply:

- It is cheaper to create a model for discussion or experiment than it is to create the real thing. Producing an architect's model of a new building is cheaper than building it in real life. Producing a diagram of how a system might work is easier than producing the whole system.
- It is easier to experiment with and modify a model than it is to do the same in real life. It is easier to rearrange the components of an architect's model than to rebuild the building. It is easier to modify a diagram than to install a new system.
- Mistakes made when experimenting with a model are less disastrous than ones made in real life. Finding that the plastic scale model or the screen image of a car will not fit into the garage is less disastrous than scraping your car against the brickwork as you drive it in. Calculating (= symbolic model) that a particular file will not fit into a given computer memory space is less disastrous than the reorganization of a public records system with questions in parliament and the fall of a government. (A completely fictitious example, but it could have happened by the time you read this book.)
- Building a model helps you understand the thing being modelled. The architect's plan helps us to see that you don't need to go up any stairs to get into the dining room. A systems diagram shows the order of processes that have to be carried out to update a customer's account.
- Models can be used for communication, education and training. When the architect's client wants to know what the building will look like, or the builders needs to know what they are supposed to be building, the model, in the form of the design plans, shows the answers. When the programmer wants to produce the system specified by the systems designer, diagrams will almost certainly be used as part of the specification.

Systems diagrams

Given that diagrams as a particular form of model have already been frequently used in this book, we can list how the broad reasons for using models translate into the need for systems diagrams:

- *Complexity* and *holism*: if the whole is more than the sum of the parts, then a description of a system and its components, one at a time in serial fashion, is not an effective way to present the qualities of the whole. A diagram can make use of all of the flat surface of a paper page or a three-dimensional screen projection to give an overall picture.
- *Definition*: if diagrams are more effective at representing the whole form of a particular system and its qualities, then they can equally effectively define existing and proposed systems, relationships, structures and processes.
- *Discovery*: it is hard to represent what you do not understand. Having to discover enough about a system to draw a diagram not only requires *heuristic* (=discovery) activities, but also implies comparison with knowledge or ideal models that we already have. Ideals imply paradigms, and comparison can imply the analysis and comparison.
- *Recording*: for a diagram to represent what has been defined or discovered about a system, it must also be a record. Systems may have both abstract and concrete components, but a diagram can record both. It can use the principles of symbolic representation to model both abstract and concrete properties of the system.

- *Communication*: as we shall see in Chapter 5, the communication of information requires a shared symbol set. Agreed conventions for the use of symbols to represent systems components can mean that diagrams act as a language for communicating information about systems.
- *Education*: one particular form of communication is involved when we attempt to implement and maintain systems. As we shall see in Chapter 8, systems development itself is a systemic process with a human aspects role. Diagrams as definers and communicators of information about systems can support this role.
- *Control*: attempting to implement a system and maintain its goals is a form of control. Diagrams can act as a particular medium for the recording and transmission of information, as part of the *control loop* that we shall cover in detail in Chapter 4.
- *Learning*: if diagrams have a control role in systems development, then at *higher-order levels of control* they can act as tools for learning. Again, we shall cover this in more in detail in Chapter 4.

Systems development

We have now referred to *systems development* several times when explaining the use of systems diagrams. Systems development is concerned with the whole process of deciding the need for a system, specifying what it must do, designing how it must do it and implementing the design.

This process will require the eventual *definition* of the system to be implemented, after *discovery* of the problems of the existing system and improvements to it have been *recorded*, so that it can be *communicated* to the potential users. They are thus *educated* into *controlling* its implementation and subsequently *learning* from their experience.

All the words in italics indicate the potential role of systems diagrams in systems development, which we will cover in more depth in Chapters 8 and 9. To prepare us for more detailed use of diagrams throughout the book, however, it would be useful to have a simple way of making sense of the many diagrams that can be used. We shall do this in the next section.

3.3.4 Types of diagram

Even the briefest look at books on systems will show that diagrams are widely used, for the reasons we have just given. What we will also soon see if we look more closely is that the range of diagrams appears to be very wide, both in what they show and how they show it.

Although the advocates of particular systems methods or the authors of some books have regularly attempted to establish standards, there is no sign of any widely accepted convention for diagramming. Hence any attempt to discuss systems diagrams in detail is in danger of becoming a mere listing of all the different conventions and styles.

There is, however, one simple but effective way to make some sense of the bewildering range. If we remember that all systems diagrams seek to present one or more properties of a system, then the range of approaches to diagramming is likely to reflect the range of systems properties. The most important of these are likely to be what the system consists of and what the system does, i.e. *structure* and *process*.

Structure

Figures 3.3 and 3.5 represent the two main ways of showing structure, that is, they represent fixed relationships between the various components of a system. The positions of the components do not represent any particular sequence of events in time or logic. There is no reason that any one particular subsystem should be in any particular place on the page, or that the shapes of the blobs in Figure 3.5 should be of any particular kind. What matters in a diagram showing structure is that we can see the relationships between components rather than worrying about how the individual components are represented.

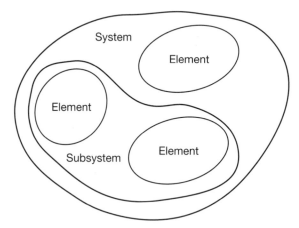

Figure 3.5 Systems hierarchy
The shapes of 'blobs' in diagrams based on the Venn convention are not significant.

The diagrams show structure by using one of two basic ways of showing relationships: by linear linkages or by encircling containment. The first method is sometimes called the digraph convention, and is illustrated by Figure 3.3. The second method is called the Venn convention, and is illustrated by Figure 3.5.

Process

The essential point about any process is that it transforms some input to a different form that we call an output. However, the input to a process will have come from some source, another component either in the system or in its environment. Similarly, the output will need a destination, either in the system or in its environment. For diagrams showing process, we therefore need some way of showing:

- individual processes
- the flow of inputs and outputs
- the sequence in which processes are carried out
- sources and destinations outside the system.

Processes, sources and destinations are usually indicated by some convention of shapes for blobs (e.g. Figure 3.5), and the usual way to show flows is by means of arrows. Sequence is then expressed by the logical connexion of processes, sources and destinations through the arrows.

Note also that sequence can be shown by an accepted convention of relative position on the page. Thus in European convention, sequence begins at the top left-hand corner and proceeds rightwards and downwards to the bottom right. However, there is no reason as far as I can see that we shouldn't go right–left or bottom up: the main thing is that the convention is understood.

Unstructured or free diagramming

Our analysis of the basic principles and reasons behind diagramming has left out one important example that we shall take up again in Chapter 8. If our need for a diagram is mainly heuristic, a convention can be dangerous in that it focuses our attention on one particular aspect. Thus attempting to diagram processes means that the system is seen primarily as something dynamic, with structure coming in later. If our heuristic aims mean that we want to keep our minds open to record anything about a situation that may be of interest, a way of diagramming that does not have a predetermined emphasis might be useful.

As we shall see in Chapter 8, such a diagram is the rich picture. Its aim is to provide a holistic, open way of recording any situation as we meet it. The lack of strict rules about what sort of symbols, words or any other way of recording can be used is deliberate. It is an attempt to prevent us from prematurely excluding things just because they can't be neatly pigeon-holed, or only selecting certain kinds of evidence. With a rich picture, we can record anything that is of interest and sort out later what sort of themes, topics or issues the picture tells us about.

Key words		
Analogue model	Emergent property	Output
Behaviour	Environment	Process
Boundary	Hard	Soft
Complexity	Hard uncertainty	Soft uncertainty
Components	Hierarchy	Structure
Concept	Holism	Subsystem
Conceptualism	Iconic model	Symbolic model
Concrete	Identity	System
Connexion	Information	Transformation process
Data	Input	Uncertainty
Dynamic	Interaction	Weltanschauung/world
Element	Model	view

Seminar agendas, exam topics and project/dissertation subjects

1 Business-to-consumer electronic commerce has now moved well beyond books, music CDs and videos. Most things that can bought in a shop can be bought on the Web. Services also are represented; particularly banking and finance. Yet what is new? Is there any real difference between Internet shopping and old-fashioned mail order, apart from speed? Are Shapiro and Vadan (1999) right when they say, 'Ignore basic economic principles at your own risk. Technology changes. Economic laws do not'? Or is the Internet more than economics?

2 Why do we seek to have definitions for terms in practical subjects? Is defining things useful? Consider the form and role of definition (if any) in engineering, medicine or the law. Talk to fellow students who study these subjects.

3 What were the sources of the systems movement? Why has it become so strong in the last three decades? Take a reader like Beishon and Peters (1972, 1976 or 1981), as a starting point; or try searching for 'systems thinking' on the Web.

4 Discuss the words holism, uncertainty and decision in relation to the three quotations at the start of this book from Lord Kelvin, Eddie Brickell and the Duke of Wellington.

5 'Many of the soft issues connected with goals have often been decided for official organizations by the government and can be less of an issue for them.' Would this be a good dissertation topic area? It is very broad; you could consider, for example, whether soft issues do get resolved or, if so, how.

Feedback on review questions

RQ 3.1 In the report on NEC, Hewlett-Packard and Oracle, the Internet is being used by businesses to deal with each other. Whatever is bought, sold or transacted, both the supplier and the receiver are businesses. Electronic commerce of this kind is therefore described as business-to-business or B2B.

An online travel agency like ebookers.com may be different. Where the customer is the final *consumer* of the product, usually individual people, such electronic commerce is described as business-to-consumer or B2C. This relationship can be reversed. Where individuals sell products or services to organizations, like an architect advertising over the Internet, a consumer-to-business or C2B relationship is possible.

Christie's, an international auction house, aims to connect individuals who have something to sell with individuals who may want to buy. Here we have a consumer-to-consumer relationship, or C2C electronic commerce.

Professor Kevin Keasey wasn't so much concerned with selling anything. Instead, he saw electronic commerce as a means of benefiting the economy and social life of a city. Not all aspects of electronic commerce are purely financial. So-called non-business EC recognizes that 'commerce' can mean *social intercourse* as well as financial transactions.

RQ 3.2 If we are thinking about the physical cupboard itself, probably not. However, what constitutes a cupboard can be very different for different people in the organization. Thus to someone planning production a cupboard is essentially a job that requires the bringing together of components like production, capacity, time and human skill, all of which are abstract – just as œ1 could be the name of something concrete or abstract depending on whose view we were taking.

The importance of deciding whether we are talking of something in concrete or abstract terms will be explained further when we consider entities in the context of data modelling in Chapter 5.

RQ 3.3 Hard properties might include physical measurements, price, weight, as well as defined properties like 'finish' or numbers of components. Soft properties might be attractiveness, convenience or fashion.

RQ 3.4 I don't think so. A door, for example, can be considered as a component of a cupboard from the moment a designer decides to make it so. An *abstract* or logical connexion has been made well before the cupboard is assembled.

RQ 3.5 To a sales manager a cupboard is probably seen as an element in the sales system, since nothing less than an individual cupboard is of much interest. To a production manager a cupboard is seen as a component of the production system, but also as being made up of components, which are the parts and subassemblies forming the cupboard.

RQ 3.6 For a system such as EDI, the transformation processes carried out will be mainly concerned with transforming abstract components such as money. As we saw above when discussing abstract components, our awareness of this transformation process is likely to come from the information we record about conceptual changes in the logical state of the system or its components, rather than any observed physical mechanism. With a concrete output from a system, like the Carry-Out Cupboards assembly process, we may watch a physical good appearing at the end. When two organizations exchange payment electronically, no physical money changes hands and there is little to be seen, but this certainly does not mean that the transformation process is 'unreal' or not 'practical'.

RQ 3.7 The concept of record itself is an emergent property, since all of the data items have to come together to make it. The *hierarchy* at its simplest is the view that the whole record is an *aggregation* of its data item components. However, we could see more complex levels of aggregation if we saw all the data about, say, stock condition as a group. Thus 'In stock', 'Allocated', 'Free stock' and 'On order' form a subgroup.

RQ 3.8 Not necessarily. Where we are concerned with a biological or ecological system the two terms may coincide. If we consider an animal or species as a system, the atmosphere they breathe, the plants or other animals they eat, and so on, are all part of their systems environment.

RQ 3.8 Where computer icons are pictures of what they represent, they are iconic models. Examples might be printers or other peripherals. However, most so-called icons are in fact symbolic, since they are signs rather than representations. Thus you don't really have a filing cabinet in your computer.

References/bibliography

Ackoff, R.L. (1962). *Scientific Method: Optimizing Applied Research Decisions*. Wiley, New York.

Ackoff, R.L. (1971). 'Towards a System of Systems Concepts'. *Management Science*. 17 (11).

Ackoff, R.L. and Sasieni, M.W. (1968). *Fundamentals of Operations Research*. Wiley, New York.

Beer, S. (1985). *Diagnosing the System*. Wiley, London.

Beishon, R.J. and Peters, G. (eds) (1972; 1976, 2nd edn; 1981, 3rd edn). *Systems Behaviour*. Harper & Row, New York.

Ben-Eli, M.U. (1988). 'Cybernetic Tools for Management: Their Usefulness and Limitations', in Sadovsky, V. and Umpleby, S. (eds). *Science of Goal Formulation*. Hemisphere Publishing, New York.

Davis, G.B. and Olson, M.H. (1984). *Management Information Systems*. McGraw-Hill, New York.

Espejo, R. and Harnden, R. (1989). *The Viable Systems Model*. Wiley, London.

Evans, P. and Wurster, T.S. (2000). *Blown to Bits: How the New Economics of Information Transforms Strategy*. Harvard Business School Press, Boston, MA.

Flood, R.L. and Jackson, M.C. (1991). *Creative Problem Solving*. Wiley, London.

Harry, M.J.S. (1990). *Information and Management Systems*. Pitman Publishing, London.

Luce, R.D. and Raiffa, H. (1957). *Games and Decisions*. Wiley, New York.

Mayon-White, W. and Morris, R. (1982) *Systems Behaviour*. Open University, Milton Keynes.

Schoderbeck, P.P., Schoderbeck, C.G. and Kefalas, A.G. (1990). *Management Systems*. Business Publications, Homewood IL.

Shapiro, C. and Vadan, H.R. (1999). *Information Rules: A Strategic Guide to the Network Economy*. Harvard Business School Press, Boston, MA.

Turban, E., Lee, J., King, D. and Chung, H.M. (1999). *Electronic Commerce: A Managerial Perspective*. Prentice-Hall, Upper Saddle River, NJ.

Ulrich, W. (1983). *Critical Heuristics of Social Planning*. Haupt, Berne.

CHAPTER 4

Management, control and information

The freedom to control freedom? Anarchists organize themselves to control the controllers of world trade

What happened

Being the host for a major world event, like the Olympic Games or a World Cup, has often been a strong aim for cities and countries throughout the globe. Sometimes it has been so strongly desired that there have even been allegations of bribery and corruption of those who choose the locations for such events.

I don't know if any pressure was exerted to locate the international talks for the Millennium Round of the World Trade Organization (WTO) in Seattle, USA, from 30 November to 3 December 1999. Now we know what happened, I suspect that many in Seattle would have liked to see the WTO go somewhere else. Just before the start of the Millennium Round, the city was astonished to find that about 50 000 critics of global capitalism had arrived threatening to paralyse the talks with 'the protest of the century'. The threat wasn't too exaggerated. Once events got underway, the *Seattle Times* was asking what the WTO was doing bringing thousands into a crowded city the week after Thanksgiving, 'mucking up Christmas shopping, immobilizing the city centre and opening the door to havoc'. The level of protest forced the WTO to cancel the opening ceremony of its meeting after protesters choked the city, preventing many delegates from leaving their hotels.

The protesters were a richly mixed gathering. There was an official demonstration of tens of thousands mounted by the trade union group, the American Federation of Labor–Congress of Industrial Organizations, but many other groups joined in. Besides steel workers demanding labour protection, there were environmentalists against the American proposal for a free logging agreement that would speed up the destruction of forests; vegans protesting against the WTO's frustration of rights for animals around the world; Dyke Action, a lesbian group opposed to free trade; the British organization Reclaim The Streets, which brings cities and motorways to a halt with its mass bicycle rides; the Kuna Indians of Panama; Zaptista Rebels of Chiapas; and a group bearing placards calling for 'China out of Tibet'. At the more vigorous end of the demonstration, what the press described as 'masked gangs of black-clad anarchists' overturned street furniture and broke the windows of multinational companies such as Starbucks coffee, Bank of America and Banana Republic.

So how did such wide-ranging and disparate groups manage to get themselves so well informed and organized to be at the right spot at the right time? For several months, hundreds of groups had developed plans to attend and disrupt the Millennium Round using the Internet. What many of the press described as 'the chaos of the past two days' was not accidental serendipity. A large range of anarchist and protest websites had hyperlinked themselves to a central website 'n30', named after the opening WTO date of 30 November. This site then acted as a central message board for the protesters. In particular, they studied Seattle's street maps and planned manoeuvres to outsmart the city police.

The police began with an energetic approach to their job. Squads wielding batons, with some carrying machine guns and CS gas, manned the streets round the convention centre. Police fired pepper spray at activists who were illegally occupying strategic street intersections. The protesters had linked arms and surrounded the Sheraton Hotel where the ministers are staying, to stop delegates, press and non-governmental organizations getting through. Riot police fired rubber bullets and tear gas in their efforts to move protesters, but many protesters picked up the tear-gas canisters and hurled them back at the police. The net effect was to increase the violence and disruption rather than to stop it. The next day, Assistant City Police Chief Ed Joiner agreed that 'in hindsight, the approach we adopted yesterday did not work'.

Meanwhile, the WTO meetings did eventually take place. On 1 December, the US Ambassador Charlene Barshefsky opened a meeting by expressing her regrets to ministers and officials who were harassed during the demonstrations. She said that the government and people of the US deplored the 'irresponsible actions of a tiny minority'.

So what is the WTO and what does it do? I've selected some of its own assertions as they were in early 2000 at www.wto.org:

> *The World Trade Organization is the only international organization dealing with the global rules of trade between nations. Its main function is to ensure that trade flows as smoothly, predictably and freely as possible. If it is successful in this, the result should be that consumers and producers know that they can enjoy secure supplies and greater choice of the finished products, components, raw materials and services that they use. Producers and exporters know that foreign markets will remain open to them.*
>
> *The result is also a more prosperous, peaceful and accountable economic world. Decisions in the WTO are typically taken by consensus among all member countries and they are ratified by members' parliaments. Trade friction is channelled into the WTO's dispute settlement process where the focus is on interpreting agreements and commitments, and how to ensure that countries' trade policies conform with them. That way, the risk of disputes spilling over into political or military conflict is reduced.*
>
> *By lowering trade barriers, the WTO's system also breaks down other barriers between peoples and nations. At the heart of the system – known as the multilateral trading system – are the WTO's agreements, negotiated and signed by a large majority of the world's trading nations, and ratified in their parliaments. These agreements are the legal ground-rules for international commerce. Essentially, they are contracts, guaranteeing member countries important trade rights. They also bind governments to keep their trade policies within agreed limits to everybody's benefit.*
>
> *The agreements were negotiated and signed by governments. But their purpose is to help producers of goods and services, exporters, and importers conduct their business.*
>
> *The goal is to improve the welfare of the peoples of the member countries.*

This is very different view from that of the protesters. I suspect that we haven't heard the last of the WTO or its opponents.

The issues raised

Interpreting loaded words and phrases

When we use words and phrases we often choose them so that they carry an emotional, as well as a strictly logical meaning. If we describe someone as 'unfriendly', there is a good chance that we are not just describing their attitude towards us: we are implying that they are not a very nice person either. In situations like these, words bring their own baggage with them in the form of some kind of implied good or bad.

Control can be seen as a word with much that *bad* to it, because it is:

- used by those in authority, like bosses, governments and dictators to force their will on others;
- a suppression of freedom and individual choice;
- rigid and inflexible;
- inhuman.

However, there is another side to this. If you are familiar with the Narnia stories of children's author C.S. Lewis (1953), consider this quote describing the management of a school:

> *These people had the idea that boys and girls should be allowed to do what they liked. And unfortunately what ten or fifteen of the biggest boys and girls liked best was bullying the others.*

Here, the lack of control looks bad. If we take the *world view*, *purpose* or *set of values* behind this quotation, *control* can be seen as a word with much that is *good* to it, because it:

- can be used by those in responsible authority, like democratically elected governments, to prevent crime and injustice;
- ensures freedom and individual choice in the face of potential bullies, bigots and undemocratic pressure groups;
- allows room for diversity and differences of value and opinion;
- ensures human rights.

The first thing we can do when considering how we deal with these apparently opposing views of control is to use our understanding of *systems thinking*, which we developed in Chapter 3. If we do this, we should recognize that control is a *concept*: *what* it is needs to be distinguished from *how* it might be implemented.

Thus *what* the Seattle police wanted to do was to control the tens of thousands of protesters. Whether *how* they did it, with tear gas and pepper spray, did result in *control* is another question. Assistant City Police Chief Ed Joiner seems to have had his doubts. Perhaps if he had infiltrated information on to the anarchist Web network, he could have substantially rubbished the whole protest operation by sowing misinformation and conflict. I suspect, for example, that not every Kuna Indian is a fan of US steel production, nor every European livestock farmer threatened by the removal of protectionism an enthusiast for veganism.

The anarchists also showed some interesting contradictions in their actions. Strictly speaking, *anarchy* means 'no rule'. Historically, anarchists have been those who reject government, or any other form of control allowing one person to rule over another. These days, anarchy is often used more loosely to mean disorder, or lack of control.

Whichever meaning we take, it's not easy to decide who was ruling and controlling at Seattle, or who was being ruled or controlled. Whatever my personal views about the WTO or the protesters' cause, it seems to me that as controllers or managers of the situation, the anarchists did better than the WTO or the Seattle police. I'm also pretty sure that the issues around the control of world trade and the power of global organizations are still going to exist long after the publication of this book.

I chose the lead-in case to illustrate that we are once again faced with *complexity*. Control seems to be something that is both desirable and undesirable, used by people who oppose it, and frequently *counterintuitive* in its results. To deal with this complexity, our first need is therefore something in the form of a set of *concepts* or a *model* that will help us *understand* the *whats* of control, so that we can make better practical decisions about *how* it might be implemented.

Box 4.1

Is dictatorship control? Some management lessons from history

A popularly repeated contemporary cliché about the Italian Fascist dictator Mussolini was that 'he made the trains run on time'. I personally can remember, as a young student back-packing my way around Germany, being assured by a lorry driver that German agriculture was managed much better under Adolf Hitler. In our own time, after the fall of Soviet communism, there are Russian citizens who demonstrate nostalgically in favour of the dictator Joseph Stalin.

The other side to such stories needs also to be noted. Mass murder by the Nazis is well documented. Volkogonov (1998) documents similar horrors about Soviet Russia under Stalin. A peasant would be sent away to a labour camp for ten years, if not shot, for nothing more than stealing a handful of wheat from the collective farm where he worked. A worker might be sent straight to prison for arriving at his factory just ten minutes late. Volkogonov comments that the *control system* was so perfect and universal, that the Russian people accepted as normal 'norm-setters, stock-takers, inspectors, and social controllers'.

If we explore historical examples like these, it is easy to conclude that dictatorship isn't nice. However, it is not just nostalgic Russian demonstrators who have a feeling that, although dictatorship may not be nice, it does get the job done: in terms of running trains, agriculture, factories and even whole societies. Perhaps you know managers who would agree.

There is, however, a simple question that challenges the assumptions behind such a view. If control, interpreted as dictatorship, is so effective, how come Hitler left Germany as a burning ruin and Stalin's communism left American capitalism as the winner of the Cold War?

In this book we offer a different answer. A *systems* view of *control* includes the components of *feedback* and *learning*. Study of dictators, such as Hitler and Stalin, shows that both had a reluctance to accept such feedback and learning. Indeed, they frequently shot their critics. Their management style could be described as very 'engaged', 'proactive' or by several other management clichés, but their *control system* was confined to one approach of implementing to goals. The goals themselves, or the ways of achieving them, seldom seem to have been questioned.

Reference

Volkogonov, D. (1998). *The Rise and Fall of the Soviet Empire*. HarperCollins, London.

What roles does information play in control?

We can see that information played many important roles in the Seattle riots.

The WTO used information to:

- project messages to the press and public about its existence, aims and what it intended to do;
- notify its members of the date, place and format of the Millennium Round;
- pick up details of the activities of the protesters;
- build up an understanding of what the protesters were doing;
- use this understanding to counter the aims of the protesters, by promoting an unsympathetic image of them and a positive image of the WTO.

The protesters used information to:

- project messages to the press and public about their existence, aims and what they intended to do;
- notify their supporters of the date, place and format of the Millennium Round;
- anticipate possible actions by the police to frustrate the protest;
- build up an understanding of how the police and authorities operate;
- use this understanding to plan even more successful demonstrations in the future to counter the aims of the WTO.

The Seattle authorities and the police used information to:

- project messages to the press and public about Seattle, the WTO Millennium Round, and the attraction and opportunities of the event;
- discover what the protesters were doing;
- reinforce their irritation and anger at the actions of the protesters;
- notify their citizens and the press of their exasperation and regret that the Millennium Round had gone so badly;
- frustrate further actions by the protesters;
- learn from their mistakes.

All of these players, and others who were involved, used a selection of ways of picking up, reviewing, communicating and acting on their information. These actions used ways of dealing with information that ranged from face-to-face contact or a press release to the global context of the Internet. What helps us understand how all the different people and organizations involved used information and different ways of handling it?

Opportunities for learning

Relationships between information, control and management

Our lead-in case has shown that three very different organizations used information as an essential component of their attempts to control the situation in Seattle and try to make it go the way they wanted.

I said *three* organizations, yet some of the language used about the protesters suggested that they weren't an organization in the conventional sense of having an official legal status, a headquarters building, headed notepaper or a copyrighted logo. Nevertheless, although the protesters were not an organization in the conventional sense, they were clearly *organized*. Although they had no managers, they were good at *management*. Although anarchists are supposed to oppose leaders or rulers, they were often more in *control* than the police were.

The WTO and the police were more conventional, official organizations, yet in many ways they were not conventional in the way they managed. Most managers don't wear uniforms or carry guns like the Seattle police. The WTO looks more like a political forum than an organization that is managed to produce a product or a service.

What I believe our lead-in case shows is that we need to have a *systems concept* of the relationship between information, control and management that is relevant to a much wider range of applications than those with explicit management or organizational *labels*. We need to look at the *whats* of this relationship, not just particular *hows*.

Learning objectives

The learning objectives for this chapter are to:

1 Identify the essential components of a systems view of management.

2 Build a systemic model of control.

3 Define the relationship between management and information using the control model.

4 Establish the lessons that an understanding of control systems behaviour can provide for management.

5 Set the boundaries of possible management control.

4.1 MANAGEMENT, INFORMATION AND CONTROL SYSTEMS

4.1.1 Management and decision making

The relationship between management, control and information

In Figure 3.4 we summarized the *hierarchical* relationship of *management, control* and *information systems*. We will now look in detail at this relationship and use it as the key to why the concept of *control* is the essential link between *management* and *information*.

In Chapter 2, we said that *management* is what *managers* do. We then asked the question 'What is *management*?'

When we looked at ways of answering this question, we saw that we should concentrate on *what* managers do, rather than *how* they, or their jobs, were described. Then we said that we needed to 'look behind the labels'. The exploration of systems thinking in Chapter 3 should now help us realize that to 'look behind the labels' means recognizing and understanding the *concepts* that link the complexity of different forms of management.

To understand why the concept of *control* is the essential link between *management* and *information*, we need to answer a question that follows 'What is management?', namely 'What *information* do managers need in order to manage?'

We shall now develop the issues and concepts of Chapters 2 and 3 to answer the two questions above by using the concept of *control*.

The definition of management

The last time we looked at *definition* was in Chapter 3, when we considered the idea of defining what we meant by the term *system*. We shall consider whether we should attempt to define the term *management* in much the same way as we did for *system*.

I think we can find from even a brief investigation that the term management is used in different ways both in academic literature and everyday life and, as we found with the term *system*, there is no universally accepted definition. Rather than attempt to produce one definition, therefore, we shall use the alternative *extensive definition* approach of Chapter 3. Hence we shall consider the common properties that a range or family of meanings can share.

Our use of the term management will be like our use of the term system in another way: we shall use *management* to describe a *concept*, not a particular way or style of doing something; hence our now familiar distinction of *what* something is from *how* it is manifested or practised.

Having settled the way in which we shall use the term management, I think that the extensive common ground found in many views is the one that I suggested in Harry (1990). There I said that a range of different management styles, from the very authoritarian to the very egalitarian, shared a common characteristic: they saw management as *an activity aimed at achieving something desirable*.

This view of management implies four important concepts that come from the following points:

1 There is *something we wish to achieve* that can be expressed as one or more *goals*.
2 We have a *meliorist belief*, that is, we believe that our *choice of actions* may have some effect on whether we achieve our goals.
3 We have a *choice of actions*.
4 We have a *decision-making ability* that enables us to make *choices*.

Hence the concepts are *goals*, *meliorist belief*, *choice of actions* and a *decision-making ability*. We shall now look at each of these in more detail.

Goals

When we described goals as something we wished to achieve, we were doing so in the context of a systems view of management. This means that our view of goals should be consistent our view of systems. In particular, we recognized that systems can have:

● *abstract* as well as *concrete components*;
● *soft* as well as *hard properties*.

The fact that systems can have concrete components means that the goals of a system may also involve concrete, physical achievements. In the context of our lead-in case, the countries of the WTO have goals in terms of the manufacturing and selling of goods. This will involve processes like the production of cars or food. These physical processes use concrete components like factories or farm machinery. Not surprisingly, much of what the management of these organizations seeks to achieve is also concrete, in terms of cars we drive or cereals we eat.

However, just as a system can have abstract components, so it can have *abstract goals*. What car manufacturers and farmers are really concerned about is not just lumps of metal or piles of grain. It is the *quantity sold*, in terms of *numbers* or *weight*, or the *money earned*, in terms of *dollars* or *euros*, that define the '*something we wish to achieve that can be expressed as one or more goals*' we talked of above. *Numbers* of cars, kilograms or dollars are abstract concepts, so goals expressed in these terms are also abstract.

As our lead-in case shows, the effects of a global economy on local economies are not always beneficial. I can give examples from my own experiences of these adverse effects. I have seen examples of workers in Russia who cannot sell the products they have worked hard to make, and I have talked to UK farmers whose food is sold for less than it costs to produce.

These Russian industrial workers and UK farmers have some important lessons for everyone who tries to manage. *Abstract* goals are not some kind of academic detail: they actually represent the reality of what managers seek to achieve. It is *sold* cars or *bought* cereals, not rusting cars or rotting grain that are the 'real' goals of car manufacture or farming.

As we continue to explore the concept of control, we shall that a key feature of abstract goals is that they are expressed in terms of *information*.

| RQ 4.1 | What abstract goals can you see for the WTO? |

Returning to my example above, did you feel some sympathy for the Russian industrial workers or the UK farmers? Having read the lead-in case, are you opposed or sympathetic to the aims of the WTO? I suspect that different readers of this book will have different opinions about such questions. To a Russian industrial worker, a high sales figure for their product may seem desirable. To a worker whose product has been displaced by a cheap Russian import, this goal looks very different. To a UK farmer with an intensive pig production system, high sales figures for pig meat may also seem a good thing. Someone interested in animal welfare might have a different view.

The possibility of *soft* and *hard* properties of systems means that goals also have their hard and soft properties. For example:

- *Hard properties*: A UK farmer with an intensive pig production system and an animal welfare campaigner would agree that a goal of producing 500 pigs per week represents an *increase* when compared with 400 pigs per week. Increases in numbers can be counted, and so represent a *hard* goal. We have no reason to believe that pig farmers and animal welfare campaigners can't count, so that is why we would expect them to agree.
- *Soft properties*: A farmer and an activist might have different views about whether such an increase is desirable. In this sense, the goal has *soft* properties, because its interpretation only means something in relation to a *world view*, *purpose* or *set of values*.

Our understanding of the properties of goals also relates to our study of systems concepts when we recall that *systems do something*, i.e. they are *dynamic* and carry out *processes*.

If organizational and business systems have a mixture of *concrete, abstract, hard* and *soft goals* that need to be managed, how does management reconcile or choose between them? If we look at the Limber Marsh Drainage Consortium in Appendix 2, it has goals relating to accessing and clearing drainage channels, in order to protect land and people from flooding. However, these goals sometimes *conflict* with its goals relating to wildlife conservation. An example of this is clearing reeds and vegetation, which helps the water flow but can be harmful to nesting birds.

We therefore have an important systems issue:

- *What does management do when faced with conflicting goals?*

We shall study this issue further in this chapter, when we look at the concept of *control systems hierarchy* and develop *a general control model*. This theoretical basis will be an important tool for distinguishing between the following:

- *Normative* goal conflicts, which come from disagreement about which *world views*, *purposes* or *sets of values* should lie behind goals that are set. Thus in the lead-in case, is freeing restrictions on world trade a desirable aim? Or is the protection of individual economies from intrusive competition a more caring ethic?

RQ 4.2 What normative goal conflicts can you see for the Limber Marsh Drainage Consortium in Appendix 2?

- *Policy* or *methodology* goal conflicts, which come from disagreement about what *method* or *procedure* should be used to determine goals, once their *normative* basis has been agreed. In terms of the lead-in case, should the WTO determine its goals by international conferences, secret meetings, a debate on the Internet or what? Should those opposed to world free trade demonstrate in the streets, stand for election, sabotage goods deliveries or go on hunger strike?

RQ 4.3 What policy or methodology goal conflicts can you see for the Limber Marsh Drainage Consortium?

- *Method* or *procedural* conflicts, which come from the *feedback* and *experience* of having used particular goals. Should the goals be *recalculated* or *reassessed*? When trouble broke out at the start of the Seattle Conference, should the organizers have resited or retimed it? If the demonstrators found that they got good publicity, should they have repeated their protests at the same location and with the same banners? Or should they have stopped?

RQ 4.4 What method or procedural conflicts can you see for the Limber Marsh Drainage Consortium?

For the moment, it is worth noting that just as a system can have a structural *hierarchy*, so the goals of an organization or business, seen as a system, can be placed in relation to this hierarchical structure. The overall, high-level *emergent property* that comes from this goal structure hierarchy we will call the *central purpose* of the organization or business system. We shall explore all this further in this chapter and in Chapter 7.

Meliorism

We said above that our view of management implies a belief that our choice of actions may have some effect on whether we achieve our goals. Such a belief is called *meliorism*. An alternative to this belief could be that our efforts are irrelevant to success. An example in the lead-in case might be if either the WTO, or those who were against its goals, believed that it *never, ever* mattered what they did, or that whatever actions they took, it would make no difference. The inevitable result of this view would seem to be 'Why bother to manage?' In this book we take the view that actions can have some effect on outcomes and that attempts at management are worthwhile. We are therefore *meliorists*, but that does *not* mean that we always expect to be successful. In Section 4.3 in particular, we shall establish the limits to what we can expect to control.

The question of whether we believe in meliorism only becomes an issue after we have identified our goals. If we don't want anything, or we don't know what we want, then concern about whether we can do something about it is irrelevant. This may sound like a purely theoretical point, but it has practical implications for both the way that we manage and the kind of *information* we need to do it. Information that helps us determine *what* our goals are needs to be available before we look for information that helps us decide *how* they might be achieved.

If we refer back to our discussion of the term *fuzzy* in the previous chapter, we can see that not knowing, or being fuzzy, about our goals may be due to unresolved *soft* issues or *hard uncertainty*.

As an example of *fuzzy* goals, the Limber Marsh Drainage Consortium may face conflicts between ecological and commercial farming interests over a proposed new drainage scheme, meaning that its goals for the scheme are unclear. The kind of information needed to resolve such conflicts may be about *soft* human values and perceptions, as well as *hard* facts of law, or the technicalities of drainage engineering.

It is unlikely that much of the information relating to the *soft issues* will be found on a computer database. However, *hard uncertainty* could arise over a specifically technical problem, like the width of a drainage channel needed to guarantee a certain volume of water flow. Past statistics on rainfall and volumes of water pumped might well help to resolve this uncertainty by enabling engineers to do calculations. Information of this kind, and methods of calculation, are just the sort of thing we would expect to be computerized. The computerized telemetry system of the Limber Marsh Drainage Consortium is just such an example.

> **RQ 4.5** Consider the statement: 'The actions of the WTO have meant that the volumes of world trade in the year 2000 are the best yet.' Consider examples of *soft issues* and *hard uncertainty* that could be raised by this statement.

As we warned above, *meliorism* only implies that our actions can have some effect; it doesn't assume automatic results. One reason for this is that any system has an *environment* over which it has little control. Hence a management system may well be disturbed and frustrated in a way that prevents it achieving what it desires. In our lead-in case, both the WTO and its opponents were doing their best to achieve their goals. However, the environment of the whole globe, such as the effects of climate and technological progress, mean that the WTO and its opponents can only do their best, they are not guaranteed success.

Choice of actions and decision making

If we know what we are trying to do and we think it reasonable to assume our actions can have some effect, then the next question is what choice of actions we make. This implies both an idea of what the choice might be and the ability to decide.

Two related major subjects called *decision theory* and *operations research* cover the methods we might use for *decision making* and our *choice of actions*.

Many books have been written on these subjects in the last four decades. I would suggest Ackoff (1962) and Ackoff and Sasieni (1968) as some of the originals. If these look like very old references, remember that *hard* subjects, like those concerned with mathematics and calculation, deal with subjects that don't change quickly, if at all. I suspect that 2 + 2 = 4 doesn't need such an up-to-date reference as does what's happening on the Internet. There is also another reason I have given these old references. The 1960s was a time when it looked like all we needed to make a success of many management problems was the right kind of *mathematical techniques* or *hard models*.

The experiences of the 1970s and 1980s led back to an older and much more human view that many problems are much more *soft* and *rich* than hard modelling can cope with.

Given the breadth of decision theory and operations research as subjects, covering choice of actions and decision making could fill a whole book. I will concentrate briefly on the three essential stages of decision making, as in Fishburn (1967) or Ackoff and Sasieni (1968), which are relevant to our information systems interest:

1 Problem formulation.
2 Model construction.
3 Deriving solutions from models.

The classic decision theory view of *problem formulation* is that *choices of actions* can be linked to possible *outcomes*, as in Figure 4.1. The nature of this link may vary according to our *degree of certainty* in our knowledge and understanding of the problem:

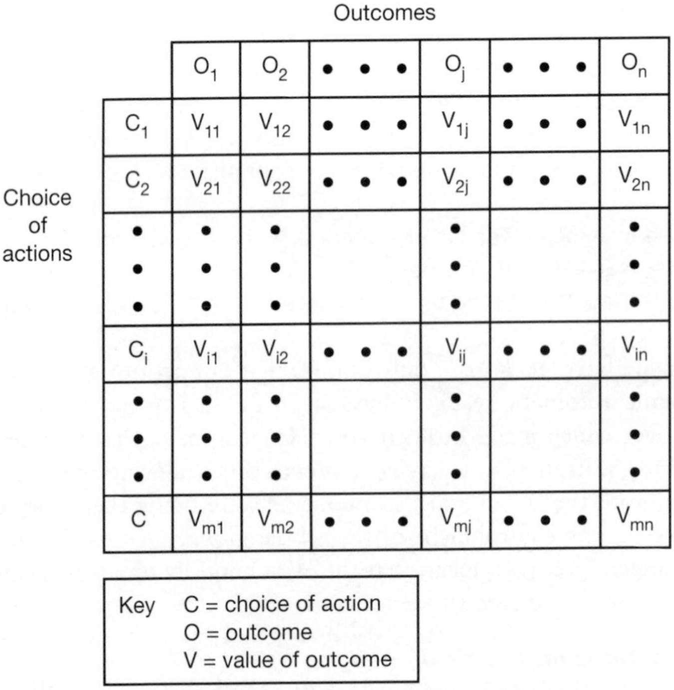

Figure 4.1 A decision theory view of problem formulation
Subscripted variables, or letters with other letters or numbers tucked into their bottom right-hand corners, are merely a way to indicate rows and columns in a matrix.

1 *Certainty*: where each *choice of action* is linked with only *one particular outcome*. Thus in a simple stock control situation, like that recorded in Figure 3.2, we know that there is a certain link between the amount of stock we decide to issue and the amount that will be left.

2 *Risk*: where each *choice of action* may result in one of *several identified possible outcomes*. Thus in the lead-in case for Chapter 2, a man may be alleged to be the father of a child by its mother. Neither outcome is certain until a paternity test had been carried out. Until then, whether this is true or not, is a question of *probability*.

3 *Uncertainty*: where the *possible outcomes* resulting from each choice of action are *not necessarily known*, and in any case we cannot assign probabilities to them. Thus the wider implications of the operations of the WTO, as well as the actions of its opponents, are not necessarily known in terms of their effects on the different processes of the global economy, integration of world trade, changes to societies, cultures and industries etc. These cannot be neatly listed as a series of possible outcomes whose probability can be estimated.

These three types of problem represent places on a spectrum, which means that real problems don't fall exclusively into one type. The less *risky* a problem becomes, the more we move to *certainty*; the more *risky* it becomes, the more we move towards complete uncertainty. Each kind of problem, however, has different information requirements, which we shall see as we follow the next two stages of decision making, involving *model construction* and *deriving solutions*.

We shall study the relationship between information and uncertainty more deeply in Chapter 5. For the moment, we can note that after *formulating the problem*, we need information on:

- the *relationship* between the *choices of action* and the *possible outcomes*. This information we use to provide our *model* of the *problem*;
- a means of *evaluating* the outcome. Decision making requires more than just knowing what choice of action produces what outcome. We have to have information about the value of the outcome to the decision maker if we are to assess its desirability or otherwise;
- a *strategy* or *policy* for *choice*. To finally decide on our choice, we have to have information about how we choose between different valued outcomes.

We shall now see what form these three information needs take for problems formulated under conditions of *certainty*, *risk* and *uncertainty*.

Decision making under conditions of certainty

In problems where there is *certainty* in the link between choice of action and outcome, the relationships are described as *deterministic*. Models of such problems often take the form of mathematical formulae, logical procedures or even just a look-up table that enables us to determine the outcome that follows a choice of action. Thus in a simple stock control example like Figure 3.2, we can model the relationship between amount issued and amount remaining as a simple formula:

$$\text{amount remaining} = \text{initial stock} - \text{amount issued}$$

However, although the method of calculating stock levels is simple arithmetic, it tells us nothing about whether a high or low stock level is to be preferred. We need a means of *evaluating* the outcome. Until we have this knowledge, we cannot decide when it is best to reorder stock, or what level of stockholding is preferred. Therefore the information we need next is how we relate a bare figure like a quantity of stock to a *measure* of *desirability* or *undesirability*. In our stockholding example this measure is likely to be cost, but the general decision theory terms for measures of desirability and undesirability are utility and disutility respectively. You may have come across these terms in your study of economics.

It is important to realize that utility is not a measure in the same objective sense that quantity or cost is a measure. The quantity '47' or the cost '£205.00' on the stock record of Figure 3.2 are all measurements in accepted units whose values can be confirmed by agreed testing methods. They are in fact hard measures in the systemic sense. Utility, on the other hand, is a general term for a measure of desirability whose actual units of measurement depend on whose concept of desirability we are referring to. Thus in our stock control example, whether we are attempting to minimize stock levels, minimize the proportion of time we are out of stock, or minimize the overall cost of the stockholding operation depends on who we are and what we see as the best policy. In this case we are dealing with a *soft* issue in the systemic sense, when we choose a measure of desirability or utility.

Not surprisingly, therefore, measures of utility can vary according to whose they are and where they are used. Note that this *soft uncertainty* does not make the concept of utility unreal. Two products in a shop or two meals in a restaurant may be the same price, but you and I might have different views about which we would prefer. When we consider the commercial effects of our choices, we can see that soft aspects of systems can still have very hard effects. We shall say more about the utility of outcomes later in this section, and in Chapter 5 when we consider the subject of risk.

Once we have the utilities of the various outcomes, we need a *strategy* or *policy* for choice. For *deterministic* problems this is normally a trivial question: we wish to maximize utility or minimize disutility. However, this may not be as obvious in practice as it may seem. If we decide that our measure of disutility is stockholding costs, then minimizing stockholding costs looks like making the obvious decision of choosing the course of action that the model says will lead to the least-cost outcome.

Nevertheless, such a relationship may not be so obvious if we have a business like Carry-Out Cupboards, which stocks hundreds of items. In that situation, literally millions of different combinations of stock levels for the different products could result in the same overall cost. Unless we are able to keep the stock levels of every product exactly at its ideal minimum or optimum level, we are left with choosing between millions of supposedly 'equal cost' suboptimum solutions. What we are now discovering is that individual measures of utility are seldom additive. To put this last statement in systems terms: the whole is more than the sum of the parts. Thus the utility of combinations of utilities, as we go up the systems hierarchy, is an emergent property.

Decision theory can therefore solve part of our management problem. It tells us how to build a model of the decision making. This model shows us what information we need to make decisions by choosing between evaluated outcomes using a decision strategy. But our systems view of management also tells us that we need to clarify what components of the systems hierarchy can deliver these different kinds of information. Clarifying our concept of control later in this chapter will be our first step towards this, and Chapter 7 will place this concept in an organizational and business context.

Decision making under conditions of risk

We saw that problems with an element of risk are those where a choice of action can have two or more possible outcomes. For these types of problem we again need information on the *relationship between the choices of action and the possible outcomes* in order to model the problem, a means of *evaluating* the outcomes, and *a strategy for choice*. Since there is no longer a single determined connexion between choice of action and outcome, however, we need one additional form of information for decision making under conditions of risk. This information will enable us to indicate how likely the various outcomes will be once we have chosen a course of action. We do this by describing the links between choice of action and outcome in terms of probabilities, and such links are called stochastic.

Probability is normally expressed as a numerical value between 0 and 1. If a particular outcome has a probability of 0, it will never happen; if it has a probability of 1, it is certain to happen. The fractional values between 0 and 1, then represent increasing levels of certainty. Thus a probability of 0.5 means that an outcome has an equal chance of happening or not. In everyday life we call this level of certainty '50–50', meaning it has a 50 per cent chance of happening. Indeed, probabilities are often popularly expressed as percentages between 0 and 100 per cent rather than as fractions between 0 and 1. However, the fractional scale makes calculations easier and is more acceptable mathematically, so we will use it.

This is not a book about probability and statistics, but it is worth noting certain basic points about probability as a concept, in addition to understanding how it is numerically expressed. Our justification for this in a book about information systems in business is that *information* about probability plays an important part in management and decision making, and modern information technology-based information systems, particularly in the form of databases, now make the provision of such information much more possible than it was in the recent past.

We can therefore consider three views of the concept of probability:

1 *A priori* (= Latin for 'from what is before') or *rational*.
2 *Empirical*.
3 *Subjective*.

A priori or *rational* views of probability are appropriate where we understand the link between a choice and its possible outcomes, so that we are able to model the process that connects them. Thus if we toss a coin, we not only know that it has two faces that can give us a head or a tail as outcomes, we also know that it is symmetrical and evenly balanced. This knowledge enables us to understand how it will spin regularly as it falls and make the outcomes of head or tail equally likely. The probabilities of 0.5 for the outcomes can be reasoned (i.e. *rational*) in advance (i.e. *a priori*) because we understand the process connecting them to our choice of action.

Empirical views are appropriate where we do not understand the process connecting choice of action and outcome, but we do have *past experience* of the results of our choices. In these situations, the process that connects input choices to the outcomes *that* are its *output* is a *black box*. (The term black box is generally used in systems thinking to describe a process that we do not understand, but one where we can observe which inputs produce which outputs.) Thus, like the Limber Marsh Drainage Consortium, I do not come anywhere near understanding that complex machine called the British weather. What I do know from past experience, however, is that if they were to schedule outdoor excavation activities for next 11 February in my area, there is a 0.2 probability of its being delayed by snow. My figure of 0.2 is based on past years' data for 11 February showing significant snow occurring 20 per cent of the time. Note that empirical probability uses the past *proportion* of times that an outcome has occurred as an indicator of its future probability.

Subjective views are appropriate where we neither understand the process linking choice of action to its possible outcomes, nor have any past experience enabling us to form an empirical estimate. In such a situation, any statement of probability is a statement of *belief* or *opinion*. If we think about some of the innovations in ICT or electronic commerce taking place at the moment, assessing the probability of whether they will still be around in 10 years' time can only be done on a subjective basis. Views about what information technology developments will occur in the next ten years or of the workings of global economics are too complex for us to understand; and as the developments are indeed new and innovative, we can have no previous experience of them.

If we consider the views of probability most likely to be useful for management, then empirical and subjective views are the best candidates. Simple processes like coin tossing, dice rolling or the collecting of coloured balls from urns are popular in mathematical texts concerned mainly with *a priori* probabilities, but organizational or business problems are usually more complex. In particular, the presence of human beings and their behaviour brings in *soft issues* that reduce the potential for clear *a priori* rationality.

The need for and use of empirical and subjective views of probability have important practical implications for the role and design of information systems. We will consider these further later in this chapter and in Chapter 5. For the moment, let us discuss the role of probability in decision making under conditions of risk.

Figure 4.2 illustrates a simple decision problem for the Limber Marsh Drainage Consortium. As the case in Appendix 2 shows, the government has encouraged the consortium to bid for additional private work where it might use its specialist equipment and skills. Just recently, an opportunity has come up where the consortium could earn an estimated £100 000 profit if it landed a particular contract. Its chance of success, however, depends on whether it is prepared spend £10 000 on detailed promotion of its bid.

Figure 4.2 summarizes this situation in terms of the general model of Figure 4.1. The choices of action are to promote the bid or not. The possible outcomes are to gain the contract or not. The values of each outcome, given the choice of action, are shown in the table. (For example, if the consortium promotes and then gains the contract, it is worth £100 000 less the £10 000 promotion cost = £90 000, and so on.)

However, Figure 4.2 does not contain all the information needed by the Limber Marsh Drainage Consortium to make its decision. It needs to know what differences there are in the chances of its gaining the contract according to whether it spends the £10 000 on promotion. Figure 4.3 shows some subjective probabilities estimated by those responsible for the decision. Essentially, they believe that they have a 50–50 chance of getting the contract with promotion, but only one in ten if they don't promote. With this information, it is possible to calculate an expected value for each choice that averages out the values of the outcomes against the probability that they will occur.

Outcome

		Gain contract	Lose contract
Choice of action	Promote bid	+ £90 000	– £10 000
	Do not promote bid	+ £100 000	£0

Figure 4.2 The Limber Marsh Drainage Consortium contract bid: value of outcomes
The possible choices, the outcomes, and the figures for the values of the outcomes have been kept simple for learning purposes. The important point of principle is that both choices and outcomes are mutually exclusive, i.e. distinct, and mutually exhaustive, i.e. cover all possibilities.

	Gain contract	Lose contract
Promote bid	$p = 0.5$	$p = 0.5$
Do not promote bid	$p = 0.1$	$p = 0.9$

Figure 4.3 The Limber Marsh Drainage Consortium contract bid: probability of outcomes
What probability values are intended to show, and how they are determined, depend on what view is taken of the concept of probability. See Section 4.2.1.

Thus choosing to promote averages out as:

Half a chance of £90 000 gain + half a chance of losing £10 000
$$= 0.5 \times £90\,000 + 0.5 \times -£10\,000$$
$$= £45\,000 - £5\,000$$
$$= £40\,000 \text{ expected value.}$$

whereas choosing not to promote works out as:

One in ten chance of £100 000 + nine in ten chances of £nil
$$= 0.1 \times £100\,000 + 0.9 \times £0$$
$$= £10\,000 \text{ expected value.}$$

If the Limber Marsh Drainage Consortium were to take straight monetary value as its measure of utility, then it would go for the promotion choice. But what if it felt that the subjective probabilities were just too woolly? One answer is to abandon any attempt to pretend they can be estimated. If this position is taken, then the problem becomes one of decision making under conditions of uncertainty, which we consider next.

Decision making under conditions of uncertainty

Conditions of uncertainty are those where the possible outcomes resulting from each choice of action are not necessarily known, and in any case we cannot assign probabilities to them.

Where all the possible outcomes are not known, we can still model the problem in terms of Figure 4.1 by listing the outcomes we do know and then adding a final general outcome that stands for all the remaining possibilities. Thus in Figure 4.2, the Limber Marsh Drainage Consortium could consider that there might be some compromise or delay over the awarding of the contract, rather than a straight outcome of gaining or losing it. In this case, it would add a third outcome called 'other' or something similar. Such a level of uncertainty usually makes a formal approach like the model of Figure 4.1 of only limited value. A better approach would normally be to investigate the problem in more depth to reduce the uncertainties. If the uncertainties were soft in origin, then an approach like the *soft systems methodology* discussed in Chapter 8 would be more appropriate.

The model of Figure 4.1 is still useful when we know the outcomes but lack any confidence about assigning probabilities. This would be the case in Figure 4.2 if we felt that the probabilities of Figure 4.3 were not very useful. In such cases, we again need information on the relationship between the *choices of action* and the *possible outcomes* in order to *model* the problem and a means of *evaluating the outcomes*, but we need a new view of strategy for choice. There are several different strategies of choice possible for conditions of uncertainty; see Luce and Raiffa (1957). We will consider the example of the maximin strategy as an illustration.

A *maximin* strategy is one where our aim is to choose the decision with the maximum utility minimum outcome. In less formal terms, we could describe this as the choice of action whose worst outcome is least bad. Consider Figure 4.2. If the Limber Marsh Drainage Consortium chose to promote, it could end up, at worst, losing £10 000. If it did not promote, the worst would be losing the contract but losing no money either. If the strategy is to choose the action with *maximum minimum (maximin)* outcome, then not promoting is the choice to make.

It is worth noting that this strategy gives a different result to assigning probabilities to outcomes in an attempt to maximize expected utility. There is no way *before* the outcome of its decision that the Limber Marsh Drainage Consortium can know which method is best. Even after the outcome, there is no guarantee that the next decision it faces will be similar. What this simple example illustrates is that decision making requires *different* kinds of information for the *different* needs of problem formulation, model construction and the derivation of solutions from them. We now need some way of understanding how these different forms of information relate to the different kinds of functional components that we find in an organization or business when we view it as a *system*. Chapter 7 will be entirely devoted to looking at organizations and businesses as systems in this way. Meanwhile, as Figure 4.4 shows, it is the concept of a *control system* that enables us to make the link between *management* and *information*.

We shall study the concept of a control system next, but we shall return to decision making in Chapter 5, after we have built up our understanding of information in the context of management.

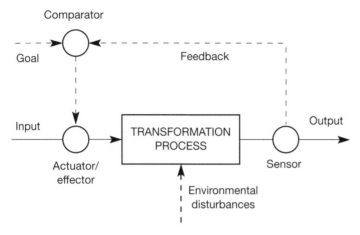

Figure 4.4 The classical control model
This title ought not to imply that this is the only form of a control model. Two features should be noted. First, the model assumes feedback, rather than feedforward, control. Secondly, the feedback is assumed to have a negative rather than a positive effect on the way that the actuator is instructed.

4.1.2 The classical control systems model

Control as a concept

The term *control* represents a central concept in this book. We will begin in this section by explaining a generally accepted basic view of the concept. In subsequent sections, I would like to develop a more complex view of my own for use in an organization or business information systems context. Although this is an individual view, I will show that each of its components is either closely related or identical to other established views.

Throughout this book it will be essential to recognize that the term control refers to a *concept* and *not* a particular *way of doing things* or a *management style*. In popular use, the word control, and the related concept of hierarchy, are used to imply a rather rigid, authoritarian approach to management. In this simplistic, stereotyped use of the word, 'management' is seen as 'the boss' who exerts 'control' by 'giving orders' that employees have to 'obey'.

I think that this stereotype is dangerous, for two reasons:

1 It fails to recognize the rich choice of ways in which control may be exerted, including ones with little trace of the bossy stereotype.
2 An assumption that 'orders' or 'obedience' are always wrong seems as bigoted as the stereotype that such an assumption wishes to condemn.

Figure 3.4 (see p. 56) has led us to anticipate that the concept of control is the link between the concepts of information and management through a systems hierarchy. In this hierarchical structure, an information system can be seen as a subsystem of a control system, and a control system as a subsystem of a management system.

To understand control as a component of management and as a concept, rather than as a management style, consider the situation described in the lead-in case about the WTO. In this context, we can show that *control* can be used to protect freedom as well as to limit it.

Many of the groups involved in the campaigning and protests against the WTO have no one in their membership called a 'manager'. They are more likely to have 'senior campaigners' or 'project officers'. Many are voluntary, egalitarian groups whose hierarchy in the everyday sense is limited to having the usual elected secretary and treasurer you find in most societies. Anybody who tried to be 'boss' would soon be rebuffed.

Despite the differences between such groups and a commercial business organization like Carry-Out Cupboards, I think it is possible to assert that many of them are very effectively managed and that their members have a very clear concept of what management involves. They are certainly committed to what they see as 'activity aimed at achieving something desirable', which is how we described management above. They have clear ideas of what things they think are 'desirable' for the ecology of the world and they act positively in trying 'achieve' them. They show themselves as *meliorists* by the fact that they thought it was worth getting together, forming their group, turning up to meetings, producing magazines, campaigning, and all the other activities that were aimed at 'achieving something desirable'.

The totality of such attempts at management by the anti-WTO groups can be seen as a complex system with various components like a human subsystem, a financial subsystem, and so on.

However, at the centre of this management system are those activities directly concerned with trying to make sure that any group achieves its aims. For an organization concerned with the effects of the WTO's decisions on the global environment these activities would include:

- Identifying which areas of environmental interest the group wishes to influence.
- Agreeing what the group is trying to achieve in these areas.
- Identifying potential disturbances and threats to their areas of interest from WTO decisions.
- Making sure they get to know about what is happening within the WTO.
- Communicating what is happening to all the members.
- Checking what is actually happening against the view the group has about what should happen.
- Having decided and agreed what should be done in the way of lobbying, meetings etc., putting these decisions into effect.

These components at the centre of the group's management activities make up an identifiable subsystem, which we shall see as an example of a control system. It is also worth noting that many of the components are concerned with the communication of information. So we would rightly expect to find some form of information system as a further subsystem of the control system.

We will now identify and explain the components of a control system. The particular model I shall use is that of *closed-loop* control with *negative feedback*, which I will call the *classical model*. There are other forms of control model, but this one is widely found in management, as well as in subject areas ranging from engineering to biology. (The terms *closed-loop* and *negative feedback* will be explained at the end of this section.)

Figure 4.4 shows the essential components of the classical model, and Figure 4.5 shows how this might be interpreted in terms of the specific example of stock control. This example can be linked in turn to Figure 3.2 and the control of stock at Carry-Out Cupboards, while our RQs will be used as a link to our WTO lead-in case.

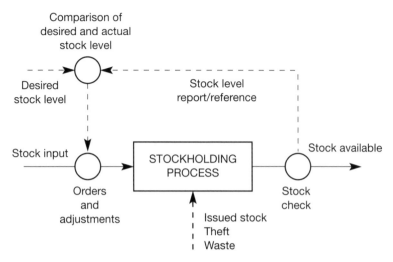

Figure 4.5 Stock control
The stockholding process is disturbed by customer demand, theft, loss and depreciation.
Inputs to the process are adjusted to turn the stock available towards the goal of a desired
stock level.

Transformation process

The first component of any control system must be something that needs controlling,
which will be some form of transformation process. In our stock example, this will be the
process of receiving stock, responding to orders and safely retaining unsold stock ready
for when it is needed. We might call this the 'stockholding process', as in Figure 4.5.

As we saw in Section 3.2.6, we are only aware of a process if we can detect some
change or *transformation* that it carries out. *Inputs* have to be transformed into
detectably different *outputs*. Stockholding as a process will transform an existing set
of stock conditions to a new one as a result of its actions in receiving and issuing
stock. In the example of Figure 3.2 such conditions would include the amount in
stock, allocated and on order.

A very important point about this example is that transformations can be *abstract*.
A stock item at Carry-Out Cupboards does not suddenly look different or undergo
any physical change when a customer buys it. Yet once sold, it is immediately transformed from being 'Free' to being 'Allocated', even though it may not be *physically*
changed until much later, when it is delivered to the customer or collected. The *logical* change of state that takes place in undergoing the abstract transformation from
'Free' to 'Allocated' is not just some theoretical concept with little practical application, however. If we ignore the logical transformation that takes place once a stock
item is sold, we can easily sell the same item more than once, resulting in chaos in our
stock control and harmful effects on our customers.

RQ 4.6 What abstract transformation process may be the concern of the WTO and its antagonists?

Goals

We have already explored the concept of goals in detail in the previous section. It is
important to note that according to Figure 4.4, goals are not actually a component of

the classical model. Instead, they are seen as something that comes from the outside and are used by it. We will explore where goals come from in the next section. For the moment, we note that the goals of stockholding might include maintaining stock levels within a desired range.

RQ 4.7 Are the goals of the WTO mainly hard or soft?

Environmental disturbances

We saw that real-life systems have an environment that disturbs them and on which they can have only limited effect. In fact, the *existence of environmental disturbances is the only reason we need control at all*. If our stockholding process could run in the confidence that nothing would ever happen to disturb it, we could set it up and leave it to run itself.

In practice, no such conditions exist. Real-life systems always have environments that disturb their processes and we need control to try to bring them back towards our goals. The stockholding process will be disturbed by such environmental factors as customer orders, theft and damage. Any attempt to predict or affect these will never be completely successful. In practice, we cannot tell customers what they must buy and when they must buy it. Despite security and care, thefts and damage can happen. A real system has to live in such a world and cope with it; hence the need for control.

It is important to note that the model distinguishes inputs from the environment, like customer orders, which are outside our control; and inputs, like orders on suppliers, which are in our control because we initiate them.

RQ 4.8 Are groups who protest against the WTO part of its environment?

Sensor

So far, we have seen the model in terms of a process that is being disturbed by the environment and we want to keep turning the output of the process back towards our goals. For a stockholding process, we want the stock available to be within certain desired levels. This view assumes, however, that we know what amount of stock is actually available. We need some way of checking this information. In practice, this will be done by someone looking, counting and recording the figure. It might be done using a bar-code reader or simply by making a mental note. The important point is that there has to be some form of *sensor* that records the output from the process.

RQ 4.9 Are media reports on the actions of protest groups at a WTO conference part of the WTO control system or the control system of the protest groups?

Feedback

Recording the output from a process is a waste of time if we do nothing with it. Our motive for having some form of sensor is that the information it gathers can be used to help make the process achieve its goals. If the sensor in our stockholding example finds that the stock available is below the reorder level, that information needs to be *communicated* to the person or department responsible for deciding when to reorder stock. Communicating sensed information for such a purpose is called *feedback*. In practice, this could be anything from one person telling another to the formal passage of a document.

RQ 4.10 If information about how well a WTO Trade Round went is gathered *after* the event is complete, is it still useful feedback that helps the WTO control its activities?

Comparator

In our stockholding example, we see feedback as communicating information about the stock available output from the process we wish to control 'to the person or department responsible for deciding when to reorder stock'. Their job is then to *compare* the value of the output from the process, which is the amount of stock available, with the goal of maintaining stock levels within a desired range. The word 'compare' is used to explain why this component is called the comparator.

It is also worth noting that the comparator works by *processing information*. This is an important point that is the start of our understanding of the relationship between management, control and information outlined in Figure 3.4. We will develop this further later in this section. Meanwhile, in the stockholding example, comparison is carried out using information about the output of the process and information about the control system's goals. The *output* from this information processing is further information in the form of a decision about whether to reorder stock and, if so, how much.

Actuator/effector

The comparator delivers information on what must be done to turn back the process output towards where we would like it to be, as expressed by our goals. This information is translated into action by the actuator or effector, which initiates or adjusts inputs to the process in a way that it anticipates will have the desired corrective effect. Thus for our stockholding example, the actuator would consist of the reordering function, which organizes the delivery of replenishment stock.

Other forms of control system

I called the control model we have just described the classical control model. This is a term of my own that I've used for convenience. We noted, however, that it would strictly be called *closed-loop control* with *negative feedback*. We'll now see why.

It is called closed-loop control because information gathered by the sensor is fed back to the comparator, which in turn passes information on to the actuator. The information flow path from sensor to actuator can be seen as a closed loop.

Another form of control is so called *open-loop* or *feedforward control*. This occurs where the actuator controls the inputs to the process but does not monitor the outputs or subsequent state of the process through sensing and feedback. Examples of this would be Carry-Out Cupboards ordering from suppliers and not checking if the goods arrived, or the Child Support Agency sending a demand for payment to an absent father and not finding out whether he ever made it.

In practice, such control is only likely to result in the outputs we desire if either:

● there are no significant subsequent environmental disturbances to the process; or
● we can predict the disturbances accurately and allow for them.

The first condition is not likely to be relevant to any but the simplest mechanical system. As we saw in Section 3.2.8, management systems have environments that disturb them. Whether it be in the context of a government body like the Child Support Agency, a commercial firm like Carry-Out Cupboards or a protest group, every system will be disturbed by its environmental components, such as global economics,

markets, law, social attitudes, climate change etc. The environment of real management systems is not some occasional inconvenience, but rather an ever-present factor
with which the management system has to be designed to cope continually. A major
tool that management uses for this is *information*, and later in this chapter we shall
study the role of information systems in helping management deal with the ever-
changing environment.

The second condition is only likely to apply where the workings of both the process
and its environment are fully understood and therefore predictable. Again, real-life
management systems are unlikely to be in such a context, particularly given the presence of *human activity systems* with their accompanying *soft uncertainty*.

Negative feedback is so called because the feedback loop works to reverse the effect
of any environmental disturbance. Thus when customer demand reduces stock levels
below the desired range, the effect of the feedback loop is to push them up again
through replenishing stock. Generally, negative feedback control has the effect of
keeping process outputs fluctuating about the desired level, as in Figure 4.6.

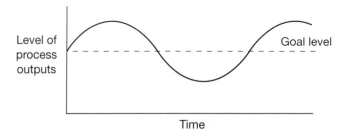

Figure 4.6 The behaviour of process outputs from the classical control model
The wavelike swing of the outputs in the diagram is intended to illustrate the principle of
oscillation about a desired, or goal, level. Each real-life example of the model will have its
own pattern. The important point is that negative feedback should result in the outputs
being continually returned towards the goal.

Another form of feedback, known as *positive* feedback, has the effect of making the
process follow the direction of the environmental disturbance. An example of this
might be the effect of investment on the profits of a firm. Greater profits can lead to
greater investment in the firm, which leads to greater profits, and so on. Similarly,
low profits could lead to less investment, which would lead to less profits. What we
notice from both these examples of positive feedback is that it has a destabilizing
effect on a process and is therefore normally undesirable. This contrasts with the popular use of the term 'positive feedback' as something 'welcome'.

Some positive feedback may be OK in the short term, such as when the more our
product sells, the more it is known, so the more it sells, and so on. However, if such
growth is *uncontrolled*, the resultant instability is likely to mean that we can't keep
our production in line with demand; or that when growth hits a saturation barrier,
the bubble bursts. The world of electronic commerce that we studied as the lead-in
case for Chapter 3 is likely to provide many examples of this. Generally, pure
positive feedback is undesirable, and we would not seek to have it in a management
control system.

RQ 4.11 Can you identify any potential positive feedback situations in the lead-in case on the WTO?

Box 4.2

How online gossip is fuelling share prices

James Mackintosh

When Reckitt & Colman agreed a £5bn merger with Benckiser of the Netherlands in July, long-suffering investors in the UK cleaning products group cautiously welcomed the move, pushing up the shares 12 per cent. But one group of investors were rubbing their hands with glee: Internet readers of the Motley Fool bulletin boards had been tipped off two weeks earlier that a merger was in the offing.

Regulators and the stock exchange are worried about leaks of insider information, although the Reckitt/Benckiser information was passed on as a 'strong rumour' by a user from Belgium operating under a pseudonym.

Such accurate forecasts are rare in the gossip-hungry world of the online discussion groups, and regulators have so far kept no more than a watching brief.

But they are worried. The power of the discussion groups has grown rapidly this year, and chief executives of small Internet companies often have to look no further than an online rumour to explain a share price move.

All the Internet forums for private investors have seen a surge in popularity in the past few months, with thousands of messages passing on rumours, tips and down-right lies every day. Now even City professionals have taken to browsing the list in the hope of uncovering useful information.

'It is outrageous some of the things people say [on the boards],' said

Matthew Orr, a partner at stockbrokers Killik & Co. 'But there is so much gossip out there it can be interesting.'

The power of the thousands of investors using the bulletin boards was shown the day after the Reckitt/Benckiser merger was announced, when the share price of Dialog Corporation, a small Internet services company, tumbled 7 per cent. The fall was traced to a message posted on the Hemmington Scott online bulletin board, which claimed – falsely – that the company's debt restructuring was in trouble. Hemmington Scott was forced to apologize and bar the sender from its systems, but the damage was done.

This is an extreme example, but there are plenty of cases of small company share prices being moved by Internet chat. Even the giants sometimes feel the effects, with rumours of a Marks and Spencer takeover reaching the bulletin boards – and the share price – days before anything appeared in the press.

In principle there is nothing wrong with exchanging gossip, opinions and rumours in an Internet chat room, any more than in a City wine bar. But the release of inside information and attempts to 'ramp' shares – drive the price up or down to make quick profits – do bother regulators.

'It is a criminal offence to manipulate the share price [to make money],' the Financial Services

Authority points out. It recommends investors stick to taking advice from properly regulated stockbrokers and financial advisers.

Andy Yates, head of operations at Digital-Look.com, which monitors chat rooms, warned yesterday inside information – as well as unfounded rumour – is becoming common.

'Rumours are often disguised to make them appear less likely to come from an insider, and anonymous nicknames are used,' he said. 'But there appears little doubt that a growing number of City professionals are using the boards.'

However, the bulletin board operators remain unworried. David Berger, head of Motley Fool UK, argues that the chat rooms are self-policing, as experienced investors tend to respond to rumours by demanding evidence.

Even the FSA says its main role at present is educational rather than about enforcement of rules. 'If people want investment advice, chat rooms are not the best place to get it,' it said yesterday.

The growing number of professional users attests to the value of the discussion groups as well as their power, according to Peter Scott, chairman of Hemmington Scott. But he repeats the health warning about the boards. 'It is a case of buyer beware.'

Source: Financial Times, 15 December 1999. Reprinted with permission.

Comment

Here is a classic example of a system with the potential for positive feedback. The danger is that rumour feeds on rumour. In an accelerating process where the more a share is talked up, the more a share is talked up; something has got to give. As with all positive feedback systems, it is potentially unstable and unsustainable.

Positive feedback rumour machines are most likely to occur, as here, where a single, selective source of feedback information is used. A wider, holistic view is likely to be more stabilizing in its effect. This happens in this example when 'experienced investors tend to respond to rumours by demanding evidence'.

The information systems component of the classical control system

Our study of the classical control model shows the first of several links in the hierarchical structure of Figure 3.4, in which an information system can be seen as a subsystem of a control system, and a control system as a subsystem of a management system. If we now consider the classical control model of Figure 4.4 in terms of information, we find that three types of information are used by the model:

1 Information about *environmental disturbances*. For our stockholding example, this would include information about customer orders, theft or damage.
2 Information about the *state of the process* being controlled, in the form of its *outputs*. For our stockholding example, this would include information about amounts in stock, allocated and on order.
3 Information about the *goals* that the process being controlled should attempt to achieve. For our stockholding example, this would include information about desired stock levels reflected by the values of the reorder level and the reorder quantity.

We also noted that information has to be recorded by the sensor, processed by the comparator, and communicated along a path through feedback from the sensor to the actuator. All of the activities by components of the control system that are concerned with information can be seen as making up a *subsystem* within the control system itself. Figure 4.7 shows what this subsystem does in the context of the classical control model. Since it is exclusively concerned with *processing information*, it seems sensible to call it an *information system*. The question then comes: is it the information system referred to in Figure 3.4, which shows the link between information and management systems? Is this information system the one that supplies the business information in the title of this book?

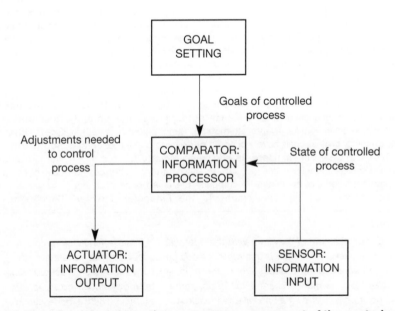

Figure 4.7 The role of the information system as a component of the control system
The main processes carried out by the information system in the context of Figure 3.4.

The answer to this question becomes clearer if we consider the role of information about goals, as shown in Figure 4.7. This shows that our explanation of the classical control model so far tells us nothing about where the information about goals comes from or how *goal setting* takes place. Figure 4.7 therefore shows us partly what an information system does, but a complete view of an information system must also explain goal setting. We will consider this next.

4.1.3 Control systems hierarchy

The role of goal setting

When we considered the nature of goals in Section 4.4.1, we used the WTO lead-in case to illustrate many of the points. There was one main event at the centre of the dramatic events of the first day. After spending a great deal of time and money organizing the Millennium Round at Seattle, the WTO *changed its mind* and gave up trying to hold its first meetings. In changing its mind, it was *changing its goals*.

In practice, changing goals isn't confined to dramatic situations like the Seattle riots. Nor is goal changing necessarily a sign of 'failure', as might have been claimed by the protesters. If in hot weather I try to keep cool and in cold weather I try to keep warm, I think few of us would see this change of goal as 'failure' or 'inconsistency'. It is the same with the management of organizations and businesses: goals have to be changed to reflect changes in their environment. Changes in the economy, the market, legislation or in public attitudes can all mean that goals have to be modified.

Even if an environment does not change significantly, there may still be good reasons for changing goals. At Seattle, when Assistant City Police Chief Ed Joiner agreed that 'in hindsight, the approach we adopted yesterday did not work', I don't think he was saying that the goal of trying to prevent or control the riots was wrong. Instead, he was recognizing the difference between *whats* and *hows*. The concept of setting the goals in terms of delivering tear gas or pepper spray needed to be changed, not the goal of controlling the riots. Even where a particular *how* has been fixed, such as sales targets for Carry-Out Cupboards, we could imagine that the original sales target goals would need to be changed because they had been badly estimated.

Goal setting may therefore range from minor modifications to goals to complete changes in direction. What all practical goal setting has in common is that it takes account of how well the control system performed with a particular set of goals. In the light of this experience, the goals may then be left unchanged, modified or completely altered. Just as classical control modifies the inputs to a process to keep it moving towards its goals, so goal setting modifies the actual form of the goals to keep them relevant to the wider aims of management.

We can therefore regard *goal setting itself as a control system*, with similar components to that of the classical control model. Where the classical model sought to control a process by modifying its inputs through an actuator in the light of feedback on the process performance, so goal-setting control modifies the goal inputs to the classical control model in the light of its performance.

Figure 4.8 summarizes in a simple way this concept of goal setting being an additional control system acting 'in addition' to the classical control model. These two forms of control can be seen as two components or subsystems of a greater whole. The control of the classical model is goal-seeking or first-order control, which takes its goals from a higher-order, goal-setting control.

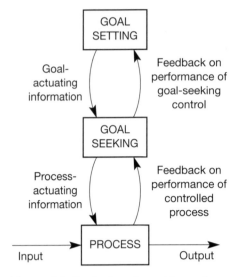

Figure 4.8 Control systems hierarchy
A goal-seeking system itself can be seen as a process. The goals for this process have therefore to come from somewhere. The concept of goal setting implies a hierarchy of control systems in which each level of the hierarchy sets the goals of the subsystem process below it. The use of the word 'below' should not be seen as a judgement of the value of each level of the hierarchy in management terms.

This concept of orders or levels of control can be extended. We said above that 'goal setting modifies the actual form of the goals to keep them relevant to the wider aims of management'. If we consider this statement, we can see that it implies that there are higher-level standards or *strategic aims* that enable us to decide which goals to choose. Thus decisions about such goals as those of the WTO in fixing a particular meeting or the sales targets of Carry-Out Cupboards have to be made against *higher* aims like the WTO's desire to promote a 'more prosperous, peaceful and accountable economic world', or Carry-Out Cupboard's aim to be a profitable company. We can conceive that goal setting itself has to have goals, and that above goal setting will be another control system that sets the goals for goal setting. Presumably, we could then conceive of a control system that sets the goals for the control system that sets the goals for goal setting, and so on *ad infinitum* (= Latin for 'to infinity')!

How, therefore, can we avoid a model of control that does not result in an endless hierarchy of orders of control? In the next section of this chapter I aim to present my own view of this in the form of a 'general control model' (GCM). But as I noted at the beginning of the previous section, although this is an individual view overall, each of its components is either closely related or identical to other views. Two additional views are particularly worth considering to show how the reasoning behind the GCM fits into a wider picture:

1 Distinguishing *automatic* and *reflective* goal changing (Schoderbeck *et al.*, 1990).
2 The concepts of *operational*, *strategic* and *normative* levels of management (Ben-Eli, 1988; used by author in Espejo and Harnden, 1989).

Automatic and reflective goal changing

We have already identified the concept of goal setting as a higher-order component of a control system that is concerned with modifying or completely changing its goals. Reference to other well-established views, as in Schoderbeck *et al.* (1990), shows that what we have called goal setting may take two different forms. We have implied this in our previous discussion, but now we need to make it explicit. Schoderbeck *et al.* (1990) present a distinction between:

- *second-order* or automatic goal changing; and
- *third-order* or *reflective* goal changing.

Second-order or automatic goal changing control is possible where:

1 All the potential set of *alternative environmental conditions* have been identified.
2 The *method* of linking *courses of action* and *outcomes* is defined.
3 The system can *store information.*

Comparing conditions 1 and 2 with Section 4.1.1 shows that automatic goal changing is only going to be possible where all the components of our *decision model* have been defined in such a way that selecting a goal can be done by calculation or some other formal procedure or *method*. It therefore becomes *automatic* in the sense that, once we have the goal-setting data, this can be fed into the agreed method and the value of the resulting goal is automatic.

An example of automatic goal changing would be setting the reorder level for stock control, as in Figure 3.2. Like in the Carry-Out Cupboards case in Appendix 1, the reorder level is set so that the stockholding process can cover the maximum expected demand over the lead time. Thus for a weekly demand figure:

$$\text{reorder level} = \text{maximum weekly demand} \times \text{lead time in weeks}$$

If there is any change in the maximum demand or the lead time, the new reorder level goal can be automatically recalculated.

However, to know that a change has taken place in any of the values used in the calculation, the second-order goal-changing system has to *store* information. How else could a change in demand or delivery lead time be noticed if we did not keep sales figures or records of supplier performance? Here we can see something very important about the role of the information system as a component of the control system that goes further than Figure 4.8. Besides processing information in support of a control system, an information system must also store it. We shall look at this aspect in great detail later in the book, particularly in Chapter 5, but for the moment we can note it as building on our understanding of the relationship between management, control and information as in Figure 3.4.

RQ 4.12   How can it be possible to know the maximum weekly demand for the formula above?

Third-order or *reflective goal* changing involves more than the automatic application of a preset method or formula. Besides the ability to set goals using a method and stored information, third-order control requires the control system to learn, so that it can choose the appropriate method when the set of environmental conditions changes. Thus second-order control can adjust a reorder level for a stockholding process using a method and stored information, but what if the method itself becomes irrelevant? If Carry-Out Cupboards found that there was no longer a market for a product and its weekly demand fell to zero, the reorder level formula above would be useless; it could produce a nonsense theoretical reorder level of zero. Similarly, if the WTO cancelled one of its conferences, any method of planning a demonstration against the conference would become irrelevant.

Third-order or reflective goal-changing control will be possible where:

1 There is a means of identifying, distinguishing, choosing and defining different methods or procedures, which we may call a *methodology*. This will be used to deliver to second-order control the appropriate method to be used where environmental conditions require a change of method.
2 Access is available to any *policies* on *soft issues* and higher aims required by the third-order control methodology to decide between methods of goal setting.

We can develop the stockholding example to illustrate these two conditions. We saw above that second-order, automatic goal-changing control is only possible within a set of environmental conditions where we can apply the reorder level calculation method and only have to accommodate changes in demand or lead time. Where the sales of a product fall to zero or a new product is introduced, environmental conditions require a different method of dealing with stock levels. How do we decide when to discontinue stocking a particular item? Do we drop the price and have a sale to get rid of the remaining stock? How do we decide on the initial stock level and ordering for a new item?

A wide range of answers is possible to these and other questions we might ask. What third-order control needs is an understanding of the choices of method available to cope with these problems and a set of principles to help choose between them. We shall call the subject that studies method in this way methodology, and note also that the existence of methodology implies that our experience of choosing and applying methods leads to a *learning process*.

Methodology on its own is not enough to enable a choice of method to be made, however. Different methods carry their own assumptions about *values* or *soft issues*, behind any method there is an implied *world view*, *purpose* or *set of values*. Thus the reorder level method of stock control assumes that we do not want to run out of stock and dissatisfy the customer and the reorder quantity will be set to minimize stockholding costs. A decision to discontinue a stock item carries with it certain assumptions about how important we think it is to continue to satisfy a minority demand. Choosing a method therefore also requires *policies* on *soft issues* and higher aims for methodology to be applied.

The concepts of second- and third-order control therefore help us to enrich our view of control and the different forms of information it uses. Our model is still incomplete, however. We are left with a need to include the role of information on world view, purpose or set of values in our model of control and to say more about the concept of learning.

Operational, strategic and normative levels of management

Before we look at these three levels of management, I would like to verify what we are not talking about. The picture of levels of management with 'strategic' at the top of some hierarchical pyramid, 'tactical' at a middle level and 'operational' at the bottom is a standard cliché, to be found in some form in many books on management, e.g. Hannagan (1998). Such a view, often with an accompanying pyramidal diagram, paints a picture of 'top management' thinking great strategic thoughts, while the lowest level just does what it is told and carries out 'operations'. Accompanying this stereotype is likely to be some assertion that the different levels of management use different kinds of information and information systems.

In real organizations and businesses it seldom works like that. So-called top management often spends much of its time engrossed in firefighting day-to-day operational crises, and middle management plots and schemes in a way that has significant effects on strategy. As to the information used by management; a great deal of strategic information flows between 'operational' staff in the company's restaurant, and a lot of tactical information is exchanged between 'top executives' in the washroom.

What the traditional, pyramid cliché gets wrong is not its recognition of the existence of strategy, tactics and operations. Rather, it confuses the *whats* and *hows* of the three levels. While there are levels of management, the 'management' referred to is what is done, not necessarily *who* does it or *how* it is done. If we concentrate on the conceptual whats of management, we do not have to get trapped into an artificial view of individual managers falling exclusively into particular categories and only being concerned with certain separate and disconnected forms of information system. We shall cover this concept in detail in Chapter 7, but for the moment we note that 'levels of management' refers to the processes of management, not a particular organizational structure, set of people or method of doing things.

If we can build up a *conceptual, systems* view of what is involved at different levels of management, we can use this as a means of building on our view of what is done by different levels of control, since we see control as a component of management as in Figure 3.4.

For an example of such a systems view, I have chosen Ben-Eli (1988). He puts forward the concept of levels of management shown in Figure 4.9. Of these levels he says, 'The pertinent point is that approaching problems that are related to each such level requires a *"different conceptual orientation"* and *"information aggregated at different levels of detail"*.' In terms of the systems view presented in this chapter, two words from this quotation are significant: *conceptual* and *aggregated*.

The use of the word conceptual shows that he is focusing, like us, on the *whats* of management rather than the *hows*. The use of the word *aggregated* makes a clear link with our concepts of *hierarchy* and *emergent property*. As we saw in Section 3.2.5, our systems view of hierarchy is different from this (the traditional view) since we see it in terms of levels of aggregation associated with emergent properties.

What management does at any level, according to Ben-Eli, and the information it uses can therefore be seen by us in terms of the *emergent properties* associated with the various levels of control that management exerts. We can thus consider how his hierarchical view of management might enrich our model of control.

Ben-Eli's levels of management are:

- normative
- strategic
- operational.

Figure 4.9 Levels of management/planning according to Ben-Eli (1988)
This is my interpretation of the original diagram in the reference. Espejo and Harnden (1989)
should also be referred to.

Normative levels of management are concerned with forming policy and deciding
how an organization should react to decisions on change and adaptability in the face
of environmental disturbances. These activities imply the concept of an 'institutional
mission' reflected in policies and commitment. The case used by Ben-Eli was a medical centre. When questions about the purpose of the centre were asked, it was first
thought that the answers to the questions were obvious and had little practical management value. In fact, more detailed investigation showed big differences in views.
Until these differences were resolved, 'practical' management of programme priorities
and resource allocation was difficult and limited.

Strategic levels of management are concerned with the integrating and co-ordinating
the many activities of an organization so that the behaviour of whole is optimized and
its overall direction is consistent with policies formed at the normative level.

Operational levels of management then implement activities according to plans that
have been co-ordinated at the strategic level.

Given these views of what the different levels do, what differences do we see
between them in terms of 'different conceptual orientation' and 'information aggregated at different level of detail'?

A *norm* is a standard or a criterion against which something is judged. We can
therefore see why Ben-Eli describes the highest level of management that decides purpose and policy as normative. In the WTO lead-in case, decisions about trade policies
could only be made after an acceptance of higher norms like the desire for 'a more
prosperous, peaceful and accountable economic world'.

However, the WTO example takes us further in understanding the difference
between normative decisions and those that follow them. Policies on free trade are
potentially not just technical questions about finance and economics. They raise

strong emotional and other soft issues, as the demonstrations showed. Besides the disputes about facts and figures or ways of doing things, there are differences of *world view*, *purpose* or *set of values*. These latter differences have to be resolved before there can be any decision on *purpose, policy* or *norms*.

Once norms have been decided, it is possible to determine a *strategy* whose goal is to make sure that the overall direction is consistent with policies formed at the normative level. Thus a country could decide that it agreed with the aims of the WTO, in terms of 'a more prosperous, peaceful and accountable economic world'. The same country might not be happy about free trade as a way for this policy to be put into practice. In these circumstances, operating outside the WTO could be seen as the best method available at a particular point in time and under particular conditions. At some future time, with a changed context or *environment*, joining the WTO or negotiating a new arrangement might be more appropriate. Thus strategy involves choosing the appropriate method of operation, given the environmental conditions, which is in line with our policy or purpose.

Once the method of operation has been chosen, then *operational* management is concerned with seeing that it is correctly carried out. Countries in the WTO are required to conform to particular standards (or lack of standards) on tariffs, product quality or labour conditions. Those outside the WTO might set these standards at different levels. *Operational* management, in or out of the WTO, is therefore mainly concerned with hard, technical decisions about conformity to *goals*. At the operational level these will involve very specific, logical, numerical measures, which are *hard*.

The need for fourth order control

If we now consider what Ben-Eli's three levels of management do in terms of *control*, we can see close links with the classical model and the concepts of second- and third-order control discussed so far.

Operational management is concerned with using a particular method to achieve goals that have been set for it. Thus the WTO might decide to begin breaking down trade barriers between two countries by allow goods up to a certain quantity to be exported before a tariff is applied. Operational management, in the form of the importing country's customs officers, would check the amounts of goods being imported. Once this number exceeded the WTO's agreed quantity, the customs would impose a tariff. In this example, operational management is principally concerned with first-order control because it is *seeking* to impose goals that are *set* elsewhere: by the WTO.

Strategic management has to choose what method or mix of methods should be operated and appropriate goals for them. Thus the WTO has to make decisions about whether to allow restrictions on completely free trade by allowing quotas and tariffs and, if so, what mechanisms should be used to support them. When this no longer looks necessary, and the WTO wants to push for greater free trade, new discussions such as the Millennium Round have to make decisions about when to withdraw quotas and tariffs. Hence strategic management is concerned with similar processes to those of *goal setting*, which we saw making up second- and third-order control.

It would not be difficult thus far to relate closely our exploration of levels of control and Ben-Eli's concept of levels of management. A further element comes into our discussion, however, when we consider the *normative* level. As we saw above, normative management processes require the resolution of *world view, purpose* or *set of values*. As we also saw when discussing second- and third-order control, our model was incomplete because we were 'left with a need to include the role of information on *world view*, *purpose* or *set of values*'.

Our exploration of management and control therefore leaves us with the recognition that the highest process in the control hierarchy will be concerned with deciding *purpose* and *policy* in the context of a stance on *world view*, *purpose* or *set of values*. I shall call the process that does this fourth-order control. In the next section, we will see how all our discussion on control can be brought together as a general model.

4.1.4 GCM: a General Control Model

Introduction to the General Control Model (GCM)

Figure 4.10 shows my model of a control system in the context of management as summarized by Figure 3.4. Although the whole of the GCM in Figure 4.10 is a personal view, I think that all of its features and components come directly from the widely used systems thinking and concepts discussed so far in this chapter. Since it is intended to cater for the issues we have raised about the nature of management and its relationship with information and control, I will explain its overall structure and then look at the details of some of its components.

The model in Figure 4.11 shows:

- the *control system* itself
- the control system's *environment*.

The control system consists of three components:

1 The *process* that is being controlled. This component represents the same concept that we have referred to throughout this chapter, as exemplified by the stockholding process, WTO and other examples. The process *transforms inputs* into *outputs* and is disturbed by the *environment*.

2 Goal-seeking control, which aims to control the process so that its outputs conform to the goals of the whole system. Again, this component is the same concept that we encountered in the classical control model. Goal-seeking control uses a sensor to assess the process outputs, and feedback from this assessment is used by the comparator to determine the deviation from the system's goals, and determine what changes to the process inputs need to be made by the actuator/effector to bring the process back on course.

3 *Goal-setting control*, which sets the goals for goal-seeking control and modifies them in the light of *feedback* on the goal-seeking control system's performance. This overall concept is one we have already discussed and would be represented by our previous examples of changing tariffs or desired stockholding levels. What is new about the GCM in Figure 4.10 however, is that goal-setting control is itself seen as a subsystem consisting of the three components of *second-*, *third-* and *fourth* order control. These additions to the classical model have been made to accommodate the other issues raised when we considered the concepts of *automatic* and *reflective* goal changing, and *levels of management*. Since these aspects of the GCM are new, we will look at them individually opposite.

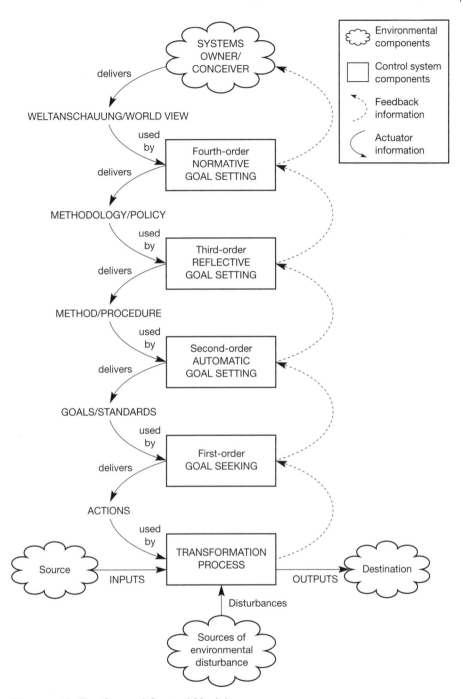

Figure 4.10 The General Control Model

This diagram epitomizes the approach I have taken to interpreting the role of information systems in business. As Section 4.1.4 shows, however, the General Control Model derives from a range of working views of control. The essential point is that the model is *conceptual* and *descriptive*, rather than *prescriptive*. It shows what goes on, rather than the physical implications of how things are done, who does them or where they are done. Real-life applications are likely to be a mixture of the conceptual processes shown.

The control system's *environment* consists of four components:

1 The *source of inputs* to the process that is being controlled.
2 The *destination for outputs* from the process that is being controlled.
3 The *source of disturbances* to the process that is being controlled.
4 The *source of the world view, purpose* or *set of values* being used by the control system.

The first three components are those we already know from the classical control model. The fourth component takes account of the need to identify how the soft issues relating to control are to be resolved. These range from specific issues such as utility or subjective probability raised in our discussion of decision theory in Section 4.1.1, to more general issues policy which we introduced in Section 4.1.3. The position taken on soft issues depends on the *world view, purpose* or *set of values* that is assumed, and this in turn depends on whose concept of the system we are taking as our model.

The General Control Model of Figure 4.10 is therefore a development of the classical control model that takes into account the need to detail the processes of goal setting by identifying three additional levels of control, and the need to link this with the *Weltanschauung* of the conceiver or owner of the system. Since these are further developments of the classical control model, we will look at them in more detail in the rest of this section. Before we do so, however, there is one feature of the General Control Model that is relevant to all the levels shown.

Each level of control can be seen as carrying out similar processes in relation to the processes at levels immediately above and below it. This relationship is summarized in Figure 4.11. Generally, the process at level L uses feedback from level L–1 and output from level L+1, to set the input to level L–1. All of these inputs and outputs are flows of information, which are processed and sometimes stored. Thus, as we saw in Section 4.1.2, defining the control model also defines the role of the *information system* as a component of the control system.

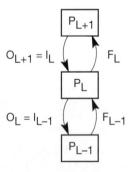

Process $_L$ uses Output $_{L+1}$ and Feedback $_{L-1}$ to set Output $_L$ = Input $_{L-1}$

Figure 4.11 A generalized model of the relationship between levels in a control hierarchy
The output from the level above is also the input to the level below.

Goal setting: second-order control

This lowest level of goal setting represents the technical or hard component of the process. It compares feedback on the performance of the goal-seeking control system with the results of using the method set by third-level control to establish the goals for goal-seeking control. The words 'hard' and 'method' are used here to show that second-order control processes work through the application of decision models, formulae or other formal procedures to produce hard goals that are used by first-order control. Given the defined, formal nature of these methods, second-order control can be seen as *automatic* goal setting.

Our previous example of the stockholding example in Section 4.1.3 can be used to illustrate the hard, automatic nature of this, the lowest level of goal setting. There, we saw that the goal of maintaining stocks within certain levels could be implemented by a reorder level calculated according to the formula:

reorder level = maximum weekly demand × lead time in weeks

In terms of Figure 4.11, the second-order (L=2) control process P_2 uses feedback F_1 data from the first-order control process P_1, in the form of weekly demand figures for the stock item in question and records of supplier performance on lead times for delivery. By application of the formula, it then delivers as an output O_2 the goal of a reorder level for the first-order goal-seeking process.

Note also that the assessments of weekly demand and lead time are *stochastic* in the sense that we explained in Section 4.1.1. This means that individual figures from the data for each instance of demand and delivery have to be *stored* in order that their probabilistic estimate can be calculated. As we saw for the classical control model in Section 4.1.3, 'a second-order goal-changing system has to *store* information'. This level of goal setting or changing can be seen as *automatic*, since once we have the data on delivery lead times and demand, the calculation of the reorder level is predetermined by the formula.

In other examples of second-order control, the *method* of setting the goal may not be a ready-made formula, but the goal setting is still automatic in the sense that the method for doing it is fixed. Thus the Limber Marsh Drainage Consortium fixes many of its goals using committees and meetings, and there are standard rules and procedures for setting the drainage rate so that the Consortium's income can cover its expenditure.

Our stockholding example, however, brings up an important practical point about second-order control and its implications for the information system. The example we used is typical of many real-life examples of this level of control. In them we find that *the data needed for automatic goal setting is already being processed by the information system, but being ignored.* Thus every time a replenishment order is made for stock and subsequently delivered, some part of the information system is recording the details in terms of product, quantities, dates etc. Similarly, every time stock is issued, the details are recorded. Thus first-order control is *already* capturing the data needed by second-order control, and all that is required in addition is that the data be stored and processed using the automatic goal-setting formula. Yet I see many organizations with computerized so-called stock control systems where goals like reorder levels are inserted manually, and any attempt at statistical analysis of past data requires a special exercise. Not surprisingly, when there are hundreds of different items in stock this exercise is often skipped and 'guestimates' used to produce reorder levels. Hence tight controls are kept on costs by strict monitoring of stock issued and delivered, but slovenly cost control is then applied to the operation of the first-order stock control system itself.

Nevertheless, the success of first-order control depends on the use of an appropriate method for setting its goals. In our stockholding example, any recalculation of the reorder level will be irrelevant if this method of stock control itself is irrelevant. As discussed in the Carry-Out Cupboards case in Appendix 1, other stock control methods like periodic reordering may be more appropriate in some situations. A complete control system therefore needs a third-order control level that produces the appropriate method for second-order control.

Goal setting: third-order control

In terms of Figure 4.10, third-order control is the process that uses the feedback on the performance of the second-order goal-setting process to modify or produce a new method for second-order goal setting.

Modification of existing methods or the production of new ones requires an input from fourth-order control. This input has to provide third-order control with a method or a policy for choosing between methods themselves. In our stockholding example, this might be a choice between a reorder level or a periodic reorder method of stock control. In the WTO example, it might be a new way of calculating tariffs or a police chief's new way of controlling protesters.

We call a method that enables us to distinguish, assess and choose between methods a *methodology* (see Chapter 8). If, however, our method of choosing between individual methods is less formal in its approach, we might use a broader term such as *policy*. In our stockholding example, the term methodology is probably appropriate because we can define quite specifically how the two systems of stock control work, and even produce formulae to calculate such critical factors as the costs of operating the various systems. For the tariff or police control method in the WTO case, it was more a question of having a broad policy of trying to promote freer trade or contain demonstrations. As we shall see in Chapter 8, what we call methods are usually very *structured*, while unstructured methods are better described as *approaches*. Methods usually consist of set procedures or formulae, while approaches rely on the more flexible application of principles.

What differentiates third-order from second-order control is the presence of *soft issues* in the third-order process. When third-order control selects a method, defines a decision model or selects an approach, judgements have to be made about soft issues such as utility, subjective probability or desirability.

Thus a decision to apply a formula to calculate a reorder level in the stockholding example can only come after we have first made a decision on the soft issue of whether running out of stock is an acceptable policy. This is because the reorder level formula is designed to ensure that stocks are replenished before we run out. If we were in a market where the demand for our product was such that we thought customers were willing to wait, we might decide not to keep stocks at all. Suppliers of luxury goods often operate such a policy. The choice of stock control formulae also requires decisions on the utility of various costs, such as those associated with stockouts and customer dissatisfaction.

Similarly, a decision by the protesters about which street junctions to block at Seattle could only follow a soft decision that some form of street junction blocking was the best policy to help foil the Millennium Round.

The presence of soft issues in the third-order control process should not be automatically confused with uncertainty in general. In Section 4.1.1, we made a distinction between *hard* and *soft* uncertainty. In the operation of world trade there is no clear formula to connect tariff levels to constraints on trade, but the connexion is a hard one, since both the tariff and the amount of goods imported by a country are variables that can be measured with objective values. However, the costs of stockouts are not measurable in the same way. A dissatisfied customer who cannot buy a product off the shelf and goes elsewhere is a cost that depends on the world view, purpose or set of values of the person assessing it.

The presence of soft issues and the need to make judgements as part of the third-order control process makes it reflective rather than automatic. The feedback from second-order control's use of any method chosen by third-order control results in *experience* and *learning*. This learning can take various forms, but all of them imply an ability to *record* and *store* both the *method* used, the *data* used by the method and the *outcomes* that resulted from the use of the method and the particular data.

Notice that while third-order control shares the need to be able to store information with second-order control, there is a difference in what is actually stored. Second-order control merely stores data such as delivery lead times or demand for stock. Third-order control records *models* of the methods that may be chosen by the reflective goal-setting process for use by second-order control. Thus stock control formulae, decision models like those of Section 4.1.1 or minutes of meetings that established the policies of the Limber Marsh Drainage Consortium on determining drainage rates are all examples of what third-order control must record. In practice, how they are stored may be very different indeed, but what is being stored is conceptually equivalent.

Here again, we see that the distinction of whats and hows means that a systems view of information can look very different from a conventional organizational view. This distinction is not just a theoretical nicety. Failure to recognize, for example, that committee minutes can be part of the information used by third-order control can mean that no *feedback loop* is established to ensure that *learning* takes place. How often do organizations use lower orders of control to ensure that every penny of expenditure is accounted for, while policy disasters costing the earth sail blissfully on without feedback, analysis and learning? I remember the operations manager of the Limber Marsh Drainage Consortium saying to me, 'Everybody knows the cost of a bag of cement.' His meaning was that the things people understand, they debate furiously; the things they are too embarrassed to admit they don't understand, they let go by without comment.

If, however, third-order control is operating successfully, this in turn means that the methodology or policies used by third-order control can be built on and developed by fourth-order control, as we shall discuss next.

Goal setting: fourth-order control

Fourth-order control decides both the range of methods and the principles for choosing between them. We use the terms *methodology* and *policy* to describe this output from fourth- to third-order control. Thus in our stockholding example, fourth-order control would decide the policy on how far stockouts were acceptable and what types of reordering procedures might be operated. In the WTO lead-in case, deciding on the desirability of the situation that 'consumers and producers know that they can enjoy secure supplies and greater choice of the finished products, components, raw materials and services that they use' is a fourth-order decision.

However, words like 'policy', 'acceptable' or 'desirability' imply soft issues. Deciding just what is, and is not, an issue, as well as deciding where we stand on the issue itself, are questions whose answers depend on our world view, purpose or set of values. At Carry-Out Cupboards, the desirability of having the range of cupboard kits in stock and available to the customer comes from a set of values that sees the company as popular, easily accessible and cheap. A country's desire to be in the WTO implies a world view that believes in closer world ties rather than less connected independence.

Goal setting	Sales example	Stock control example
Normative	*Should we trade using credit? What level of risk can we accept?*	*Should we hold stocks? What risk of stock-out can we accept?*
Reflective	*Should we use post codes? Client income? How do we then calculate the credit allowed?*	*Should we operate a reorder level system, a reorder period system, or what?*
Automatic	*Apply formula to post code, income or whatever to determine limit.*	*Given the data, what should be the reorder level, reorder period etc?*

Figure 4.12 Normative, reflective and automatic components of goal setting
These are just some of the possible examples for sales and stock control. Whether or not such questions are formally posed, all goal setting will have these components.

Another form of soft information that fourth-order control must deliver, as its contribution to goal setting through third-order control, is information that defines the values used in building the decision models selected by the third-order control process. The decision theory explained in Section 4.1.1 requires information that evaluates outcomes and defines decision strategies. It may also require subjective estimates of probability. All of these components of a decision model depend on the world view, purpose or set of values of the decision maker and the feedback from the use of methods by third-order control.

Fourth-order control is therefore essentially concerned with the *translation of values* into practice. Values differ between individuals, and an individual's values may change over time and in different circumstances. To complete our understanding of the whole control model, we need to identify *whose* values the control system seeks to implement. We call this person or group of persons the *systems owner/conceiver*. For reasons we will explain next, we take the owner/conceiver to be a component of the control systems *environment*, not of the control system itself.

Systems owner/conceiver

We established in Section 3.2.9 that what a system is seen to be, and what properties it is considered to have, depends on whose view or concept of the system we are taking. To call such a person or group the *systems conceiver* is therefore natural enough, since what the system is seen to be is their *concept*. But why the term *owner*?

The answer to this question comes from the fact that we are considering a control system *that* is acting as a component of *management*. If we look at the role of the descending levels of control, we see a sequence of control functions that takes a set of values expressing a world view, or purpose, and ultimately implements these in the process being controlled. In a management context, whose values would we expect these to be? The answer is that person, or group in the wider management system, who has power to influence the control system, but over whom the control system itself has only limited influence.

Box 4.3

Rightsizing the womenswear market

Juliette Jowit and Peggy Hollinger

When Marks and Spencer first started selling its famously British knickers in Asia, it hit a minor hitch. With the Asian derrière somewhat smaller than the British bottom, the company's range was inappropriate for the market.

Clothing retailers have long had to face up to the fact that sizes need to be adjusted for different markets. M&S's response was to introduce smaller sizes and increase its range of petite clothing

Until now, most UK retailers have not sought to adjust for regional differences at home. Yet the publication, after five years' research, of Britain's first 'body map' could offer the potential for retailers to do just that.

Professor Stephen Gray, of Nottingham Trent University, has measured more than 10 000 women, aged 15 to 85, in the first serious attempt to evaluate modern body shapes in some 50 years. He found women were remarkably different from north to south: Walsall women have the widest hips, Midland women the biggest breasts, Newcastle lasses are heaviest, Streatham girls tallest and those in Cardiff and Glasgow the shortest.

Moreover, in the 50 years since the last national sizing survey, more sedentary life-styles, bigger meals and regular snacking have made the average woman bigger, especially around the hips.

Yet most mass market clothing is based on patterns devised for an era when women were a different shape. For example, there has been no change to the traditional 36-24-36 bust-waist-hip formula that defines a size 12 to take account of wider hips. Prof Gray, who has set up an independent company, Computer Clothing Research, estimates that fewer than one in 10 women match all three measurements of their dress size.

Retailers know there is a problem but are not sure how to rectify it, even with the body map. The prospect of using the research to introduce a wider size 12 in the north and a slimmer fitting 12 in the south fills most with dread.

The implications for stock would be enormous and could cripple many retailers, according to one clothing executive. 'To move from five sizes to seven means you would have to increase your stock by 40 per cent,' he says. 'But you would not increase your sales by the same amount.'

He adds that the proportion of people who would fit the new sizes would be so small that the cost of distributing and holding the stock in a national chain would be prohibitive and would have to be reflected in the selling price.

Hilary Riva, managing director of womenswear at Arcadia, which owns Top Shop, Dorothy Perkins, Principles and Evans, says retailers are already dealing with regional differences by introducing different trouser lengths and new ranges such as petite. Here the proportions are different from traditional patterns. 'The biggest problem for anyone outside an average is the proportion,' she says. 'You can be a size 20–24 and still be a petite.'

One large national retailer decided to use the information gathered only from its own stores, because it had a clearly defined customer base of a certain age with its own specific average sizes. 'Where your body mass lies is quite different depending on your age,' it says.

The new sizing survey could, however, give many women, particularly larger customers, a better fit by pinpointing how proportions change according to size.

At the moment, patterns are based on the average size 12 and sized up or down by subtracting or adding two inches to the key measurements. But women do not put on or lose weight evenly, and heavier bottoms and busts tend to sag, redistributing the wider measurement lower down the body. This causes armholes to gape because shoulders do not grow in proportion to busts, and front hems to rise as stomachs stick out most.

Using this information to make more sophisticated patterns is the best solution for retailers, says Prof Gray, who maintains that despite regional differences women mostly have the same proportions.

In doing so retailers could achieve better customer loyalty and potentially win new custom, especially as the results could be analysed to match their target spenders.

Even now, for some retailers the prospect of trying to introduce more sizes is not unreasonable. Mail order companies, for example, could afford to introduce a far greater range of sizes, lengths and shapes because they are able to hold stock centrally.

But in the end it is unlikely there will ever be a perfect fit on the high street. 'Every woman is a different shape,' says one retailer. 'It's just that a size 12 is what fits the greatest proportion of people out there.'

Source: Financial Times, 30 August 1999. Reprinted with permission.

▶

Comment

Here is a very interesting, and quite complex, example of goal setting *in a stock control context.*

The first lesson we learn from the General Control Model of Figure 4.10 is that goals are unlikely to stay the same in a changing environment. Thus the environment of female body size and shape has changed 'in the 50 years since the last national sizing survey'. If goals are to be modified to keep them relevant, there has to be feedback on the goal-seeking process and this feedback has to be stored and processed to set new, relevant goals.

The 'large national retailer' who 'decided to use the information gathered only from its own stores, because it had a clearly defined customer base' had a good information system to support its goal setting. Yet many other stores had no such thing, hence Professor Gray's opportunity to do it for them.

The second lesson is the need to distinguish reflective and automatic goal setting. Once there is a method of translating body measurements into the right sized and shaped garment; goal setting can be automatic. In this situation we just convert data about women's measurements into how many garments of various sizes we need to match our market. Provided we get feedback on how women's measurements are changing, we can make the appropriate adjustments to the amounts of various sizes we expect to stock and sell.

However, Professor Gray's research and feedback from the salespeople shows that the old formulae for determining garment shapes and sizes no longer look relevant. What is needed here is reflective goal setting that looks at feedback on the results of using a particular method to set goals. Where the feedback suggests that the method needs changing, we are into methodology or the study of method, hence reflective goal setting.

Professor Gray's research indicates that in the past the information systems to support goal setting were spasmodic or absent. The clothing stores used a feedforward control system that, not surprisingly, got left behind by environmental change.

Conventional organizational views of management would take this group to be 'high-level management' or the directors of the company. More paranoid views might invent some 'ruling class' or hidden conspiracy. A systems view would recognize that the world view, purpose or set of values taken on by the control system is an *emergent property* resulting from the views of a range of environmental components coming together. This range is likely to include both formal and informal social coalitions and structures whose rich variety might, in any particular case, give some support for organizational, paranoid, Freudian and just about any other view that provides some insight into the different theories that might be implemented in real organizations or businesses. Even systems like those in Box 4.1, with the most severe dictatorial management like Hitler's Germany or the Stalinist Soviet Union, did not perfectly reflect the world view, purpose or set of values of a single systems owner. As the control system was implemented other values infiltrated the system: how else did opponents resist and even diffuse the effects of such regimes?

The systems owner/conceiver of Figure 4.11 is therefore seen as a component in the environment of the control system, which itself is likely to be a subsystem of the greater whole of the organizational or business management system.

Hard and soft information in the General Control Model

Our analysis of the General Control Model of Figure 4.10 shows that both hard and soft information flows are processed by any management control system. If we look at the information flows and their environmental sources, we can see that they have two sources:

1 Information from the systems owner/conceiver about the world view, purpose or set of values to be used by the control system.
2 Information about disturbances to the controlled process from the systems environment.

The effects of these two kinds of information flows work in opposite directions:

1 As we saw above, the control system attempts to implement the choice of *world view*, *purpose* or *set of values* of the *systems owner/conceiver* at the fourth-order level, through to the actions carried out by the actuator at first-order control level. In any control system there is this *soft* input from the first source above, which results in a cascade of policy, method, goals and actions.
2 However, *hard* information comes from the second source above about disturbances to the process being controlled. This results in a succession of feedback paths from first- to fourth-order control levels, whose effect is to modify goals, method and policy in the light of experience.

The General Control Model shows a management control system as something that is dynamic and adaptive and it *learns*. Thus at the higher levels of method and policy we can see this overall process of modification in the light of experience as one of learning. It is important to note that this learning process is not confined to objective, technical, exterior learning associated with hard information and 'facts'. There is also an implication from the presence and role of soft information in the model that subjective, personal, interior learning can take place. The model does not require us to ignore the role of personal or self-management as part of the whole management process.

Specialist components of information systems

I am going to sound aggressive, but I think that I can justify my assertions. We are now going to cover a subject area where the systems approach advocated in this book clashes with many popular texts with the words *information* and *systems* in their titles. I did make some of the points, that I am about to repeat, in previous editions. I believe that the developments in information systems since the first edition in 1994 have now been justified.

I hope you will not interpret my message as self-aggrandizement. The important point is that the half-dead nature of what I cover in this section is an excellent illustration of how dangerous *labels* are as a guide to *what* is happening in the fast-changing world of information and communications technology, applied to management.

As explained in earlier editions, the General Control Model also enables us to relate various kinds of *supposedly separate* or *different* forms of information system such as:

- decision support systems
- executive information systems
- expert systems.

These are just one set of falsely separating labels to describe how parts of the management control process might be carried out.

Decision support systems (DSS) are designed to support the decision-making processes of management. The word 'support' is emphasized because DSS do not replace management decision making, but are intended to help in the decision-making process itself. The most common way in which they do this is to automate the type of decision model we discussed in Section 4.1.1, so that managers can test the potential results of setting particular values to their choices as actuators in the control process. DSS do this by automating the decision model through the use of computer software.

Examples of this at very different levels might include:

- The use of computerized models designed to reflect the effects of removing tariffs on world trade in emerging economies.
- How a manager at Carry-Out Cupboards could use a computerization of the reorder level formula on a spreadsheet to work out whether a particular reduction in lead time was worth a particular increase in price by a supplier.

What all DSS have in common, however simple or sophisticated, is that they enable management to try out the 'what if' of decisions through the convenience of an automated model. In terms of our General Control Model, this represents the use of computerized support for goal-setting second-order control.

Executive information systems (EIS) are usually described (e.g. Laudon and Laudon, 2000), as being principally concerned with providing a wide variety of summarized data that will enable management to plan strategically. This strategic planning checks and ensures that the various functions of the organization are properly co-ordinated, and that the organization is going in the right direction in terms of markets and opportunities. Typical information to be summarized might relate to competitor performance, the legal context, the economic environment or market preferences. Generally, EIS are designed to process data summarizing the performance of the whole organization in relation to its environment. In order to carry out this function, such a system usually takes the form of a set of software that can access the database of the organization to obtain the data it needs to summarize.

At first sight, such a description of EIS enables us to place it clearly in the General Control Model as supporting the fourth-order level of control. In terms of the model, the EIS provides feedback on the performance of the whole in relation to its environment and enables any changes of policy to be made. A danger comes, however, when many well-established and respectable books on management information systems picture EIS in the stereotypical context of the non-systemic organizational hierarchy of which we were critical in Section 4.1.3. The danger of this approach is that the logical *what* of an organizational activity becomes identified with a particular *who* or *how*. Thus Laudon and Laudon (2000) see EIS as the concern of 'top management' or 'chief executive officer plus staff'. This may be true of many organizations, but it is not a necessary characteristic when we view an organization as a system.

Automatically linking the conceptual *what* of strategic policy formulation with a particular *who* or *how* can dangerously suggest that small organizations or businesses do not need or do not have a fourth-order level control function. Such a view is not only false from an academic systems viewpoint, it can also lead to poor practical management. In a small business like MX Marketing in Appendix 3, a busy man such as Ben Lister with limited clerical support might particularly benefit from access to software and a database that could summarize competitor performance, the legal context, the economic environment or market preferences. The fact that it might not be economic for him to own it is a separate issue of the *how*, not the *what*. Once he recognizes that MX Marketing has a need for fourth-order control just like any other managed organization, he might consider access to government and other information that is available on the Internet. Automatically associating EIS with the 'top management' of large organizations could mean that important information systems opportunities are lost to smaller organizations like MX Marketing.

Expert systems can be placed in the context of the General Control Model once we recall the role of learning in higher-order control. So far, we have implied in all our descriptions of the development of methodology at the fourth level, and definition of method at the third level, that this development and definition are done by the human components of the system. Expert systems are attempts to model the human ability to use reasoning and acquire knowledge. Thus in our stockholding example, we saw the identification of the different methods of stock control and the choice of method as a human activity. Expert systems software would seek to gather information from the user about how the different methods worked and the rules or reasoning used when choices were made. The so-called *knowledge base* of the expert system stores both rules to represent human reasoning and semantic nets to represent how the different components of this knowledge can be classified and inter-related.

The systemic view of management presented in the General Control Model is therefore intended to represent the *logical* or *conceptual* relationship between management, control and information to be found in any organization or business that claims to be managed. The particular *ways* or *hows* may vary, but our aim is to recognize underlying common systems structures.

4.2 INFORMATION, THE ENVIRONMENT AND CONTROL SYSTEMS BEHAVIOUR

4.2.1 The environment and essential forms of management information

We set up *control* as the key concept that helps us understand the link between *management* and *information*, as in Figure 3.4. We then used the General Control Model of Figure 4.10 to enable us to classify and appreciate the *different forms* and *roles* of information that are used by management.

From the General Control Model, we can see that *all* information of interest to management is about one or more of the following:

- goal setting
- goal seeking
- the environment.

We established the roles of *goal setting* and *goal seeking* in management, and determined the role of the *information system* as a component of these processes.

However, as we saw in Section 4.1.2, 'real-life systems have an environment that disturbs them and on which they can have only limited effect', and so 'the existence of environmental disturbances is the only reason we need control at all'. Hence information about the *environment* is essential to any form of management that hopes to have any control over the processes it manages.

Given the importance to management of information about the environment, we shall devote the whole of this section to answering two questions:

1 What sort of information does management need to have about the environment, and how can it use this information to deal with *environmental disturbances*?
2 How can management use this information to design *control systems* with the best *response* to environmental disturbances?

Before trying to answer these questions, we need to remind ourselves of some basic systems concepts:

- The *environment* of any system has *more effect* on the system than the system does on its environment. For example, the state of the global economy or the UK market will have more effect on the fortunes of Carry-Out Cupboards than Carry-Out Cupboards will have on the global economy or the UK market.

- The *components* of any system *interact* with each other, and often these interactions *conflict*. For example, the sales manager of an organization such as Carry-Out Cupboards might like to see a full range of products on display at every outlet, with high stock levels, to guarantee immediate satisfaction of demand and ensure maximum sales. The finance manager might like to limit the range and amount on display to control stockholding and floorspace costs.

- The overall *behaviour* of any system is an *emergent property* resulting from both the internal *interaction* of its *components* and the *external* interaction with its *environment*. For example, the overall behaviour of the sales of Carry-Out Cupboards' products will be the result of internal actions, such as how well they are designed and made, and of interaction with the environment, including changing consumer tastes or their purchasing power.

Understanding systems behaviour in the light of these concepts is the key to understanding the role of information in control and management systems, and hence to answering our two questions above. What we called 'external interaction' will relate to our first question, about *environmental disturbances*. What we called 'internal interaction' will relate to our second question, about *control systems response*.

4.2.2 Information and managing environmental disturbances

Let's begin with a couple of examples:

- The market for Carry-Out Cupboards products represents a component of the environment of that organization. The management of Carry-Out Cupboards may sometimes be baffled, frustrated or annoyed at the way its customers behave, but that does not mean that it can do nothing about its market. The history of business is full of examples of entrepreneurs who persuaded the market to see it their way and buy their products.

- The WTO has world opinion as one of the components of its environment. It may not be always able to swing opinion its own way, but the management of the WTO can see many examples in history of public opinion being persuaded and changed.

These examples illustrate the fact that, although there are limits to the effect a management system can have on its environment, managers of organizations do not have to be completely helpless or passive in the face of environmental disturbances.

If we consider what management can do to *deal with* environmental disturbances, I would suggest that there are three different ways:

1 *Influencing* environmental disturbances.
2 *Anticipating* environmental disturbances.
3 *Accommodating* environmental disturbances.

We shall now look at each of these in turn and give examples of what they mean.

Influencing environmental disturbances

I suspect that the WTO doesn't like the idea of high-profile demonstrations against its activities by that component of its environment called 'hostile world opinion'. Nor would Carry-Out Cupboards like the idea of the customers in its market environment deciding they don't want to buy its products. Unless the management of these or any organization, have abandoned any idea of *meliorism*; they will first think in terms of *influencing* their environment.

There are many ways in which the management of an organization can try to influence its environment, but here are some examples to illustrate the concept. To understand these examples, we should recall that all systems contain components, and that these components themselves can be systems that are subsystems of the whole. We can therefore see the environment of any system as being a wider or greater system, which contains various systems as components.

For business systems like the WTO or Carry-Out Cupboards, the environment is likely to contain, among other elements:

- human systems
- political systems
- financial systems
- physical systems.

If business systems want to try to *influence* their environment, they may do so by trying to influence one or more of these systems in that environment.

A widespread example of trying to influence environmental *human systems* is advertising. The potential customers who make up the market may not be buying one of a particular company's products because either they haven't heard of it, or they believe that they don't want it. Advertising tries to influence both of these disturbing properties of the environment by sending out *information* that:

- tells the market that the product exists. Sponsorship of sport is an example of this: it concentrates on putting information about a name or logo in front of the market;
- persuades the market that the product is desirable. Television adverts are an example of this. They may use *hard* information, like describing the size of a cupboard; or they may use *soft* information, like using the picture of a smart person furnishing their house with Carry-Out Cupboards' products.

In Chapters 5 and 6, we shall explore further what is involved in the *communication* of information, and the *bias* it can contain.

The concept of influencing environmental *political* systems can be illustrated by the WTO lead-in case. Both the management of the WTO and those who were managing the protest realized that the political environment could significantly affect their attempts to achieve their goals. The protesters realized that a colourful demonstration consisting of a wide range of groups, from Kuna Indians to US steel workers, could influence world politicians that their goals should be supported. Given that the then US President, Bill Clinton, subsequently turned up at Seattle to express reservations about world free trade, perhaps the demonstrators did have some influence. When Ambassador Charlene Barshefsky opened a meeting by expressing her regrets to ministers and officials who were harassed during the demonstrations, she was courting the media in an attempt to persuade them that the demonstrators were badly behaved and undemocratic.

Attempting to influence environmental *financial systems* is a particularly common tactic used by the management of organizations who have financial goals. Price cuts, special sales or supposedly advantageous credit terms are all examples of how an organization like Carry-Out Cupboards would try to seduce customers who are reluctant to spend their money into buying its products.

Would the protesters against the WTO have found it as easy to organize their demonstrations if the WTO had held its meeting on a remote polar island, rather than Seattle? Would potential UK customers of Carry-Out Cupboards be willing to travel to a store in eastern Russia to buy its products? The *physical systems* environment can have a strong effect on what management can control. Management can have some influence on its environment by choosing such things as physical location. The whole phenomenon of large, out-of-town shopping centres is an attempt to influence the car-owning customer by providing physical convenience.

Anticipating environmental disturbances

However much we try to influence a component of the environment, like a market or a political situation, our ability to do so will ultimately be limited. By its very nature, the environment is those things that have more effect on the system than the system does on them. Where we can't influence, we have to do something else to enable the system to manage in the face of environmental disturbances. One important thing we can do is to try to *anticipate* what these disturbances might be.

Thus Carry-Out Cupboards may not be able to *influence* its customers completely in terms of which products they buy. Some products will rise in popularity, while others will fall. There is a limit to what the marketing function of Carry-Out Cupboards can do to influence this. However, if market research data can enable the organization to *anticipate* what changes in sales are likely, stocks and production can be adjusted to ensure that there are enough of the products that are rising in popularity, and that there is not a surplus of less popular items.

There are two important ways in which environmental disturbances can be anticipated:

- forecasting
- built-in variety.

Forecasting enables us to anticipate what outputs will be needed from a process so that inputs can be set in a form now that will result in the desired output at some time in the future. Carry-Out Cupboards orders stock, or starts constructing a new warehouse, just as its raw material suppliers plant trees, in anticipation of what they will require by the time that delivery of stock takes place, the building is complete or the trees have matured.

It is essential to note that forecasting is only necessary because control systems contain *lags*. If we could instantly magic up completed products, finished buildings or mature trees, then environmental disturbances in the form of increased demand for products, storage space or raw materials wouldn't matter. In real-life control systems, however, it takes time for:

- the *transformation process* to change *inputs* into *outputs.*;
- the *information system* to carry out the *closed loop* from *sensor* to *actuator/effector*, which enables the outputs to be adjusted to respond to environmental disturbances.

The lag in a control system is therefore the time taken from sensing the output to carrying out the feedback loop and transforming the input into corrected output.

It is also essential to note that forecasting can be involved in *goal setting* as well as goal seeking. Thus if Carry-Out Cupboards uses forecasting to predict changes in the demand for various products, then goals like sales targets, stock levels or production schedules will be changed in response to the results of the forecasting. For the organizers of an international conference like the WTO, forecasting will help them set their goals in terms of accommodation for delegates, schedules for media briefings or security controls in anticipation of protests.

If forecasting is involved in goal setting or *higher-order* control, then the information that it uses must come from the results of *feedback* from *goal-seeking* control being *stored*. Thus for Carry-Out Cupboards, forecasting of sales is the analysis of trends and other movements shown by records of data for past sales of a product. All of this data is likely already to be being recorded for other purposes such as keeping accounts, monitoring sales performance etc., so all that remains is for the information system to contain a subsystem designed to pick up and analyse data for forecasting purposes.

RQ 4.13	What other components might there be in forecasting?

We shall go further with this concept in Chapter 5. There we shall see that a modern database makes storage and analysis of things like sales data much more possible than in the past. Modern databases remove many of the old restrictions of having data compartmentalized and therefore hard to integrate and analyse.

Another way of anticipating environmental disturbances that is less specific and more open than forecasting is building variety into the control system. Forecasting something like the sales of a particular product, or the number of delegates at a conference, assumes that we already know which particular variable the environment is going to disturb. In the two examples we've just given, this would be how many cupboard kits are sold and how many delegates will turn up at the conference.

But supposing that Carry-Out Cupboards isn't sure that the most important environmental disturbance with which it will have to deal is some change in its sales? It might instead be new government employment legislation that will drive up production costs. Supposing that the WTO doesn't know whether its main worry is a shortfall in the number of conference delegates, rather than an increase in the numbers of demonstrators? In such situations, the most important control problem is that we don't know what we should be forecasting. For Carry-Out Cupboards, it might be government policy rather than consumer behaviour. For the WTO, it might be organizing relations with the Seattle police, rather than negotiating with Seattle hotels.

In such situations, what we need is not forecasting of *one type* of environmental disturbance, but a way of covering a range or *variety* of possible environmental disturbances. We will develop the concept of variety more deeply in Section 4.3, but for the moment we can note the following points:

1 Management and organizational systems have environments that can disturb them in different ways. Thus Carry-Out Cupboards can find its success disturbed by government legislation as well as changes in customer tastes. The WTO can find that a conference can be messed up by poorly predicted attendance, as well as street demonstrations.

2 It is not always possible to determine the main disturbances that should be forecast. If Carry-Out Cupboards focuses on a big advertising campaign just when new safety legislation is likely to disrupt its production, it could have problems satisfying demand for its products. If the WTO spends its time allocating hotels to delegates without assessing the affect of the demonstrations, it could have problems getting delegates into hotels.

3 The greater variety of ways a system has for dealing with environmental disturbances, the more likely it is to be able to accommodate the disturbances. If Carry-Out Cupboards or the WTO has a variety of activities, intended to cover a wide potential range of environmental disturbances, it is more likely to able to deal with, or *accommodate* them.

That final use of the word *accommodate* leads us on to the third way in which management can deal with environmental disturbances.

Accommodating environmental disturbances

When we talk about 'accommodating' environmental disturbances, we are talking about a two-way process, or an *interaction*. The two components of this interaction are:

- what the *environment* does to disturb the system;
- what the *system* does in response to the disturbances of the environment.

When two components like these come together, our understanding of systems concepts would expect there to be an *emergent property*. This emergent property is called *systems behaviour*. Dramatic examples of this can be found in the lead-in cases of the Child Support Agency or the WTO Seattle conference. When both these organizations were disturbed by political and social attitudes – disturbances that they had neither successfully *influenced* nor *anticipated* – they had to *accommodate* them. The accommodation in each case was not something disconnected from the environmental disturbance. Whom the CSA appointed as a new director, or how the WTO rescheduled its programme and its locations, were interactive responses to the environment in the form of public reaction.

Management often has to design a system that has to accommodate environmental disturbances that cannot be totally influenced or anticipated. In such circumstances, the management of the system has to answer the question:

How can the system be designed to result in the optimum (= best) behaviour in response to disturbances from the environment?

There are two concepts that can help management answer this question:

- buffers
- control frequency.

We will devote the rest of this section to exploring the role of buffers, and then cover control frequency in the subsequent section.

An example of *buffers* is what we do when we hold stock, as in the Carry-Out Cupboards example in Appendix 1. If we wish to satisfy a demand under conditions where we cannot exactly co-ordinate the demand with supply, stocks are essential. In most business situations this condition applies. We cannot determine when customers should come to us and what they should buy. They are part of the environment and their disturbances to the system cannot be totally *influenced*. I find it hard to imagine that the management of Carry-Out Cupboards, or any other organization, could send out men with fierce dogs to force its customers to come to the local store and buy what they are told. And as to the ability of management to *anticipate*, even if good forecasting tells us that we are going to sell 10 of a particular product in a month, we don't know when the individual items will be required.

The only way to deal with the limits of influencing and anticipating the environment, if we want to be able to satisfy demand immediately, is to accommodate the unforeseen by holding items in stock.

Many business books give the impression that stock is somehow a 'bad thing' to be avoided. This is very simplistic, and a good example of the difference between *reductionism* and a holistic, *systems* approach.

Let's first look at the arguments against stock. Critics of stockholding rightly point out that holding stock costs money. It costs money to have storage space, to heat and ventilate, or to keep secure, as well as all the other things necessary when holding stock. Any reduction of stockholding can reduce such costs. The big management credo of the 1980s, JIT (= 'just in time'), was a concept that tried to address the costs of stockholding. The idea of JIT is that, instead of holding stocks, we ensure that the delivery of an input arrives 'just in time' to meet the needs of the transformation process that converts the input into the desired output.

In the Carry-Out Cupboards example, management would avoid holding large amounts of the cupboard components, in the form of such things as doors or hinges, waiting for the assembly and packing process. Instead, it would co-ordinate the arrival of what was needed by the assembly and packing programme so that the components arrived 'just in time' for the operations of assembly and packing.

However, it is unlikely that if the assembly process for a particular kit needed four hinges every minute, separate delivery vans with four hinges on board would arrive at one-minute intervals. Also, at the retail outlets, we would not expect to find empty shelves that would suddenly contain the particular kit a customer wanted just as they asked for it. The fact is that the pure concept of JIT is rarely possible because stocks are essential when we have to *co-ordinate different patterns of supply and demand*, as in Figure 4.13. Thus we have to have a stock of four hinges before we have enough to make up a kit, and we probably need many more than that before we can justify a van delivery. In practice, therefore, it is only possible to co-ordinate the different patterns of supply, e.g. by the van load, and demand, e.g. by assembly quantities, by holding stock.

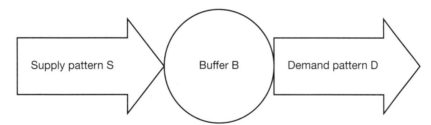

Figure 4.13 The role of buffers
Buffers act as a mechanism for enabling the interaction of different patterns of supply and demand. They are most likely to be needed where at least one of these patterns is outside the control of management. Customer demand would be a classic example.

Where both the supply and demand processes can be controlled by the system, then although a pure concept of JIT cannot be applied, it is possible to minimize stock-holding by tightly co-ordinating supply and demand schedules. The use of supply *chain management*, as in Appendix 1, is an important example of how an information system can support this. However, when either the input or the output of a process cannot be controlled, it is no longer a question of *minimizing* stock levels but rather of *optimizing* them. Thus Carry-Out Cupboards may be able to control the pattern of input of kits into its retail outlets, but it cannot control the output pattern of customer demand. The stockholding aims of the retail outlets will therefore be to ensure that they can meet a variable, uncontrolled range of customer demand by holding stocks as a buffer. A very small buffer will mean that sudden increases in customer demand may not be met. A large buffer may be able to accommodate a very big increase, but will involve us in high stockholding costs.

Figure 4.14 illustrates the principle. With stock levels very high we incur high stock holding costs. With very low levels we increase the chances of stock-outs and the costs associated with lost sales, bad commercial image, delayed production etc. The overall relationship between the total cost of the stockholding operation and the stock level shows a potential minimum that balances these costs. This is an optimum, or best balance quantity, not a minimum.

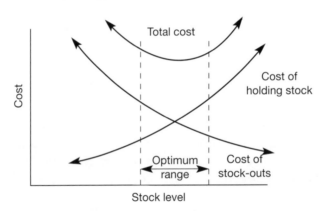

Figure 4.14 Optimum stock level
Holding stock is not automatically undesirable, as some of the poorer advocates of financial accountancy might imply. Stocks have an important role to play as buffers between different patterns of input and output. The aim should be to optimize stock levels, not always to eliminate them.

4.2.3 Information and control systems behaviour

Control frequency and the costs of control

There is an old country saying that 'the best fertilizer is the farmer's boot'. Its meaning is that those fields where the farmer walks and takes the trouble to check are the fields that will do best in growing crops. As a principle of management control, whether in farming or any other business, very frequent checking seems like a good thing. But is it? In this section we will consider how often the 'boot' of management control should tread on a particular 'field' of a process we wish to control. How often it does is a measure of *control frequency*.

When we use the term control frequency we refer to how often in a particular time interval the sensor of a control system checks the value of the *outputs* from the *transformation process*. This value is then *fedback* and used by the *comparator* to instruct the *actuator/effector* on what modifications have to be made to the *inputs* to the transformation process. As we saw in Figure 4.7, this sequence of activities represents the contribution the information system makes as a component of the control system.

'Very frequent checking' is therefore a colloquial way of describing a high control frequency. If we go close to the limit of checking all the time, then the control frequency is near its highest value and can be considered as continuous. To understand whether or not high frequency or even continuous control is always desirable, we can return to our WTO and stockholding examples.

Values of imports and exports between countries can go up and down month by month, and still end up with little overall change year by year. Governments' attitudes towards liberalization of trade will depend on what they see as the long-term economic opportunities for their exports, and the threats posed by growth in imports. Trade ministers do not necessarily need to know their daily export figures, nor do they need to be asking for weekly WTO conferences to be continually changing the rules. Indeed, if ministers did behave in this way, they would probably cause more instability and damage to the economies of their countries than if they had merely left matters alone.

Similarly, in a stockholding example like Carry-Out Cupboards, we might consider that a retail outlet manager had suffered a mental breakdown they had their staff continuously counting and recounting the amount of stock on the shelves.

Both the stockholding and WTO examples show that in practical applications of control systems, the operation of the information system component contributes its own costs to the cost of control. High-frequency control may bring good crop yields to our farmer and his boot, but much of the profit from these yields can be absorbed by the time and money spent travelling around the farm on inspection visits. Similarly, stock checking cuts down the costs of stock-outs, theft or wastage; but stock checking itself costs money.

Box 4.4

Rats are neophobes

Rats are a pretty successful management system. Every human being in London lives quite close to at least one of them. Yet if rats had the motto 'innovate or die', I wonder if they would have done so well.

If we take 'neophobe' to mean 'fear of the new', then rats do show that characteristic. Put something new, like a trap, into a rat's environment, and its first reaction will be one of suspicion. Rats don't like new things and will carefully negotiate around the trap. It will probably take two weeks before a rat feels relaxed about such a new intruder into its environment.

Yet 'innovate or die' seems to propose something different. It implies that the more receptive that the rat is to the new, the more successful it, and therefore all of the rat kingdom, is likely to be.

Such is the ratty problem. Innovative rats can soon die out because their desire for the new leads them into the trap first time. The rats who are too persistent in rejecting the new are likely to fail in finding new food sources, and new mates.

The answer to this apparent conflict between neophobia and innovation is to be found in the rubber stamp of operational research, Figure 4.20. In practice, the surviving rat knows how to make the balance between too hasty innovation and excessive neophobia.

For 'rat' read 'management'.

RQ 4.14   How often do you check your bank balance?

Optimizing total control costs

Figure 4.15 summarizes the costs that have to be considered when deciding on control frequency. The horizontal scale represents how frequently output from the transformation process is sensed, fedback and used to determine the adjustments made to the inputs by the actuator. The extreme left of the scale represents a frequency of zero, i.e. *never* checking. Moving to the right along the scale represents increasing frequency, to the point that the checking is virtually continuous.

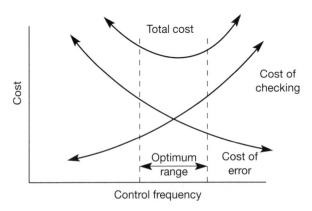

Figure 4.15 Optimizing control frequency
The particular shapes of the curves will vary in individual real-life examples, but the principle behind the general form will always apply where the cost of checking rises with control frequency and the cost of error falls. In these situations the total cost curve will be concave upwards, with a minimum corresponding to an optimum control frequency. I have indicated a range containing the optimum, rather than the optimum itself, to imply that in real life exact estimation of optimum control frequency is unlikely.

The cost effects of frequency are measured by the vertical scale. By 'cost' we mean the broadest hard and soft senses of the word. Hence soft costs of aggravation and inconvenience would be included as well as hard costs like money or time.

If we now consider the effect of control frequency on the total costs associated with running a control system, we can see that this total cost is a combination of two components:

1 The *cost of checking*, which is made up of costs associated directly with operating the control system itself. In the stockholding example, these would be the costs of counting, calculating and recording stock levels, as well as keeping track of stock issued, reordered and delivered.
2 The *cost of error*, which is made up of the costs associated with any failure to achieve the control system's goals perfectly. In the stockholding example these would include the costs of being out of stock, like lost sales and customer ill will; and the costs of being overstocked, such as obsolescence, extra storage or tied-up capital.

The *cost of checking* will be greater the more frequently we check, since every check made requires further counting, calculating etc., as above. The *cost of error* works in the opposite way. The less frequently we check, the more likely it is that stocks will run out because they have not been reordered, or stock levels will become too high because no check has been made on falling demand.

If we look at the *total costs*, we can see that they tend to be higher at very high and very low control frequencies. This is because at low frequencies the cost of error becomes large, and at high frequencies the cost of checking becomes large. Between these extremes, we can see that there is a range of frequency corresponding to lowest overall cost in operating a control system.

In theory, the total cost relationship of Figure 4.15 has a single minimum or *optimum* value. In practice, the presence of both soft costs and hard uncertainty means that it would be impossible to calculate with complete confidence the control frequency corresponding to minimum cost as an exact value. It *is* possible, however, to take the principles illustrated by Figure 4.15 as a guide to what kind of information on costs is needed if we are to attempt to estimate a good choice of control frequency.

The role of the information system in control frequency

Besides helping to show what we need to know about costs when trying to optimize control frequency, the analysis of Figure 4.15 tells us something about the role of the information system in this optimization. If we look back to Figure 4.7, we can see that the feedback loop from sensor through to actuator is one of the main roles of the information system as a component of a control system. If we consider the activities whose costs make up the *cost of checking*, they are all activities that the information system carries out on this loop.

Practical decisions about control frequency based on costs must therefore take account of a total cost that includes the cost of checking. Since all of this latter cost arises from the operation of the information system, understanding the role of the information system, and the kind of information it uses, is a significant element in designing control systems for management.

One important example of assessing the cost of this role is the issue of whether we use *real-time* versus *batch processing* when operating an information and communications technology-based system. To understand this issue, we should first check on the meaning of the term real-time processing, since it is often used incorrectly.

Real-time processing should refer to situations where any change in the state of a system being controlled is immediately reflected in the information stored about the state of that system. In the stockholding example, this would mean that any addition or withdrawal of stock would be immediately sensed, fedback etc. by the information system so that the record of the amount of stock held would always be up to date. Modern retailing systems do this by integrating EPOS (electronic point-of-sale) systems with their stockholding and logistics. When we take our goods to a checkout, the bar-code reader electronically registers the goods we have bought and this information is electronically communicated to the computer system, which updates the stock record almost immediately.

Real-time processing implies that the *control frequency* is very *high*, with very *short lag*. Every time there is a stock movement, for example, the information system will immediately process the information about additions or withdrawals. As we saw above, such a high control frequency is likely to be expensive in terms of the cost of checking in Figure 4.15. For a manual system, it implies that the people involved have always to be available to collect and process data. For an automated system using a computer, both the people and the equipment involved have to be continually on call and ready to respond. Since this often means that computers have to be continually connected on-line, the term *on-line* is sometimes wrongly used to mean the same as real time.

Batch processing is different. Batch processing systems record and then store information gathered by the sensor. This stored information accumulated over a period makes up a batch, which is used by the comparator at the end of the period to decide the information that is passed on to the actuator for modifying the inputs to the process being controlled. In the stockholding example, this would correspond to keeping records of stock issued and received from suppliers, and then updating a stock record such as that in Figure 3.2. This might be done at the end of every day or only once a week. The longer the period between updates of the stock record, the *lower* the *control frequency* and the *longer* the *lag*.

Batch processing can lower the cost of checking, since the information system does not have to incur the cost of comparison and actuation of the reaction to every unpredictable disturbance from the environment the moment it occurs. Instead, the accumulated record of disturbances can be processed at a time *chosen at the convenience of the information system*. Thus batch processing in a stock control system would be able to choose when updating the stock record was done, and so give the opportunity for using much more modest and economic clerical or computer facilities that did not requires the system to be continually ready and on-line for processing. We shall explore the control principles behind deciding sizes of batches of information, or how long we accumulate them, in the next section and in Appendix 1.

Batch processing and real-time information systems

If the cost of checking was the only cost to be considered when deciding the frequency of control, then it would be hard to see any role for real-time information systems. However, our study of Figure 4.15 tells us that the *cost of error* also has to be considered.

When we look at some kinds of real-life control systems, the cost of error associated with low control frequencies is not acceptable. Most forms of booking system are good examples of this. Imagine telephoning an airline to see if there were any seats left on a particular flight and being told, 'Well, there were a couple available the last time we checked so it might be OK'! It would be equally inconvenient for the airline to advise you not to book with them just in case the seats had been taken up. Airline booking systems therefore need to ensure that what is recorded accurately reflects the state of the system being controlled. As we saw above, this means that they need real-time processing.

Even systems that do not need every update of their state to be immediately recorded in real time still have limits on how out of date the record can be before the cost of error makes total control costs too high. It may not be necessary to update stock records every time there is a stock movement, but failure to update records over long periods could mean that wastage, theft and other costly happenings could be taking place without being detected. Generally, the longer such things go on unchecked the worse their effect, so there will always be some economical limit to the time between processing batches of update information.

The period between batch processing may also be governed by the fact that a particular process being controlled is just a component of a wider control system. Thus a stockholding system may check all the stock movements that have taken place in a day's trading, and update the stock records at the end of each day so that any replenishment orders can be placed on a daily basis. Here, the stock control system is a component of a wider logistics and supply system. The retail outlets of Carry-Out Cupboards are in this position. Another example might be a payroll system.

This would save all the time sheets for its employees for a week and then use them to calculate total hours worked, overtime, etc. for the wages payment at the end of each week. The wider context of personnel relations and employment law means that a weekly batching period for the payroll control system is imposed on it by its environment.

Whether the information system supporting a control system is real-time or batch processing, our study of the workings of the information system reveals an important principle about the way in which information systems capture, store and process information, which we will consider next.

The role of transaction and master files

The previous section has expanded our understanding of the role of the information system as a component of the control system. It has also enabled us to look more closely at the different ways in which an information system may work in such a role. In particular, we began to look in more detail at the way in which information systems *capture*, *store* and *process* information in real-time and batch processing systems.

Both ways of making an information system work as a component of a control system aim to do the same thing. Data captured by the sensor has to be fedback and processed by the comparator, to enable appropriate information to be passed to the actuator. For the comparator to do its work of instructing the actuator, it has to know about the *state of the system* being controlled. Thus the aim of stock control, for example, is to maintain stock levels within the range set by the system's goals. This is done by issuing the appropriate information about what stock may be released in response to demand and when replenishment stock should be ordered from suppliers.

The essential component of any such procedure, therefore, is having a record of the state of the system. The difference between real-time and batch processing lies in whether that record is continually up to date or updated on a periodic basis. This difference arises in turn from whether *capturing* data and *processing* the *record* of the state of the system take place together or not. Thus in stock control, is data captured about stock movement used immediately to update the stock record, or is the data recorded for use at the end of the day?

Both ways of processing therefore differ in the way they co-ordinate the treatment of:

- data captured by the sensor about *changes* to the state of the system being controlled;
- information on the *state* of the system used by the comparator for comparison with goals and instructions to the actuator.

In real-time processing, the data captured is used immediately to update information about the state of the system. In batch processing, however, the captured data is stored and then used at a later time to update information on the state of the system. This separation means that batch processing systems record data and information on two types of file:

- transaction files
- master files.

Transaction files record data captured by the sensor about *changes* to the state of the system over the batch processing period. *Master* files record information about the state of the system at any one point in time. Thus a record of the amounts of stock issued in response to orders during the day and quantities delivered from suppliers would be a transaction file. A record showing how much was in stock, on order etc., as in Figure 3.2, would be recorded in a master file. (Note that what is shown in Figure 3.2 is therefore incomplete, since it does not include an indication of when this record was last updated.)

How batch processing uses these two types of file is shown in Figure 4.16. It is worth clarifying two important points that have practical implications for our treatment of *records, files* and *databases* in Chapter 5.

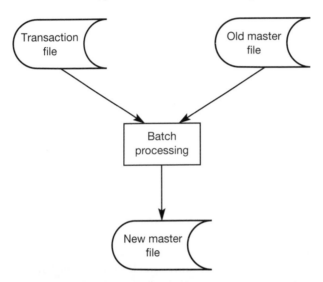

Figure 4.16 The standard model of batch processing
Some version of this diagram is found in most books on computer-based information systems. The old standard symbols for a file are an example of the carryover of old. The shape of the symbol is chosen to represent pictorially a stack of disks. We no longer automatically link an information system concept with its physical manifestation in this way, as we shall explore further in Chapter 6.

First, you will find that many books on data processing attempt to make the distinction between transaction and master files essentially *relative*. Thus transaction files may be described as containing 'temporary' or 'short-term' information, while master files contain information that is 'permanent' or 'long term'. Such descriptions are confusing and disguise a distinction *in principle* between the two types of file and their roles. Transactions take place over a period of time and are *dynamic*: they reflect changes. A master file reflects the state or condition of the system at a point in time. The *behaviour* of the system is represented or *modelled* by the information system processing the two kinds of file, as in Figure 4.16.

Secondly, it is important to realize that, as so often in this book, we need to distinguish between the conceptual, logical *whats* and the concrete *hows* of the system. Although transaction and master file information can be logically distinguished, a particular physical record may contain both kinds of information. Thus a monthly statement of an account for Carry-Out Cupboards from a supplier, such as Figure 4.17, might include a list of deliveries during the month in question as well as a statement of any payment and the amount owing at the end of the month. The details of deliveries and payment represent transaction data, while the final statement of the amount owing is master file information. The first shows changes over a period of time, the second shows the state of the system at a particular point in time.

SAXUN OFFICE SUPPLIES

21 Saxun Way
Viking Trading Estate
North Coates
Barsetshire
BA99 9ZW

Telephone: (0176) 992992

Fax: (0176) 993993

VAT Reg. 478 8748 44

Carry-Out Cupboards
Cowford Business Park
Kirton
South Riding
SR77 7DQ

Account No. C2256
Page 1 of 1

28.05.01

STATEMENT

Date	Type	Reference	Status	Debit	Credit	Balance
05.02.01	Invoice	1820	Paid	15.43		
11.02.01	Invoice	1832		68.24		
22.03.01	Invoice	1864		94.16		
28.03.01	Cr. Note	1866			10.00	
06.04.01	Invoice	1872		23.23		
27.05.01	Invoice	1892		48.29		
27.05.01	Receipt	Cheque	Alloc.		16.24	

THREE MONTHS & OVER	TWO MONTHS	ONE MONTH	CURRENT MONTH	TOTAL DUE	223.13
67.43	84.25	23.16	48.29		

Payment due 28 days from date of invoice.
Payments received after the end of month are not shown on this statement.

Figure 4.17 A typical customer account statement
Note that much of what appears on this document, and how it appears, is not determined by the information system's designer but by the business and legal environment. The implications of this for systems designers are considered further in Chapter 8, when we distinguish derivative and innovative methods for information systems development.

Any attempt to refer to transaction files and master files in terms of *how* information is actually recorded can confuse *what* the information is and what it is being used for. Such a view stems from the days when the term *file* referred to a particular reel of magnetic tape on which the information was recorded. Thus the data on a transaction file (i.e. one tape) was fed into the computer to process the master file (i.e. another tape). We know that modern systems do not work like this. As we shall see in Chapter 5, a file in a modern *database management system* is purely a *concept* used to explain the logic of data processing and does not necessarily exist as a separate physical thing, like a tape, that we can identify.

In case any of this section seems rather theoretical and new, consider some very conventional financial accounting concepts that have been used for centuries: the *balance sheet* and the *profit and loss account*. A balance sheet records the state of the company at a particular point in time (e.g. 'as at 31 December 2001'). The profit and loss account records the transactions for a company over a period (e.g. 'for October–December 2001'). Long before computers, therefore, the logical concept of a list of transactions being used to update a record of the state of the system was well established. Note also that this process has been developed to ensure financial *control*.

Box 4.5

Real-time accounts

Peter Martin

It is high time companies abandoned their annual reports and provided shareholders with more frequent information.

Why do today's high-technology companies report to their shareholders on a rhythm derived from the agricultural calendar?

Or, to put it another way, when will bosses who lecture their subordinates on the overwhelming need for speed and real-time data start to deal with their owners on the same basis?

In short, when will the annual report meet its well-deserved end?

These questions were sparked by a recent UK government report on reforming company law.[1] They are relevant to any company anywhere.

The report devotes only one paragraph to the issue. It highlights three trends – the pressure for more frequent reporting, the existence of powerful software to manage company finances and the availability of the Internet – and asks whether these together 'raise questions as to

the appropriateness of aspects of company law for the information age'.

Let no one ever say the English are losing their talent for understatement. In fact, these three trends completely undermine much of current practice in accounting, auditing, corporate governance and investor relations.

At least the report recognized the issue. Other standard-setters, wrestling with arcane aspects of corporate process and accounting conventions, risk missing the big picture. Finance directors, accountants, regulators and stock exchanges must seize the opportunities created by the intersecting trends identified in the report.

Consider what is happening. Big companies are creating, at accelerating speed, integrated computer systems such as SAP. These greatly simplify the task of preparing accounts. By forcing companies' global operations into a single reporting framework, they eliminate

much of the laborious reconciliation and consolidation that delay corporate results.

Much internal reporting in big companies is moving on to a faster timetable. Auditors are struggling with concepts such as continuous auditing, in which they certify and monitor the overall quality of the financial reporting system, carrying out random tests to ensure its integrity.

Constantly updated internal information, standardized internal systems and continuous auditing create the possibility of more frequent release of audited information to shareholders.

US companies routinely report every quarter; there is no reason why they could not promptly shift to a monthly cycle. British companies usually report every six months; they should move to quarterly reporting immediately, with monthly frequency a realistic target.

Continental European companies still often give really comprehensive figures only once a year – but since SAP is a German company it is hard to believe that they do not have much more frequently updated internal numbers that they could, if they chose, reveal to the world.

There is no point in releasing information much more speedily just to give the financial press something to write about. It makes sense only in the context of a transformed relationship with shareholders.

The package of information that shareholders receive should – as Alan Benjamin of the software company QSP suggested in his contribution to an earlier British study – include realistic performance indicators of a non-financial sort: market share, quality ratings, customer turnover and so on.[2] It might, as a US Financial Accounting Standards Board study is considering, include 'forward looking information' such as 'opportunities and risks and

management's plans including success factors'.[3]

And it should certainly make access to these data accessible to users. Glossy annual reports and glamorous websites do not achieve this. At least US companies are forced by the Securities and Exchange Commission's Edgar system to file standardized reports in an electronic form. But for the most part these are merely annual or quarterly reports that capture and manipulate.

An imaginative company would make its existing data available on its website in manipulable formats, such as spreadsheet files. Long-run data in a standardized format are also badly needed. Once these steps are taken, the way is clear for more frequent reporting.

Today's annual report is like a Victorian snapshot, an artificial

moment in time, laboriously processed. Just over a century ago, the Lumiere brothers broke free to bring us the motion picture. Business activity, the life that films capture, is a flow, not a series of discontinuous steps. It is time for corporate reporting to make that switch.

References

1 *Modern Company Law for a Competitive Economy*, Department of Trade and Industry, 1999. www.dti.gov.uk.
2 *The 21st Annual Report*, Institute of Chartered Accountants in England and Wales 1998. www.icaew.co.uk.
3 *Business Reporting Research Project*, Financial Accounting Standards Board. www.fasb.org.

Source: *Financial Times*, 2 March 1999. Reprinted with permission.

Comment

This is good example of how information and communications technology-based information systems can affect the issue of real-time versus batch processing. Before ICT, producing a set of accounts or some other assessment of a company's performance was a major manual clerical exercise. In terms of Figure 4.15, the cost of checking was high. In all but the most volatile or risky businesses, the potential cost of errors was not big enough to justify a full analysis of the company's position anytime someone fancied knowing. Given that the law required annual reporting

of accounts, it therefore made sense for most companies to produce a set of accounts once a year only.

Modern software and ICT have now changed this balance. If the company's information system is working in real time anyway, the extra cost of producing a computerized analysis is low. More frequent reporting or even reporting on demand are real possibilities. Add to this the integration of internal information systems with the Internet, and the annual 'Victorian snapshot' turns into a continuous movie.

Lags in the control system loop

When discussing the need for forecasting, we said that it was only necessary because control systems contain *lags*. In Section 4.1.2, we showed how the classical control system of Figure 4.4 contained a loop. This loop is formed by the interaction of the outputs from the transformation process with its inputs through the information path from sensor to actuator. The concept of a lag in such a loop is a recognition that it takes time for the transformation process to change inputs into outputs, and for the information system to process information through the sequence from sensor to actuator. Thus in a stock control system it takes time to accept deliveries, move stock on to shelves and into bins, take stock out of storage and deliver to the customer, record stock levels, compare then with the desired range of stock levels, and implement any reordering procedure.

We have just used a stock control example to illustrate the concept of lags in the control system loop, but what would be the lags in the control system that the WTO tries to operate?

The effect of any lag in the control system loop is to *delay* the effects of any control action. The outputs from the processes being controlled are always the result of trying to make the state of the system correspond to what was thought desirable at an earlier time by the comparator. This was decided on the basis of feedback resulting from what the sensor picked up even earlier. In everyday terms, we could describe the effect of lags on control systems as meaning that we are always trying to sort out yesterday's problems. In the analysis of the Carry-Out Cupboards reordering procedure in Appendix 1, we show that there can be lags in the system due to the time taken from deciding replacement stock was needed to receiving its delivery. These lags would mean that deliveries received by both the retail outlets and the central assembly and packing facility would be those that were relevant to some previous state of the stockholding process. In the time taken for the reordering and delivery loop to function, however, customer demand may have changed and different reorder quantities might be appropriate.

Generally, the effect of a lag in a control system loop is to introduce instability into the behaviour of the system. This takes the form of increasing the *fluctuations* of the outputs from the system in its attempt to achieve its goals. The greater the lag from sensing the output from a process to modifying the input, the greater the time for the environment of the system to change, and the greater those changes may be. This in turn increases the potential deviation of the system from its goals and the need for greater changes to the inputs by the actuator.

A particular example of the potential effects of lags in the control system loop can be seen in the Carry-Out Cupboards example in Figure A1.3, but we can see many examples of this principle in various parts of our lives. Most processes that we seek to control, not just in business, take time. Inputs are not immediately transformed into outputs. It takes time to make products; educate and train people; build schools, hospitals, roads, power stations and factories; grow food and trees. In most transformation processes, there is a lag between input and output.

There is also a further contribution to the lag from the information system that closes the loop between sensor and actuator. It takes time to assess the market for products and to develop and design them. Our buildings have to be authorized, sited, planned and financed. In my lifetime, it has taken decades for the political system to respond to the disappearance of natural woodland and plan for new broad-leaved forests in my country. Meanwhile, the conifer forests that are now sneered at by some conservationists are the output from a control loop that began in the First World War, when it was realized that Britain imported over 90 per cent of its timber.

Thus a control system loop in real life has built-in lags that are often measured in years, but when we look at these lags we find that they are made up of two components:

1 The time required for the transformation process.
2 The time required to operate the data capture and information processing from sensor to actuator.

Component 1 is often something fixed by technical or natural restrictions: there tend to be limits on the rate at which buildings can be built, people can be educated or trees grown. Indeed, it is impossible to make some transformation processes take less time: you can't change a child into an adult overnight.

Component 2, however, represents the contribution of the information system to the control loop. It is potential improvements in this component that interest us as students of information systems. We have already seen how forecasting and buffering can help with anticipating or accommodating the effects of lags. In the next section, we shall consider how certain principles can be incorporated into the design of information systems that can reduce the effects of lags in the control system loop by *reducing* of the time taken for the information system to cover the loop from sensor to actuator. In particular, we shall see how *sequence* of a system's *process* and the *hierarchy* of its *structure* can affect the time taken for an information system to work.

The effects of sequence and hierarchy on lags

Our investigation of the effects of control frequency and lags in a control system did not always make a clear distinction between controlling the *behaviour* of a whole system, and controlling an output from a particular process carried out by a *component* of a system. This was because the principles that we established about the effects of control frequency and lags can be applied both to the individual outputs of component processes, and to the *emergent property* of *behaviour* that comes from connected multiple inputs and outputs of the individual subsystems components of a system. Thus the behaviour of the profitability of Carry-Out Cupboards will be an *property* that *emerges* from the interaction of sales, stockholding, logistics, financial control etc. On a larger scale, 'free trade' will be a behaviour of the global commercial system coming from the interaction of national economies and WTO rules about trade.

The concept of systems structure involves two ways of connecting systems components: *horizontally* and *vertically*. These refer to the *systems hierarchy*.

A horizontal connexion, in terms of systems behaviour, would be between two processes at the same level of the systems hierarchy. A vertical connexion would be between two transformation processes at the same levels of the hierarchy in terms of the General Control Model.

Figure 4.18 shows how there might be a horizontal connexion between processes in a situation like that of Carry-Out Cupboards, where a retail outlet, a warehouse or a factory acts as both customer and supplier according to whether we consider its inputs or its outputs. Figure 4.18 is a more generalized version of Figure A1.4.

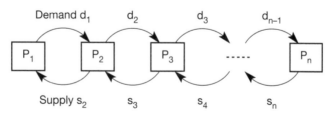

Figure 4.18 Interacting processes in sequence
In real life every cycle of supply and demand will involve a lag.

Our study of control systems hierarchy led to a generalized model of levels in a control hierarchy, as in Figure 4.11. In this model, overall control exerted by management can be seen as being made up of a series of individual instances of the classical control model, each with its process and control loop linked vertically. This looks rather like Figure 4.18 rotated through 90 degrees.

The effects of both types of connexion on behaviour can be understood together if we note that the essential point is that the processes are linked in *sequence*. Thus the output from one process becomes the input to the next and so on, either between processes at the same level of the hierachy or between processes at adjacent levels. Each has a *loop*, whether it is the closed loop of classical control or the demand/supply loop between adjacent horizontal processes. Each loop has the potential for a lag, and the behaviour of the whole system will be an emergent property resulting from the interaction of the individual levels of the control system or adjacent processes acting as components of this whole. Thus the effect of a lag in any individual process or level of control will *interact* with the effects of lags in other levels or processes, to have an *overall* effect on the behaviour of the *whole* system.

The example of stockholding for Carry-Out Cupboards in Figure A1.4. shows how lags in interacting processes in sequence can lead to instability, as shown in Figure A1.3. A simple step disturbance in the input at one end of the sequence leads to increasingly complex disturbances as it is fed through each process with its *lag*. What we have in Figure 4.18 is a generalization of this kind of interaction, where a series of processes in a system *interact* with one another. What can be demonstrated mathematically, but we already have a hint of in Figure A1.6, is that every addition to the sequence of processes results in a further directional movement in the effects of the disturbance. Thus Figure 4.19 is a generalization of Figure A1.6 in the same way that Figure 4.18 is a generalization of Figure A1.4.

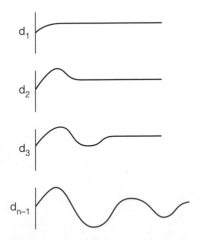

Figure 4.19 The responses of a sequence of processes to an initial disturbance
As we move from process p_n to process p_{n+1}, the change from disturbance d_n to disturbance d_{n+1} involves an extra movement in direction of the disturbance.

The essential lesson from the principles behind Figures 4.18 and 4.19 is that every addition of a process to the interacting chain increases the potential instability of the system both in terms of its severity, shown by the 'size' of the fluctuations, and its complexity, shown by their 'pattern' of peaks and troughs.

The significance of this general analysis of systems behaviour for the development and implementation of an *information system* comes from looking at how information flows through the sequence of processes. What we see is that the information output from one process becomes the information input for the next. Hence the *further* two processes are *separated* along a sequence, or up and down a control hierarchy, the *greater* the *destabilizing* effect of this method of transmitting information. The answer to this problem is to reduce the overall sum of the lags by giving decision making and communication access to information through a *common database*. When information systems are designed so that all the processes in a *chain* or all levels of a control hierarchy have direct access to information, cutting out all intermediate transmissions reduces the cumulative lag effects of Figure 4.19. The example of *supply chain management*, which we cover in Appendix 1, is a practical example of this.

Trade-off and optimization

Figures 4.14 and 4.15 look very similar because they are just two examples of a standard control principle, shown in Figure 4.20. When we study control systems, we find that this principle occurs in many forms. It shows that often when trying to design a control systems, we find that a variable whose value we can set as part of our controlling actions has a dual effect. Its effect on one set of costs is to increase them as the variable increases, while its effect on another is to decrease them as the variable increases. The total effect on costs of the choice of value for the variable implies that there is a *trade-off* between these opposing costs, which can give us a lowest cost or *optimum*.

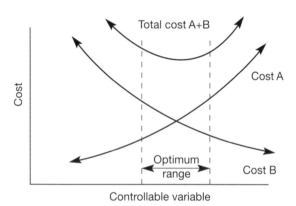

Figure 4.20 The 'rubber stamp of operational research'
Figures 4.14 and 4.15 are just two examples of the concept of optimizing control systems. In these and further examples in this book, the basic format consists of one variable that increases cost and another variable that decreases it. In all cases, the total cost has a concave upward shape that implies a minimum.

Since knowing the particular form of these relationships in any control situation depends on information, the information system has a role in optimizing the behaviour or performance of the control system as well as the transmission and storage roles we have considered so far.

Not surprisingly, versions of Figure 4.20 will crop up elsewhere in this book. Its universality has led to its being called a 'rubber stamp', in the sense that it can almost automatically be applied to a range of control situations.

Box 4.6

A letter from the Duke of Wellington to the British Government in Whitehall, London, August 1812

Gentlemen,

Whilst marching from Portugal to a position which commands the approach to Madrid and the French forces, my officers have been diligently complying with your requests, which have been sent by H.M. Ship from London to Lisbon and thence by dispatch rider to our headquarters.

We have enumerated our saddles, bridles, tents, tent poles, and all manner of sundry items for which His Majesty's Government holds me accountable. I have dispatched reports on the character, wit, and spleen of every officer. Each item and every farthing has been accounted for, with two regrettable exceptions, for which I beg your indulgence.

Unfortunately the sum of one shilling and ninepence remains unaccounted for in one battalion's petty cash and there has been a hideous confusion as to the number of jars of raspberry jam issued to one cavalry regiment during a sandstorm in Western Spain. This reprehensible carelessness may be related to the pressure of circumstances, since we are at war with France, a fact which may come as a bit of a surprise to you gentlemen in Whitehall.

This brings me to my present purpose, which is to request elucidation of my instructions from His Majesty's Government, so that I may better understand why I am dragging an army over these barren plains. I construe that perforce it must be one of two alternative duties, as given below. I shall pursue either one with my best ability, but I cannot do both:

1 To train an army of uniformed British clerks in Spain for the benefit of the accountants and copy-boys in London, or, perchance
2 To see to it that the forces of Napoleon are driven out of Spain.

Your most obedient servant,
Wellington

Comment

Ancient history? Not if we consider some of the changes that have taken place in the management of British public services in recent times. The demands for accountability have increased the burden of formal reporting procedures. Similar examples can be found wherever top-level management is trying to control costs by demanding more information. But gathering information about costs itself involves costs. In Wellington's time these costs came from ships sailing to Lisbon from London and riders crossing mountains. Today, nurses may spend time filling in forms rather than attending patients, teachers may be collecting data rather than teaching pupils, while police write about arrests rather than making them. We cannot manage without information, but the costs of control must be balanced against their benefits.

Incidentally, the Duke was a good holist. He recognized that information, useful or otherwise, is as much to do with the hard counting of tent poles as the soft assessment of officers' spleen.

4.3 LIMITS TO MANAGEMENT CONTROL

4.3.1 Control and cybernetics

Our analysis of the concepts behind the General Control Model has shown the details of the relationship between management, control and information. It has also distinguished the different kinds of information and their role in the control system's hierarchy. In Chapter 5 we shall look more closely at some of the properties of information itself, and in Chapter 7 we shall look further to see how organizations and businesses can be regarded as systems, using the concepts of the General Control Model.

If our view of information systems in organizations and business is to be based on the principles of this model, it is finally worth noting the kind of model that it is in terms of management and systems thinking. I think that reference to a range of very different works on the subject of management and systems – such as Beer (1985), Espejo and Harnden (1989), Flood and Jackson (1991) or Schoderbeck *et al.* (1990) – would describe our model as essentially *cybernetic*.

The word cybernetic comes from the Greek for a governor or steersman. It therefore seems very appropriate for our view of management as one based on *meliorist belief* and functioning through *control*. The Greek vision of the steersman who believes it to be worthwhile (i.e. *meliorist*) trying to steer the ship (i.e. *control*) towards a desired harbour (i.e. *goal*) in the face of disturbing winds and currents (i.e. *environment*) chimes in quite well with our view of management. What we do not accept from this analogy, however, is the assumption that the ship must be propelled by slave oarsmen under the steersman's whip. As frequently repeated above, we take control to be a concept, not a particular management style. Control does not automatically equate with coercion.

4.3.2 Requisite variety and Ashby's Law

Much of our explanation of the control concept has concentrated on examples of controlling a particular process, such as stockholding. We have considered how some simple action, like reordering stock, can be used to control such a process. I chose simple examples because our main aim was to understand the various components that make up the concept of control. However, we did also see that control concepts can help us understand a much more complex situation, like that faced by the WTO.

In practice, management is involved in controlling much more than a single process and has to deal with a much greater *variety* of systems behaviour than a particular form of stock movement. Thus besides stock being supplied, stored and subsequently sold, a stock control manager can expect to deal with theft, damage, returns from customers, returns to manufacturers, obsolescence, changes in demand and price, changes in legislation regarding storage conditions, and many other aggravations that make the job much more *complex*. If all the manager can do in response to this is to decide whether or not to reorder, their control over the stockholding system is likely to be very limited. Generally, there will be limitations on control whenever the process under control has a wider *variety* of ways in which it can behave than the variety of ways the controller has of controlling it.

Ashby (1963) recognized the importance of the relationship between the variety of actions available to the controller and the variety exhibited by the system they are trying to control. *Ashby's Law of Requisite Variety* states:

> *Only variety can destroy variety.*

Thus if a stockholding process can produce a *variety of behaviours* arising from theft, damage etc., as above, then management will *require* a corresponding potential *variety of control actions* to control these behaviours. If managers want to 'destroy' the potential variety that comes from theft, damage etc., they have to have a sufficient or *requisite* variety of security, inspection and other methods to deal with them.

This law has *major practical implications* for what management can, *and cannot*, hope to control. While Ashby's Law implies that complete control is only possible where the controller can match the variety of the system they hope to control, in the complex, holistic world in which business management operates, such matching of variety is very rarely possible.

Many of the situations described in the WTO lead-in case illustrate this point. The amount of variety than can be thrown up by the complex global system of public opinion, markets or economic circumstances is far greater than the relatively limited range of bureaucratic procedures available to the organization of the WTO to deal with them. This applies at any level, not just the global one. At Seattle, the authorities learned that a crowd of demonstrators can throw up more variety than one police officer.

Box 4.7

Big guys and little guys: America Inc. votes for Ashby

America, Inc., 'The Corporation for All Americans', believes that large transnational corporations have more flexibility, and can out manoeuvre, less robust nation states. This is because no nation state has as much requisite variety as a large transnational corporation that transcends national boundaries and legislative authority.

Hence Ashby's Law of Requisite Variety implies that the control of transnational corporations will only be possible with a transnational government or a transnational corporation of equal or greater requisite variety. America Inc. conceives of a new 'General Interest' corporation; with millions of small investors, buying dividend-based rather than appreciating stock, and capable of redistributing power and wealth quickly and peacefully. Newly empowered citizen-owners, as stakeholder-stockholders, would then be very potent in positively influencing the behaviour of the existing, more narrowly focused, 'special interest' transnational corporations that currently dominate the globe.

As America Inc.'s 'short version' of Ashby's Law states, 'A lot of little guys can band together and win over a few big guys.'

Source: Adapted from www.phoenixlive.com/phoenixguild/america.html.

Comment

This sounds like an interesting idea, and it wouldn't be the first to attempt to apply Ashby's Law and other cybernetic principles to society and politics. The question is whether when the small guys get themselves organized, they just end up with about the same variety as the organizations they seek to control. Thus, in the past, dinosaur capitalist corporations have spawned dinosaur trade unions.

The book to read on designing freedom is Beer, S. (1974) *Designing Freedom*, Wiley. New York.

Ashby's Law therefore shows us that attempts to control any but the simplest, lowest-variety systems will have limitations *in principle*. It isn't just a lack of more hard work, greater thought or improved motivation that limits our ability to control: it is a fact of life. Just as many demonstrators can throw up more variety than one officer, so many employees can act with more variety than one manager, or many customers represent more variety than one product can satisfy.

So has our study of the concept of control been the study of a myth? Experience shows that it has not. Our lives, not just in management and business, are filled with examples of successful control. Police officers cannot always control crowds, traffic or criminals, but our streets are not in a state of continual anarchy. Stock controllers cannot absolutely guarantee that goods will not be damaged or stolen, but trillions of dollars' worth of successful trading takes place every day. The point about Ashby's Law is not that it says that control is impossible, but that it is *limited*. This limit will be set by the degree to which the *variety of the controller* can match the *variety of the process under control*.

If we seek to increase our ability to control, we therefore need to raise the limit set by the difference in variety between the controller and what is controlled. We can do this in two ways:

1 By increasing, or *amplifying*, the variety of the controller.
2 By decreasing or *attenuating*, the variety of what is controlled.

Either or both of these actions will increase the variety that the controller can destroy or absorb.

Amplifying the variety of the controller can be illustrated by looking at the police versus demonstrators fixture in Seattle. Seen as collections of similar human beings, thousands of demonstrators represent more variety than hundreds of police officers.

Hence Ashby's Law tells us that the police can't absorb the variety of the demonstrators. However, this only remains true if we assume that one human being, called a demonstrator, represents about the same amount of variety as another human being, called a police officer. If we equip the police with radios and helicopters, then one officer has a much greater variety of potential control actions than an unequipped, unco-ordinated demonstrator. In such a situation, the police have increased or *amplified* their variety, particularly in terms of their communications ability, to absorb that of the demonstrators.

What was really significant about the demonstrations from an *information systems* standpoint was the way the demonstrators amplified their variety by exploiting the Internet. Far from being low-variety subjects with their choices limited to whether or not they shouted and carried a banner, the demonstrators used information and communications technology to overcome the limits set by their geographical dispersion, lack of communication and limited information about what the WTO and the Seattle police were doing. Many of the demonstrators may have thought of themselves as anarchists and anti-organizational, but in Seattle they were some of the best managers on the block.

The principle of *attenuating the variety of what is controlled* is illustrated by the very names of both the examples we have used in this chapter: the World *Trade* Organization and Carry-Out *Cupboards*. Thus the WTO knows that it cannot hope to control the actions of every member of the human race all of the time. If it seeks the goal of 'a more prosperous, peaceful and accountable economic world', it has to do so by focusing on a limited or *attenuated* selection of variables for it to control. So it cannot hope to monitor every imported banana or exported car, but it can set overall tariffs and quotas and monitor these. Carry-Out Cupboards cannot manufacture every possible product and individually satisfy every possible customer, but it can concentrate on the production of a limited range of related products, and try to control the sales of these to a *segment* of the *market*.

This last point is a classic illustration of attenuating variety. Rather than attempt to absorb separately the variety of individual human customers, we reduce the variety of what we hope to control by using a simpler concept called a 'market', whose variety is confined to some variable such as 'monthly demand' that we have a chance of absorbing.

As with amplifying variety, so it is with attenuating variety: *information* plays a central role. Whether it is demonstrators dealing with police or manufacturers dealing with a market, the ability to capture, store and process information is essential to successful management. We already established this essential role for information when considering the concept of control. The concept of requisite variety adds to our understanding of this role by revealing the:

- *potential* and *limits* for the usefulness of information; and that
- *level of detail* of information that is useful.

What all of our lead-in cases so far and many of our examples have shown is the potential that modern information and communications technology has to raise the profile of these issues. In our next chapter, therefore, we will explore in detail the concepts that enable us to manage the capture, storage and processing of information in a way that exploits such technology.

Key words

Actuator	Goal seeking	Output
Buffer	Goal setting	Process
Comparator	Hard uncertainty	Rational
Control	Input	Risk
Decision theory	Lag	Sensor
Deterministic	Master file	Strategic
Disutility	Meliorism	Subjective
Effector	Normative	Transaction file
Empirical	Operational	Transformation process
Feedback	Operations research	Uncertainty
Goal	Optimization	Utility

Seminar agendas, exam topics and project/dissertation subjects

1 The General Control Model of Figure 4.10 is my creation, albeit from various sources. A critical analysis of its features in relation to an organization you know could be a useful exercise. How would you modify it?

2 Investigate the stock reduction/elimination system known as 'just in time' or JIT. Does it contradict the concept of buffering set out in Section 4.2?

3 Study the workings of an example of commercial stock control software. Does it really *control* stock in terms of both goal seeking and goal setting, or does it merely use input information to update stock records?

4 How does an organization that you are familiar with actually make forecasts? What are the relative roles of 'guesswork' or 'feel', and the use of formal mathematical methods in forecasting? Why does it work the way it does? Is it working in the best way?

5 Take the 'rubber stamp' of Figure 4.20 and see if you can find examples of it in quality control, financial control or controlling the government of a country by the choice of timing for elections.

Feedback on review questions

RQ 4.1 Terms like 'policy', 'agreements' or 'rights' represent things that the WTO would like to achieve and maintain. They can therefore be seen as goals. However, they are concepts rather than something concrete or physical, and hence *abstract*.

RQ 4.2 There are possible conflicts between the needs of agriculture, conservation, residential housing and industrial development, hence we have potential *goal conflicts*. Also, there is no generally accepted set of values that tells us how many rare plants are worth how many tonnes of food, or whether a house is more important than a tree. There are therefore potential conflicts based on *world view*, *purpose* or *set of values, i.e. normative*.

RQ 4.3 Even where there is agreement about norms, such as deciding to protect a rare plant species, there can still be choices about the methods available. Thus, would we be willing to use mechanical methods of controlling the invasion of more common species in order to protect the rare species? Or are mechanical methods themselves anti-environmental? Would it be more environmentally friendly to use manual methods, like hand weeding and cutting with scythes?

RQ 4.4 In our previous RQ we considered the example of protecting a rare plant species. Suppose we decided to use mechanical methods: should we operate on a regular seasonal basis? Once a month? Only after birds have nested? When?

RQ 4.5 Examples of *soft issues* would probably start with us asking whether increased success for the WTO was a good thing anyway. Even for those who thought that it was, there is no unquestioned agreement that *volumes* are a better measure than *monetary value*, and in any case how are the volumes measured? Tonnes, number of items or what? Thus is 10 million tonnes of wheat more significant than 10 million tonnes of soya beans? *Hard uncertainty* then arises from how accurate our data is. Could 10 million tonnes actually be 9.9?

RQ 4.6 Perhaps the main abstract transformation process that is if concern to both the WTO and its antagonists is changing people's opinions. Related to this are the legal and political changes that each party would like to see.

RQ 4.7 The goals of the WTO are a good mix of hard and soft. Soft goals like 'policy', 'agreements' or 'rights' have to be *implemented* or *manifested* as hard goals like tonnes of wheat or numbers of motor cars. What is significant is the *hierarchy* of these goals. *High-level, soft* goals like policy have to be translated into low-level, hard goals like tonnes. As we see in the General Control Model, this hierarchical goal structure is common to all control systems.

RQ 4.8 The key point here is whether, or what, control there is over the groups by the WTO. If there is little or no influence or control, then the groups are part of its environment. However, it is not unknown for big organizations to recruit protesters or to incorporate them into the organization's activities to make them effectively part of the system.

RQ 4.9 They can be both. The protest groups and the WTO can use them to plan and control their operations, thus the same report can have more than one role.

RQ 4.10 If the information is *stored* it can be reviewed and used as a basis for *learning*. It is then useful feedback that helps the WTO to *set future goals*, which it uses to control its activities.

RQ 4.11 Violence breeds more violence. The more people who know about the WTO, the more people there are to inform others, so the more people will know about the WTO.

RQ 4.12 The short answer is that we can't. Perhaps a better phrase would be the maximum likely demand. 'Likely' could then be defined as something that would not be exceeded more than one week in, say, ten. A stochastic analysis of past data could then be used to determine this demand level. There is a vital role here for *forecasting*.

RQ 4.13 No good holist would expect forecasting to be purely a hard, quantitative procedure. Anticipating future trends in sales of goods that depend on social fashion, ethical perceptions and other soft questions of world view, purpose or set of values requires an input from the higher levels of the General Control Model, not just monitoring past sales statistics.

RQ 4.14 When it seems that it is a long time since I did it? When there's been a major transaction? On a regular basis? As with our stock control examples, I suspect we try to balance the cost of checking against the cost of what might happen if we don't. Note that our bank balance is an *inventory* or *stock* of money.

RQ 4.15 When I said 'the control system that the WTO tries to operate', I was implying a false assumption that the WTO is concerned with just one control system. There are in fact at least two obvious examples of control system. First, there is the control of trade and the attempt to make it conform to the WTO's goals; this is mainly goal-seeking control. Then there are the various political systems that are concerned with setting goals. The goal-seeking control will have quite a long lag, since data like trade figures takes time to accumulate, let alone act on. Lags here could easily be in years rather than months. The political goal setting takes even longer. The so-called 'round' of trade talks at Seattle was just one round out of several that have spread over decades.

References/bibliography

Ackoff, R.L. (1962). *Scientific Method: Optimizing Applied Research Decisions*. Wiley, New York.

Ackoff, R.L. (1971). 'Towards a System of Systems Concepts'. *Management Science*. 17 (11).

Ackoff, R.L. and Sasieni, M.W. (1968). *Fundamentals of Operations Research*. Wiley, New York.

Ashby W.R. (1963). *An Introduction to Cybernetics*. Wiley, New York.

Beer, S. (1974). *Designing Freedom*. Wiley, London.

Beer, S. (1985). *Diagnosing the System*. Wiley, Chichester.

Ben-Eli, M.U. (1988). 'Cybernetic Tools for Management: Their Usefulness and Limitations', in Sadovsky, V. and Umpleby, S. (eds). *Science of Goal Formulation*. Hemisphere Publishing, New York.

Espejo, I. and Harnden, R. (1989). *The Viable Systems Model*. Wiley, Chichester.

Fishburn, R. (1967). *Decision and Value Theory*. Wiley, New York.

Flood, R.L. and Jackson, M.C. (1991). *Creative Problem Solving*. Wiley, Chichester.

Hannagan, T. (1998) *Management: Concepts and Practices*, 2nd edn. Financial Times Pitman Publishing, London.

Harry, M.J.S. (1990). *Information and Management Systems*. Pitman Publishing, London.

Laudon, K.C. and Laudon, J.P. (2000). *Management Information Systems*. Prentice-Hall, Upper Saddle River, NJ.

Lewis, C.S. (1953). *The Silver Chair*. Geoffrey Bles, London

Luce, R.D. and Raiffa, H. (1957). *Games and Decisions*. Wiley, New York.

Schoderbeck, P.P., Schoderbeck, C.G. and Kefalas, A.G. (1990). *Management Systems*. Business Publications, Homewood, IL.

Volkogonov, D. (1998). *The Rise and Fall of the Soviet Empire*. HarperCollins, London.

CHAPTER 5

Building information and communication

The climate is changing – as usual

What happened

Given that Greenland is mainly covered with a huge white ice cap, why is it called 'green'? One theory I heard was that the name was a con trick. The first Vikings to find it, just over 1000 years ago, thought that by describing the place as 'green' it would encourage other people to go and settle there. Another theory is that the land was indeed green at that time. The world has been both warmer and colder than it is now, and there was a warm period about the time that Leif Ericson got as far as Canada via the Viking settlements in Greenland. However, the increasingly cold winters in the thirteenth and fourteenth centuries, and the long supply lines from Europe, meant that the settlements were eventually wiped out. The cooling trend that hit the Vikings was itself reversed by the mid-eighteenth century, and this was well before industrialization or the exploitation of fossil fuels. So is climate change a cyclical process that's always been around? Could temperatures start falling again in the next hundred years? What does research tell us?

By 1996, five years of research, carried out by some 2000 scientists working for the Inter-Governmental Panel on Climatological Change (IPCC), had come to the following essential conclusions:

- The world's climate is changing due to global warming.
- Greenhouse gases resulting from human activity are a significant contributing factor to the change.

These conclusions merely confirmed the IPCC's previous 1990 predictions and reinforced existing strong beliefs. Thus in 1994, the Stitching Greenpeace Council of Amsterdam published *The Climate Time Bomb*, an extensive catalogue of news reports covering upsets and disasters in agriculture, insurance, international finance, ecology, human health, energy resources and many other areas, all resulting from the effects of climate change. In similar disaster mood, Sir John Houghton of the UK Royal Commission on Environmental Pollution warned that flooding in Bangladesh and Southern China could lead to mass migration and wars over water supplies.

But what is 'warming'? A European Union study of currents in the North Atlantic has highlighted the potentially contrasting effects of the 'warming' scenario. The melting of the Arctic ice fields could act against the incoming flow of the warm Gulf Stream currents (responsible for the temperate climate of a large part of western Europe). Such cooling could offset the effects of global warming, as far as western Europe is concerned. We could have a colder western Europe in a warmer world. This and other European slants on climate change can be found on the European Union's official website, www.europa.eu. They appear under the ostentatious title 'European saves the world', which sounds like something serious and dramatic.

Meanwhile, across the Atlantic, www.globalwarming.org takes a more sceptical view. It criticizes then US president Bill Clinton for signing international, legally binding agreements at the December 1997 Kyoto Conference. It challenges the assumption that global warming is real and that it is caused by human activity. The site's authors ask whether the potential damage caused by global warming would be greater than the damage caused to the US economy by severely restricting energy use. They also contest whether the actions called for by the Kyoto Agreement will significantly reduce greenhouse gas emissions worldwide and prevent global warming. They look at answers to three questions:

- Is global warming occurring?
- Are humans causing the climate to change?
- If global warming occurs, will it be harmful?

Challenging whether there is global warming at all, they quote 'Accu-Weather, the world's leading commercial forecaster', as saying that global air temperatures have only increased by 0.45 degrees Celsius over the past century. This is based on data from land-based weather stations, which are subject to the 'heat island effect' around major cities. By contrast, satellite data indicates a slight cooling in the climate in the last 18 years. Computer models designed to predict warming are limited by our incomplete understanding of the effects of cloud formations, precipitation, the role of the oceans or sun cycles. Oddly, as computer climate models have become more sophisticated, their predictions have been less dramatic.

As to whether humans are causing the climate to change, www.globalwarming.org points out that 98 per cent of total global greenhouse gas emissions are natural (mostly water vapour) and only 2 per cent are from man-made sources. Given that 70 per cent of the warming in the last century occurred *before* 1940, it can hardly be blamed on the upsurge in greenhouse gas emissions from industrial processes that occurred after that date.

Even if global warming occurs, will it be harmful? Globalwarming.org thinks that the idea of massive melting of the ice caps and flooded coastal cities is 'mere science fiction'. Sea-level rises in the past are attributed to warmer and thus expanding oceans, not to melting ice caps. Health fears are 'fear mongering', and larger quantities of carbon dioxide in the atmosphere and warmer climates could be a good thing: they would lead to an increase in vegetation.

What do I think? The systems concept of *positive feedback* could be summarized by the statement 'the more rabbits you have, the more rabbits you have'. The point is that rabbits result in more rabbits, until something else from their environment, like disease, hard winters or predators, intervenes to disturb the rabbit system.

Is the number of people talking about global warming a rabbit population? It suspect that positive feedback could be at work, in the sense that the more people who tell each other about global warming, the more people will tell each other about global warming.

But what about the *statistics* for temperatures and sea levels? Are all the *experts* who are warning us about warming *wrong*? Am I abusing my role as an author to rubbish *accepted* views about climate change, because they might threaten the value of my property, which is *only* three metres above sea level? Before you think I've gone crazy with all those words in italics, I've deliberately laid them on to introduce some of the issues that come up when we try to build up our information on this or any other subject.

The issues raised

Value judgements and information
In the last paragraph of the lead-in case I put several words in italics. The reason I did so was to draw attention to the way in which *value judgements* can creep into language that pretends to be sensible, or even scientific. Let's now look at those words.

Statistics is a collection of mathematical techniques for determining the mathematical characteristics of collections of figures, or data. Sometimes, as in that last paragraph, people talk about 'statistics' when they mean the data itself rather than the techniques for processing it. Whichever meaning we take for the word, statistics alone doesn't show anything. It is our *interpretation* of the statistical analysis of the data that *infers* meaning. It is one thing to analyse data and discover that the average of two sets of temperature data are different; it is something else to interpret those averages to mean that we can expect continued increases in temperature in the future. The way we choose to interpret will depend on our *world view*, *purpose* or *set of values*. All statistical interpretation therefore contains a *soft* component, and how we deal with this is an issue affecting how information is built.

This brings us to the experts and whether they can be *wrong*. Although my knowledge of statistical techniques is well up to university standard, I am not an expert. There are plenty of advanced mathematical techniques that I don't understand and that I would probably get wrong if I used them. So when it comes to calculating various complex features of temperature data, the experts are likely to get it right and I am likely to get it wrong. But I don't know of any expert who is more capable than I am of deciding whether I personally want my house to be flooded. The issue of understanding how information is built also includes the issue of who builds what.

Once the issue of how the information is built has been clarified, there is a further issue of how it is *communicated* and *received*. I talked about 'accepted* views about climate change'. Accepted by who?' Information isn't just built to be forgotten about: it is communicated from one person to another. The way that it is communicated and received will affect the message that is transmitted. Thus my saying '*only* three metres above sea level', rather than '*a full three* metres', made the information communicated sound very different. Beside the building of information, there are issues associated with how it is communicated.

Opportunities for learning

The issues raised mean that we are looking ways in which we can deal with:

1 The *complexity* of information: *hard* complexity, in terms of handling large amounts of data; *soft* complexity, in terms of identifying the world view, purpose or set of values present as components of information.

2 The *communication* of information and how its meaning can be *determined* and *distorted*.

In this chapter we will therefore begin by seeing how information can be built up from hard and soft components. We shall then explore a model for communication between a single sender and a single recipient, before developing our ideas about communication to cover complex communication networks.

Learning objectives

The learning objectives in this chapter are to:

1 Establish the concepts and language used to describe stochastic and complex information.

2 Identify the form and roles of soft information components.

3 Specify a model of a communication system in the context of management and control systems.

4 Reveal the implications for the concept of information that come from identifying the role of the components of a communication system.

5 Epitomize the role of standards in enabling the management of complex communication networks.

5.1 BUILDING INFORMATION

5.1.1 Information-building concepts and their importance for understanding communication systems

Information as a constructed or built emergent property

In Chapter 3 we established the essential systems concept of *emergent property*. We saw that where components come together, the *whole* can have properties that none of the components possesses separately. One of the most important examples of emergent property in this book is *information* itself. Thus separate letters can mean nothing, but brought together they have meaning as a word. Similarly, words can be brought together to form sentences that have meanings not possessed by the separate words. But information isn't just verbal. Coloured dots, or pixels, mean little separately, but brought together they can form an informative image. Sounds can be brought together to form speech that carries a message.

Human beings have always communicated or received information using all their five senses: sight, touch, hearing, smell and taste. Recent important developments in

ICT have meant that technology itself has become more capable of dealing with this complex human mixture. Old views of business information, which saw it as essentially words and numbers shown on a screen or printed on paper, are now only part of the story. Information processed by ICT systems has become a rich, *multimedia-*based concept. We can make sense of this complex richness by using the systems concepts of Chapter 3.

RQ 5.1 Is rich, multimedia-based information necessarily superior, from a management viewpoint, to simpler text-based or number-based information?

We saw in Chapter 3 that an emergent property, like information, comes from connecting components together. We also saw, however, that the particular way in which they were connected could result in different emergent properties. The way that components are connected, or the *structure*, has just as much effect on what emergent property we get as does the nature of the components themselves.

If we want to understand how any particular information emerges as a property, we need to answer two questions:

1 What are the *components* of information?
2 How are these components connected as a *structure*?

When we try to answer questions like these, we are effectively analysing how information is *constructed* or *built*.

Reasons for understanding how information is built
Why should we bother with analysis and understanding of information-building concepts? I think that we have already hinted at some of the reasons. The information handled by modern ICT systems is becoming increasingly:

● rich
● abstract
● complex
● communicated.

By the term *rich* we mean varied and wide-ranging. In this *multimedia* age, information and communications technology is no longer confined to processing information that can be put into a computer through a keyboard, i.e. letters, numbers and a restricted range of symbols. Let's look at an everyday source of management information like an employee record. Twenty years ago, even if such a record was computerized at all, it would normally be restricted to text and numerical items like the person's name, address, qualifications and salary. By the late 1980s, progressive organizations may have included a picture of the employee on their record, but the chances were that it would only be printed out in monochrome. Today, a person's record could include a colour video of their recruitment interview or working skills, which could be accessed over the Internet by a manager anywhere in the world. Nor is the rich information available to management confined to records of things already in existence. *Virtual reality* enables someone like a training manager to test out proposed facilities and equipment even before they exist. Any view of management information that cannot identify and put a structure to this richness will not be able to exploit the potential of modern information and communications technology.

A further important property of information comes from its frequently *abstract* or *weightless* character. Information has always been an abstract concept that can be expressed in various ways. Thus it can be spoken or written, for example. What is important about the advent of information and communications technology is that information is much more frequently *processed* or *stored* in abstract form. As we saw in Chapter 3, this means that it is virtually *costless to reproduce* and can be almost *instantaneously transmitted*. In a networked context, it can be effectively *ubiquitous* in the sense that it doesn't seem to be fixed in one place at any one time.

Once again, in such an information world, old ideas constructed in terms of physical forms of information, located at particular places, fail to see why globalizing phenomena such as electronic commerce are taking place.

There has always been complex information. Indeed, it was the complexity of the information that the Second World War code breakers had to deal with that led to the development of the first computer. Modern business information can be much more complex, but the power of information and communications technology has also grown. For the early code-breaking pioneers, the challenge was to develop the technology to handle the complexity. Today, it is the technology itself that is the *source* of the potential complexity we have to handle. The need, therefore, is not a technological but a *conceptual* one. What ideas or models can help us make sense of what is sometimes described as 'information overload'? How can we see information as something clearer than a mass of multimedia material? We have established the fundamental concepts of *systems* and *control* to help answer this question. Now we need to see what can be learned further as we apply and develop them.

Finally, the *communication* provided by networked information technology means that answers to a management question like 'What information is available to me?' have changed significantly in less than a decade. As we discussed above, the information human beings have communicated has always been rich, when they have been near enough to see, touch, hear, smell and taste. The important changes we are experiencing in communications technology are enabling much of this richness to be incorporated into communication when two or more people are:

- *incontiguous*: not present in the same place;
- *asynchronous*: not present at the same time.

Older technologies, like radio or telephone, have enabled people who are not in the same place to communicate, just as sound recording has not required them to be present at the same time. What is new about more recent communications technology is the rich mix of sound, sight etc. that can be flexibly combined with choices as to time and place. Box 5.1 gives some examples.

Box 5.1

New pointy thingy and the human touch

Imagine you wanted to write something on paper. Suppose someone suggested that you got a willing friend to let you use their hand. You take their hand in your hand, and then use your hand to make their hand pick up a pen. By guiding their hand with your hand, you can make their hand write what you want.

Crazy? Why not just pick up the pen with your own hand and write? Well yes; but now consider what we do when we use a mouse. Instead of moving the pointer around the screen, we push a mouse that moves the pointer.

An example like this shows how easy it is for us to consider that what information and communications technology can achieve is supposedly 'new', when a moment's thought reveals that it in practice it does something old in a new way.

However, let's not dismiss the mouse. Selecting, dragging, pulling down menus and activating procedures with a left or right click is not quite the same as the clumsy process of moving a friend's hand around.

The important point about ICT-based communications is not that they enable something entirely new, but that they can strikingly alter the way that communications can work. Just as a simple computer mouse has altered the way we communicate with computers, so the Internet has altered the way we communicate with each other.

There are two particular criteria that can help us question how information and communications technology makes a difference between:

- e-mail and sending a letter;
- chat programs and talking to people in a pub;
- newsgroups and gossip;
- bulletin boards and sticking up a notice;
- voice mail and getting a friend to pass on a message;
- digital information services and giving someone the figures on paper;
- videoconferencing and a meeting;
- dataconferencing and sitting down at a desk to go over some figures.

The differences relate to *timing* and *location*. Just as I can receive an e-mail anywhere in the world *when* I like, not just at my home address, so with *all* the Internet facilities listed above. A further advantage is that in order for mail, voice, video, data etc. to be transmitted over the Internet, it has to be *encoded* in digital form. This means that if we want to carry out further storage or processing, our information is already in the right form. Thus, for example, data that is the subject of data conferencing can be further manipulated by spreadsheets or database software.

5.1.2 The anatomy of information

So far we have established that the information processed by modern ICT systems can be very rich in its nature, but that like all information it is an *emergent property* that results from the bringing together and interaction of components in a particular *structure* or relationship with one another. Figure 5.1(a) shows the general systems concept, while Figure 5.1(b) gives some examples for text, verbal and visual information.

The fundamental point of this *systems* view of information is that it is a concept. Like any other concept, it must be *someone's* concept, and it will reflect a *world view*, *purpose* or *set of values*. As we saw in Chapter 4, all information has its *soft* or *normative* properties. If we also see information as an emergent property resulting from components and structure, then we need to understand how different norms can result in different views of what the components and structure should be. In the following sections, we shall look at how different norms can affect our choice of the components and the structures used to build up information.

(a)

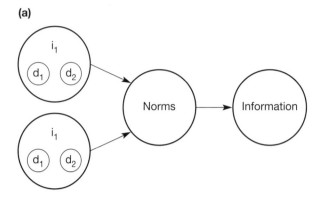

Key:

d_1, d_2, ... etc. = data elements
i_1, i_2, ... etc. = information components

(b)

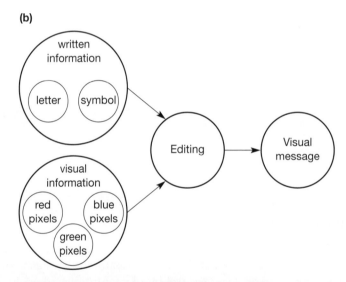

Figure 5.1 Constructing information from data
What data is selected and the way it is assembled into information involve assumptions about what is important. Hence all information contains a normative basis that depends on someone's *world view*, *purpose* or *set of values*. Figure 5.1(b) shows an example for visual information.

5.1.3 Normative properties of information

As far as the components of information are concerned, normative properties can especially enter their anatomy in two ways:

1 How components are *named*, *labelled* or *presented*.

2 How they are *selected*.

Labels and loaded meanings

Our first lead-in case was about an organization that called itself the *Child Support* Agency. It would take a brave person to say that they didn't like children or animals, so we might decide that any agency that claims to support children must be a good thing. As we saw in Chapter 2, however, the agency could have been labelled something like the 'Payment Enforcement Agency'. That doesn't sound so nice: on the whole, people don't like paying and they don't like being forced. In an example like this, we can see that the labelling of the word *components* that go to make up the *whole*, in the form of the agency title, has a strong effect on the *information* communicated. My dictionary tells me that a child is 'a young human being below the age of puberty', but I don't think that's entirely why the politicians chose the word in the title.

All information can be seen to be potentially *soft* once we realize that when we use words, we find that they often carry emotional, ethical and other meanings with them that go beyond a *hard*, logical definition. The choice of the labels for the components of information therefore loads the information with particular soft properties. I find that words like 'old', 'football' or 'vegetarian' carry associations with them that go beyond anything a dictionary could deal with. Matters become further complicated when we find that people don't agree on what these extra ingredients of the meaning can be. An example of this from my experience is the word 'sophisticated'. I was told that it comes from 'sophist', an ancient Greek word for people who are clever at arguing, but not necessarily honest. So if someone described me as 'sophisticated', I wouldn't be too pleased.

RQ 5.2   What do you see as some of the loaded words in the lead-in case to this chapter?

So far, we've just looked at the potential loading of information based on words or *labels*; but visual and other *multimedia* information can be loaded in the way that it is presented. Early television adverts for the Child Support Agency, for example, selected images and voice tones that suggested 'support' rather than 'money extraction'. An important *management* issue that comes from examples like this is that modern networked ICT systems have a much greater ability to load information. The Seattle protesters in the WTO lead-in case could have organized themselves with old-style 'snail mail' and telephone calls. The representatives of the WTO could have posted a notice on a noticeboard explaining their views. In practice, it was the rich mix of the Internet and modern media that enlivened the Seattle activities.

We shall look at some other examples of the potency of rich, multimedia-based information later in this section. Meanwhile, what are the different ways in which information can be loaded? Here are some important ones:

● Hyperbole
● Question begging
● Special pleading
● False objectivity
● False concatenation.

Hyperbole is the use of exaggerated ways of representing information. An example of this is the word 'trauma'. My maternal grandfather was a soldier during the First World War. He was buried alive in the ground for three days by an exploding shell. When he was found he could not speak. It took ten years, a loving wife and many doctor-prescribed daily pints of Guinness to restore him to something like the person he was before his traumatic experience. Meanwhile, nearly a century later, I find the word 'trauma' used by the media to mean just about any emotional upset.

The reason for this change in the meaning of words is that those who use them have a management purpose, based on their *world view*, *purpose* or *set of values*. I'm try-ing to manage you, the reader, by communicating my view of what I think trauma really is. Someone wishing to set up a counselling service for potential customers who have difficulty with the stresses of divorce or bereavement might have another view.

Whatever our view, what is important is that we recognize the potential loading that hyperbole can apply to information. This will apply even more strongly in an age where the richness of possible management information increases the potential for hyperbole. The Seattle riots looked like a major reverse for the aims of the WTO, but was that hyperbole created by the richness of the information the media could por-tray? The management of the WTO needs to look very carefully at the anatomy of its information before deciding how important the riots were.

Given that this is the best book you've ever read in your life about business infor-mation, let's be honest, only someone with learning difficulties could find fault with the way I've identified and explained my subject so far...

Don't worry if you found that last sentence rather alarming: you've just been submitted to *question begging*. This is where information is presented as the unchal-lenged answer to a question we haven't even had time to ask. In the previous paragraph, the phrase 'given that' *preempts* any questioning. It suggests that, something is a fact before any testing procedure has been carried out. You've also been subjected to *special pleading*. 'Let's be honest' is trying to plead, or persuade you, that any attempt to disagree with me means that you are dishonest.

Words commonly used to block out challenges to interpretation are 'only', 'merely', 'simply', 'just' or 'no more than'. In the lead-in case, global warming is 'mere science fiction' according to those who oppose the 'fear mongering' of the 1997 Kyoto Conference. The richness of multimedia can make special pleading and pre-emption even more effective. None of the mothers or children portrayed in TV promotions for the Child Support Agency was anything other than young and appealing in their appearance. How could one possibly feel anything but sympathy?

False objectivity occurs where something that is a matter of opinion is presented as a fact. It can come from *false definition*; where something, or somebody, is described as 'the' fact, phenomenon, expert, authority or whatever. When I research material on global warming, I find that people's opinions frequently quote someone who is 'the expert', 'the respected authority' or 'the acknowledged leader', in the hope that we will accept their opinion without further argument. Such false objectivity often comes when *descriptive* analysis of data is confused with *inferential* analysis. We shall say more about this later in the chapter.

Another form of false objectivity is the use of *deceptive abstraction*. By using the word 'it', rather than 'he', 'she' or 'they', we can hide the personal and therefore *soft* nature of people's opinions. 'It is accepted' or 'it is now agreed' are examples of this deception. Our question should be 'who accepted?' or 'who agreed?'

False objectivity is an especial danger in today's rich information media. Every pic-ture, sound recording, video etc. is *somebody's* camera angle, sound edit or zoom. But modern ICT brings a major opportunity to counteract this. *Interactive* multi-media can give some of the selecting and editing power to the user.

False concatenation is where we link things together to imply that they share something in common that in fact they don't. An example I heard recently of this was the statement 'gays, women and other minorities'. Since the person who made this statement was referring to the UK, then it is hard to see how women, who make up the majority of the population, can be a minority. I suspect that the speaker was confusing issues of minority with issues of discrimination. However, much false concatenation is deliberate. Many of the issues covered in our lead-in cases provide examples of this. In the Child Support Agency case, the fact that fathers were 'absent' could be easily joined to the idea that they were 'irresponsible'. Yet many fathers had already made financial arrangements for their children, only to be charged a second time by the CSA. Again, the fact that electronic commerce is more 'modern' or 'faster' than traditional cash transactions does not make it automatically the best way of doing business. Are all those concerned about the objectives of the WTO potential rioting anarchists like the people shown in the news? Is the argument about whether there is global warming the same argument as whether such warming is a bad thing?

All of these ways in which the soft properties of information can be skilfully *distorted*, *captured* or *owned* were available to any person or group long before the advent of information and communications technology. The important difference that we are now experiencing comes from the *richness* of the information that the technology can handle. The success and effectiveness of communicating information grow with the ways in which it can be reinforced. *Reinforcement* is the concept the more of our senses we can apply to communication, the more effective the communication is likely to be. A simple educational example is that a lecturer who supports their spoken material with visual material on a screen tends to communicate better than one who just talks. The multimedia implications of this concept are still just beginning to be explored. All management activities that depend on communication are likely to be transformed by it.

5.1.4 Capturing the data

The effects of measurement and observation on certainty

We saw in Chapter 4 that *uncertainty* comes from various forms of *environmental disturbance*. We also saw that *communication*, in the form of feedback, is a vital component of the information system that forms a subsystem of a control system. Successful control therefore requires that we successfully gather information through the *sensor* component of the control system and transmit it to the *comparator*, using some form of *communication system*. Figure 5.2 shows how Figure 3.4 can be extended to show the role of a communication system as a component of a management system through the hierarchy of information and control.

We have already seen how *soft* uncertainty enters information via norms and values. However, there is an another important principle that means that information will have an element of *hard* uncertainty, however carefully we design and operate the sensing and feedback of information, or try to avoid bias and spin.

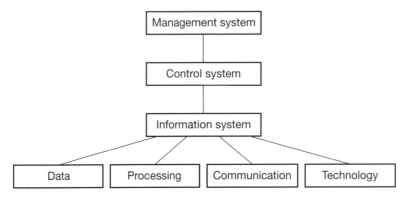

Figure 5.2 Communication as a component of an information system
This structural diagram enlarges on Figure 3.4.

This principle can be summarized as:

All observation disturbs what it observes.

I will use two very different examples to illustrate this principle. The first comes from atomic physics, and is known as the *Heisenberg Uncertainty Principle*. Werner Heisenberg set this out in 1927 when discussing whether it was possible in principle to have *exact* data about such properties as the movement and position of small atomic particles like electrons. What he showed was that the only way you could find out where an electron was and where it was going was to make it interact with something else. You might try getting it to 'reflect' a small amount of radiation and reveal itself and its movement. After all, the way we see something is because it reflects light, which our eyes then pick up and use to deduce its presence as a cat or a computer keyboard.

However, there is a difference between cats and keyboards and electrons. Cats and keyboards are big things in atomic terms. They contain billions and billions of electrons. When light hits a cat it doesn't feel a thing; or when it hits the keyboard the keyboard isn't disturbed. For an electron, however, a small amount of radiation is a bit like one snooker ball is to another snooker ball. When the radiation bounces off the electron, it also knocks the electron away to somewhere else. So when the radiation returns from being reflected by the electron, the electron has moved off somewhere else. Our observation can only tell us where it was, not where it is now. We might try to get over this by using very 'gentle' radiation that wouldn't disturb the electron, but alas, the equivalent of 'gentle' radiation is rather like a snooker ball stuffed with feathers, because its ability to bounce or reflect accurately is much reduced. So it doesn't disturb the electron much, but the way it is reflected gives less reliable, blurred results.

Thus our example shows that it is impossible, even in principle, to devise an experiment that tells us exactly where an electron is and where it is going. Modern physics, in the form of the Heisenberg Uncertainty Principle, recognizes this and always talks about electron movement in terms of *probabilities* rather than certainties. As we have seen, the word *stochastic* is used to describe data and information that talks in terms of probabilities.

Modern physics may seem a long way from management, but in fact a similar principle also applies to social observation. In 1924 some famous experiments were carried out at the Hawthorne plant in the US whose original objective was to adjust such factors as plant lighting with the aim of improving worker performance. After many complex adjustments to the tests, it was found impossible to separate the effects of one particular adjustment from other factors. Indeed, improving the lighting in one situation had the same effect as not improving it somewhere else. The Hawthorne researchers found it impossible in particular to separate the effects of their presence in the measuring process from the values of the measurements themselves.

In everyday life we are aware of this principle from our own experience. Doing something when you are watched is not the same as doing it privately, and if someone is recording the results of their observation, our behaviour is likely to be even more distorted.

For information systems in business, therefore, with the inevitable human component, the concept of certainty of information is limited. Whether the uncertainties matter, however, depends on the costs associated with them, as we saw above.

Classification and hierarchy: dealing with complex information

One of the important ways we deal with complexity in information is to place things in *classes* and *categories*. Thus in a business like insurance, where decisions have to be made about the cost of cover for millions of individual people, some way has to be found of estimating an individual's lifespan, their likelihood of having a car accident or their probability of being burgled.

One thing that is not possible in those circumstances is to have vast amounts of detail on each person. What insurance companies do is the same that we do as individuals: they *classify* their experience so that they can use commonly shared characteristics as a basis for simplifying the processing of large amounts of information. Once you know that a particular person falls into the classes of 'male' and 'aged 23', you can use the results of processing data about previous 23-year-old males to estimate how likely it is that he will have a car accident and what the cost of repair is likely to be. This information can then be used to estimate what amount of money you will require for annual car insurance.

Such information and calculations are regularly used successfully in business. A whole insurance and pension industry has ended up being the majority owner of British industry on the basis of being able to deal with complex, *stochastic* information. However, where I think modern popular thinking has become confused is in not distinguishing between classifying information, and stereotyping individuals. Stereotyping does occur and its result can be the Nazi death camps in the Second World War, but there is also a constructive and positive way in which concepts of *classification* and *hierarchy* can be used. In this section I want to distinguish some elementary points that will add to our concepts of hierarchy and that we can take up in Chapter 9.

One simple piece of classification that a pension fund might use is that women form a group of people who live longer than men. Is this stereotyping? After all, my father lived longer than my mother, so in one sense it seems to be untrue. There are two important points that help us analyse such questions. The first comes from the systems concept of *emergent property*. What is called something like 'expected male lifespan' is not the property of any man, any more than having 2.4 children is the property of any family. Instead, 'male lifespan' is the emergent property that comes from the *aggregation* and *processing* of *component* data. Stereotyping occurs when we transfer properties appropriate to one level of the systems hierarchy down to an individual component.

A second potential cause of confusion is the failure to recognize two different types of hierarchy. When studying systems, we have used a concept of hierarchy based on levels of *aggregation* or being part of some greater *whole*. Another concept we shall come across when we study *object-oriented methods* in Chapter 9 is a hierarchy that deals with components as a kind of a *general class*. The fact that a component can be seen as a member of a part of a hierarchical *whole* does not imply that it automatically has properties in the way that it would from being a member of a particular *kind* or *class*.

5.1.5 Methods for building data into information

Why we aggregate data

Is the world warmer than it was last year? Our lead-in case seems to imply that it is, but what is the detailed, accurate information? The only way we could really answer that question is to produce a vast list of data for every temperature reading for every weather station in the world for every day of this year and last. Even that wouldn't be entirely detailed and accurate, because it wouldn't cover variations within the day. Even if we had such data, we'd probably fall asleep or die before we had read it all, and almost certainly we'd forget what last year was like by the time we'd read about this year.

In terms of Ashby's Law of Requisite Variety, our brains don't have the ability to absorb that amount of detail. What we need is some way of *aggregating data* into a form that is *information*, rather than confusion.

The mathematical subject of statistics provides techniques that enable us to deal with large amounts of data in a way that means we can make sense of them. The subject divides into three components:

1 Descriptive statistics.

2 Inferential statistics.

3 Decision theory.

Descriptive statistics provides us with ways of talking about large amounts of data in a simple, low-variety way that we can understand. Thus instead of all the temperature data for a particular year or place, we can use some measure of their overall size, level or *central tendency*, like an average or mean. Instead of trying to take in the complexity of the variation in levels of temperature, we can use some measure of dispersion of the data above and below the mean, like a *variance* or *standard deviation*. We can also summarize the data using various diagrams, like bar charts or pie charts.

Once we've summarized our data, using descriptive statistics, we are likely to find patterns or relationships. We might find that for a selection of cities in the world, the average temperature in the previous year was higher than it was in the latest year for which we have data. Does that mean that any city in the world also experienced a similar increase? When we ask questions like these we are trying to make *inferences* from the data. *Inferential statistics* provides us with mathematical techniques that enable us to talk about what is *probable* or what is *likely*. Inferential statistics therefore deals with *stochastic* information.

If descriptive statistics show that most parts of the world are warmer now than they were previously, inferential statistics can give us some *probability* of what that might mean for areas where we don't have the data. Such a situation is fuzzy because it has both *hard* and *soft* uncertainties. The *descriptive* statistics show us the uncertainty that comes from trying to infer conclusions from hard, *stochastic* data. But we now have to decide what *risk* or *uncertainty* we are prepared to accept when making *inferences* from the aggregated descriptive data. This involves *decision making*. *Decision theory* provides the analytical tools for dealing with such management problems.

What comes out of our analysis so far is that aggregating data into information introduces an element of *fuzziness*, both *hard* and *soft*.

The fuzzy nature of all information

At the end of the last section we established the principle that all information will be fuzzy. This is because all systems have environments that disturb them. The need to aggregate information comes from the need for management to accommodate the uncontrollable aspect of human nature, which limits our mental ability to cope with large amounts of data.

This aspect then introduces uncertainty about:

1 What the information is, in terms of aggregated data.

2 What interpretation and meaning should be given to such information.

Uncertainty about what the information is in terms of *aggregated data* results from what *method* we use to aggregate the data. Whatever the method is, it means that the information contains *hard uncertainty* and is *stochastic*. Thus there are different ways of aggregating the same data to produce different descriptions of the central tendency of global warming, like 'higher on average' or 'lower on average'. But descriptive statistics gives us different measures for this, like the *mean*, *median* or *mode*.

Whatever we think the information is in terms of the way we aggregate the data, we then ask what *interpretation* and *meaning* should be given to such information.

Uncertainty about what the information *means*, or how it should be *interpreted*, comes from soft issues emanating from *world view*, *purpose* or *set of values*.

We will now look more closely at how *hard uncertainty*, in the form of stochastic information, can be described and dealt with. Our main approach to soft issues will be in Chapter 8.

Describing stochastic information

In Section 4.1.1 we established that describing *stochastic* information involved talking in terms of *probability*. Although we saw that there were different types of probabilities in terms of how their values were arrived at, the value of a probability was an expression of how likely it was that something would happen or would be the case.

If we apply the concept of probability to the stochastic nature of hard information, it means that any piece of information is an expression of something that we think is probably the case, and that in principle could be assessed or measured to find out if it was. Thus we believe that the amount in stock in Figure 3.2 is 470 packs. But what if it isn't? Or what if it isn't quite or is nearly the case? To understand the answers to questions like these, we first need to distinguish between:

● continuous variables; and
● integer variables.

Continuous variables are those whose values can vary over a range without any gaps or breaks. Thus the volume of fuel that a petrol station might have in stock could be any value within the capacity range of the storage tanks. It would not have to be an exact number of gallons or cubic metres.

Integer or *discrete* variables are those whose values are confined to whole numbers. Thus the number of hinges or packing cases held by Carry-Out Cupboards would be a whole number, a stock record saying that there were 3.475 hinges in stock would be nonsense.

A special case of integer variables are zero–one variables. These are integer variables that can only take the values 0 or 1, as their name implies. In situations where we are concerned simply with whether something is a fact or not, true or false, making 0 stand for false and 1 stand for true is a convention known as *boolean* variables.

| RQ 5.3 | If customers of Carry-Out Cupboards were asked how important they thought it was to know the origin of the materials of which the cupboards were made, with what kind of variable would the survey be dealing? |

When we come to describe *hard* stochastic information in terms of the probability that it is correct, the particular way we do so depends on the form of variable used to express such information.

For integer variables, including zero–one variables, all we do is assign a probability to each possible value of the variable to show how probable it is.

Thus we might use past figures on customer demand to estimate the *empirical* probability of different demand levels (an integer variable) in any particular month, as in Figure 5.3. We might also use similar past data to estimate the probability that a reported stock figure would change or not (boolean variable) due to customer demand between stock checks, as in Figure 5.4.

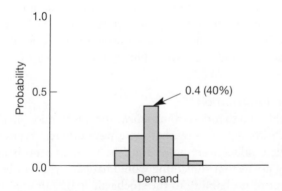

Figure 5.3 The empirical probability of different demand levels (1)
Shows how probable different levels of demand are, based on past data. The particular demand levels are a textbook example, but the fact that they sum up to a value of p = 1 is an essential part of probability theory.

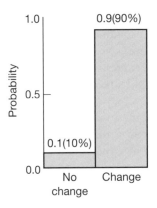

Figure 5.4 The empirical probability of different demand levels (2)
Compared with Figure 5.3, this example shows a probability distribution based on the concept of a Boolean variable, change/no change or yes/no, rather than a range of values for a variable.

For *continuous* variables the situation is a little more complex. Thus if quality control at Carry-Out Cupboards was checking on the small variation in the length of a cupboard door cut from board during manufacture, it would expect some variation about the official dimension laid down in the design. Here there is no reason for it to be an exact number of millimetres, it might be anything in a range. The way we can describe this is in terms of *probability density*, as in Figure 5.5. What probability density shows is the *continuous* change in the probability of a variable having any value over the possible range. The changes in probability, like the changes in measurement, do not go in steps like in Figures 5.3 and 5.4. The maths of this theory is quite difficult if you don't know calculus, but the idea is simple enough. The higher the probability density curve in any range of measurement, as in Figure 5.5, the more that range of measurements is likely to occur.

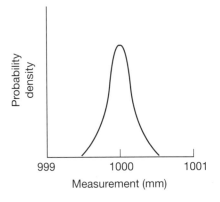

Figure 5.5 A probability distribution for a continuous variable
The changing level of probability for different values of the measurement is shown by the probability density curve. Ranges of measurement corresponding to high levels on the curve are more likely than those where it is lower.

What the common theory behind Figures 5.3 to 5.5 does show is that real life information has to be thought of in terms of how probable it is that it is correct, rather than that it is correct, full stop. For this reason, we strictly ought to describe all values for variables in terms of estimates or averages, yet we don't. Why is this? To understand the answer to that question we need to recognize a further concept from probability theory.

Figure 5.6 shows information about the same example as Figure 5.3 but with different data. Here the data shows both a narrower range of possible values and one particular value with a very high probability. The overall shape of the distribution is narrower and more peaked. Both of these features work together in showing more certainty in the information given by Figure 5.6 than that in Figure 5.3 about the demand for the product. Generally, the taller and narrower a probability distribution like Figures 5.3 or 5.6, the more *certainty* it provides. Conversely, the wider and flatter it is, the less certainty it provides. For continuous variables the same principle applies. Thus curve A in Figure 5.7 shows a situation where there is a high probability that the dimensions of a product will be confined to quite a narrow range of variation. This gives us a high level of certainty as to what the dimensions of the product might be in practice. Curve B, however, is wider and flatter, with the implication that a much wider range of values for the measurement is possible and we can therefore be less certain what sort of value a particular measurement might take.

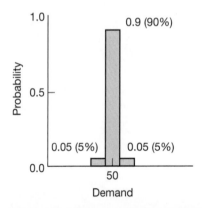

Figure 5.6 The empirical probability of different demand levels (3)
This distribution of demand levels has less dispersion than Figure 5.3, and enables more certainty in estimating possible levels of demand.

Stochastic variables therefore need some additional way of description beyond estimates of their likely value or average size. We need also to take account of the degree of *variation* that can occur about that estimated level or average. As we saw above, these are called *measures of dispersion*, and the most common one used for the kind of data we have described is the variance. Generally, the greater the variance, the greater the level of uncertainty associated with stochastic information.

So, returning to our earlier question, why don't we always talk in terms of estimates and averages? Why do we treat much information as if it were correct? The answer is a combination of two factors:

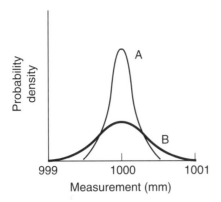

Figure 5.7 Two possible probability distributions for a continuous variable
Both distributions have the same average value, but distribution A is less dispersed than distribution B. As with the comparison of Figures 5.6 and 5.3, the less dispersed distribution A enables more certainty in estimating demand levels than distribution B.

1 The size of the variance in much data can limited by appropriate use of control. Thus an engineer at Carry-Out Cupboards can keep the dimensions of a cupboard so close to the nominal that you or I as a customer wouldn't notice the difference. Even where the engineer fails, the quality control is unlikely to let the cupboard pass inspection.

2 Even where the variance in data is large enough to be noticed, the costs of the uncertainty it causes may not be important. I'm sure Carry-Out Cupboards don't mind too much if it only has 1345 pairs of a particular hinge rather than the 1346 it estimated.

What both of these factors imply is that it is the *balance* of the *cost of control* and *the cost of error* associated with uncertainty that matters, not the uncertainty in itself.

RQ 5.4 Can you identify the central control systems principle in the last paragraph?

Entropy and the usefulness of information

The lessons we learned from considering Figures 5.3, 5.6 and 5.7 have an implication for the concept of the *usefulness* of information. Being told that the demand for a product could be anywhere between 0 and 100 in a particular month and that any one figure was as probable as another is less informative than being told, as in Figure 5.6, that it will be a figure between 49 and 51, with a 90 per cent probability of being exactly 50.

Communication theory has taken a version of a concept called *entropy* from physics to express this idea. Entropy can be used as a measure of the fuzziness of information and therefore of its usefulness to us in terms of the level of certainty it brings. Note that here we are not talking about the certainty associated with one value of probability, but of the overall certainty provided by a combination of probabilities in distributions like those in Figures 5.3 to 5.7. We might instinctively feel that Figure 5.6 is more informative and certain than Figure 5.3, or that in Figure 5.7 curve A gives more certainty about measurements than curve B. But how can we express this formally as a measurement? The answer is entropy. When calculated (according to a formula I won't bother you with: see Shannon (1963) for a thorough mathematical background to communications), entropy takes account of the degree of peak and spread in a distribution in such a way that flat, uninformative distributions have high entropies and more peaked, informative ones have low entropies. Since entropy is a strictly a measure of the uselessness of information, its reverse, called negentropy, is sometimes used instead. Generally, the more entropy in a system the more fuzzy, decayed and useless it is. The purpose of a good information system is therefore to keep entropy at an optimum level that balances the costs of certainty against the costs of uncertainty and error.

Setting boundaries

In our lead-in case we asked whether the Earth is getting warmer. Our study of how we aggregate data has shown that the answer to that question can be very complex, and it depends on how we interpret *soft* as well as *hard* uncertainty. We promised to look further at dealing with soft decision making in Chapter 8. For the moment, however, it is important to understand a particular soft issue that has to be decided before any attempt to aggregate data using the statistical techniques that we've outlined. This issue is one of *boundaries*.

When we aggregate data, we have to make assumptions about what data should be included and what left out. Is the planet getting warmer? The answer looks different according to where we put the boundary for the data we include. If we compare the average temperature for the last century with that for the one that ended in AD 800, we get a different view from comparing just the last two centuries.

Any attempt at using data for time series analysis aimed at *forecasting* comes up against this soft issue. What data do we include? What periods are significant? How long does a figure have to go on increasing before we decide that it is a trend? The answers to questions like these are not to be found in mathematical theory. Instead, they depend on why we are making the forecast or what the analysis is for. That is why our view of information has to be related to the General Control Model of Figure 4.10 and our wider *management* aims. In Chapter 8 we consider this further.

5.2   COMMUNICATING INFORMATION

Figure 5.8 shows a model of a communication system. Since we shall use this to understand a range of different examples, I shall refer to it as the General Communication System Model. We will begin by looking at the overall form of the model and then at its components.

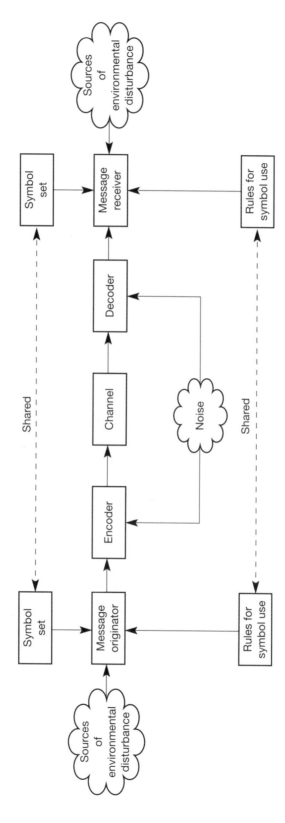

Figure 5.8 The General Communication System Model

As with the classical control model of Figure 4.4, this represents a version of a widely-held view. The annotation of the diagram might be improved by showing that a 'shared' symbol set could also be described as a 'closely approximated' symbol set.

The General Communication System Model

An important feature of the model that should be noticed from the beginning is that it is a model of a *system*. We can therefore expect it to have all the systemic properties that we introduced in Chapter 3.

Although I shall present the model in a way designed to support the objectives of this chapter and the book generally, the form of the model and the names of its components are very similar to those you will find in standard books on information systems, so the General Communication System model is not as individual to this book as the General Control Model.

Like the General Control Model, the General Communication System Model derives originally from hard engineering systems applications. Names like *channel* or *encoder* referred to technical equipment. But as we used control to represent a *concept* rather than a particular physical application or management style, so we shall take communication as a concept that can be applied more widely than physical systems like telephone lines or cable networks. As with other systems, we focus first on the General Communication System Model as a logical *what* rather than a particular physical *how*.

Once we recognize that the General Communication System Model is a model of a system, then all we have said about the practical implications of a systems approach in Section 3.1 apply to it. The implications of components, connexion, structure, hierarchy, process, interaction, holism, emergent property, behaviour, environment, identity, boundary and conceptualism are all relevant to understanding the implications of the General Communication System Model. We will look at these concepts as they arise.

At this point, however, the most important practical implication of the concept is one that it shares with other business systems. This is that any attempt to develop and implement a communication system as part of an information system must take account of its *holistic* nature. It will have both abstract and concrete components, and it will involve *hard* and *soft* issues. Consequently, attempts to establish or improve communication that ignore either the technical or the human aspects of the system and their interaction are likely to be inadequate or to fail altogether.

Message originator and receiver

The first systems concept that is relevant is that communication is an *emergent property*. Putting aside trite jokes about schizophrenia, it takes at least two people for communication to occur: we don't see someone communicating alone. The minimum requirement of communication is therefore an *originator*, or *sender*, and a *receiver*.

I have given the alternatives originator and sender to distinguish between whose message it is and who, or what, sends it. This recognition of the original source of a message is one essential if it is to be correctly *interpreted* and *understood*. I put those last two terms in italics to refer back to the analysis of the *soft* issues about information that we covered above. As we saw, two people can use the same words to mean very different things, so knowing who is using them is essential for a correct interpretation of a message. Just as every system reflects someone's *world view*, *purpose* or *set of values*, so too does communicated information in the form of messages.

We also saw that this principle governed what data was collected, processed, stored and output; how it was assembled into a whole structure to form information; and what role this information played in the wider control and management systems.

Here we see the concept of a message as part of a communications system illustrating the same principle. Just as the model of any system reflects the views of its owner or perceiver, so the meaning of the information in a message will reflect the intentions of its originator.

When we consider the roles of all who are involved in the workings of an information system and the implications for systems development in Chapter 8, we shall find that identifying the roles of originators and receivers is as important as understanding procedures. Many systems development methods have important first stages that record and analyse such flows and roles in the existing information system as a prelude to specifying improvement. We shall also see that good systems methodology generally recognizes that we need to understand the soft issues behind what people seek, or do not seek, to communicate about their needs from a system and their role in it.

Shared symbol set and rules for use

The implication of needing to know the originator of a message is that, without this information, the receiver will not be able to interpret its meaning. Understanding the purpose or norms of the originator enables the receiver to resolve the soft issues behind the use of words and language; or for visual information, it helps us interpret symbols and images.

However, it is not only necessary to know who is sending a message for the receiver to interpret the soft components of information; you also need to have some common ground of understanding to interpret the hard data. An upper-case *H* is a letter that occurs in both the Latin and Cyrillic alphabets, but in Russian it stands for the sound made by a Latin *N*. *Nada* is a word in both Spanish and Russian: in Spanish it means 'nothing', in Russian it means 'necessary'. 12/1/01 means 12 January 01 in Europe and 1 December 01 in the US.

Even before we enter the minefield of norms and biases, we need two further components to enable successful communication:

1 A shared set of symbols.
2 Shared rules for symbol use.

Thus for communication using language, a shared set of symbols implies that people have to use the same alphabet and words. The shared rules for symbol use imply in turn that there is agreement on such matters as spelling, pronunciation, or which direction the writing flows on the page. For electronic communication, we need conventions on how such things are translated into digital signals.

Where legitimate differences exist in the form of spoken language, we may want to remove the potential this gives for poor communication and misunderstanding by adopting a formally agreed standard. As we saw in Chapter 3, diagrams provide one means of overcoming ambiguity when seeking to communicate information about systems themselves. In Chapter 9, we shall find that other tools may be used for this purpose. Thus communicating clearly what a process does in a system may require us to adopt an exclusive set of defined words and ways of using them called structured English. Such a tool is designed to ensure that the originator, in the form of the systems developer, successfully communicates a definition of what a process should do to the receiver, in the form of the systems builder or computer programmer.

Encoder, channel and decoder

The processes called *encoding* and *decoding* may be required in the General Communication System Model for two related reasons:

1 The originator and receiver have different ways of *describing* or *recording* information.
2 The *communication channel* transmits information in a different form from the way in which the originator or receiver describes or records it.

A universal example of the first reason is provided by the existence of computer programmers and software. The role of the programmer came from the need for encoding and decoding, indeed, we call what a programmer ultimately produces 'code'. Computer code is essentially a set of instructions in a digital form that a computer can understand, recorded in an electronic medium that it can read. Human beings, however, issue instructions in the aural/oral medium of speech and the visual/touch media of typing and writing, and record them on the medium of paper or brain memory. The job of a computer program is to enable human keystrokes, mouse movements or voice instructions to be *encoded* into digital signals that the computer can understand. Digital signals from the computer have in turn to be *decoded* into visual material on the screen, aural warning beeps or print-outs.

The encoding and decoding needs of the *communication channel* have become a major issue since the advent of *networked* information technology. The majority of telephone communication channels transmit signals in *analogue* rather than the digital format used by most information technology. The need for a modem, when we want to connect to the Internet, comes from the fact that the digital information on our computer needs to be *modulated* or encoded into a form that telephone lines can transmit. Similarly, the computer on the receiving end needs to *demodulate* or decode the analogue signals into digital. Hence the word modem comes from *modulate/demodulate*.

We shall look at some of the more complex Internet aspects of shared symbol sets and encoding/decoding in the next section. Meanwhile, it is essential to recognize that a *channel* is a concept and is not necessarily a *concrete* thing. Consider the phrase 'I heard about it through the usual channels'. The channels of communication referred to here are the conceptual communication links between human beings, often called the 'grapevine'. We also hear people say things like 'I can't get through to you', when there has been an argument or misunderstanding. What is being communicated here can be things like words or body language using one or more of our senses. You might encode your anger into louder sounds or a pointing finger; I decode them into the feelings that you have. In none of these human communication examples is it necessary to have a formal, fixed, concrete connexion, but there is a communication system nonetheless.

I think the most important implication of these concepts for information systems in business comes when we consider the wider communication system that includes both human and information technology components. In this situation, the sequence of encoder–channel–decoder represents a major connexion between sources of hard and soft problems and issues. The computer system is a mechanical device that operates according to set rules of logic and predetermined standards. The human activity system that has to interact with this computer system so that they both act as components of the wider information system works on the basis of taste, judgement, beliefs and other factors depending on the *world view*, *purpose* or *set of values* of those involved. In Chapter 8 we shall find out what *methodology* is available to support the design of information systems where the human and the technological interact.

We have seen earlier in this chapter that information is an emergent property resulting from bringing together data components. We also saw that the nature of any information, in terms of what it tells us and what we can do with it, depends on how data is brought together. Chapter 6 will give examples of how the choice of method used to build individual data components into information depends on both the logical view or model (the whats) of the information, and the physical medium (the hows) used to record it. For the communication of information, therefore, the logical model implies a shared symbol set and rules for originator and receiver, and the medium implies a channel.

Chapter 7 will show that once we see a business or organization as a system, new technological development can be used to provide a common channel for communication for very different originators and receivers. This does not always represent a 'solution' or a 'facilitation', but rather the need sometimes to deal with contemporary information systems in a different way from the old ones.

Sources of environmental disturbance and noise

We have already established that the occurrence of the word system in the title General Communication System Model means that all those properties of a system that we covered in Chapter 3 would be exhibited by a communications system. We also asserted in Chapter 3 that no real-life system, like a business system, could be a closed system. All real-life systems have an *environment* that disturbs them and over that they have only limited influence or control.

These properties and principles are shown to apply to communication systems when we consider:

- the *effect of environmental disturbances* on the message originator and receiver;
- the phenomenon of noise.

Environmental disturbance of the message originator and receiver means that in practice neither of these components is a fixed entity whose position or behaviour never changes. Where the originator or receiver is human, this means that such factors as tiredness, dishonesty or inconsistency can be present in the message before encoding or can be paced into its interpretation after decoding. It also means that although the General Communication System Model talks of 'shared' symbol sets or rules for use, in practice we might do better to add the phrase 'a close approximation to'.

The term noise is used to refer specifically to the environmental disturbances affecting the encoder–channel–decoder sequence. In the original technical applications of communications, these effects would literally have been the noise we hear when atmospheric electrical effects result in interference on a radio channel. The term was then extended to cover the effects of interference generally, whether or not they resulted in actual aural noise. We shall take it even further to include interference in the channels of human communication. If we consider the extension of the concept to cover the range of communication that takes place in information systems in business, we can also see that noise comes into the disturbance of the encoder–channel–decoder sequence of human communication in the form of such factors as tiredness, dishonesty, inconsistency, prejudice or the bias we have already mentioned above.

Environmental disturbance and noise can therefore be associated with:

- the *hard* technological components of the communication system, such as malfunction of equipment, power failure or accidental damage;
- the *soft* human components of the communication system, resulting from unintended disturbances like tiredness or accident; or intended disturbances due to maliciousness or dishonesty.

When we consider them in the context of information and communications technology systems in business one significant set of practical implications of the effects of environmental disturbance and noise on the encoder–channel–decoder sequence relate to *security*. Any system of security has to address the whole sequence of encoder, channel and decoder. It therefore requires:

- boundary controls
- encoding and decoding controls
- communication controls
- storage and database controls.

Boundary controls aim to prevent disturbances from getting into the communication system from the outside. They can be concrete, like locking a computer room or making communication lines inaccessible. They can be abstract, like using encryption codes. Note that the term *boundary* is used in its conceptual systems sense, so that not all boundaries are physical things located in space.

Devices such as passwords and encryption are designed as *logical* barriers to access to conceptual divisions of a communication system. Thus two computers physically connected to the same remote machine may have different selections of access to its information. In the next section we shall see how the concept of *ubiquitous software* extends the concept of systems boundary well away from a simple physical interpretation.

Encoding and decoding controls aim to prevent disturbances caused by the human–machine subsystems that do the encoding and decoding. At their simplest level, these could be things like automatic spelling and grammar checks, or validation checks that ensure that the different data components making up message information are consistent. For example, the delivery date on an order must be later than the order date, or the age of a child lower than that of its parent.

Communication controls are concerned to see that what is received from a communication channel is what was sent. At a physical level, the process of *attenuation* means that communication signals weaken and die away as they travel along the channel. Even if the signal is potentially readable by the receiver, it has to be receiving. This means that sending and receiving have to be *co-ordinated*: either by the receiver being active when the message arrives, or by there being some form of storage to *buffer* the different patterns of sending and receiving.

Storage and database controls ensure that when we do need to store messages, before or after they are sent, they are not lost or corrupted.

Box 5.2

Business-only web auctions to shake up supply prices

Carlos Grande

Internet auctioneers are planning to bring 'dynamic pricing' to construction, transport and raw materials markets through business only online auctions. Companies will be able to bid live over the Internet for goods from concrete to container ship capacity via two business web auctioneers being launched. Both Bidbusiness.co.uk, a UK Internet start-up, and Bid.com Europe, an offshoot of a Canadian web auction software company, believe business-to-business sales will outstrip business-to-consumer auctions pioneered by Internet companies such as eBay in the US and QXL.com in Britain.

On the new sites business will vie to outbid each other for supplies, and in so-called Dutch or reverse auctions, to underbid rivals to win customers looking for the lowest prices. 'Fixed pricing will not survive the Internet,' said Aidan Rowsome, managing director of Bid.com. 'Whether you are a freight cargo company or a hotel chain, you cannot maintain a ratecard when you are faced with mass demand from the Internet.'

While companies such as QXL handle goods and are thereby saddled with warehousing and shipping costs, neither Bid.com nor Bidbusiness will carry stock. Instead, they will process auctions and take a commission on sales. Bid.com Europe plans to co-operate with manufacturers to co-brand web sites. It predicts the first will be launched early next year, and identifies freight, travel, utilities and advertising as key early auction markets.

Bidbusiness.co.uk is testing its web site, with 10 auction categories from minerals to waste disposal and commercial property, for launch next month. It forecasts taking a cut of 5 per cent on small-volume sales. 'For commodity goods, internet auctions offer a much more efficient way of matching buyers and sellers,' said Andrew Biggs, managing director of Bidbusiness.co.uk.

Terry Maguire, managing director of Concorde Electronics, which auctions second-user computers via the Internet, said: 'We also use a conventional fax shot to 12 000 customers but the online auction is a much cheaper way of finding sales leads. The challenge for many small companies will be if they get their first customer in Venezuela via the web, are they ready to deliver there?'

Source: Financial Times, 12 November 1999. Reprinted with permission.

Comment

Auctions are a good example of a new information and communications technology 'how' for implementing a very old information systems 'what'. Traditional auctions consist of an auctioneer who sells by exchanging shouted messages with potential buyers. Such auctions have covered a wide range of products from cattle to life assurance policies to antique furniture. The important common property of traditional auctions has been that auctioneer and buyer have had to be within shouting distance and present at the same time. The Internet means that 'shouting' can now take place across the globe, with everyone's contribution being made at their own place, time and convenience.

What the article does not always detail is how far the various systems go beyond just being an electronic acceptor of bids. Just as a human auctioneer encourages the bidding and can identify and coax potentially interested bidders, so good ICT systems will learn about bidders' interests and behaviour to encourage future business.

Many of these security issues apply even more strongly when more than one sender and receiver are involved. We will develop this theme further in the next section.

Another important practical implication of recognizing the inevitability of error creeping into the communication of information relates to the development of information systems. We shall consider this in Chapter 9. Although systems development is concerned in its early stages with specifying what an information system should do, no systems design is complete in practical terms unless it also includes provision for accommodating what to do when errors occur.

Lags in the system

One final important concept that applies to communication systems, as it does to other systems, is *lags* in the transformation process. We saw in Chapter 4 that this is important in control systems. Once we recall, however, that a major example of a communication system in this context is the feedback loop, then the implications of lags in a system that we covered before will have their equivalents here.

The main implication we will focus on here is one linking up with the consideration of the stochastic nature of information that we introduced above, and adding to our previous study of it. The transformation process of encoding the message, transmitting it along a channel and decoding it will always take time in a real-life communication system. There will be a lag between the originator's and the receiver's perception of the message. This means that even if noise does not distort the message in any way, the information that it seeks to transmit may be in error.

We can see examples of this if we return to the role of communication in the feedback loop of a control system. Here the communication system is acting as a subsystem of the control system. In a stock control example like that illustrated by Figure 3.2, the sensor may correctly pick up the figure for the amount in stock and there may not be any noise error introduced by the figure being copied incorrectly or misunderstood when spoken. However, by the time that a comparator, like a stock control clerk working with a software package, has acted as receiver and used the figure to decide on stock allocation, further stock movement could have made the figure out of date. The role of shared databases in Chapter 6, and supply chain management in Appendix 1, can reduce this aspect, but it cannot always eliminate it. The stochastic nature of information means that 'total quality' of information will always be a myth in real information systems, whatever the consultants and politicians would have us believe.

5.3 NETWORKS AND MULTIPLE COMMUNICATION SYSTEMS

5.3.1 Modelling networks

Compared with systems that correspond to the single-channel General Communication System Model, networks have two important properties that increase their complexity. If we want to ensure that communication is successful over a network, we need to:

- *distinguish* between many possible *senders* and *receivers*;
- *route* messages over the network so that they arrive *safely* at their *intended destination*.

To understand how these complexities are dealt with, we need a *model* of networked communication, just as we had one for single-channel communication. However, before we look at any network model, we need to check what we mean by the term *network*. Doing this brings us back to our familiar systems distinction of the logical *whats* from the physical *hows*.

I suppose that the obvious examples of what we might call a network would be a local area network (LAN) in the building where we work, or the Internet that we access from our computer at home. Yet if I connect to the Internet using a computer at my workplace, am I on a LAN or the Internet or both? When I get home and connect to the Internet, I use the same line that I also use for telephone calls. Is it really the telephone line that connects me to the Internet?

Our now familiar holistic systems view answers questions like these by recognizing that *connexion* is an *emergent property* that requires both concrete physical connexion, like the telephone line, and abstract logical connexion, like having the right connecting instructions in the software we use. Any systems model of a network must therefore cover both its *concrete* and *abstract* components.

5.3.2 Properties of network models

Any *systems* model of a network will not only have to enable us to distinguish the various concrete and abstract components, it will also need to show us how the components are connected and how they interact. We recall from Chapter 3 that how components are connected is called the system's *structure*, and how the components interact determines process. Internationally agreed models defining these characteristics of network systems are called *reference models*.

The need for reference models arose in the late 1970s and early 1980s when both the types and numbers of ICT networks were growing rapidly. These included Local Area Networks (LANS), Metropolitan Area Networks (MANS), Wide Area Networks (WANS) and Wireless Networks. All of these could then be connected by an inter-network, or the Internet as we now call it.

The purpose of a reference model was to establish international standards that would ensure compatibility of all the various hardware and software network components. Two major examples of such models are:

- OSI (Open Systems Interconnection);
- TCP/IP (Transport Control Protocol/Internet Protocol).

The TCP/IP model tended to develop piecemeal with the development of the Internet itself, while the OSI model was a formal international attempt to set up a standard by the ISO (International Standards Organization). As Tanenbaum (1996) points out, the OSI model came too late and it has failed to become standard. We shall follow a 'hybrid' model proposed by Tanenbaum, which concentrates on the essential features for any reference model.

5.3.3 Network model layers

We said that any reference model would have to cover the structural relationship of both concrete and abstract network components, as well as the process interactions between them. Network reference models do this by using the concept of *layers*. Figure 5.9 shows the model proposed by Tanenbaum. It is essential to understand that the layers are a systems *concept*, not necessarily things we can see or touch.

Each layer is a systems component whose actions contribute to the emergent property of *communication* that we want from the system as a *whole*. The reference model defines *what* each layer has to do in order to make its contribution to the whole system. It also defines the ways in which the layers can communicate and interact with each other through the layers' interface. *How* individual layers do what they are supposed to do are each a layer's own business, as long as it gets the job done. Provided that it conforms to the ways of communicating across the interface to other

Layer	Name
5	Application
4	Transport
3	Network
2	Data link
1	Physical

Figure 5.9 A hybrid network reference model following the principles of Tanenbaum (1996)

layers, a layer can change how it works without affecting how other layers work. To illustrate these concepts, let's look at some examples for each layer.

The physical layer

As with any form of communication, networks have to have some form of physical channel along which the data can flow. Examples include:

- wireless transmission
- telephone wires
- ISDN
- cellular radio
- communication satellites.

The job of the physical layer is to carry out the procedures, or *protocols*, that ensure that the data transmitted by the sender corresponds to the data arriving at the receiver, regardless of the type of channel used. *How* this is done is of no interest to the other layers, nor is the physical layer interested in what the other layers are up to. Thus my telephone line isn't interested in whether it's transmitting my voice in a telephone call or the e-mail from my computer. Also, when my software sends e-mail across the Internet, it isn't interested in whether the physical layer is using telephone wires or wireless transmission. And I didn't have to change my e-mail software when the telephone company installed a different kind of line in my house last year.

The protocols to which this and other layers conform when carrying out their processes are like a black box to the next-door layers with which they communicate.

The data link layer

Physical channels alone are not enough for communication. The physical layer transmits data, in the form of digital bits, without any regard to their overall meaning or structure. The data link layer has the job of creating and recognizing the beginning and end of any whole group, or frame, of data that has an overall meaning. This is done by attaching special bit patterns to the beginning and end of the frame.

There is also a need for error detection and correction. If the frame boundary bit patterns occur accidentally in the data, the data layer must be able to stop these patterns being incorrectly taken to be frame boundaries.

The network layer

The layers considered so far could equally apply to single-channel communication between one sender and one receiver. As we stated above, a network contributes problems associated with having many possible senders and receivers and more than one *route* through the network.

In particular, the network layer uses:

- *Routing algorithms*, which calculate the route that data should best take through the network.
- *Congestion control*, which prevents packets of data getting in each other's way and blocking the system.
- *Address reconciliation*, which covers problems that can arise when a packet has to travel from one network to another. If the protocols differ, so that the addressing used by the second network is different from the first, the network layer needs to overcome such problems and enable heterogeneous networks to be interconnected.
- *Accounting*, which enables different owners of different parts of the network to toll or charge data passing over their section.

The transport layer

Having said that there are problems associated with having many possible senders and receivers and more than one route through the network, it is more important to see these network properties as *advantages*. The transport layer seeks to exploit these.

Thus there can be more than one way through a network, from a particular source to a particular destination. When a connexion requires a high throughput, the transport layer might create multiple network connections, dividing the data among the network connexions to improve the throughput.

The complexity of a network can also enable multiple connexions entering and leaving each host.

Box 5.3

MIME: Multipurpose Internet Mail Extensions

When e-mail began on ARPANET, the ancestor of the Internet, e-mail was confined to text encoded using the ASCII *symbol set*. This effectively meant that the only symbols that could be in an e-mail were what was on a 'qwerty' keyboard. Furthermore, the *language* used in messages was US English.

Now that e-mail is global, neither that symbol set nor that language are necessarily shared. Messages are now sent and received in:

- languages with accents, like French or Turkish;
- alphabets that don't use the Latin script, like Arabic or Russian;

- languages without alphabets, like Chinese;
- non-text format, like audio or video.

MIME (Multipurpose Internet Mail Extensions) is a convention that extends the old ASCII-based RFC 822 format rather than totally replacing it. It introduces encoding rules for non-ASCII messages so that they can be added to the message body. By not deviating from the old RFC 822, MIME messages can be sent using the existing mail programs and protocols.

The application layer

The application layer is probably the one we are most aware of as business users. The applications referred to include:

- electronic mail
- Usenet news
- the World Wide Web
- multimedia.

This layer is also concerned with managing network security and the domain name system.

Much of this is familiar to Internet users, but from an information systems viewpoint there are two significant features and developments that we need to watch:

- ubiquitous software
- multimedia.

We shall look further at these in the next section.

Box 5.4

Thus links with Nokia to deliver WAP services

Thus plc today announces that it is to provide mobile access to web-based services using Wireless Application Protocol (WAP), in a technology link-up with Nokia.

Two out of five people in the UK own a mobile phone and it is widely recognized that WAP offers an easily accessible platform to open up web-based services to this large and growing market.

Using equipment supplied by Nokia, Thus is developing WAP services both for existing customers of its Demon Internet service provider business as well as for wider application to the corporate and SME business market. It is expected that the WAP services will be available, initially to Demon customers, by the summer.

Demon customers will be able to read and reply to e-mail and access WAP-enabled content from their mobile phones. In addition, Demon will enable corporate customers to host their corporate intranet sites on its servers, allowing their employees to gain access to their corporate intranets from their WAP enabled mobile phones. Early applications for business customers include providing employees mobile access to company news, employee contact directories and business critical information.

Wireless Application Protocol is an open global standard for accessing information over a mobile phone or other wireless network.

In the same way as a modem dials an Internet Service Provider to access the Net, a WAP enabled phone will dial a WAP gateway service. This allows the user to access content and send e-mail from their handset. WAP-based technology enables the design of advanced, interactive and real-time mobile services, such as mobile banking or Internet-based news services, which can be used in digital mobile phones or other mobile devices

Source: Demon press release, 2 March 2000

Comment

This is just one example of the next major development in information and communications technology systems. The potential ubiquity of communication systems, when neither sender, receiver nor network channel is fixed, means that networks take one further step away from the located models of communication. When the Demon press release talks of such applica- *tions as mobile banking, it is just scratching the surface. We are moving towards the potential for any kind of information anywhere. As far as* management *information is concerned, this implies that* management itself *has the potential to break away from being something that is done in a particular office or in any particular place at all.*

5.3.4 **New views of communication**

Ubiquitous software

By *ubiquitous* software I mean software that is not fixed to one computer and can operate anywhere on a network. Historically, software has been something that is loaded on to a computer, where it enables that particular machine to implement what the software is intended to do. The advent of programming languages like *Java* has removed the simple rigid link between the computer hardware and the software that it uses. When Java is used on the Web, for example, a browser can download a piece of application software (an 'applet') to the client machine, where it can be used to carry out the application.

Thus if a purchaser wants to order a product from a supplier, they can click on the appropriate link on the supplier's web page, and a form will appear on the purchaser's screen. Also, unseen to the purchaser, software will be downloaded to automate and support the form-filling process. When the form is completed, the information it contains will wing its way to the supplier's order-processing system. There is no reason this process shouldn't be automated further. The supplier's applet could be authorized to access the purchaser's computerized stock and payment systems and do the whole thing without human intervention.

The potential for software to carry out an application anywhere on a network opens up new flexibility in the way business information systems can work. Instead of every organization having to have all the applications software it might ever need stored on its system, applications could be accessed and used from the Internet when needed. Essentially, the potential power of an information system would be the power of the Internet itself. Even if only part of this potential could be realized, it would still be much greater than any one organizational system could hope to achieve.

This kind of mobility of software breaks down concepts of communication based on concrete, physical views of its structure and processes. Instead of information being processed in one fixed place, communicated to another fixed place and then processed again, the fixed link between place and processing has gone. Words like 'on' my computer or 'on' the Internet are concepts rather than statements about location. If I access a website and it downloads an applet that enables me to play a piece of music stored on a machine in Moscow, 'where' is the music? 'On' the Web? 'On' my machine? 'In' Moscow? 'In' my head?

Multimedia

This last example leads to the second main area of potential development in information systems. We emphasized earlier in this chapter that information is a *rich* concept that can involve all the senses. The fact that in the past information and communications technology confined its attention to words and numbers was a technological rather than an unchangeable restriction. New forms of information and communications technology now enable *multimedia* communication.

The advent of MPEG (Motion Picture Experts Group) standards for compressing images and sound files enables transmission of videos over the Internet while maintaining their quality. It may not seem obvious that we would want to go further and incorporate other senses like touch. But consider business needs like education and training: having an actual *feel* for pressures and movements is an important part of the use of simulators, for example. Surgeons, pilots and many other professions already use them. The combining of virtual reality with Internet communication has enormous potential: learn to do an operation anywhere in the world? Technician in Surrey repairs oil rig in Siberia?

If there was one area where I would emphasize the importance of concepts and systems thinking as a tool for understanding, it would be networks and communications.

Key words

Boolean variable	Integer variable	Probability density
Channel	Interpretation	Receiver
Communication	Kind of hierarchy	Shared rules for symbol use
Continuous variable	Measure of dispersion	Shared symbol set
Decoder	Messenger	TCP/IP
Discrete variable	Negentropy	Uncertainty principle
Encoder	Noise	Understanding
Entropy	Originator	Variance
Environmental disturbance	OSI reference model	
Fuzzy	Part of hierarchy	

Seminar agendas, exam topics and project/dissertation subjects

1 When discussing how measurement or observation disturbs the object of attention, as in Section 4.1, we said, 'Doing something when you are watched is not the same as doing it privately, and if someone is recording the results of their observation, our behaviour is likely to be even more distorted.' Identify a piece of published management research that has relied on the observation of human beings. Is it invalidated by the principle we have just stated?

2 Take a TV advert, a political web page or a newspaper leader as a subject. Try analysing it for hyperbole, question begging, special pleading, false objectivity and false concatenation.

3 Have you followed a course in statistics or quantitative methods as part of your management studies? Revisit your notes and other material. Can you identify issues of hard and soft complexity in the areas you studied?

4 The next time you come across a widely publicized report in the news media, examine the role of descriptive and inferential statistics in the report. How was the data selected?

5 Research the history of the OSI reference model for network communication. Has it been a failure?

6 Prepare an argued case in favour of the destruction of the Internet.

7 Compare what has been said about communication in this chapter with your coverage of the same topic in your HRM studies.

Feedback on review questions

RQ 5.1 A good example of where management would want to avoid such richness is in statistical surveys like opinion polls or market research. By deliberately narrowing down questions and focusing answers on specific choices, pollsters hope to eliminate much potential ambiguity in their results. So instead of asking a question like 'What do you think about global warming?' and videoing the subsequent rambling monologue, the question might be 'Which of the following best expresses your view about global warming: "I am very concerned", "I am slightly concerned"?' and the answer recorded by an interviewer using a standard form.

It is important to note that a *reduction* of the richness of information is aimed for when management has clear ideas about its goals and the nature of the problem. When management is trying to sort out what the possible problems are and what its goals might be, a richer and more open use of media may be better. See the discussions of *rich* pictures in Chapter 9.

RQ 5.2 It looks like the Vikings might have got in first with 'Greenland', if their aim was indeed to promote the place! I guess that 'time bomb' doesn't sound terribly neutral: is warming something that is going to suddenly explode, or will it be slow at first and then gather speed? 'Greenpeace' sounds more seductive than, say, the Society to Explain and Convince People about Complex Ecological Issues. 'Europe saves the world' doesn't sound too modest either. Meanwhile, we notice that computers that run man-made models full of man-made assumptions are 'sophisticated': ought we therefore to believe them?

RQ 5.3 It would depend on the question they were asked, but I would expect it to be some form of integer or discrete variable. If the question asked whether they thought it 'very important', 'important', 'not very important' or 'completely irrelevant', then we see four discrete possible values for a reply. If the survey asked for 'yes' or 'no' (which no good survey would), it would be zero–one. I think it very unlikely that interviewees would be asked to reply on a continuous scale from 0 to 10 that included the possibility of 5.288347.

RQ 5.4 See Section 4.2.3 and 'Trade-off and optimization'. Here the cost of control increases in terms of the frequency, effort, manpower or money put into it. The cost of error decreases in relation to the same. The optimum cost will be the minimum of the combination of the two.

References/bibliography

Johnson, R.A. and Wichern, D.W. (1996). *Business Statistics: Decision Making with Data*. Wiley, New York.

Kosko, B. (1993). *Fuzzy Thinking*. Flamingo, London.

Shannon, C.E. (1963). *The Mathematical Theory of Communication*. University of Illinois.

Tanenbaum, A.S. (1996). *Computer Networks*. Prentice-Hall, Upper Saddle River, NJ.

CHAPTER 6

Modelling and managing data

Changes at Norris Trainers

What happened

Friday 13 August turned out to be unluckier for some than for others at Norris Trainers, the big sports equipment retailers.

It was also a bad day for PQ Plastics. It had been a supplier to Norris Trainers for many years, but its recent quality and delivery performance had become so bad that Norris's chief purchasing manager Keith Patel persuaded his directors that the PQ Plastics contract should not be renewed. PQ Plastics was replaced by NM Moulders. This led to changes in the sports shoe range that Norris offered to its customers, but products manufactured by PQ Plastics were replaced, where possible, by the nearest NM Moulders equivalent.

Friday 13 August was a day of friction between the finance section and computer services. A young financial graduate trainee called John MacLeod tried to be innovative at a routine computer users' meeting by suggesting that that the recording of sales figures and amending of stock level records should only need one entry into the computer system. At present, when any item was sold at a retail outlet it was recorded as a sale on the sales file and the stock file was separately amended with a copy of the same figure. Computer manager Guy Henessy said he already realized this, but the present system could not accommodate the suggestion in a practical and economic way; it could only be achieved by writing special software. Since this was not the first time that Guy Henessy had killed off one of John's ideas, John lost his temper and made sarcastic comments about 'dinosaur systems'. For him, it was not a very constructive end to the week.

For someone else in the finance section, however, it was a lucky day. Jane Isherwood was on leave getting married. She and her husband moved into a new house, and she took on her husband's surname to become Jane Berlin.

For sometime after Friday 13 August Keith Patel found that changing from PQ Plastics to NM Moulders created a lot of work for the computer and clerical staff updating important computer files. It wasn't just a question of modifying one computer file by replacing the name and details of PQ Plastics with those of NM

Moulders. Details of PQ Plastics appeared on three separate files and each of these had to be modified, often with the same details. PQ Plastics appeared on a file used by purchasing to identify which suppliers could supply what kind of product together with a quality rating of past performance. It also appeared on an accounts file that was used to ensure correct payment for goods supplied. Finally, the stock file had to have the new NM Moulders products added to it. Those products previously supplied by PQ Plastics were left on file until stocks ran out. Since the stock file identified the supplier of each item, a special new file was created to show which NM Moulders products could act as substitutes for the old PQ Plastics ones.

Guy Henessy did his best to accommodate the changes brought about by Keith Patel's decision on PQ Plastics, but there were problems. Since many of the details of NM Moulders' products appeared on more than one file, there were errors and inconsistencies in the records of such items as product code numbers, product descriptions and prices. These errors and inconsistencies were either a result of mistakes made in the original data entry, or failure to update all three files at the same time when changes were made. Guy Henessy's problems were not helped when John MacLeod pointed out to Keith Patel that this wasn't the only example of how the appearance of items in more than one file caused problems.

Jane Isherwood found that her next salary was paid correctly into her bank account in her new name of Jane Berlin. Unfortunately, her change of name was not picked up in time by personnel to appear in the new internal phone book. The phone book was produced every two months by a section of the personnel department that printed out names from a personnel records file that was separate from the payroll file. Both files contained personal details like name, age and address, but the personnel records file kept details of employees' careers and their qualifications, while the payroll file covered payment and tax. Jane remembered to inform payroll of her new situation because she was anxious to be taxed and paid correctly, but she did not officially inform personnel until later. In the following two months Jane had to put up with various irritations arising from having different surnames and different addresses, until both files and the new phone book were updated and consistent with each other.

The issues raised

Like in all of the lead-in cases, the selection of events described ranges from very public events, like the strategic commercial deal, to individual events like a change in one person's private life, yet each event raises the same issues at its own level of importance.

The big-bust up with PQ Plastics and Jane Isherwood's marriage were both inputs from Norris Trainers' environment that disturbed its operations and required changes in the way it would have to manage those operations in the future. As we saw in Chapter 4, an essential component of any management system is the hierarchy of goal setting and goal seeking within the control system. Within such a control system, an essential component is the information system, whose job is to provide the information that enables the control system to work. We also saw that the information used by any control system is concerned with:

- goal setting
- goal seeking
- the environment.

The changes resulting from the PQ Plastics affair and Jane Isherwood's marriage involved all three types of information.

Goal-setting information had to come from the wider system to those subsystems at Norris's concerned with purchasing, accounting and stock control. The information defined the new range of products to be bought, stocked and sold. It gave quantitative details on pricing, costs, desired stock levels and all other details defining what the various processes controlled by the various subsystems were trying to achieve.

When Keith Patel and his clerical staff carried out the various tasks needed to update the computer files, they were implementing the changes in those goals that were recorded on the computerized information system.

When Jane Isherwood got her personal and tax details changed on the payroll file, she was modifying the goals of that particular process by redefining what name, tax, bank account number etc.

Goal-seeking information, which helps to control the behaviour of processes such as purchasing, accounting and stock control at Norris's, continued to be used in controlling processes aimed at the new goals as it had for the old ones. One example was that purchasing continued to record such details as quantities bought and prices paid to NM Moulders, as it had done previously for PQ Plastics when it was a supplier.

Similarly, payroll continued to collect the necessary information on hours worked or expenses incurred in order to calculate pay and tax for the new Jane Berlin in the same way as it had for the former Jane Isherwood.

An example of information that enables the control system to identify, anticipate and allow for the effects of disturbances from its *environment* was that recorded on the quality and delivery performance of PQ Plastics. It not only enabled Keith Patel to pick up individual lapses by PQ Plastics, it also gave him a more strategic picture that justified choosing a replacement supplier with anticipated long-term benefits.

Personnel and payroll both had the means of reacting to disturbances from the environment such as changes in personnel employed, names and addresses, hours worked, tax coding etc., but the method of gathering the information and updating records was not always reliable, as Jane found out.

Our information and control systems view of the situation at Norris Trainers included four issues that frequently arise when we considered the role of information as a component of the business control system:

1 How can information be described, defined or explained in terms of the data from which it is constructed?
2 How can information be recorded?
3 How can information be manipulated or processed?
4 How can possible answers to issues 1–4 be co-ordinated into a successful overall approach to the description, recording and manipulation of information?

Opportunities for learning

To understand issue 1, we should recall the systems concepts of structure and emergent property covered in Chapter 3 and then used to help our understanding of the relationship between information and data. We saw that information could be regarded as a property that emerged from the whole when component elements of data were brought together in a particular relationship or structure. If we take this view of information, one way in which we can consider how it could be described, defined or explained in terms of the data from which it is constructed would be to consider:

- What are the elements of data that go to make up the information as a whole?
- What is the structural relationship between these elements of data?

An example of data elements from the Norris case might come from quoting the phrase 'the quality and delivery performance of PQ Plastics'. When Norris's needed some way of assessing this, it had to decide what goes to make up 'quality' and 'delivery performance'. But 'quality' and 'delivery performance' would need in turn to be defined in terms of how many late deliveries, how many products with faults, which shoes were sent to the wrong place at the wrong time etc., etc. In other words data, in the form of quantitative figures or qualitative description, had to be assembled to make a whole like 'the quality and delivery performance of PQ Plastics'.

RQ 6.1	Can you suggest some examples of this issue for Jane Isherwood?

An example of a structural relationship from the Norris case might come from thinking about Jane Isherwood's salary. She was being paid an annual salary of £19 000. If we look at these figures as data, we have a 1, a 9, and three 0s. We could put these elements together as 120 different combinations:

£91 000

£90 100

£10 900

etc.

However I think we can see that the way they are put together, or the structure, can make a very big difference to what the whole combination of data means: £91 000 and £10 900 are made up of the same individual elements of data, but the information they transmit, in terms of 'Jane Isherwood's salary', is very different.

To understand how information can be recorded (issue 2), we need to recall the essential distinction between 'whats' and 'hows' that we introduced in Chapter 3 and go on repeating throughout this book. It may be that 'what' information Norris's management needs for its stock control will include details made up of data such as product code number, product description and price. Although these details will take on just one particular value for any product at a particular time, 'how' they are recorded may vary considerably. To form a stock record containing such details, they could be recorded by typing them on a card to be inserted into a box file, or they could be hand written on a paper sheet that goes into a ring binder. In the case of Norris's, they were in fact recorded as magnetic fields on computer storage.

Recognizing that the data making up particular information can be recorded on different media is only part of the 'how' issue. There is also the question of how it is actually recorded on the chosen medium itself. Given that we may be using a card index for our records, there is then the question of how the data making up the information is laid out on the card itself. We could arrange items like product code number, product description and price in many ways on the card, and we could use many different formats, typefaces and formats to do so. This may seem like getting down to trivial details that could easily be sorted out by someone interested in designing forms, but if we consider storage on magnetic media like computer disk, we shall see later in this chapter that the issue is important. Data on disks is not and cannot be recorded in the same arrangement as it would appear on a screen or a print-out. Far from being a problem, this actually enables computer-based information systems to be released from the constraints placed on the manipulation and processing of information by the old paper-based systems. We shall see more about this when we come to issue 3.

There was one other aspect to the 'how' issue that arose in the Norris case. The friction between John MacLeod and Guy Henessy, as well as Keith Patel's problems, stemmed from the fact that the same information was sometimes recorded more than once on the same medium. In Jane Isherwood's case it was recorded more than once and on two different media.

Hence issue 2 can be seen to arise in different ways:

- What medium (or media) should be used to record the data comprising the information we want to use?
- What physical arrangement, format or structure should be chosen?
- What duplication (if any) of recording should occur?

Whatever issues arise concerning the description or storage of data, we are only interested in the data in the first place because the right selection of data assembled in the right structure will provide the information needed to enable us to manage. This need to select, assemble and generally process brings us naturally to issue 3: how can information be manipulated or processed? In considering this issue we can take both information and data together. Whether we are considering the processing of elements of data like individual numbers or information like a complete personnel record, the principal questions as to how we manipulate or process are the same.

The replacement of PQ Plastics by NM Moulders as a major supplier meant replacing details of PQ Plastics' products with those of NM Moulders on three of the existing files. This involved various actions. For each of the new NM Moulders products the computer and clerical staff had to *create* new records. Once the old PQ Plastics range was finally cleared out, they would have to *drop* the old records. In the meantime, they had to alter the format of the existing records by adding new data showing which new products were the equivalents of the old ones. Once an equivalent product was found, it would be necessary to *select* its record from the file to find out details of its price, stock level etc. As further NM Moulders products were added to the range, it would be necessary to *insert* them in the file and to *delete* old ones. Where prices or stock levels changed it would be necessary to *update* the file entries.

This description covers just some of the actions that had to be carried out when processing data at Norris's, but they are good examples of the actions that are common to any information system, whether computerized or not. I haven't just put the words that describe these actions in *italics* to emphasize them: they are in fact a selection of commands from a widely used standard data definition, manipulation and control language called SQL. (Smart people pronounce SQL like the word 'sequel' to show they know something about its ancestry, but people like me seem to get by calling it 'ess kew ell' without too many problems.)

This consideration of issue 3 implies that we will need to look in more detail at the principles that enable us to make sense of how information can be manipulated or processed. That leaves us with the issue 4, which asks how possible answers to issues

1–3 can be co-ordinated in a successful overall approach to the description, recording and manipulation of information.

Issue 4 is illustrated by the argument between John MacLeod and Guy Henessy, where both of them realized that the recording of sales figures and amending of stock level records should only need one entry in the computer system. The issue is also illustrated by Keith Patel's experiences in having to modify three computer files, each involving the same information. What issue 4 shows is that even when we have decided on how information can be described, defined, recorded, manipulated and processed, we are left with problems that arise if it is stored in more than one place. When this happens we are likely to find:

- Processing becomes more complicated because we have to repeat the same or similar processes for each record of the same information.
- This complication of the processing gives extra opportunity for errors or inconsistencies to creep into the recorded information.
- Recording the same information more than once uses extra storage space.

When considering issue 3, we saw that a wide range of processes is likely to be carried out in practice by information systems. Some of these, such as updating data, are likely to occur very frequently. It make sense, therefore, to minimize unnecessary duplication or redundancy in recording information. Since this recorded information is made up of individual items of data, we shall need to consider how the recording of data can best be done to minimize unnecessary duplication. Putting this issue in the appropriate technical way, we need to consider how best to management our *database*.

Learning objectives

The learning objectives for this chapter are to:

1 Understand how the concepts of entity, attribute and relationship can be used to describe how data can model information.

2 Distinguish the main types of data models: hierarchical, network, relational, object-orientated and semantic.

3 Identify those parts of the theories of relational algebra and relational calculus that help to understand how data can be described and manipulated.

4 Understand the principles of managing data to meet the needs of an information system as implemented in the main features of a database and database management system (DBMS).

6.1 DATA ANALYSIS AND DATA MODELLING

6.1.1 The elements of data

We have already recalled the concept, established in Chapter 3, that information can be regarded as a property emerging from the whole when component elements of data are brought together in a particular relationship or structure. In this section, we will see just what these elements are and how we can describe their relationship.

A starting point for understanding the elements of data in these terms is the review of information we first carried out in Chapter 2. There we found that all the forms of information we considered as relevant to management are about something. Management uses information about customers, products, employees, items of equipment and many other things in order to set its goals and attempt to achieve them in the face of disturbances from the environment. Whatever this 'something' is, and which the information is 'about', we term an *entity*. If we consider the example of Carry-Out Cupboards, a cupboard, a customer, a supplier or a supplier's account would all be entities about which we would need information.

RQ 6.2 What is the relationship between the concept of an entity introduced here and the concept of an element used to describe the smallest component of a system in Chapter 3?

Entities may be of different types. A cupboard, for example, is a *concrete* entity: it is something we can see and touch. Figure 6.1 shows the details of some cupboards sold by Carry-Out Cupboards, with various characteristics like surface finish or height. A supplier's account, however, is an *abstract* concept. When we talk about the characteristics of a supplier's account we would be concerned with quantities of items supplied, dates or amounts of money. Entities are not always inanimate things, whether concrete or abstract: we often need to have information about people such as employees. Nor need entities be components of the system of interest: the suppliers of Carry-Out Cupboards may be outside the Carry-Out Cupboards system, but they are part of its *environment*, about which we need to have information.

STYLE	SIZE	SURFACE FINISH	HEIGHT	FITTINGS	PRICE £	SITING	STOCK CLASS
Calabria	3S	Veneer	3480	Triple/A/S	215.00	Lounge	LG
Calabria	3S	Antique	3480	Triple/A/S	205.00	Diner	DN
•	•	•	•	•	•	•	•
•	•	•	•	•	•	•	•
Classic	1S	Fabric	870	Single/S/S	100.00	Diner	DN
•	•	•	•	•	•	•	•
•	•	•	•	•	•	•	•
Country	1H	Floral	870	Single/N/H	90.00	Diner	DN

Figure 6.1 Details of some cupboards sold by Carry-Out Cupboards
The whole of this 'C' range (Calabria, Classic, etc.) is shown in Figure 6.14.

Whatever the different types of the entities we decide are of interest to us, the reason for our interest is the same. The entities are considered to be relevant because certain information about them is also relevant: we need it to define goals, control behaviour and cope with environmental disturbances to the system. The information we need to have about an entity we call its *attributes*. Thus we need to have information about the attributes of surface finish and height for a cupboard to decide whether it is suitable for a particular market, or we might need to know its surface finish and height in order to check that the customer receives the correct product.

Just as entities may be concrete or abstract, so attributes may be either or both. The cupboards in Figure 6.1 have concrete attributes like surface finish or height, but they also have abstract attributes like price or stock class.

Having identified the concepts of entity and attribute, we then need to make a further distinction. Entities and attributes can be regarded as sets made up of particular *instances* and *values*. Thus Figure 6.1 shows *n* different individual *instances* of the *entity* 'Cupboard'. Similarly, for a particular cupboard in Figure 6.1 the *attribute* 'surface finish' may take on a particular *value* like 'Floral' or 'Veneer'.

Entities do not merely exist as a collection of instances within a particular system. If they are *components* of a system, we would expect them to be *connected* together either physically or logically, as we saw in Chapter 3. In the Carry-Out Cupboards case, we would expect each instance of the entity 'supplier' to be associated with the occurrence of another entity called 'account'. We therefore see a *relationship* between the two entities. The particular form of this relationship we call its *degree*, depending on the number of entities involved. Since it would be unusual in normal practice for a supplier to have more than one account, or still to be a supplier without having an account at all, we describe the relationship as having a *degree* of *one-to-one* (or 1:1), since one supplier goes with one account and vice versa.

Relationships may be to other degrees. Thus the relationship between 'Central Assembly and Packing' and 'Retail Outlet' is *one-to-many* (1:*n*), since one central assembly and packing facility at Carry-Out Cupboards supplies many retail outlets. For the entities 'Cupboard' and 'Part', however, the relationship is *many-to-many* (*m:n*), since a particular cupboard may contain more than one kind of part, and one particular part, may go into more than one kind of cupboard.

Besides having degrees, relationships may be compulsory (sometimes called *mandatory*) or *optional*. Thus the relationship between supplier and account is compulsory because it is not possible to be a supplier without having an account. The relationship between 'employee' and 'retail outlet' would be optional, however, because not all the employees of Carry-Out Cupboards work in the retail outlets.

Like other kinds of systemic relationships, relationships between entities are sometimes better shown using a diagram (see Chapter 3). Figure 6.2 shows some common conventions used for diagramming data relationships, whether entity relationships (ER) or entity attribute relationships (EAR). Figure 6.2 also shows examples of these conventions to describe the assembly and packing operations at Carry-Out Cupboards.

Box 6.1

Labour signs database deal with IBM and Oracle

David Wighton

All Labour party constituencies are to be linked to a national campaigns database under a £1m deal signed with International Business Machines and Oracle, the computer software and services companies.

The new system will allow Labour headquarters to see trends in any street in the country allowing campaign strategists to target political messages at certain groups and maximize turnout. Labour claims the move will put the party at least 10 years ahead of the Conservatives in terms of campaign technology.

'This will take us up to the level of the best direct marketing firms. It is the biggest investment we have ever made, and the first strategic partnership with business for the Labour party,' an official said.

Labour has already announced separate plans to save £800 000 a year by contracting out its membership system to a private company.

A study by KPMG, the management consultants, said the improvements the party wants to make to its membership services would increase its spending from £1m to £1.8m a year, but that a specialist private company could provide them for little extra cost. The party decided last month to put the contract out to tender.

Source: Financial Times, 21 June 1999. Reprinted with permission.

Comment

Our study of the construction of information in Chapter 5 should tell us that the phrase 'The new system will allow' was well chosen by David Wighton. There are two reasons for this:

1 The database itself will only contain data attributes of voters that 'Labour headquarters' decide are important. There remains the dilemma that attributes are not worth putting on the database unless they are significant, and it may not be obvious until they are put on the database. Good old political instinct will still be needed.

2 To 'see trends in any street' means deciding what a trend is. As we saw in Chapter 5, a trend is about inferential statistics, not an absolute to be defined by mathematics.

Labour will do well to integrate this information technology support for its political management, but it enhances existing components of political decision making: it does not replace any of them. Should Labour make the mistake of thinking otherwise, then watch this space. Some old-fashioned high-variety human systems could catch this variety reducer out.

6.1.2 Data models

We covered the subject of models and modelling in Chapter 3. In relation to *data modelling*, it will be sufficient to recall that a model is a way of representing and describing a view of something. In this case that 'something' is the whole collection of data that we need as the potential components we bring together to form information. We call this 'collection of data' the *database*, and understanding the way a database can be described, defined or manipulated is only possible if we first understand more about the modelling of data itself.

It is also important to note that we described a model as 'a view of something' rather than 'the view', because the way we look at data will depend on who we are and what we want to use it for.

If we consider the concepts of *entity*, *attribute* and *relationship* that we have just covered, they were essentially *high level* and *abstract*. We used them to describe the data in *logical* terms. This kind of analysis and description is about what entities have what relationship with what other entities, and what attributes are associated with them. I don't think I need to go on putting the word 'what' in italics any more to make the point that a logical view of data is about 'whats', and that this needs to be

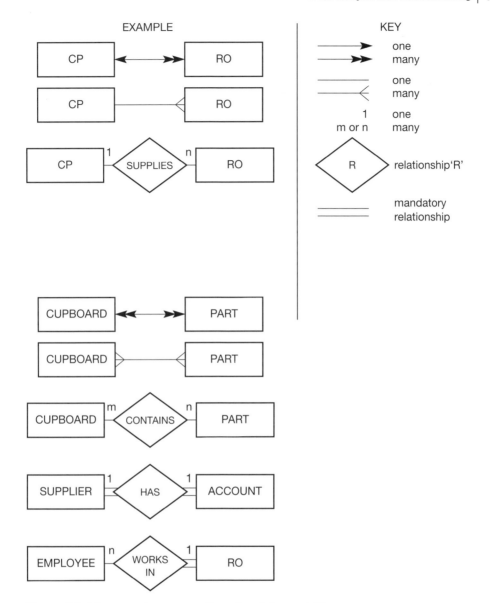

Figure 6.2 Diagramming conventions for data modelling
As with other diagramming conventions, it is unlikely that one convention becomes a universal standard. What is important is to recognize the essentials that any convention must cover. Here, the bare minimum is a way of representing *entities* and the *relationships* between them.

distinguished from the physical view of how the data is recorded, accessed or transmitted. When we described the relationship between supplier and account in the previous section, we said nothing about whether this account was recorded on computer disk, printed out as a document or recorded on a card file. Still less did we get involved in the details of how the data would be physically arranged on the disk, accessed by the software or laid out on the document.

We can therefore make a distinction between *high-level*, *conceptual* or *logical* models that describe what view a user may have of the data, and *low-level*, *physical* models that describe how the data is recorded, accessed or transmitted as a result of *implementation* by a computer specialist.

This reference to implementation reveals the need for a third type of model that can make the link between a very abstract, logical view of the data and the way in which it is physically recorded. Our high-level view of the data may show that there is a one-to-many relationship between the entities retail outlet and employee at Carry-Out Cupboards. It may also show a one-to-many relationship between central assembly and packing and the retail outlets. What this high-level view does not give us, however, is some logical structure or descriptive *schema* to direct us in the ordering and arranging of this data when we come to record it physically. Thus there is nothing in the ER or EAR model of Carry-Out Cupboards that tells us whether we should keep individual *records* of retail outlets with lists of employees on them, or whether we should have separate records for employees with their attributes.

The third type of model that enables us to translate the high-level concepts of the ER or EAR model into a logical description of how the data will be represented we might call an *implementation* model. We shall consider some examples in the following sections, and look more closely at some of the terms like record and schema that we introduced in this section to see how they relate to the different views of data given by the models.

6.1.3 The hierarchical data model

The use of the word *hierarchy* to describe this data model is a good example of the danger we noted in Chapter 3 of a term having different meanings according to where it is used. It may have several meanings in the systems context, as well as in everyday life. In Chapter 3 we discussed two meanings of the term hierarchy, before favouring its use to describe the concept of *levels of aggregation* within a system, rather than the popular everyday meaning associated with the concept of *levels of command*. In Chapter 5 we then distinguished *part of* and *type of* hierarchies.

The term *hierarchical data model* uses the description 'hierarchical' to describe a model as having a tree structure. If we consider how a tree is made up, we can see two examples of the same structure. One trunk or base leads to many branches and each one branch leads to many twigs. Below ground, one base sends out many roots and each one root has many smaller ones leading from it.

RQ 6.3   What kind of hierarchy is that?

In our tree example, the words 'one . . . many' occur several times, and this is one of the essentials of the *hierarchical* or *tree* data model. In such a model the entities are all connected in terms of one-to-one or one-to-many, there are no many-to-many relationships. Figure 6.3 shows the essentials. The tree is made up of a hierarchy of elements called nodes, with a single topmost node called the *root*. (Yes, it does seem odd that the root is at the top of the tree!) All the nodes except the root have a node above them which is called a *parent*, and each parent may have nodes immediately below it called a *child*. (Parents without children are sometimes called leaves because they are correspondingly at the very end of branches.) The other important feature of this data model is that *a child may only have one parent*.

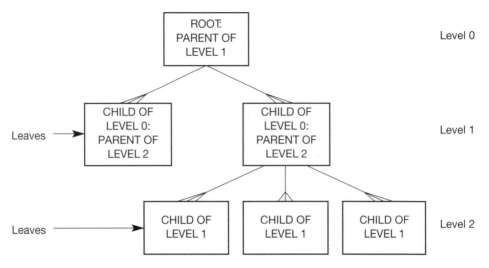

Figure 6.3 The diagramming and labelling conventions for a hierarchical or tree data model
An important feature of this data model is that a child may only have one parent.

These features appear to make this form of data model contradict real life. As we have seen above, many-to-many relationships are frequently found in practice, and child entities may resemble real-life children by having more than one parent. So how does the model cope? We will use Figures 6.4 and 6.5(a) and 6.5(b) as examples. They show some of the entity relationships for the central assembly and packing facility (CP) of Carry-Out Cupboards. In this example, the entity 'operation' has two parents: 'operator' and 'production facility'.

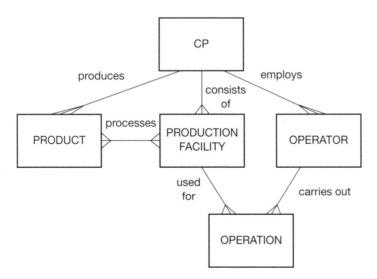

Figure 6.4 Some of the entity relationships for the central assembly and packing facility (CP) of Carry-Out Cupboards
In this example the entity 'operation' has two parents, and there is also a many-to-many relationship between 'product' and 'production facility'. (Appendix 1 explains the function of the CP within Carry-Out Cupboards.)

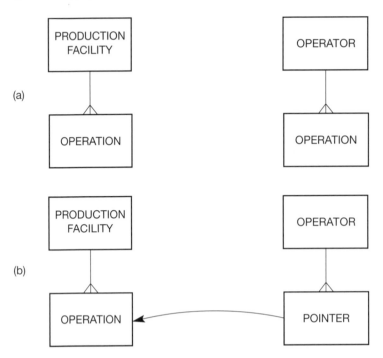

Figure 6.5 Resolving the phenomenon of two parents in a hierarchical model
This can be done in two ways: either by the use replication, Figure 6.5(a), or by the use of a pointer, Figure 6.5(b).

The phenomenon of two parents can be represented in two ways: either by the use of *replication*, Figure 6.5(a), or by the use of a *pointer*, Figure 6.5(b). Replication is essentially solving the problem by separating the model into disjointed components. This can hardly claim to be a systemic approach, since connexion is an important property of any system. The use of pointers is better from a systemic viewpoint because it retains the important quality of connexion, but it does introduce a soft issue as to which entity is seen as the source and which is the destination of this connecting pointer; terms like *source* and *destination* carry a very strong *world view* with them.

The use of a pointer would not solve the problem of many-to-many relationships like that between 'product' and 'production facility' in Figure 6.4; since each production facility would need to be connected to each product and vice versa. A solution to the problem is available if we look again at the many-to-many relationship. It is possible to see the relationship itself as an entity, which may or may not have a corresponding physical equivalent in real life. What connects the various products with the various production facilities is their coming together when any product is processed by a particular production facility. We could call this coming together a *production order* or *job*. We could then use this new concept or logical entity to modify the model as in Figure 6.6, and replace the many-to-many relationship with two one-to-many relationships. This modification still leaves us with two parents, but we have already seen how a pointer can deal with this. (It is worth noting that the new conceptual or logical entity production order or job is also one that would have a physical representation as a document or screen in the physical system of Carry-Out Cupboards; see Chapter 7.)

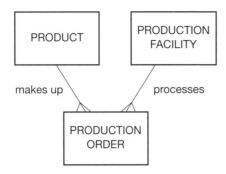

Figure 6.6 Resolving a many-to-many relationship with two one-to-many relationships
Note that this example of modification still leaves us with a two-parent relationship. This could be resolved by the use of a pointer, as in Figure 6.5(b).

A hierarchical model constructed in the way described so far will show the logical or conceptual relationships between entities. Once these have been defined, an *implementation* model can be used to develop a description of the *database* to be used by the information system. The basis of this implementation model will be a *hierarchical schema*. Such a schema uses the logic of the hierarchical model as its basis and then describes how the data is organized within this structure. Figure 6.7 shows the basic principles and a simple example of this.

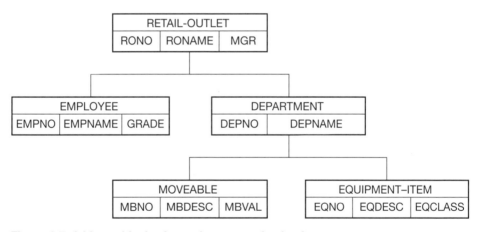

Figure 6.7 A hierarchical schema for a part of a database
Such a schema uses the logic of the hierarchical model as its basis and then describes how the data is organized within this structure.

The smallest element in the schema is a *field*. This represents the smallest unit of data that can be referenced separately and is used to hold the value of a single *attribute* found in the EAR model. All of the fields referring to a single *entity* are grouped together to form a segment. One of the fields within a segment, called the *sequence field*, is used for ordering segments of a given kind.

Each *segment* therefore consists of *fields* holding the *values* of the *attributes* of one of the *entities* that forms a node in the hierarchical model. The tree structure of the hierarchical model is then reflected by the definition of *logical database* records, which consist of a named hierarchies of related segments. The whole logical database is made up of these logical database records.

The implementation of the hierarchical data model is carried out with the use of *data definition* and *data manipulation* languages, which define the features of the schema (Figure 6.8) and enable access to the data stored in the hierarchical database. A major example of such a language is DL/I, which is used by IBM's so-called Information Management System (IMS). This had its origins over 30 years ago. I use the phrase 'so-called' about it here because I think the whole point of what we have established in Chapter 3 makes a management information system much more than software or a computer system. I am not trying to denigrate this application of the model, however. I think that Bowers (1988) expresses the practical history very well when he explains that 'hierarchic structures are intrinsically user-oriented: organizations are arranged in hierarchies, filing cabinets are arranged hierarchically; even books are essentially hierarchic. It has long been known that cross-references are difficult to deal with – indeed, it is questionable whether people can maintain adequate mental representations of information plexes other than hierarchies.' The reference to 'plexes' leads into the next model.

```
SCHEMA NAME = CARRY-OUT-CUPBOARDS

HIERARCHIES = HIERARCHY1, HIERARCHY2, HIERARCHY3

RECORD
        NAME = RETAIL-OUTLET
        TYPE = ROOT OF HIERARCHY2
        DATA ITEMS=
                RONO        INTEGER
                RONAME      CHARACTER 15
                MGR         CHARACTER 30
        KEY = RONO

RECORD
        NAME = DEPARTMENT
        PARENT = RETAIL-OUTLET
        CHILD NUMBER = 2
        DATA ITEMS =       INTEGER
                DEPNO       CHARACTER 25
                DEPNAME
        KEY = DEPNO
```

Figure 6.8 Hierarchical Data Definition Language
This shows how some of the features of the schema of Figure 6.7 might be defined using such a language. For more detail, try Elmasri and Navathe (1989).

6.1.4 **The network or plex data model**

One of the problems we found with the hierarchical model was that relationships were ambiguous where a child had more than one parent. The arbitrary choice of parent and the use of a pointer rather put us in the position of a divorce court judge deciding who should have custody of the child and who would be allowed access rights. To pursue that analogy further, as with human parent–child relationships, it is not always obvious in a database which way the allocation should be made. It might therefore be sensible, to accept the concept of multiple parents and consider a data model that recognizes this directly: a network or plex data model.

The essential concept behind the network is that of a set. A set consists of two entity types between which there is a one-to-many relationship. The entities at either end of this relationship are referred to as the *owner* and the *member* respectively. Since a data model is likely to represent more than a single relationship between two entities, models are usually created by identifying set types and building them up into a model. The conceptual link that allows this building up is that *entities may belong to more than one set type as owners or members*. Figure 6.9 shows part of the central assembly and packing facility example of Figure 6.4 interpreted in this way.

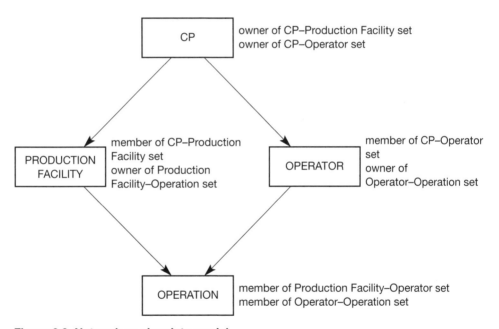

Figure 6.9 Network or plex data model
A network version of the central assembly and packing facility example of Figure 6.4.

In describing this model we need to distinguish the set type from a particular *instance*. Thus in the example of Figure 6.9, there will be more than one instance of the set type operator–operation. There is more than one operator at the central assembly and packing facility, and each of these might carry out more than one operation, so we would expect many separate instances of an operator carrying out an operation.

The network model still retains the problem of many-to-many relationships that we found with the hierarchical model, but this can be resolved in a similar way to before.

Figure 6.10 shows the network equivalent of Figure 6.6, where the introduction of the entity production order enabled us to resolve the many-to-many relationship into two one-to-many relationships in terms of a network model.

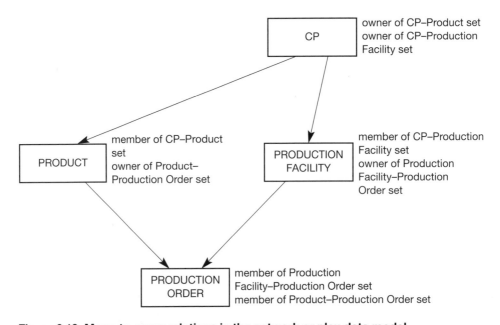

Figure 6.10 Many-to-many relations in the network or plex data model
This is the network equivalent of Figure 6.7, where the introduction of the entity 'Production Order' enabled the resolution of a many-to-many relationship.

Like the hierarchical model, the *implementation* of the network model brings its own terminology. The smallest element is a *data item*. This represents the smallest unit of data that can be referenced separately and is used to hold the value of a single *attribute* found in the EAR model. Unlike the hierarchical model, however, the network model allows for multiple values of an attribute. If these are all of the same type, e.g. different values for the attribute 'orderno' for the entity 'production order' in Figure 6.11, then the data items can be grouped together as a *vector*. If the data items are all of different types, e.g. the different types of values for the attributes 'opno' and 'optype' of the same entity, then the data items are defined as a *repeating group*.

All of the data items referring to a single entity are brought together as a *record*, which can therefore be a collection of *data items, vectors* or *repeating groups* in various combinations. A data item within a record used for ordering or selecting records is called a *key*. A set is then a named collection of records forming a two-level hierarchy, as explained above, with one record type defined as the *owner* and one or more record types defined as the *members*. Figure 6.11 gives an example of a network database schema from our central assembly and packing facility example.

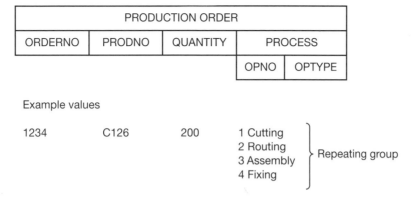

Figure 6.11 A network database schema
Again based on the central assembly and packing facility example. 'Grouting' is the operation that forms the channels in the chipboard sheet material used to fit sheets together.

RQ 6.4 What kind of hierarchy is referred to here?

The network model described in these terms is sometimes referred to as the CODA-SYL or CODASYL-DBTG model. As with the hierarchical model, the implementation of the network data model is carried out with the use of a data definition (DDL) and a data manipulation (DML) language. For most implementations of the CODASYL model the DML is hosted in a high-level language such as COBOL, so that accessing and processing the database are conveniently integrated with other programmed tasks. Figures 6.12 and 6.13 give examples of DDL and DML for a network schema.

```
SET NAME IS OPERATOR–OPERATION
    OWNER IS OPERATOR
        ORDER IS SORTED BY DEFINED KEYS
    MEMBER IS OPERATION
        KEY IS ASCENDING OPNO
```

Figure 6.12 Network Data Definition Language
This example refers to part of Figure 6.9.

```
OPEN: A file or set of records is opened, i.e. made
  available for an application program to use.
MODIFY: The values of specified data items of a specified
  record occurrence are replaced with values in the program
  work area.
DELETE: A specified record occurrence is removed
  from the database, and relationships involving it are deleted.
CLOSE: A file or set of records is closed, i.e. made
  unavailable to an application program.
```

Figure 6.13 Network Data Manipulation Language
These are just a selection of commands. This sample should be compared with Figure 6.22.

6.1.5 **The relational model**

Although the two models we have looked at so far have been widely and successfully implemented, they both have a potential weakness in relation to one of the issues we raised at the beginning of this chapter: change in the contents and use of the database. As in the Norris Trainers case, most databases don't stand still.

The kind of change we saw at Norris Trainers and are considering here isn't just that associated with first-order control like updating stock levels or customer accounts. It also involves higher-order control changes like adding new types of data and requiring new forms of output from new ways of processing the database.

The results of such changes in practice has been that databases tend to become bogged down and cumbersome. The number of logical linkages tends to grow every time a new application is added, because fresh ways of querying the database are required from an increasing range of data types. We often find in other applied fields of management or technology that once a particular approach to a problem becomes too complex, inflexible and costly to operate, new ways are found to get around the problem. So it was with databases: a new approach based on a *relational* model was proposed by Codd (1970) that overcame the limitations of using hierarchical or network structures. Understanding why an approach based on the relational model has an advantage over the others comes from noting a limitation that these previous approaches share. Both of them think in terms of an ultimately *implementable physical* structure, rather than concentrating specifically on the structure of the *data* represented. The relational model concentrates on the *logical* description of the data from the user's viewpoint and is not linked to any one particular *physical* representation. (There are many ways in which a relational database can be physically structured.)

The essence of the relational data model is the two-dimensional *flat table* or *flat file*. We can use Figure 6.14 as an example. It shows the selection of the details of cupboards from Figure 6.1. We recall that each of the columns of the table corresponds to an attribute of an entity, in this case a cupboard. All of the values in a particular row correspond to one particular instance of that entity, and all the instances go together to make up a whole concept or an *emergent property*, which in this case is the whole collection of products we call 'cupboards'. In the relational model such wholes are called relations, and in Figure 6.14 shows the particular *relation* we could call *cupboard*.

A database constructed from relations of this kind is called a *relational database*. Modelling a relational database requires no other device than the flat table itself. As we shall see later in this section, even complex relationships like many-to-many can be represented without resorting to pointers or other complicating devices. The attraction of the relational model is this simplicity and elegance, and I notice that the adage 'great engineering is simple engineering' has been rightly applied by Martin (1976) to the principles behind the relational model.

Given the central role of the relation, we need to understand the terminology used to describe its components and characteristics. If we call the whole of a flat table like Figure 6.14 a *relation*, the each of its rows is called a *tuple*. A tuple is described as an N-tuple according to the number, N, of attribute values represented. The tuples in Figure 6.14 are 8-tuples. It is important to note that a tuple is an *unordered* row of values rather than a structured record. This flexibility is important, because it indicates the potential that a relational database has for presenting data in different ways

STYLE	SIZE	SURFACE FINISH	HEIGHT	FITTINGS	PRICE £	SITING	STOCK CLASS
Calabria	3S	Veneer	3480	Triple/A/S	215.00	Lounge	LG
Calabria	3S	Antique	3480	Triple/A/S	205.00	Diner	DN
Calabria	2S	Veneer	1740	Double/A/S	185.00	Lounge	LG
Calabria	2S	Antique	1740	Double/A/S	150.00	Diner	DN
Classic	3S	Veneer	3480	Triple/S/S	200.00	Bedroom	BD
Classic	3S	Antique	3480	Triple/S/S	190.00	Lounge	LG
Classic	3S	Fabric	3480	Triple/S/S	180.00	Diner	DN
Classic	2S	Veneer	1740	Double/S/S	135.00	Bedroom	BD
Classic	2S	Antique	1740	Double/S/S	125.00	Lounge	LG
Classic	2S	Fabric	1740	Double/S/S	120.00	Diner	DN
Classic	1S	Fabric	870	Single/S/S	100.00	Diner	DN
Classic	1S	Floral	870	Single/S/S	80.00	Kitchen	KT
Classic	1H	Floral	870	Single/S/H	85.00	Kitchen	KT
Country	2S	Fabric	1740	Double/N/S	100.00	Kitchen	KT
Country	2S	Floral	1740	Double/N/S	100.00	Diner	DN
Country	1S	Fabric	870	Single/N/S	80.00	Kitchen	KT
Country	1S	Floral	870	Single/N/S	80.00	Diner	DN
Country	2H	Fabric	1740	Double/N/H	110.00	Kitchen	KT
Country	2H	Floral	1740	Double/N/H	110.00	Diner	DN
Country	1H	Fabric	870	Single/N/H	90.00	Kitchen	KT
Country	1H	Floral	870	Single/N/H	90.00	Diner	DN

Figure 6.14 The 'C' Range of Carry-Out Cupboards
The background to the principle of exploiting permutations of components to make a complete range of products can be understood in the context of the Carry-out Cupboards case of Appendix 1.

to accommodate the differing views and needs of various users. In our cupboard example, a customer might want to think about price and surface finish before considering the model, while a stock clerk might start by looking at the stock class. By not imposing a concept of the 'best' or 'correct' order on the components of the tuple, we make these differing views possible.

A particular column of the relation is called a *domain*. Note that this refers to the whole set of attribute values represented, and that we envisage the individual values in each of the tuples as being selected from this whole. A particular tuple can be regarded as a *mapping* between the domains from which the values are drawn.

One or more domains in a relation will be chosen because their individual values enable us to identify a particular tuple uniquely. What is chosen is called the key of the relation. We shall say more about this when we look further at the concept of *normalization* in the next section.

The use of conceptual wholes like relation, domain etc. is an essential characteristic of the relational model. As we shall see in Section 6.2, to regard the database in terms of sets and wholes enables the application of mathematically based, precise notations for describing relations and for performing operations on them.

The number of components in a relation is described in terms of its *degree*, representing the number of domains, and its *cardinality*, representing the number of tuples.

So does the relational model described above fulfil the objectives we have given it for dealing with problems like *'The number of logical linkages tends to grow every time a new application is added because fresh ways of querying the database are required from an increasing range of data types'*? I think the answer to this question is a clear 'no'. We know that the relational model gives us an open decision as to which domains we may include in a tuple according to our needs. If we return to our cupboard example of Figures 6.1 and 6.14, we saw that a customer might want price and surface finish but not technical details like stock class, while a stock clerk would want to identify a particular cupboard and know its stock class. Decisions like these affect what particular form a relation should take in terms of the number and values for these data items in the tuples. Without any consistent way of defining the possible form of the resulting flat tables, we could end up with one of two possible complications to the model that would make it unwieldy or messily complex. One complication comes from trying to see the database as one large flat table, the other comes from trying to see it as several smaller individual ones.

If we try to control the model by viewing all the attributes of all the entities as being in one flat table like Figure 6.14, we don't actually have one relation at all. This point will become clearer if we look more carefully at Figure 6.14. First, we can see that it contains several *repeating groups*. Thus the style 'Calabria' occurs many times because that particular style comes in several sizes and with different surface finishes. We can also see that there are different kinds of relationship or *dependencies* between the domains. Thus the value for stock class is automatically determined by siting, so this latter domain can be considered as somehow secondary to or dependent on the former.

One single large table therefore tells us about several different things. A particular individual combination of style, model and surface finish indicates the existence of a particular cupboard, whereas siting or price tells us more about a cupboard already on our list. Our use of the phrase 'several different things' indicates that a flat table like Figure 6.14 does not represent just a single relation: parts of the table can be seen as relations in their own right. We shall look at this more rigorously when we come to consider the subject of normalization later in this section.

What if we look at the database in terms of several smaller tables, each containing only that selection of domains of interest to a particular user? We might have style, model, surface finish and price for the accounts people, or everything except stock class for salespeople and customers. If we try this approach we introduce a new complication. Once we use more than one table to express our view of the different relations in the database, we nearly always find that some domains occur in more than one table and introduce the complication of having the same data repeated several times in different parts of the model. This brings with it the potential for inconsistency and unnecessary redundancy.

RQ 6.5 What examples of this can you find in the lead-in-case?

There are therefore problems and benefits whichever way we view the database: as one table or as many. It would be useful to have a set of principles to enable us to come up with a representation that recognized the different relations present in the database while avoiding the complications of duplication and redundancy. Booch (1991) puts this point very succinctly: 'The simplest yet most important goal in database design is the concept that each fact should be stored in exactly one place.' If this simple principle can be implemented, it provides a database that:

- eliminates redundancy and potential storage requirements;
- simplifies the process of updating the database;
- makes it easier to prevent inconsistencies within the database.

The process of *normalization*, referred to above, attempts to define a relational database in a way that has these qualities. The next section will look at the principles behind normalization using an illustrative example.

6.1.6 Normalization

Figure 6.14 shows a particular range of cupboards sold by Carry-Out Cupboards. Different details can be selected to express different users' views of what it contains, but as we saw in the previous section, the aim of normalization is to produce a model that eliminates redundancy, reduces potential storage requirements, simplifies the process of updating the database and makes it easier to prevent inconsistencies within the database.

The process of normalization exploits the essential property of a relational database that all the component relations can be redefined in terms of flat tables in a way that brings the advantages of eliminating redundancy. To achieve this redefinition, certain features in the original table have to be recognized and dealt with separately in the stages of the normalization process. The stages in this procedure result in the definition of a series of *normal forms* (NF) called *first* (1NF), *second* (2NF) and *third* (3NF) normal forms respectively:

- Stage 1 Remove repeating groups.
- Stage 2 Remove partial dependencies.
- Stage 3 Remove transitive dependencies.

The particular normal form we derive at each stage represents the removal of some redundancy from the relational model and a step towards the aim of redundancy elimination. If we are to understand how the passage from 1NF to 3NF in the normalization process removes redundancy, we need also to understand the difference between *redundancy* and *duplication*. In Figure 6.14, for example, many of the details of the cupboards appear to be duplicated – but are they redundant? The key to answering this question is the concept of *dependency*. We have to ask whether the particular value for a duplicated data item depends on the value of another.

The difference between redundancy and duplication can be illustrated by returning to Figure 6.14. Does the fact that a cupboard is in the *Classic* style imply that its Surface Finish will automatically be *Fabric* or vice versa? If we consider the frequently occurring value *Fabric* for the attribute Surface Finish, we can see that the value of one does not depend on the value of the other. The elimination of all cupboards with a *Fabric* value for *Surface Finish* does not eliminate all *Classic* cupboards in terms of their *Style*. Similarly, there will still be cupboards with *Fabric* for their *Surface Finish* if we eliminate the *Style* called *Classic*. Since the duplication in these examples does not come from any dependency, it does not represent something about the structure of the relation that needs identifying and separating to remove redundancy.

This last point does not apply to the relationship between *Siting* and *Stock Class*: the values of these attributes always go together. If we get rid of all the cupboards whose *Siting* is *Lounge*, we also automatically get rid of those whose *Stock Class* is *LG*. Once we recognize the structural dependency of *Stock Class* on *Siting*, then knowing that the siting is, say, *Lounge* automatically also tells us that its *Stock Class* is *LG*.

Given this distinction between *duplication* and *redundancy*, we shall see that they do not have the same significance for the normalization process. Normalization only seeks to eliminate duplication where it is redundant.

We are now ready to consider the stages of the normalization process that are the most important. Other subtleties can arise when we look at particular cases, but our Carry-Out Cupboards relation of Figure 6.15 will illustrate the main concepts.

To establish models in 1NF, 2NF and 3NF respectively, we apply the three stages given above to the relation *Cupboard* of Figure 6.14.

Stage 1 requires the removal of *repeating groups*. This is done by separation into different tables, each of which represents a relation with this feature removed. The *Cupboard* relation of Figure 6.14 contains two repeating groups, one of which happens to lie inside (or is *nested* in) the other. The repeating groups are separated one at a time, with each separation producing a new relation. The two relations then produced contain:

- the *key* of the original relation, plus any attributes that depend on them;
- the key of the original relation, plus those attributes forming the *key of the repeating group*, together with the attributes of the repeating group.

In the case of the *Cupboard* relation of Figure 6.14, the application of these procedures for each repeating group eventually produces three tables. The first contains *Style* and any (if there were any) attributes uniquely determined by it; in this case that's zero. The second consists of the remaining attributes, with a key made up of *Style* and *Surface Finish*, but this second table needs to be split again to remove the nested repeating group to allow for repetitions due to the value of *Size*. The result is a second and third table that take on the principle of the 'key of the original relation, plus those attributes forming the key of the repeating group, together with the attributes of the repeating group'. Hence the relation *Application*, with *Style* and *Surface Finish* as the key, and a new version of the *Cupboard* relation, with *Style*, *Surface Finish* and *Size* as the key.

Before going on to the next stage of the normalization process, it is worth seeing how the concept of a key to a relation can be developed further. Once we start on the process of breaking down a previous relation into component relations through normalization, we find that one or more keys of a previous relation may appear with new keys to form an overall key to the new relation. Thus in Figure 6.15, the original key *Style* of the *Cupboard* in Figure 6.14 reappears with *Surface Finish* as the combined key to the *Application* relation. Similarly, *Size* has been added to form the key of the new version of *Cupboard*. A key of an original table passed on down to a component table in the normalization process is called a *foreign key*.

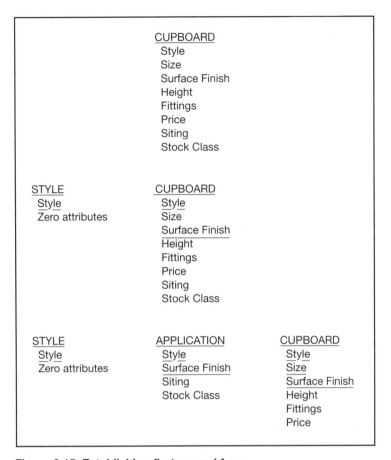

Figure 6.15 Establishing first normal form
Removal of repeating groups, e.g. more than one different version of style and surface finish, or even of one style, surface finish and size.

Stage 2 of the normalization process requires the removal of *partial dependencies*, again by separation into tables representing relations with this feature removed. In systemic terms, these can be seen as components of the original concept of a relational database. The concept of partial dependency can be understood by looking more closely at the terms *dependency* and *partial* in turn. The dependency referred to is the dependency of the non-key attributes on the value of the key attributes. Thus for the new version of the Cupboard relation in Figure 6.15, the values for *Height*, *Fittings* and *Price* will depend on the particular *Style, Size* and *Surface Finish* of the cupboard concerned.

However, we need to make a distinction between attributes whose value is determined by that of all the key attributes, and those whose value is determined by just some of them. In the *Cupboard* relation of Figure 6.15, the value for the attribute *Price* depends on the individual values of all three key attributes: variations in style, size and surface finish can all affect the price. The value of *Height*, however, is only dependent on *Size*: once we know the size of the cupboard we know the height, regardless of its particular surface finish or style. Where the value of a non-key attribute depends on anything less than the entire key, we call this dependency partial. In our examples from Figure 6.15, the dependency of *Height* on *Size* is such a partial dependency.

RQ 6.6   What form does the dependency of Fittings take in this context?

Any partial dependencies found in a 1NF table are removed by forming them into new separate relations. Thus Figure 6.16 shows the previous *Cupboard* relation of Figure 6.15 split to form two new relations, *Size* and *Model*. The new relation *Size* shows the partial dependency of *Height* on *Size*, while the new relation Model covers the partial dependency of *Fittings* on *Style* and *Size*. The removal of any partial dependencies from a 1NF relation then leaves it in 2NF, as in Figure 6.16.

STYLE
Style
Zero attributes

APPLICATION
Style
Surface Finish
Siting
Stock Class

MODEL
Style
Size
Fittings

SIZE
Size
Height

CUPBOARD
Style
Size
Surface Finish
Price

Figure 6.16 Establishing second normal form
Removal of partial dependencies, e.g. height does not depend completely on style, size and surface finish.

Stage 3 of the normalization process involves the removal of any *transitive dependencies* from the 2NF relations. As in the previous stages, this is done by separation into tables representing relations with this feature removed. Transitive dependency occurs when the value of an attribute does not depend *directly* on the value of the key. Instead, we have a relationship where the value of one attribute depends on that of another, and then the value of this second attribute depends on that of the key. We can see an example of this in the *Application* relation of Figure 6.16. In this relation, the value for *Stock Class* depends entirely on that for *Siting*, but *Siting* itself is not a key for the relation: it depends in turn on the key attributes *Style* and *Surface Finish*.

Figure 6.17 shows our original *Cupboard* relation transformed into a series of tables in 3NF and Figure 6.18 summarizes how these link together. The result of the normalization process is a set of relations reflecting the properties of the key and nothing else, and thereby achieves our goal that each fact should be stored in exactly one place. This now means that we have a database that eliminates redundancy, reduces potential storage requirements, simplifies the process of updating and makes it easier to prevent inconsistencies arising within the database.

There are more complex issues associated with normalization that we have not covered, including Boyce-Codd Normal Form and the possibility of 4NF and 5NF. For a more

STYLE
Style
Zero attributes

APPLICATION
Style
Surface Finish
Siting

MODEL
Style
Size
Fittings

SIZE
Size
Height

SITING
Siting
Stock Class

CUPBOARD
Style
Size
Surface Finish
Price

Figure 6.17 Establishing third normal form
Removal of transitive dependencies, e.g. stock class is entirely determined by siting.

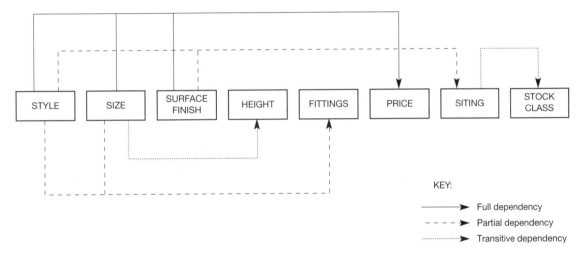

Figure 6.18 The relationships of third normal form
'The key and nothing but the key.'

rigorous, mathematical treatment of normalization, try Stanzyk (1990). For a refreshingly practical and sceptical view of databases and normalization, try Veryard (1984).

6.1.7 Semantic models

In the previous sections, we have shown some of the development that has taken place in thinking about the principles behind databases concepts as well as studying the details of particular models.

In studying hierarchical and network data models, we frequently emphasized the important principle of distinguishing between the *logical* and the *physical* database, but a link between the logical and the physical still remained. When we considered, for example, how data could be *accessed* in a structure, we were still thinking in terms of how the database would be implemented.

When we moved on to the relational model, we took a further step in making the distinction between the logical and the physical by concentrating specifically on the structure of the data represented in the database. Why did we do this? The answer is that the elegant principle 'each fact should be stored in exactly one place' brings the advantages of eliminating redundancy, reducing potential storage, simplifying processing and preventing inconsistencies. Thus even with the strongly logical rather than physical emphasis of the relational model, issues of *implementation* are still present in our discussion.

To understand why the models we have studied so far continue to lack something, we must return to the original reason for our interest in them. We decided to study data models in the wider context of information and information systems. We followed up our assertion in Chapter 3 that information could be regarded as a property emerging from the whole when component elements of data were brought together in a particular relationship or structure, and we decided that all the forms of information we considered as relevant to management are *about something*. The limitation of the models we have studied so far is that their emphasis tends to be on the data structure, rather than on the information in which the user is interested.

RQ 6.7 How could this be interpreted in terms of communication between the user and the computer system and the General Communication System Model of Chapter 5?

The *semantic data model* (SDM) attempts to shift the balance of emphasis away from a mainly logical, disconnected view of data structure towards an emphasis on the meaning of the data for the user. If we take the *Concise Oxford English Dictionary* definition of *semantic* as 'relating to the meaning of language', we would rightly expect a semantic data model to be based on principles deriving from the user's view of the meaning of the data.

The SDM is defined in terms of *classes* and *attributes*. As in other models above, these attributes are characteristics of entities, but with the important proviso that the entities correspond to objects in the *real world*. It is this concentration on real-world objects, rather than logical entities conceived for the convenience of the data model, that gives the SDM its user-meaning emphasis. *Classes* are collections of entities that share the same set of *attributes*. The SDM then follows the conventions of the EAR model in describing entities, attributes and relationships, including the possible diagramming conventions of Figure 6.2.

We can take a simple example from Carry-Out Cupboards to illustrate these concepts. Possible classes of products sold by Carry-Out Cupboards might be:

1 Cupboards.
2 Furniture.
3 Freestanding Cupboards.
4 Hanging Cupboards.
5 Tables.
6 {Cupboard Number CA3SVR, Cupboard Number CL3SVR, Cupboard Number CL2SVR, Cupboard Number CA2SVR}

The difference between the last class in this list and the others illustrates an important principle in the way we can define classes. One way is to define a class by listing all of its members, as in 6 above. This way of definition is not very helpful, because it does not answer the question 'Why is it in this class?' A better way is to define membership in terms of some property that each member of the class must possess, and that non-members will not, as is done in 1–6 above. Such membership properties will be represented by a set of shared *attributes*. Thus all members of the class 'cupboard' will share the attribute 'door', which will not be applicable to 'table'.

This concept of *class* can then be naturally extended by adding the concept of *subclass*. Figure 6.19 shows how this might occur. Where all the members of a class are also members of some other class, the first class may be taken as a subclass of the second. Thus 'freestanding' cupboards are a subclass of 'cupboards'. It is possible for a class to be a subclass of more than one other class. Thus the subclasses of table called 'square folding' or 'circular folding' can both be placed in the 'folding' category, or individually classed as 'square' or 'folding' respectively.

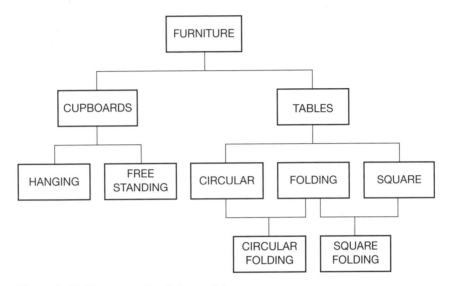

Figure 6.19 The semantic data model
Examples of classes and attributes in terms of the products of Carry-Out Cupboards.

Another important feature of the SDM is the way in which it regards and represents *relationships*. This goes beyond the definition of basic logical characteristics like the degree of a relationship or whether it is compulsory or optional. It also goes beyond what we could hope to cover in a non-specialist book like this, but we can at least understand some basic issues.

More developed forms of the SDM would recognize how different kinds of entity may be related through different kinds of relationship. Consider Figure 6.19 again. If we decided to carry out an operation like deleting 'tables' from our database, we would automatically get rid of 'circular tables' too; but what about the effect on, say, 'suppliers'? These may be represented in an associated class divided into subclasses like 'fittings suppliers', 'materials suppliers' and so on. How would the deleting of 'tables' from the database affect 'suppliers', if at all? Should this mean that certain suppliers should be eliminated? Might an irrelevant supplier be left on the database? Generally, how do we ensure that in processing the database we also maintain its consistency and integrity?

To ensure that these goals are achieved, the SDM categorizes relationships and defines what types of maintenance of them is required and allowed. Thompson (1989) looks at this in some detail.

6.1.8 **Object-oriented models**

We introduced the concept of hierarchy in Chapter 3 and classification in Chapter 5, and we indicated that they form the important basis for an object-orientated approach to systems development that we shall consider in Chapter 9. It therefore makes sense to leave further detailed treatment of the object-orientated view of data and information until then. Meanwhile, I think we have covered enough of object orientation to understand the important basic principles behind an *object-orientated database*.

RQ 6.8 What kind of hierarchy has just been referred to?

When considering the SDM, we emphasized how it represented yet a further move away from thinking about the data to thinking about what the data represented. This can be seen as a process of abstraction as far as the hard computer system is concerned. Questions of how data is stored and accessed, which still featured in the hierarchical or plex models, have virtually disappeared from our view of how the data is modelled when we use the SDM. By distinguishing different kinds of entity and relationship types, we have a richer model that is able to reflect the different qualities of the real life being represented. This can be illustrated by comparing the term 'cupboard' as it appears in the relational model examples of Figures 6.15–6.17 with the SDM example of Figure 6.18. The examples of Figures 6.15–6.17 focus much more on kinds of relation than they do on kinds of cupboard. This is not the case with the SDM example of Figure 6.18: this looks much more like cupboards as we would regard them in practice.

The SDM still has a drawback. Consider the question of manipulation of data. When the models we have described so far involve the creation, deletion or updating of entities, there are other processes that follow from them. Thus if we are creating a new cupboard, we might need to check whether it is a replacement for a previous model or whether some of its components and materials come from existing suppliers. The processes that carry out these checks are governed by the type of entity with which we are dealing. Recognizing that a particular entity does or does not belong to particular class will determine which operations are needed. Thus the next stage in the modelling of data is the *integration of defining data modelling with data operations*.

Object orientation can enable this, and the wider systems development context of Chapter 9 should show how this can be the case.

6.2 DATABASE PROCESSING AND MANIPULATION

6.2.1 **Database language principles**

We introduced the subject of data languages when considering the hierarchical data model. We saw that the implementation of the model required the use of data definition and data manipulation languages. A *data definition language* (DDL) defines the *structural* features of the model of the database, while a *data manipulation language* (DML) defines how the data can be accessed and manipulated. We should now add a third type of data language to our list, a *data control language* (DCL), which controls access to the database and helps ensure security.

It is worth noting the order in which we mentioned these three types of language, since it reflects something about their relationship to each other in terms of their function. We can explain this by using the analogy of a room plan of a building.

Control of the security of a building requires knowledge of the siting of the entrances and how rooms and passageways are connected. We need to know about structure and access before we can control security. So with a database, the form of the DCL will depend on the structure and access to the database defined by the DDL and DML respectively.

If we pursue our building room plan analogy further, we come up with an important issue about the relationship between the DDL and the DML. In our building, we might say that the structure of the building determines the access. For example, if the bedrooms are upstairs and the living room is downstairs, then this structure for a house defines that access to the bedrooms is achieved by the process of going up the stairs first. By analogy in the database, since the DDL defines the structure of the database and the DML deals with *process*, we would expect the form of the DML to depend on the form of the DDL.

However, this conclusion that structure determines process is only half of the relationship between them. In our building analogy, we can see that it could be the other way round. If it is not easy for me to go upstairs because I use a wheelchair or suffer from arthritis, then I might choose a house structured in a way that means I don't have to use the stairs at all, e.g. a single-storey bungalow. In database terms, we might say that rather than seeing the DDL as determining the nature of the DML, data *structure* and data *processing* are *complementary systemic properties* affecting each other.

This inter-relationship of structure and process enables us to look at data languages in complementary ways. One way is to start directly from a process viewpoint and look at the principles determining the types of operations that can be carried out on a database. Alternatively, we can consider how we might define the relationships behind a database structure and use this to define principles for processing the database.

The way in which either of these approaches can be applied depends on the particular data model with which we are dealing. We mainly focus on the relational data model for the rest of this section, because it is a model with wide-ranging application and support. Semantic and object-orientated models may challenge the ascendancy of the relational model in the future, however.

We shall therefore consider two theoretical foundations:

1 *Relational algebra* as a way of looking at the principles determining the types of operations that can be carried out on a database.
2 *Relational calculus* as a way of defining the relationships within a database structure and using these to define ways of processing the database.

6.2.2 Relational algebra

Relational algebra begins by recognizing that the relations that make up a relational database are sets. It then defines *operators*, which can be applied to relations to form other relations:

$$\text{relation}_a, \text{relation}_b \rightarrow \text{set operator} \rightarrow \text{relation}_c$$

There are five standard set operators that are the same as those found elsewhere in set algebra, plus three operators that are specific to relational algebra. We can illustrate what these operators do by referring to Figure 6.14.

The standard operators are:

- UNION: Brings two relations together into one united relation. For this to be possible, both the original relations must be *union compatible*. This effectively means that they must have the same attributes ranging over the same domains. Thus Figure 6.14 could be seen as the union of two separate relations: one containing all the 'Country' cupboards and the other containing the rest of the range.
- DIFFERENCE: The difference between one relation and another will be a resultant relation that only contains those tuples not present in the second relation. In terms of Figure 6.14, the difference between the relation shown and one containing only 'Country' cupboards would be a new relation with no 'Country' cupboards.
- INTERSECTION: The result of applying this operator to two relations is to identify which tuples are present in them both. An intersection of Figures 6.14 and 6.20 would be a relation containing only 'Calabria' cupboards in 'Veneer' and 'Antique'.
- PRODUCT: This results in a relation whose attributes represent all the possible combinations of those attributes in the original relations. Figure 6.21 gives a simple example.
- DIVISION: This is essentially the reverse of PRODUCT. Thus in Figure 6.21, if we divided the relation 'Style.Surface Finish' by, say, 'Style', it would result in the original 'Surface Finish' relation.

STYLE	SIZE	SURFACE FINISH	HEIGHT	FITTINGS	PRICE £	SITING	STOCK CLASS
Calabria	3S	Veneer	3480	Triple/A/S	215.00	Lounge	LG
Calabria	3S	Antique	3480	Triple/A/S	205.00	Diner	DN
Calabria	2S	Veneer	1740	Double/A/S	185.00	Lounge	LG
Calabria	2S	Antique	1740	Double/A/S	150.00	Diner	DN
Classic	3S	Floral	3480	Triple/S/S	180.00	Diner	DN
Country	3S	Fabric	1740	Double/N/S	100.00	Kitchen	KT
Country	1H	Floral	870	Single/N/H	90.00	Kitchen	KT

Figure 6.20 Selection from the C range
An *intersection* of this selection and the table of Figure 6.14 would be a relation containing only 'Calabria' cupboards in 'Veneer' and 'Antique'.

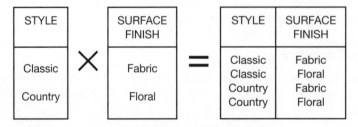

Figure 6.21 An example of the PRODUCT operator
This results in a relation whose attributes represent all the possible combinations of those attributes in the original relations.

In addition to these standard operators, the three operators specific to relational algebra are:

- SELECT: This applies a predicate, or condition, to a relation to select a subset of its tuples. The general definition would take the form:

$$\sigma_{<condition>}(<relation\ name>)$$

An example applied to Figure 6.19 might take the condition 'Style = Calabria' for the relation 'Cupboard', which would result in a list of cupboards in the 'Calabria' style.

- PROJECT: This simply extracts a subset of the attributes of a relation. Here the general definition would take the form:

$$\pi_{<attribute\ list>}(<relation\ name>)$$

An example applied to Figure 6.19 for the attributes 'Style' and 'Size' of the 'Cupboard' would result in a table consisting of the first two columns of the figure.

- JOIN: This is used to combine two relations on the basis of the value of a shared attribute. The general form is:

$$R \bowtie <JOIN\ CONDITION>\ S$$

- where R and S are two relations. Thus one relation (R), listing 'Style' and 'Size', could be joined with another relation (S), listing 'Style' and 'Surface Finish', via their common value of 'Style' (which is the JOIN CONDITION), to form a new relation with the attributes 'Style', 'Size' and 'Surface Finish'.

Elmasri and Navathe (1989) do a very thorough job on relational algebra and many other topics in the field of database management.

6.2.3 Relational calculus

We explained above that relational algebra is a way of looking directly at the operations or *processes* that can be carried out on a database. However, we saw earlier that defining the *structural* relationships within a database will also imply how a database can be processed and can be used as a basis for process definition.

Relational calculus uses the latter approach. Our earlier analogy of the room plan of a building showed that defining the *structural* relationship between the components of the building automatically implied what *processes* might be applied to access it. So although relational calculus is relational (concerned with *structure*) rather than *procedural* (concerned with *process*), it can be used to define the processes used in database manipulation.

Relational calculus *itself* is therefore *non-procedural*, even though we know that our interest in it is based on a desire to derive principles for processing databases. We can refer to a commonly used concept in this book: relational algebra is concerned with *how* we retrieve data from the database structure, while relational calculus specifies *what* data in the structure we wish to retrieve.

The formal specification of relational calculus may be alarming for those who find mathematical formulae daunting. For example, Elmasri and Shamkant (1989) do a thorough job when they state that a general expression of the tuple relational calculus is of the form:

$$\{t_1.A_1, t_2A_2, ..., t_n.A_n \mid COND(t_1, t_2, ..., t_n, t_{n+1}, t_{n+2}, ..., t_{n+m})\}$$

and then go on to define the various components of this heavily subscripted formula, but this perfectly correct mathematical language is not something that everyone would want to tackle.

However, the *concepts* behind relational calculus are not that difficult to grasp once we get past the conspiratorial pedantry of the mathematics. Thus in the Carry-Out Cupboards selection of Figure 6.14, we might want to find out what cupboards, if any, of the 'Country' style were available in the 'Fabric' surface finish. We could put this more formally by stating 'retrieve *any tuple* from the cupboard relation, *given that* the values for *style* and *surface finish* are 'Country' and 'Fabric' respectively'. So we query the database to find out the values of the *attributes* (hence 'A') of some *tuple* (hence 't') variable *given* (that's what the symbol 'l' means) that a certain set of *conditions* (hence 'COND') applies.

The calculus is therefore essentially built up from the concepts of tuple variables and conditions (also called *well-formed formulae*). Each tuple variable ranges over a particular database relation and can take as its value any individual tuple from that relation. We then use a condition to identify any tuples that fit the criteria we lay down for the query. The essential ingredient of the complex formula above then becomes:

$$\{t \mid COND(T)\}$$

so that:

$$\{t \mid cupboard(t) \text{ and } t.style='Country' \text{ and } t.surface\ finish='Fabric'\}$$

defines the tuples in the cupboard relation that meet our conditions.

For most users, however, neither the relational algebra nor the relational calculus represents a convenient language for accessing or processing a database. It makes sense, therefore, to develop data manipulation languages that are much easier for the user to use, but at the same time to ensure that these user-friendly DMLs are based on the correct rigour of relational algebra or calculus. In the next section we shall look at some examples of this principle.

6.2.4 Database language applications

We have already established the principle that relational algebra is concerned with how we retrieve data from the database structure, while relational calculus specifies what data in the structure we wish to retrieve. If we decide to design a *user-friendly* DML, it makes sense to avoid the need for the user to specify how the data is to be retrieved from the database. Users are mainly concerned with queries like 'What accounts are overdue?' or 'What cupboards are available in a Veneer surface finish?' and, provided that the DML can get the answers out of the database, they don't want to be bothered with how the answers are retrieved.

Given this emphasis on whats rather than hows, it is not surprising that the most popular commercial DMLs are high-level, *declarative* languages that require the user to declare what result they want from a query. Given the distinction we made between relational algebra and relational calculus in respect to hows and whats, we can also see why several of the most popular declarative DMLs derive their principles from relational calculus. QUEL and SQL are two examples of such languages, although SQL is less closely linked to relational calculus than is QUEL. (The degree to which such a language can express any query that can be expressed in relational calculus is called its degree of *relational completeness*.) QUEL is both a DDL and a DML.

A sample QUEL query such as:

RETRIEVE (CUPBOARD.SIZE)
WHERE CUPBOARD.STYLE='Country' AND CUPBOARD.SURFACE
FINISH='Fabric'

shows how closely it corresponds to our relational calculus examples above, while being a high-level language that is easy to understand. There is also an embedded form of QUEL, known as EQUEL, which is explained below.

SQL was originally called SEQUEL (Structured English QUEry Language) and was developed by IBM. It is used by several popular database management systems, including DB2, ORACLE and INGRES (available as an alternative to QUEL). SQL offers all the three components that make a full database language: a data *definition* language (DDL), a data *manipulation* language (DML) and a data *control* language (DCL). Figure 6.22 gives some examples of commands from each.

COMMAND	DESCRIPTION
SQL Data Definition Language	
CREATE TABLE	Creates a table and defines its columns and other properties.
CREATE VIEW	Defines a view of one or more tables or other views.
ALTER TABLE	Adds a column to, or redefines a column in, an existing table.
DROP	Deletes a cluster, table, view, or index from the database.
SQL Data Manipulation Language	
INSERT	Adds new rows to a table or view.
SELECT	Performs a query and selects rows and columns from one or more tables or views.
UPDATE	Changes the value of fields in a table or view.
SQL Data Control Language	
GRANT	Grants access to objects stored in database.
COMMIT	Makes database transactions irreversible.
LOCK TABLE	Locks a table and thus permits shared access to the table by multiple users while simultaneously preserving the table's integrity.
REVOKE	Revokes database privileges or table access privileges from users.

Figure 6.22 A sample of SQL commands
SQL provides a complete range of commands capable of data definition, manipulation and control. See Perry and Lateer (1989) for the full list.

The ORACLE language is a popular example of the implementation of SQL. Besides the use of SQL, it provides other enhancements, including:

- SQL*FORMS: a means of creating record input/output formats that bypasses the clumsy procedures of many general-purpose languages.
- SQL*REPORTWRITER: for incorporating various SQL queries into producing a report.
- SQL*MENU: enables the user to produce automated friendly applications through creation of supporting menus.
- SQL*CALC: spreadsheet software that can use the data resulting from SQL-based queries of a database.
- PRO*C: an example of embedding (see below).

These are just *some* examples from *one* particular choice.

The examples show that, for most practical applications, the data definition and manipulation capabilities of languages like QUEL and SQL need to be enhanced by broader programming capabilities. This need can often be fulfilled by general-purpose languages like C. As our ORACLE example of PRO*C implies, this is because DMLs require other features if they are to be more widely used in developing applications such as more complex calculation procedures, or sophisticated printing and displays. We can express this need by saying that a DML may be *relationally* complete without necessarily being *computationally* complete.

It is common practice, therefore, to embed DMLs in a general-purpose language, called a host. Where this is done, the data retrieved by the DML can be processed using the wide range of functions and procedures available from the general-purpose language. When embedding takes place, statements from the embedded language are included in the host language program, but are identified by some distinct prefix character or command so that the preprocessor can distinguish them.

Box 6.2

Data mining, not size, brings results on the high street

Susanna Voyle

Marks and Spencer is to overhaul its system for supplying merchandise to stores following a trial which had produced big increases in sales.

Under the new system – begun at the end of January in 31 outlets – stores are grouped according to a series of criteria, including the demographics of customers, their lifestyle and working patterns – and supplied with clothing accordingly.

The changes to the old system – under which stores were sent merchandise according to their sales space – are the most visible sign so far of M&S's promise to become customer-focused.

Some of the results of the trials will be announced tomorrow when M&S unveils the results of its rebranding exercise, which involves the demotion of the St Michael brand and changes to the distinctive green carrier bags.

Jan Bromilow, store manager for Marks and Spencer in St Helens, Lancashire, one of the trial sites, says the new system has made a huge difference because for the first time stores are being given clothing tailored to the needs of local customers.

She has just delivered a near-five-fold rise in sales of women's clothing to her bosses. The rise in sales of men's wear at the store may not be

quite so eye-grabbing in comparison – but 46 per cent is not to be sneezed at, in what all retailers admit is a very difficult clothing sector.

The traditional M&S system of supplying clothes goes some way to explain the troubles the group has suffered. Stores were banded according to their retail footage – and all stores of the same size were sent the same clothes for sale.

For example, Guildford in southern England was grouped with Blackpool in the north-west. The trial, involving all types of store, has produced such startling effects so quickly that M&S has shrugged off its traditional caution and speeded up the plan to introduce it to all stores.

Many more outlets will have the system in place for the autumn clothing collection, with all 300 coming under the scheme for next spring's ranges.

Geoff Rowbotham, who heads the team at the group's Baker Street headquarters implementing the changes, says: 'We have talked a lot about being a customer-driven business – and this is what we mean by that.'

In St Helens, Ms Bromilow says that under the old system her store used to receive mainly leisure wear – more casual clothing, usually separates. Her increase in sales had come because they have been supplied with more suits and co-ordinated clothing for both men and women. She cites swimsuits, which St Helens was not allowed to sell under the old system until after Easter. Now they have them all year round – and sales have leapt.

Not only have sales risen year-on-year, the average value of a basket of goods purchased has gone up from £10 ($16) to £13.10. That means the store is attracting new customers – and persuading existing shoppers to spend more.

Mike Davies, who manages several M&S stores in the north-west, says that in the group's glory days customers who couldn't find what they wanted in their local store were prepared to travel to a bigger M&S. Once the decline set in, with all the attendant bad publicity, instead of travelling to another M&S, customers deserted the group for high street rivals.

The trial has also had a big effect on the mood among store staff, who have been weighed down by the group's highly public travails as well as the uncertainty created when retail entrepreneur Philip Green was stalking the group.

'It has been fantastic for morale,' says Ms Bromilow. 'The feeling is: They must really believe in us if they are starting to invest in us.'

Mr Rowbotham says the new categories for stores were reached after detailed customer research – both with existing shoppers and those not using M&S. The group also used data from its charge card records.

'We have always known who shops in our stores – what we have never known is who doesn't,' he says. 'We profiled all 300 of our stores and natural groupings started to emerge.'

The trials have covered just women's wear and men's wear so far, but Mr Rowbotham says they could be extended to all the ranges – including food. It is also likely to be used for the group's overseas operations.

And it is not just small stores, such as St Helens, which will benefit. Mr Rowbotham says that the group's two biggest stores – Manchester and Marble Arch in London – may both be huge, but their customers probably need different merchandise.

'In future, no two M&S stores will be the same,' he says. 'Nobody will run the full M&S range.'

Source: Financial Times, 21 March 2000. Reprinted with permission.

Comment

Data mining is used to describe the process of trying to discover descriptive *statistical patterns and trends in database data, like 'demographics of customers, their lifestyle and working patterns'. Data mining can then be integrated into a wider system of knowledge management (KM).*

Knowledge management takes over from database management and data mining once we take up the descriptive *statistics that make up the database and process them to draw* inferences *that can be used for* decision making, *like deciding to sell swimsuits all year round. The ability of modern database management systems to overcome the old file processing systems (Figure 6.24) means that it possible to share and collaborate in amassing knowledge across the organizational and geographical boundaries of an organization.*

Where KM systems are integrated with networks, management can be provided with knowledge portals. *These are like large electronic directories that catalogue and categorize information, which is structured with a* taxonomy *that reflects the particular management focus of the user.*

KM uses two main types of software tools:

1   Data mining tools. *These automate the process of discovering patterns in the data.*
2   Query and reporting tools. *These allow the user to find answers to questions about data patterns already being suspected. Apparent inferences can then be statistically tested.*

6.3 DATABASE SYSTEMS

6.3.1 Database management versus traditional file processing

So far in this chapter we have developed our understanding of data because we see it as the building material that we can put together to form the information we need for management of a business or organization. In this section, we consider how our stock of 'building material' that we call our *database* can itself be *managed* as a *system* to produce this necessary information. Not surprisingly, such a system of controlling our database is called a *database management system* (DBMS).

Why is the distinction between *data* and *information necessary*? Even something as authoritative as the United Kingdom Data Protection Act (DPA) of 1984 asserted in one of its opening paragraphs that 'Data is information'. In fact, I think the fact that the legislators who drew up the act got so confused is a good example of why we need not only to distinguish between data and information, but also to distinguish the traditional technology-centred *file-processing* view from a modern *database management* approach. We will continue a little further with the DPA example to consider some of the issues that create the need for both of these distinctions.

The stated purpose of the DPA is to reassure people that data held about them on file can be openly checked by its subjects as a safeguard against there being a false record of the information held about them. We would agree that false data will result in false information, since information is an emergent property that results from the coming together of its data components. If the nature or value of any one of these components is changed, then it will affect the nature or value of the whole. Wrong data on a credit file about what accounts I have paid, or not paid, will give wrong information about my creditworthiness. This far, the confusion of data and information by the DPA does not seem to matter, but we need to consider two further questions to see why it does matter:

1 What do the terms file and record mean, if anything, in the context of contemporary systems practice?
2 If they mean something different, or no longer mean anything, what concepts do we now use to understand the accessing and processing of data to provide the information we need?

We have already given answers to the first question when we considered various data models in previous sections of this chapter. The terms file and record are still used in some of these contemporary models, but a clear distinction is made between *physical* and *logical* views. A logical view of data is about whats, and this needs to be distinguished from the physical view of how the data is recorded, accessed or transmitted.

We saw that in everyday use a file is seen as a source of information about a number of people or things, present as a series of records. Furthermore, both the records and the file would be seen in physical terms. The file might be a box with the records as individual cards inside the box, or the records might be areas of magnetic patterns on a disk. The important point about the physical view is that it binds up the *logical* connexion between records in a file, and data items within a record, with the form of their *physical* connexion on the recording medium.

The traditional technology-centred file-processing view sees the terms record and file completely in these physical terms. It is a classic example of the 'carry-over' effect of redundant concepts from an old technology into a new one that we discussed in Chapter 3. The early computer systems of the 1960s took over a physical view of record and file from manual office systems. So just as a box file was filled with individual record cards in sequence, so a magnetic tape had blocks of records following each other in sequence. It was normal practice to use the terms tape and file interchangeably. When I first worked in computer systems, a request like 'get me the On-Order file' meant 'get me that tape spool'. The analogy with the old manual systems was not perfect, however: the size of records and the size of blocks did not necessarily coincide. It was rather like the individual record cards in a manual filing system not always coinciding with individual records.

The analogy of computer systems with manual systems was further broken down with the increased use of direct access disk storage. This happened for two reasons. First, the removal of the need for sequential storage meant that all the components of a record need no longer be adjacent; indeed they were often fragmented and scattered all over the disk. Second, the increasing storage capacity of disks meant that one disk could contain many files. At this stage, physically identifiable files consisting of physically identifiable records still remained, but the form of physical connexion had become potentially so much more complex that the analogy with manual systems had almost disappeared. This was rather like parts of different individual records being recorded on the same card in a manual filing system.

As we followed through our study of database models, we found that more recent views of databases saw things less and less in this physical way. Instead, if the terms file and record were used at all, they referred to a concept. From this information perspective, it makes no difference whether the records making up the file of, say, Carry-Out Cupboards products are on a computer or in a friendly old moth-eaten cardboard file. As long as we can end up with details of the style, model and surface finish of some cupboard we are interested in, it will still be the same information. The file and record medium has changed, but the contents of the files and records have not.

But if we see information as a property that emerges when data is brought together, we are now considering the second question we asked above as to what concepts we can therefore use to understand the accessing and processing of data once the physical view of files and records has gone. This can be answered by considering what the phrase 'when data is brought together' means in a computer systems context.

To understand this next issue, consider the principle behind two types of coffee-vending machines illustrated in Figure 6.23.

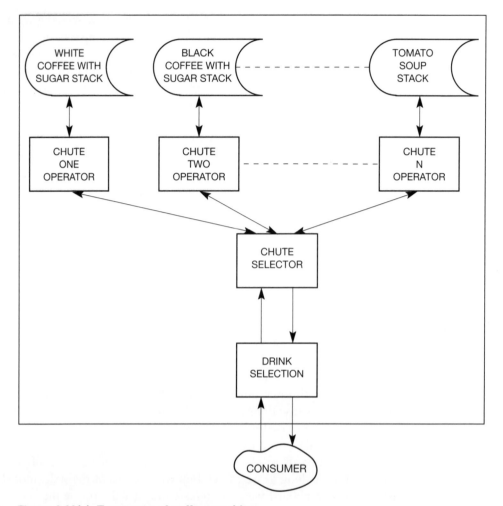

Figure 6.23(a) Two types of coffee machine
The first type (a) has drinks ready-mixed in cups and the ability to choose one.

The first kind of coffee-vending machine has separate columns containing plastic cups already filled with the ingredients. There is one column of cups for every available combination. If you decide that you want white coffee with sugar, the machine gathers a cup from the appropriate column, fills it with lukewarm water and throws it down the delivery chute.

The second kind of coffee machine does not have ready-mixed combinations. Instead, the potential ingredients are kept separate. If you decide that you want white coffee with sugar, what I will call for the moment 'a little green man' (in my experience coffee machines are very sexist) inside the machine pulls the necessary levers to send water, whitener, sweetener and coffee powder down the various chutes into a previously plummeted plastic cup.

The first thing to notice about these two examples is that the experience of a cup of coffee is an emergent property of either of the coffee machine systems described. Consuming the ingredients separately and washing them down with a cup of warm

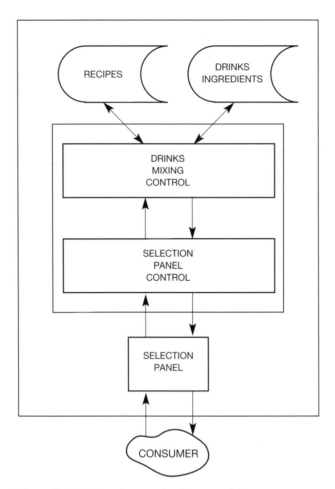

Figure 6.23(b) Two types of coffee machine
The second type (b) has potential ingredients with the ability to select them and make up the desired drink when required.

water is not the same as the holistic experience of sampling them together as an output of a machine (albeit almost as revolting).

If we put aside the warm water from our previous examples, we find that there is an important conceptual difference between the two systems for producing the *emergent property* known as 'a cup of sweet white coffee'. In the first kind of machine, the mixture is already physically there (water apart) waiting to be served on request. The second kind of coffee machine, however, does not contain any cups of coffee. Instead, the second kind of coffee machine contains a logic with the potential to produce one.

This difference goes an important stage further. Let us suppose that neither of the present machines can produce black coffee with sugar. To meet this new need, the first kind of machine will have to physically introduce a new column into the machine containing the appropriate ingredients ready mixed in a cup. The second machine will need no such major physical change; instead, the system will merely have to be instructed with a new logic that 'sweet black coffee' means a different combination of pulling the existing physical levers by the 'little green man'.

If we look at the first kind of machine described, we can be clear about what drinks are stored ready for delivery: they are physically present in separate columns within the machine. This kind of machine is analogous with the old technology-centred file-processing view of recording and accessing data. The ready-assembled, physically linked components of white coffee with sugar are the equivalent of the physically linked data item components of a record, labelled ready for access and processing.

With the second kind of machine it is different: the machine does not physically store any drinks at all. Instead, it stores the ingredients plus the logical ability to produce the whole range of drinks. Modern database management systems work on a similar principle to the second type of coffee machine when accessing a database. Instead of having actual physical records on the recording medium, they use the medium to hold individual data items which can be 'brought together' by the 'little green man' (i.e. the database software) in any form the user requires.

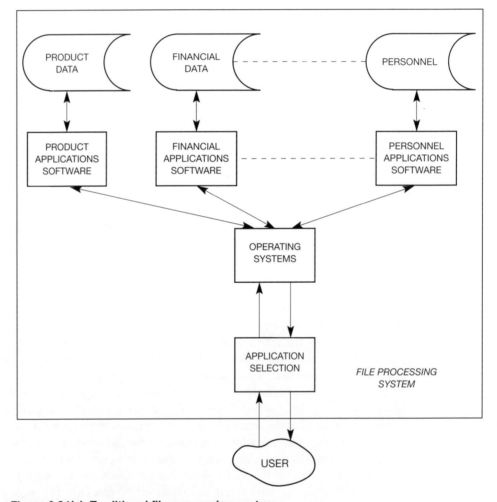

Figure 6.24(a) Traditional file processing system
The file processing system uses ready-made files designed to fit the appropriate applications software.

For a modern database managed by a DBMS, what is physically recorded is not records, but individual items of data. When the user asks for a record, the data items making up the record are assembled by the DBMS. This means that neither the computer nor its recording devices actually contains records, any more than our second type of coffee machine contains the various drinks. Instead, a database contains the potential to produce any kind of information 'drink', in the form of an assembled record, that can be assembled from the data items by the DBMS.

Figure 6.24 shows the two views of accessing and processing data that we have discussed: the technology-centred file-processing view and database management. Having made the case for the database management approach, we will now look more closely at the typical components of a complete database system. In doing so, we will consider some of the wider management implications of the use of such a system.

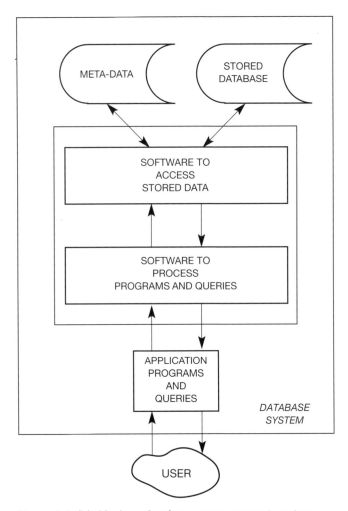

Figure 6.24(b) Modern database management system
The database management system stores all data as a common resource that can be accessed, assembled and processed according to the particular application need.

6.3.2 **Structure and application of database systems**

Figure 6.24(b) shows that the a database system has two main components:

1 The *database*.
2 The database *management system*.

The *database* consists of two components: stored data, and meta-data, which defines the characteristics of the stored data.

The range of data stored is determined by the needs of the wider information system of which the database system is a component. These needs in turn are determined by the needs of the various management subsystems, like the financial subsystem, personnel etc., which we shall discuss in detail and give examples of in Chapter 7. For the moment, however, we can note some important issues that come from applying a management systems view.

We can begin by recognizing that all the data in a database is there for a purpose, but we need to recognize how different these purposes can be. Each data item is a potential building block for some form of information that management needs in order to exert control. As we saw in Chapter 4, the concept of control brings with it the concept of hierarchy. This means that a particular data item may play very different roles according to the nature of the user.

Consider, for example, a data item whose value records the sales of a particular cupboard in a particular month by Carry-Out Cupboards. The sales figure could be used at a *goal-seeking* control level to feedback data on the performance of the retail outlets with a view to controlling stock levels. It could be used at a *goal-setting* level as part of an analysis of customer demand aimed at setting future production targets. It might be used at a much more strategic level as part of a study to consider the future of the whole Carry-Out Cupboards product range. The concept of *data mining* is an example of using analysis of data in a database to achieve the *learning* that is part of any control system.

Such needs as those in our example were present long before anyone invented modern database systems, but the important point is that the coming of modern database systems makes them so much easier to fulfil from one common database. A systems view of management will recognize the different needs of the different functions and their interconnexion within management in a way that a departmentalized, organizational view of management will not. The success of a modern database system therefore depends on its being accompanied by a modern systems view of management. As so often in this book, we emphasize that the information system is a component of the wider management system.

The management systems view that all the data on a database is there for a purpose linked to one or more management functions has important implications:

1 The principles for *defining* the contents of a database and the process of *constructing* it should reflect the needs of the wider management system. This principle implies that any *method* for the development of a database system will include previous stages that analyse the needs of the business or organization concerned. In Chapter 8 we shall say more about this when we study information systems development methodology.

2 Control over the *manipulation* and *use* of the database should be set in the context of *user support* rather than the convenience of computer specialists.

In real life it doesn't easily happen this way. Information technology professionals, like many others, understandably seek to protect their interests when these are in conflict with the wider management system. But this book is about information systems in business and takes the wider view; so I make the point, and we shall develop these issues further in Chapter 8. It is worth noting in the meantime that specialist information technology follows the history of other specialist technologies in gradually becoming subservient to the wider need that it satisfies.

RQ 6.9　What other 'specialist technologies' would you quote to support this last statement?

Besides the data itself, the other component of the database is the *meta-data*. If we consider a parts database for cupboards, it will contain data about the parts that make up a particular cupboard. The *schema*, as explained above, will define the ordering and arranging of this data in the data model and will enable us to understand the relationship of the parts to one another, and how a cupboard is made up. Just as a database contains data and has a schema, so we can have a further database describing the database itself and containing the schema as part of its data. Data that describes the database in this way is called *meta-data*.

We have already looked at particular examples of the software used by database management systems. Generally, as in Figure 6.24 (b), we classify the software as either *processing software* or *accessing software*.

Processing software can take different forms depending on the sophistication and needs of the user. High-level software taking user-friendly forms has been designed to help casual users query and process the database. In particular, declarative (see previous section) or so-called fourth generation languages (4GLs) enable the user to do this using English-like statements. Even easier forms of software use graphical interfaces with icons, menus or some combination of any of these. More specialist users may use host application programs in general-purpose computer languages that have the ability to interface with the accessing software, usually through embedded DML statements, as described above. The accessing software would normally be the DML itself (see Section 6.2).

There is one further important aspect of DBMS software that we have not discussed. The user-friendly nature of much of the high-level software means that detailed knowledge of computing is no longer needed to create working computerized information systems that use the database. When we come to studying the subject of systems development in Chapter 9, we shall see that prototyping or the use of CASE tools makes possible much closer links between those who design and build information systems and those who use them.

Key words

Attribute	First normal form	Relational algebra
Cardinality	IMS	Relational calculus
CODASYL	INGRES	Relational database
Data control language (DCL)	Intersection	Relationship
Data definition language (DDL)	Join	Repeating group
Data description language	Mapping	Replication
Data item	Network	Schema
Data manipulation language (DML)	Normalization	Second normal form
Database management system (DBMS)	Object-orientated model	Segment
	ORACLE	Selection
	Parent/child relationship	Semantic model
	Partial dependency	Sequence field
Degree	Plex	SQL
Difference	Pointer	Third normal form
Division	Product	Transitive dependency
DL/1	Projection	Tuple
Domain	QUEL	Union
Duplication	Redundancy	Vector
Entity	Relation	

Seminar agendas, exam topics and project/dissertation subjects

1 Which microcomputer database packages are you familiar with in popular business use? Are they based on a relational model?

2 Investigate the development of a successful database management system in an organization or business to which you have access. Who decided what entities and attributes should be in the model? The developer? The user? The co-operation of both? How was the co-operation organized?

3 Investigate the statements to be found in Appendix 1 of Veryard (1984) that are critical of formal techniques of normalization:

(a) They are not sufficient.
(b) They are rarely applied vigorously.
(c) They are only based on an intuitive connexion between EAR modelling and normalization.
(d) Codd's theory is mathematically questionable.

You may not have the technical ability to analyse them all, but see how more informed professionals react to them and try to form an opinion.

4 In a survey of the whole of British agriculture as part of a wider EU survey, farmers had to identify attributes of their fields like area and crops grown. Find out about this IACS survey of 1993 and ask the question 'What is the entity field?' How did the British government answer that question?

5 How can a database of visual material be modelled? Consider finger printing of the faces of wanted criminals.

6 Get individual members of your seminar group to investigate their rights under the Data Protection Act. Let everyone try independently to find out their credit rating and report back their experiences. Does the Act protect you?

Feedback on review questions

RQ 6.1 If we consider her in terms of being an employee who wanted to be 'correctly paid', then the emergent property of correct payment meant the bringing together of correct, up-to-date personal details like name, bank account number, tax code etc. In Jane's case, as in any other attempt at a successful whole, one erroneous component destroys everything. 'Minor details' of data can destroy the effectiveness of large information wholes.

RQ 6.2 I think they are the same concept in that we use both terms to describe the smallest item of interest. A practical difference might be that when we look at an applied database, as we shall later in this chapter, there has to be a common view of the information system for it to work. What constitutes an element of a business seen as a system can be much more diverse, as we saw in Chapter 3.

RQ 6.3 This looks like a 'level of command' type of hierarchy, in the sense that the flow of supporting nutrients and the control of behaviour goes from trunk to branches and from branches to twigs.

RQ 6.4 This looks to me like a 'part of' or aggregation hierarchy, because the records at the 'lower level' are members of the 'higher'.

RQ 6.5 The repeated appearance of details about PQ Plastics on three files. Jane's surname appearing in at least two different places.

RQ 6.6 This is also a partial dependency because it is governed by Style and Size regardless of Surface Finish.

RQ 6.7 This has similarities with the shifts experienced in the form of computer languages and the development of GUIs. The encoding–decoding emphasis is moving away from computer system convenience towards human convenience, as computer technology becomes more able to adapt through faster processing and larger storage capacity.

RQ 6.8 Sorry that I asked what 'kind' of hierarchy. It was an unintended pun. It was indeed a 'kind of' hierarchy.

RQ 6.9 The most obvious to me is the motor car. Early owners had to understand how their vehicles worked and what to do when they frequently went wrong. Today, you don't even have to know how to change gear if you get yourself an automatic, let alone be familiar with what's under the bonnet.

References/bibliography

Booch, G. (1991). *Object Oriented Design*. Benjamin Cummins, Redwood City, CA.

Bowers, D.S. (1988). *From Data to Database*. Van Nostrand Reinhold, New York.

Codd, E.F. (1970). 'A Relational Model of Data for Large Shared Data Banks'. *Commun.* ACM 13 (6).

Elmasri, R. and Navathe, S.B. (1989). *Fundamentals of Database Systems*. Benjamin Cummings, Redwood, CA.

Hernandez, M.J. (1997). *Database Design for Mere Mortals: A Hands-On Guide to Relational Database Design*. Addison-Wesley, Reading, MA.

Martin, J. (1976). *Principles of Database Management*. Prentice-Hall, New York.

McFadden, F.R., Hoffer, J. and Prescott, M.B. (1999). *Modern Database Management*. Addison-Wesley, Reading, MA.

Perry, J.T. and Lateer, J.G. (1989). *Understanding Oracle*. Sybex, San Francisco, CA.

Stanczk, S. (1990). *Theory and Practice of Relational Databases*. Pitman Publishing, London.

Thompson, J.P. (1989). *Data with Semantics*. Van Nostrand Reinhold, New York.

Veryard, R. (1984). *Pragmatic Data Analysis*. Blackwell Scientific, Oxford.

Veryard, R. (1992). *Information Modelling*. Prentice-Hall, Upper Saddle River, NJ.

CHAPTER 7

Organizations and information systems

A simple commercial transaction?

What happened

I was buying a book over the Internet for the first time. It wasn't anything very unusual or expensive, but I found that the supplier had it in stock at a more competitive price than the shop I have dealt with before. Since I live in a country area, many specialist things I buy have to be ordered over the Internet and delivered. This is usually a straightforward process of accessing a web page, quoting an account or credit card number, and awaiting delivery. I find that the increase in the range and quantity of delivery services has made living in the countryside and running a business much easier in the last ten years. Occasionally we get a van driver who hasn't heard about maps, but most of them find no problem in whisking around village lanes and up farm tracks to deliver everything from thermal underwear to a piece of computer equipment.

Two days after I ordered my book, therefore, I was not surprised when a delivery van turned into my drive, and a driver I recognized from a previous delivery jumped out. She walked briskly round to the back of the van, opened up the doors, handed me a packet and asked me to print and sign my name. Although I find most of these drivers very friendly, they are usually in a hurry. I suspect this is connected with the fact that their companies compete on the basis of speed of delivery. I notice, for example, that when I sign the delivery document the time as well as the date of delivery has been entered by the driver.

Although I am usually friendly as well, I've learnt to be more assertive on the question of signing before I've had time to check that the correct item has been delivered. While I was doing this, the driver returned to the cab and brought back a map. She was trying to find someone whose address gave only a house name and our village. Needless to say, everyone knows everyone in a village and I was able to direct her. So with a revving of a diesel engine the van was down my drive and off.

The issues raised

The title of this lead-in case and its brevity are designed particularly to emphasize simplicity. Given the role of these introductory cases as raisers of issues, you will not be surprised that I now intend to show that what we have described is in fact quite a complex combination of potential data processing procedures hidden behind a simple commercial transaction. We can understand this by considering the implications of two key events.

The first key event took place when I confirmed that I wanted to buy the book and placed my order on the Web. Although this simple transaction was recorded on a standard form with customer and product details, it represented data coming into the seller's information system that could do much more than make sure I got the product and the seller got the money.

We should notice first that it wasn't an order for any product, but for that particular book at that particular time in its market life, at that particular price, and against a particular promotional background in terms of the way it was advertised and sold. Data like this on the sale of the product had now been captured by an information system that was capturing similar data on other sales and on other products. The system wasn't just finding out about one transaction, it was also potentially building up an understanding of a whole set of products and markets. If I didn't keep the security level on my Web browser so high and I wasn't so paranoid about cookies, I guess that I'd be contributing a lot more information about buying habits to Web market watchers' sites like DoubleClick.

The next thing to note is that it wasn't anyone buying the software: it was me. The data on the standard form would say something about me, such as where I live and my postcode; or that I chose to pay by a credit card, with its associated credit limit and implied credit rating. Such data has the potential to tell the supplier something about what sort of customer is buying what sort of product. Hence the data recorded for this, as for any sales transaction, isn't just to be used for the *goal-seeking* control of ensuring delivery and payment, it also represents potential *learning* about markets that can be used to set goals.

We can look further by considering what the software did when I enquired and placed the order. When it confirmed that the book was in stock and I placed my order, although nothing physical happened to the book itself, it immediately changed its conceptual state in the stock control system. We can understand the distinction between the conceptual and the physical in terms of Figure 3.2 and the description of standard stock control procedures in Appendix 1. Once a stock item is sold it goes from being 'Free Stock' to being 'Allocated', thus reducing the stock level by one unit. If this had resulted in a complete stockout or a fall below the reorder level, my simple commercial transaction would have acted as an actuating trigger for the reordering mechanism. Whatever the details of how my book supplier's stock control system worked, my order was not only data to be used in the *goal-seeking* control of ensuring appropriate stock levels. As a piece of sales data for a particular stock item, it would also contribute to forecasts and estimates of demand used to set reorder levels as part of the *goal-setting* process of stock control.

To the person in the book supplier's storerooms, my order represented the use of human resources rather than a sale. Together with all the other orders placed that day, it was data relating to the amount of moving and packing that had to go on. Data on sales for the store management represented potential information to be used in human resource management for planning of such things as the size of workforce needed and the use of seasonal or temporary labour. It also was needed for decisions on facilities such as storage space.

Even as a commercial transaction, however, my order may not have been as simple as ensuring I got my book and the supplier was paid. Had I been a fraudster or bad debtor, my transaction would have been one piece of data to have gone into any of the goal-setting processes associated with credit control.

Once my order had been accepted and the package made ready for delivery, a double copy of the order form was now passed on to the delivery firm. When the order was delivered to me and I printed and signed my name, a second key event took place.

For my delivery driver, as for the supplier's store management, the data on the order form represented a job. My address implied certain details about mileages and times that affected the incentives and payment of the person making the delivery. Once I signed the double copy of the order form, the copy retained by the delivery driver was the feedback needed by the delivery company to help control a number of processes. These included confirmation to the supplier that the delivery firm had fulfilled its contractual obligation, and confirmation to both the driver and those who paid her that she had done the job in a certain time.

There was another copy of the form, however. This was the one I retained. As a self-employed person I need to keep my own accounts for tax purposes. The book represented part of the expenses that I incurred in carrying out my business. So my copy of the document represented *feedback* on my expenses that I could use as part of my financial system. If the Inland Revenue should require confirmation of the expenses involved in my business of writing this book, my copy of the document would also be a component of their control system feedback.

The central message that comes out of this simple lead-in case is that *the nature of information is defined by its management and organizational use.*

Thus there is no such thing as exclusively 'marketing', 'stock control', 'financial' or whatever information. As we saw in the lead-in case, my so-called simple transaction information was potentially useful for sales, marketing, human resource management, logistics, stock control, purchasing and supply management, credit control, in fact, a whole range of the bookseller's management activities.

What we have seen is that *labels* applied to information can be misleading and restrictive. The analysis of what happened in the case brings us back to the distinction of *whats* and *hows*, and the *conceptual* nature of any system. As long as we see the order form on the Internet, the delivery van coming up my drive and the book, we are fooled into thinking that the information involved is concerned solely with order processing and delivery. Once we realize that the data components of that information can be assembled and used in other ways, we can fully exploit the potential of information and communications technology. This becomes possible once we see organizations as systems and see the boundaries between their different activities as conceptual *whats* rather than physical hows.

We made a start to this process in Chapter 2 when we saw the limits of the traditional hierarchical triangle model of management in Figure 2.2. In Chapters 3 to 5 we established the basic concepts of systems thinking and used these to understand the role of the information system as a component of the wider management system through the concept of control. In Chapter 6 we explored models of how information could be built up from its component data. In that chapter we once again found that the distinction of whats and hows was important in separating the logical and physical views of data. The important concept of a database, with its implications of information as a organizational resource, was only possible once we had made this distinction.

What our lead-in case is now showing is that the wealth of concepts we have developed in Chapters 2 to 6 can only be specifically applied to understanding information systems in management once we have clearly resolved two issues:

1 How can an organization or business be seen as a system?
2 How can we distinguish the different roles of those involved?

Opportunities for learning

As we saw in Chapter 2, most of the classic books on management information systems try to marry a conventional, organizational view of the business with a computerized interpretation of information systems. In this chapter we shall consider how the concept of a system can integrate the way in which an organization or business is viewed and the role of the information system within it. This will then prepare us for Chapters 8 and 9, were we shall study how information systems can be defined, developed and implemented to support the management of organizations and businesses.

Learning objectives

The learning objectives for this chapter are to:

1 Build a generally applicable systems model of organizations and businesses, based on the concepts and principles of Chapter 3 to 6.

2 Interpret both profit-motivated businesses and alternatively motivated organizations in terms of this model.

3 Understand the distinction between the conceptual nature of the model and its specific manifestations.

4 Use the model as a means of understanding the role of information systems in the management of organizations.

7.1 THE ORGANIZATION AS A SYSTEM

7.1.1 Conventional and systems views of organizations

In Chapter 4 we saw how a hierarchical concept of control, as in Figure 4.10, enabled us to make the connexion between information and management. At each of the levels of the control hierarchy, the information system was seen as a subsystem of the control system. We also saw how the hierarchy of control systems led to a relationship between the level of control, the nature of the control exerted and the type of information used.

In this chapter we shall show how the typical main functions of a business can be understood in systems terms, and hence how a business or organization can be viewed as a management system. We shall then see what forms the hierarchy of control systems can take within this management system, and the different kinds of practical function the information system has to carry out as a component of control. Throughout this chapter I will use the term 'organization' to stand for both commercial businesses like Carry-Out Cupboards and non-commercial organizations like the Child Support Agency or Limber Marsh Drainage Consortium.

When we take this very broad view of what can constitute an organization, we will be using the now familiar principle that the description of a system as a concept can be very different from its physical or concrete materialization. In particular:

- The structure of any particular organization when it is seen as a management system does not necessarily have the same named components as those shown on the official organization chart or printed on notices above the doors to its various departments. MX Marketing is an example of this principle. It is a small company of two to three people working from a base of a single office. They are selling products, one of which they designed themselves. Such a small team covers all the functions of a business by each person taking several responsibilities. Just looking at one individual from the team of three: Ben Lister could answer questions like 'Who's the boss?', 'Who's the marketing manager?', or 'Who was the designer of this product?' by saying 'It's me'.
- We shall see how the processes carried out by different organizations can be interpreted in terms of common systems principles. Thus when we discuss such diverse organizations as commercial companies, hospitals or official government bodies as systems, we shall see that they share certain common underlying conceptual similarities. This does not mean, however, that we regard these organizations as the same. We shall equally acknowledge the assertion that in concrete, physical terms they are very different. We may, for example, describe both the treatment of patients in a hospital and the packing and assembly of products at Carry-Out Cupboards in terms of them both being processes. We are not implying, nevertheless, that we think that how these processes are carried out should be at all similar, or that we would have the same attitude to what is being 'processed'.

In Chapter 2 we introduced the idea that language can be misleading not only if we do not distinguish whats and hows, but also between the particular hows themselves. This latter point happens to be particularly important when changes in technology take place. Consider a piece of advanced modern technology like a new nuclear submarine, with its deadly and sophisticated weapons. Despite this modernity and sophistication, when a submarine moves it is described as 'sailing'. When this word is used, no one envisages the captain parading on deck with orders to raise the mizzen or pull up the spanker: to quote some old sailing ship terms. Even so, some old fashioned language prevails and we continue to talk of a submarine 'sailing' not 'fissioning' its way out to sea.

As we saw in Chapter 6, this retention of previous language is not confined to traditional professions like the British Royal Navy. Managers still happily refer to 'files' on their computers, even though such files have no more reality than the sails on a nuclear submarine. We warned in Chapter 2 that using the old thinking can be both helpful and dangerous at times of transition. We saw that a computer that presents so-called icons of folders, filing cabinets and a wastepaper basket on a desktop can help users interpret the new technology that they do not understand in terms of the old that they do. Again in Chapter 6, we warned of the dangers of confusing the logical form of a database with its particular physical implementation.

In the field of information and the management of organizations, the retention of old models can be even more inhibiting. Information has *emergent properties* that mean that advances in the media used for its *physical* manifestation actually make for *qualitative* changes in the nature of information itself. Replacing a filing cabinet with storage on disk, like replacing sails by nuclear power, is not just a quicker way of doing the same job: it actually leads to *new possibilities* for the whole system.

The nuclear power of a submarine not only drives the ship faster than sails, it can also generate power for heating and lighting as well as replenishing its internal atmosphere. This in turn results in a whole system that does completely new things compared with former ships. Nuclear power not only breaks through the surface movement limitations of wind and weather, it also sends the submarine under water or ice caps, and even allows it to sit for days on the sea floor.

Similarly, advances in information and communications technology and the advent of the Internet don't just provide a quicker way of ordering books or keeping accounts. As we saw in the lead-in case for Chapter 3 and our study of networked communications in Chapter 5, *physical boundaries* are being replaced by *conceptual boundaries*. Things like departments and organizations are less likely to be identifiable as a room or a building. Teams or communities are no longer necessarily people gathered in one place. The old management vocabulary doesn't always fit any more: like the filing cabinet icon, it can be misleading.

So the danger is that we have the 'nuclear power' of modern information and communications technology attached to a 'sailing ship' language for a view of management in organizations. We may have grown out of thinking in the old terms of file processing into the new view of a database management system, but we still think that, say, 'finance' is the name of a department on a company organization chart, or 'marketing' the name of a nice new office building set well apart from the factory.

If we are to replace old computer data processing ideas with an information systems view, we also need to replace an organization chart or physical picture of management with a systems view. Otherwise we shall be fitting nuclear reactors to a wooden sailing ship. Thus if a systems view of information is to be presented, it is inconsistent to try to marry this to a non-systems view of organizations.

It is possible to take our analogy further. Some may fear that nuclear power, even when used peacefully, can be potentially dangerous. Likewise, developments in information and communications technology can also be regarded with suspicion. However, far from being an argument against taking a modern systems view of information and organizations, this fear makes such a view even more important. If we wish to protect ourselves against a threat, we need to face it and understand it.

General Montgomery, an important British army commander in the Second World War, always had a photograph of his main German military rival General Rommel to look at when he was planning his strategy. At the very least in self-defence, modern management needs to have a picture of 'the enemy' in the form of understanding modern approaches.

More positively, there is another important reason for seeing beyond a physical system to what is actually going on. Failure to discern the logical system behind the physical system can greatly reduce the chances of successful *systems development*, as we shall see in Chapters 8 and 9.

7.1.2 The components of a systems view of organizations

One way of seeing an organization as a system is one I first published in Harry (1990) and will develop further in this chapter. The important principle behind this view stems from the aim to see an organization as a system. If we do this, it follows that our view will incorporate the systems properties we introduced in Chapter 3.

One of the important systems properties we shall use in forming our view of organizations is that a system 'does something', i.e. carries out *processes* and exhibits *emergent properties*. If we then go on to consider systems that are managed, the concept of management brings with it the General Control Model of Figure 4.10 and the concept of *purpose*. In Section 3.2 we explored the concept of purpose in building up the model and saw that the purpose of an organization reflected the *world view*, *purpose* or *set of values* of the systems owner or perceiver. We also saw that this was translated down the control hierarchy into information specifying *methodology* and *policy*, *methods* and *procedures*, *goals* and standards and, finally, information on the *actions* to be carried out by the *transformation process* of the system.

If we view a managed organization as a system, therefore, we see it as something that tries to carry out processes with the purpose of producing emergent properties reflecting the aims and values of the systems owner, in the context of an environment that disturbs those processes. Our use of the term emergent properties and processes reflects the fact that an organization seen as a system will share the property of all other systems in consisting of at least two, and usually many, components. These will be both abstract and concrete, as well as hard and soft.

To make sense of the complexity of such a whole, we can first distinguish two main components of an organization when seen as a system, as in Figure 7.1:

1 A *central-purpose subsystem* that justifies or explains why the whole organization as a system exists at all.

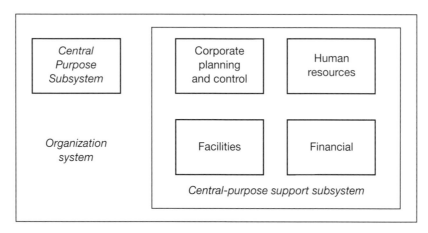

Figure 7.1 A systems view of an organization
A first step in identifying the major components distinguishes a *central-purpose subsystem*, which justifies or explains why the whole organization as a system exists at all, and a *central-purpose support subsystem*, which makes possible and supports the activities of the central-purpose subsystem.

2 A *central-purpose support* subsystem that makes possible and supports the activities of the central purpose subsystem.

Central purposes will differ according to the kind of organization we are considering.

RQ 7.1 What would you see as the central purpose of:

1 Carry-Out Cupboards?
2 The Limber Marsh Drainage Consortium?
3 MX Marketing?
4 The Child Support Agency?

Although central purposes of different organizations may themselves be very different, they all have the common property that without a central purpose, the need for the organization would disappear.

It is also important to note that central purpose is a *holistic* concept that may be an *emergent property* consisting of several components. Thus I was once asked whether an organization might not have more than one central purpose. For example, a firm might make roof racks for cars that it could either fit to customers' cars, or sell to customers for them to fit themselves.

RQ 7.2 Is the central purpose of this firm to sell or to fit roof racks? Or again, a hospital may carry out medical tests and give emergency treatment too. Which is the central purpose?

I would add further to what I have asserted about the central purpose and say that if an organization has no discernible central purpose in this holistic sense, why are we viewing the organization as a *whole* in the first place?

The *central-purpose support subsystem* makes possible and supports the activities of the central-purpose subsystem so that the whole organization will function as a system. It is important to note here that our systems view of hierarchy does not see the word 'support' as implying judgement about the relative importance of the central-purpose and central-purpose support subsystems. We see the whole, which is the sum of these two components, as 'the greater', not either of the components.

Figure 7.1 also shows the *four components* of the central-purpose support subsystem:

1 A *human resources* subsystem, which provides the human power and skills that the central purpose requires.
2 A *facilities* subsystem, which provides the equipment, machinery, land, buildings and all the other inanimate, concrete components that provide resources to support the central-purpose subsystem.
3 A *financial* subsystem, which provides the financial operations to support the central-purpose subsystem.
4 A *corporate planning and control* subsystem, which provides the goals for the organizational system as a whole, and attempts to control the outputs from the systems components so that the behaviour of the whole system meets the organizational goals.

It is important to note that the *corporate planning and control* subsystem will cover the *coordination* and *decision making* that affect the form of interaction of two or more of the central-purpose, human resources, facilities and financial subsystems (Figure 7.2).

As we shall see later in this chapter, these subsystems exert *goal-setting* and *goal-seeking* control over their own processes. The higher orders of control of the General Control Model of Figure 4.10, which are concerned with co-ordinating goal setting through establishing methodology and policy in relation to the systems *world view, purpose* or *set of values*, is the task of the corporate planning and control subsystem.

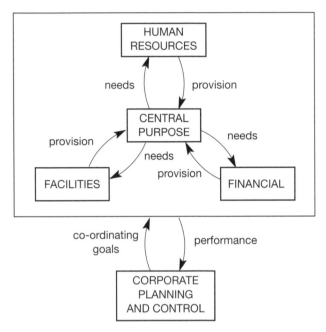

Figure 7.2 The interaction of the organizational systems components
The human resource, facilities and financial subsystems support the central-purpose subsystem, with the corporate planning and control subsystem co-ordinating the whole.

We can consider an example to illustrate this point. Let us examine the decision making involved if the Limber Marsh Drainage Consortium were considering buying a new excavating machine. The central-purpose subsystem would decide what sort of machine was wanted and what operations it had to perform. The facilities subsystem would have the job of acquiring the machine and ensuring it was kept in working order. The financial subsystem would have the job of paying the supplier for it. But the whole decision as to which machine to buy in terms of its technical abilities, reliability and financial costs requires a decision that *co-ordinates* these different goals in the context of the wider organizational system.

Figure 7.2 illustrates the relationships between these subsystems. It shows that the human resources, financial and facilities subsystems have a service or supporting role for the central-purpose subsystem. In each case, the central-purpose subsystem has needs that it communicates to the appropriate supporting subsystem. Note that the communication of these needs is an information flow, and that the role of the information system will be to ensure that such information is gathered and communicated.

Given that Figure 7.2 illustrates the role of the corporate planning and control subsystem in co-ordinating the goal setting of the individual subsystems in a way that is consistent with those of the organization as a whole, each of the subsystems will then need its own *control hierarchy* of goal setting, and goal seeking, which we will now consider.

7.1.3 A general model for organizational subsystems

A general systems model of the central-purpose and its three supporting subsystems can now be built from the relevant concepts of *systems hierarchy* and *control* from the General Control Model of Figure 4.10. We will call this the General Model for Organizational Subsystems (GMOS), and its general form is shown in Figure 7.5.

The first of these concepts are the simple ones of *goal-seeking* and *goal-setting* control, as illustrated by Figure 7.3. The *process* that is being controlled in each case will depend on the subsystem we are considering. Thus for the central purpose it will be the satisfying of a market, the provision of a service etc. as discussed above. For each of the supporting subsystems it will be the provision of the human resources, facilities or financial needs of the central-purpose subsystem.

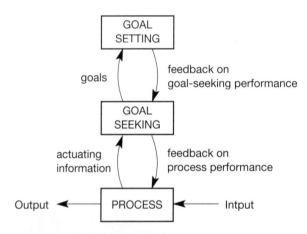

Figure 7.3 Goal-seeking and goal-setting control
This repeats the principle of Figure 4.8, but here the flow of input-process-output is shown right to left for subsequent convenience.

The next concept we need to introduce is one we have not discussed in any detail so far, which is the *interaction* of the various component subsystems with the whole system's environment. This can be generally illustrated by Figure 7.4. Examples of such interaction

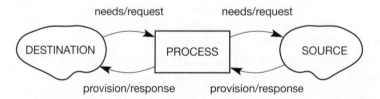

Figure 7.4 Interaction of a systems process and its environment
The process will have needs that its environment can supply as well as itself acting as a supplier of needs to its environment. Thus a manufacturing process will have material needs arising from its aim of meeting a need for the product manufactured.

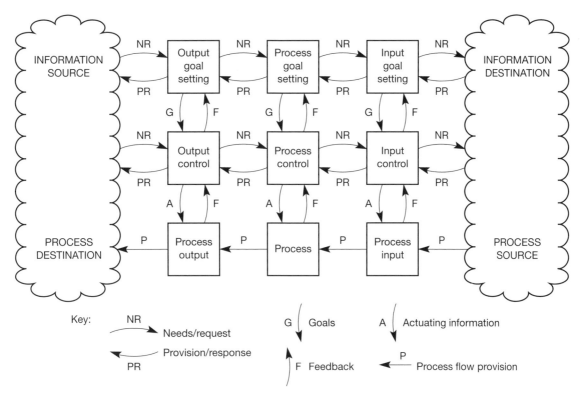

Figure 7.5 A General Model for Organizational Subsystems (GMOS)
This is built on the fundamental concepts of control, as presented in Chapter 4, and the concept of interaction with the environment of Figure 7.4.

would be the need to pay suppliers by the financial subsystem or to deliver products to a customer by the central-purpose subsystem of a manufacturing organization.

One further point will enable us to understand the General Model for Organizational Subsystems of Figure 7.5. When we consider the processes of any of our subsystems, we will find it useful to distinguish input and output components from the process itself. The process will be what the subsystem does as its main function within the organization, while the input and output components represent the interaction of the various subsystems with the environment. Thus, for example, the facilities subsystem of Limber Marsh Drainage Consortium has as its main process the support of the central-purpose subsystem by maintaining plant and equipment. But it also has to interact with the environment by receiving new equipment from suppliers or disposing of old equipment.

When we bring these concepts together to form the General Model for Organizational Subsystems of Figure 7.5 we see:

1 The *vertical* groupings of the components representing control systems with their hierarchies of *goal setting* and *goal seeking*. Each of these three is an instance of the control model of Figure 7.3, for input, process and output subsystems respectively.
2 The *horizontal* groupings of components representing the needs/request-provision/response relationships that track the effect of environmental disturbances. These groupings represent an expansion of the model in Figure 7.4, to cover the stages of *input*, *process* and *output*.

We will now look at how each of the central-purpose and supporting subsystems can be interpreted in this systems model of organizations.

7.2 THE CENTRAL-PURPOSE SUBSYSTEM

7.2.1 The general model of the central-purpose subsystem

If we intend to illustrate how the central-purpose subsystem of an organization can be interpreted in terms of the General Model for Organizational Subsystems, it will be useful to choose one particular organization as an example. This will be easier for one whose central purpose is marketing and manufacturing, so we will choose Carry-Out Cupboards as our example. We can then use the contrasting non-commercial, public-service example of the Limber Marsh Drainage Consortium to make additional points.

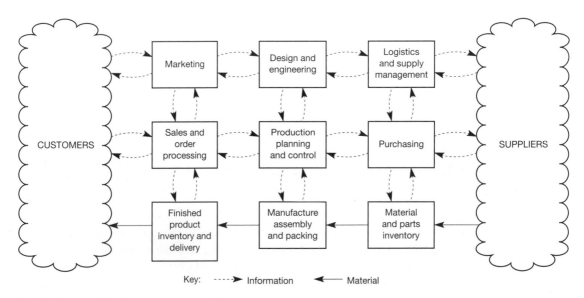

Figure 7.6 An interpretation of the central-purpose subsystem of Carry-Out Cupboards in terms of the GMOS

It is important to note that the names given to the various processes refer to what they do, rather than to names of departments or locations. Thus the finished product inventory and delivery function is shared by both the CP and the ROs (see Appendix 1).

Figure 7.6 shows how the model in Figure 7.5 could be interpreted for Carry-Out Cupboards and many other production- or manufacturing-based organizations. The components of the subsystem have been given names that commonly correspond to those frequently used to describe practical functions. It is vital to remember, once again, that we are referring to what goes on in the subsystem, not where it is done or who does it. Furthermore, to avoid confusion, throughout this section we will assume that the term 'system' refers to the whole central-purpose subsystem at this level of the hierarchy, and use 'subsystem' to refer to the partial aggregations of its components.

As we established above, an important aspect of Figure 7.5 is the way in which the components can be grouped into subsystems. This may be done either vertically or horizontally in terms of the diagram, but each way represents an important property of the central-purpose system that we will now consider.

We shall focus on the vertical grouping of components into three subsystems and emphasize the control model relationship. We shall look at these three subsystems in turn to get a broad picture of their main components and what they do. We shall also consider how they interact with each other horizontally in terms of the environmental disturbance, needs/request-provision/response model of Figure 7.4. In addition to this broad view, a detailed systematic run through the information flows as illustrated by Carry-Out Cupboards is to be found as part of Appendix 1.

Box 7.1

Time for Auntie to quit the slow lane and drive to market

Martin Dickson

With one very notable exception, shares in Britain's big media businesses leapt this week on news of the proposed US merger between America OnLine and Time Warner. The odd man out was the UK's largest media organization, the BBC, which does not, of course, have any shares to be traded. It is high time it did.

The AOL deal may or may not prove a model for the rest of the communications industry – strong arguments can be mounted on both sides – but it does show that if a business wants to be a serious force in the new global media industry it needs three important attributes: great flexibility, since no one really knows what the future holds; deep pockets to snap up assets, though these should be filled with share certificates rather than cash, to permit painless equity for equity swaps; and a strong international reach.

The BBC possesses none of these, but it could if the British establishment heeded the wake-up call of the AOL deal and started thinking seriously about privatizing the second largest media group in Europe after Germany's Bertelsmann.

Instead, it is engaged in a tortuous debate over how to fund the BBC's digital television expansion plans, earnestly trying to decide whether aun-tie will spend the money wisely, or fritter it away on gin, and whether she should be forced to raise some funds herself by selling off part of the family silver or becoming a little more (but not too much, dearie!) involved in that dangerous bingo-like activity, 'commerce'.

The BBC has big ambitions for digital television, which will transform viewing patterns over the next decade, offering vast numbers of channels, access to archives of programming, and convergence between the Internet, broadcasting and personal communications devices. It has already built up an impressive Internet presence with its BBC Online site. But its plans will cost a lot and it argues that without adequate funds it will be condemned to a slow demise.

Last summer a government committee headed by Gavyn Davies, the economist, recommended it should get an additional £150m–£200m a year, through an additional licence payment from subscribers to digital television and should sell, or inject private capital, into its commercial offshoots.

Commercial digital broadcasters oppose the licence payment, saying it will hamper them in winning subscribers. The Commons select committee on culture is also against, arguing that it will slow the take-up of digital television, which the gov-ernment is keen to promote, and that the corporation – scornfully dismissed as a digital 'follower' rather than a leader – has not made an adequate case for funding. The government is still agonizing, but a decision is due soon.

Seen from a distance, however, the protagonists look rather like a family standing in the path of a hurricane, squabbling over the right way to build a Heath Robinson escape vehicle while wilfully ignoring the sports car parked nearby, fuelled and revving. That sports car is privatization.

For the BBC, it would solve at a stroke its perpetual cash shortage. It could aggressively exploit its superb brand name, expand into digital, and bid more aggressively for talent, shows and sports fixtures. It would have a currency with which to snap up other businesses and become a genuinely global force. Helpfully, it has in Greg Dyke, the new director-general, a leader whose career has been spent in the private sector.

For policymakers, there should be numerous attractions. First, MPs would no longer debate the validity of the BBC's ambitions like central planners from another era. The market would decide. It would also force greater efficiency on the corporation,

▶

which film-makers complain is still over-bureaucratic.

Alas, however, privatization is not a live political issue because the government and most of the establishment believe the BBC should remain a public service broadcaster, with a duty to 'inform, educate and entertain', enriching viewers' lives in 'ways that the market alone will not'. As such it is also supposed to exert an influence for good on private-sector broadcasters, whose instincts are supposedly for the cheap and vulgar.

But this argument is simply out of date. First, no one seems able to define very clearly what public service means in an age of infinite choice. Second, the very idea smacks of elitism from another age: let them eat our cultural cake. Third, in the digital age people will simply not watch the BBC if it does not provide what viewers want, leading eventually to a licence-payers' revolt.

Finally, it is a national myth that the bulk of BBC's service nowadays 'enriches viewers' lives in ways that the market cannot'. Quality is in the eye of the beholder, but a dispassionate Martian comparing BBC TV with commercial rivals would be hard put to notice any significant difference. Auntie's news is usually less sharp than ITN's (I've commented before on its lamentable coverage of finance) and prime-time is stuffed with slow-moving 'comedies' notable mostly for pre-adolescent sexual smut. Radios One, Two and Five are quite as banal as anything to be found on commercial channels.

Admittedly, there are a few remaining pockets of genuine 'enrichment': parts of Radio Three and Four and a scattering of scientific and educational programmes. But these could be protected, as part of a privatization licence, or subsidized by public subscription, as in the US. And the government could temper quality concerns by holding a golden share in the privatized company, at least for its early years.

So instead of doling out another grudged slice of licence-payers' money for the BBC, Tony Blair should be announcing its liberation. Of course he will not, given the Labour party's reflex belief in the nanny state and the Conservatives' knee-jerk support for anything wrapped in the Union flag.

The next root-and-branch reassessment of the corporation's role and financing is not due until its 'charter review' (a tellingly antiquated phrase) in 2004–06, by which time the world will have changed greatly and auntie will be much more at risk of the marginalization it fears so much. The hurricane is coming.

Source: Financial Times, 15 January 2000. Reprinted with permission.

Comment

We can expect to get a lot more agonizing about the BBC. A major reason for this is that many of the worthy people concerned about its future are still thinking in old ways. The important systems point about the BBC is that it has two kinds of information at the centre of its activities:

1 Information that it needs in order to manage its activities, just like any other managed organization.
2 Information that is its product: news, entertainment etc.

Big changes in information and communications technology have greatly altered the way we handle all kinds of information. For the BBC this has meant that the two kinds of information, which are conceptually different, are often physically mixed together on a common information technology.

An example of this is the Electronic News Production System, ENPS. This stores multimedia news material electronically and also provides the programme producer with a platform to assemble and schedule items from the stored material to make up programmes. Thus the product information, like a news report, is running within the same software environment as the management information, like a schedule.

However, just consider how this can be taken a stage further in this networked world of ours. Why do we need a producer? Why not open the database of material to the Internet? This would enable the public to assemble and view what they wanted when they wanted. Where now is the 'public service' direction for the BBC? To hang on to its material and tell the public what they can have and when? Or to let the public choose?

7.2.2 The central-purpose output control subsystem

The *output control subsystem* is concerned with output from the central-purpose system to the environment. For Carry-Out Cupboards, this will involve selling products at the retail outlets to the customer.

| **RQ 7.3** | Why do we consider the output control subsystem first? |

Goal-setting control for this subsystem will involve deciding on the type and quantity of products to be sold. This top-level process is carried out by *marketing*. In everyday life the terms marketing and selling are often used to mean the same thing, but for a professional manager this is bad practice because an important distinction can be made between the two terms. Systems thinking also leads us to make a similar distinction to that made by professional management. This can be clarified if we compare marketing with the first-order control and goal-seeking process of sales and order processing.

Sales and order processing is concerned with selling products from the existing range to customers. Marketing is concerned with establishing what products we are going to make in the future. To do this, it gathers information about unfulfilled existing or future customer needs using market research, and defines what characteristics particular products would have to have to meet them. These characteristics are usually defined as high-level emergent properties like 'value' or 'appeal', although marketing people would probably not use the term emergent property.

In the case of Carry-Out Cupboards, market research might reveal a trend towards more open, bright kitchens with a high-technology feel to them. This might be linked with a move away from a darker, wood-veneer, cottage style. Furthermore, this trend might be seen at its strongest among a younger group of society who cannot afford luxury items. The output information from the marketing process would take the form of criteria like 'lots of glass', 'simple geometrical shapes', 'primary colours' or 'economy before elaboration', rather than defining low-level details like how doors are fixed, handle design shapes or colours, or what proportion of the product cost can go on packaging. It is the next process of design and engineering that would take the information from marketing about what sort of product was needed and use it as a high-level specification to create a specific design for a cupboard. Marketing would also assess the potential size of the market in terms of sales, and details of the potential customer, including type and location.

The results of the decisions by marketing will be a product range aimed at an identified market and will represent goal setting for sales and order processing. *Feedback* on control performance for these goals will be the *statistical data* on sales, which will normally be held on some form of *product file*. This data will be periodically subject to *sales analysis* and the results used by marketing to decide about modification or additions to the product range. This is how Carry-Out Cupboards might confirm the drift away from 'cottage-style' cupboards.

> **RQ 7.4** What are the equivalents of these processes for the Limber Marsh Drainage Consortium?

Goal-seeking control is carried out by sales and order processing. Customer orders are environmental disturbances to the subsystem because they are inputs outside its control, and the disturbance comes in the form of the orders themselves and their changing demand patterns. The subsystem attempts to influence the environment, however, by carrying out actions like sales *promotion* or *advertising*. Note that the particular desired form of these actions, and the original decision to carry them out, are goal-setting processes originating from marketing.

Getting products to customers is carried out by the *finished product inventory and delivery process*. This takes as its inputs the cupboards from the assembly and packing process, and outputs them by handing them over or delivering them to customers. It is the retail outlets of Carry-Out Cupboards that do this.

How is this goal-seeking control process carried out by MX Marketing, and who does it?

The control exerted over finished product inventory and delivery by sales and order processing in practice requires information to be recorded about both product and customer. We can list some of the typical names for the documents, files and their computer screen equivalents. While in any computerized or networked organization much of this information will be electronically filed and processed, *hard copy*, in the form of documents, will frequently be used in conjunction with these files. Often the screen version will replicate the document itself.

Examples of ways used in practice to communicate and store such control information include:

1 *Product file/stock record* (Figure 3.2 on p. 51). Kept by the producer as a list of the products available for sale to potential customers. Gives details of the product identity and qualities by use of code number, description, type or category, dimensions etc. May also contain information about costs, price, source, reorder quantities or procedures and quantities in stock. Frequently mixes the functions of physical movement and stockholding with financial accounting and sales recording. Carry-Out Cupboards would certainly have one of these, and it would usually be kept as a regularly updated computer printout to enable retail outlets to know what was available.

2 *Customer file* (Figure 7.7). Kept by the seller. Gives details of customer identity and location, products bought, creditworthiness and performance, means of contact and market category. Often overlaps and confuses in its actual physical format the financially precise customer accounting functions of the financial subsystem that are strictly concerned with recording who owes whom for what supplied when. These latter functions would be recorded in the sales ledger. Carry-Out Cupboards would not normally have one of these because most of its sales are retail, i.e. direct to the final customer. However, most commercial transactions are done on credit, so one business selling to another would certainly keep some form of this.

3 *Invoice* (Figure 7.8). Details what has been supplied, when, and the financial amount owing as the result of a particular delivery. May or may not accompany

Customer No:	BA 6489	Name:	Barkages Ltd
Delivery Address:	Station Yard South Stoke Lifton	Address:	Barset House High St Lifton
Post Code:	NL21 7WB	Post Code:	NL20 67S
Area:	20	Product Groups:	A, C, F
Credit Level:	10	Discount Code:	12.5

Figure 7.7 Customer file
Kept by the seller as a means of recording details about a customer and supporting marketing and sales functions. In practice, this usually overlaps the customer accounting functions of the financial subsystem. A distinction might be made between information that generally applies to the customer, and information that refers specifically to financial transactions.

SAXUN OFFICE SUPPLIES

21 Saxun Way
Viking Trading Estate
North Coates
Barsetshire
BA99 9ZW

Telephone: (0176) 992992

Fax: (0176) 993993

VAT Reg. 478 8748 44

INVOICE

Carry-Out Cupboards
Cowford Business Park
Kirton
South Riding
SR77 7DQ

Date: 11.02.01

Number: 1832

Account No. C2256

Quantity	Description	Product Code	Price	
1	Kayware Mouse	I	59.34	59.34

Total Goods	59.34
VAT	8.90
Total	68.24

Figure 7.8 An invoice

This informs the customer what goods have been sent out and what is charged for them. As with Figure 4.17, much of what appears on this document, and how it appears, is not determined by the informations system's designer but by the environment. Thus Customs and Excise has specific rules about what must appear on the invoice of a company that is registered for VAT.

the products/goods, hence a delivery/goods received note goes with goods supplied to confirm/check physical delivery. Again, this is normally associated with commercial sales on credit, but Carry-Out Cupboards would use these for customers who had ordered for delivery on credit.

4 *Statement* (Figure 4.17 on p. 133). Reviews and aggregates on a periodic basis (cf. Chapter 3 and the concept of batch processing) the information supplied by a series of invoices. Carry-Out Cupboards would only use this for commercial operations as before, but in everyday business relationships this is a standard document.

5 *Remittance advice*. Confirms the delivery of payment in a similar way to the delivery note confirming delivery of the goods. Used in connexion with 3 and 4 above.

An important point comes out of our consideration of these typical documents and files. When we look at their contents, some of the data they contain seems more relevant to the *financial subsystem*. According to our systems view, the central-purpose output control subsystem is concerned with controlling the *delivery* of the product or *service* to the customer; not with ensuring payment.

This apparent confusion disappears once we return to our distinction between systems as concepts and their particular physical implementation, which we introduced in our lead-in case. One physical document can play many systems roles within an organization, just as a person can.

The potential range of roles that conventional documents and procedures like those above can play is a good example of why our conceptual, systems view of organizations is important. If particular documents are seen as the 'property' of some particular 'department' or management function, the data they contain is similarly departmentalized. Instead of being part of the organization's database or information resource, the data they contain is only exploited to provide the information needs of one of the conceptual subsystems. If this happens, much of their information value to the whole organizational system is lost. If we were developing a new or improved information system, as in Chapter 9, we should need to keep this important point in mind.

RQ 7.6 Would a non-commercial organization like the Limber Marsh Drainage Consortium have any equivalents of the above documents?

7.2.3 The central-purpose process control subsystem

This will control the heart of what the central-purpose system actually does. For an organization like Carry-Out Cupboards, it is concerned with producing products in response to the output needs identified by the central-purpose subsystem output control system. *Goal setting* is carried out by *design and engineering* using a high-level specification produced by marketing. This specification then acts as a starting point for producing a design defining which particular product we have come up with to meet the market need.

In our Carry-Out Cupboards example above, marketing came up with concepts like 'lots of glass', 'simple geometrical shapes', 'primary colours' or 'economy before elaboration'. We said that it was the job of design and engineering to translate these concepts into details like how doors are fixed, handle design shapes or colours, and determining the method and style of packaging consistent with the proposed cost for the product.

The *output* information from design and engineering will also include details of parts and materials, which *logistics and supply management* will use to decide on sources of supply, as we shall see below. For Carry-Out Cupboards, these details will form a high proportion of the output from design and engineering, since the product is mainly assembled from components made elsewhere. For organizations whose central purpose includes more manufacturing processes, however, design and engineering would need to define them.

Generally, the design and engineering process is only complete when enough information has been produced unambiguously to define the product and how it should be made. (I once read a good summary of the relationship between marketing and engineering in a student's answer paper. She said, 'marketing is the idea: engineering is the fact'. Alas, since it was in a finals paper, I never had a chance to ask her where the quotation came from.) The same statement could be made about the design and engineering of an *information system* as a product, which we will see in Chapter 9.

The *production planning and control* process will take as goal-setting input the definition of the product design from design and engineering. This will contain all the information needed to make the product. Production planning and control will also take a needs/request input from *sales and order processing* on how many of each product are needed to meet customer orders and when. Both of these information flows will be used to form a *production schedule* that *manufacture and assembly* will seek to meet. This production schedule will also produce an output to *purchasing* of a *parts and raw materials* schedule to meet the needs of manufacture and assembly.

Feedback by production planning and control to design and engineering will give information on the experience of making the product. This experience can result in learning better ways to design and make products in the future. Response on how manufacture and assembly is meeting the production schedule may be used by sales and order processing in turn to respond to customer queries about delivery dates.

Inputs to manufacture and assembly will consist of the raw materials and parts needed to make the product and the outputs will be the products themselves. It should be remembered here that we are only considering the central purpose and that interaction with the other subsystems of the organization will involve support from human resources, facilities and finance.

Typical names for the documents and files, and their computer screen equivalents, used in practice to communicate and store control information by the central-purpose process control subsystem might include:

1 *Production schedule/plan* (Figure 7.9). Defines how much of what product should be made when. The term product here will include parts, quantities of substances or assembly of components.
2 *Batch/job ticket* (Figure 7.10). Allocates a particular part of the production plan to a particular operator or some component function within the central-purpose process control subsystem. Has a mixed systems role, since it may be used to control the physical production process as well as the performance of the people involved and the financial aspects of their payment.
3 *Operations sheet/card/list* (Figure 7.11). Defines what physical operations must be carried out to produce the product. Is combined interest to both the human resources and engineering supervisory functions in order to see that the job is carried out. Has heavy implications for the operators and their representatives as defining what it will be like to do the job concerned.
4 *Engineering drawing/design*. Defines what the product processing system must produce, and is used in conjunction with the operations sheet that defines how it is produced.

PRODUCTION SCHEDULE

Production Facility: Packing

Date: 19.7.01

Time: 1000hrs

Day Number: 256

Day / Prod. code	256	257	258	259	260	261	262
C127	50			100	100	50	
C156	100	100	50			50	100
C218		50	100	100	50	50	50

Figure 7.9 Production schedule /plan

Used to define how much of a product, a part or an assembly should be made and when. May be expressed in diagrammatic form like a Gantt chart.

BATCH/JOB TICKET

Number: 256/12

Date: 19.7.01

Day Number: 256

Quantity	Code	Description	Facility
50	C127	Classic Single/S/S	Packing

Figure 7.10 Batch/job ticket

Identifies an operation or set of operations that have to be carried out on a product, or batch of products, as part of the production process. In this example, 50 C127 cupboards have to be packed. Note that this is one of the jobs specified by the production schedule of Figure 7.9.

5 *Clock cards and time sheets*. Record when the operators concerned with product processing are functioning. Combines and confuses several different subsystems concerned with product planning and control. The central-purpose process control subsystem uses these to monitor production performance. It is also used by the human resources subsystem to check for attendance, absence, sickness ... etc. The financial subsystem may use it to calculate wages or other payment and deductions.

OPERATIONS LIST

Product Group: All S/S Cupboards

Facility: Packing

Op. No.	Operation Type	Time
1	Check components complete	1.00
2	Fix wrapping	3.30
3	Assemble container	0.30
4	Pack	0.30
5	Inspection	1.00
6	Seal	0.30
	TOTAL	7.00

Figure 7.11 Operations list
Defines the operations that have to be carried out to complete some particular job. Besides defining the methods and facilities used, it may also define the times required. These may be used in helping to plan the production schedule as well as determining the amount of time the operator has to be paid for the job. When used for both of these purposes, there is an inherent tension between the interests of the operator, the financial subsystem and production planning and control.

Again, we notice how often in conventional physical forms of information systems the whats and hows become very mixed. Any attempt at systems development that aims to be successful for the whole organization must take account of this. Ignoring the fact that a particular document has, say, human resource implications as well as financial ones can result in the information system's working very differently from what is intended.

7.2.4 The central-purpose input control subsystem

In a production-based organization like Carry-Out Cupboards, this subsystem is concerned with ensuring the supply of parts and raw materials needed for manufacturing the product.

As we saw above, the *goal-setting* control is carried out by *logistics and supply management* using the output information from design and engineering to decide on sources of supply for materials and parts. This information is used by *purchasing* together with details on the *production schedule* from production planning and control to produce an *order or procurement schedule* on suppliers. It is worth recalling here that the issues faced by purchasing in deciding how much and when to order are an example of classic stock control, which we considered in Chapter 4. The *performance of suppliers* in terms of delivery times and product quality will form the *feed-*

back to logistics and supply management, which enables poor suppliers to be dropped and new ones investigated. This process of supplier assessment is sometimes called *vendor rating*. Note that it represents feedback on the goal-seeking performance of this control subsystem.

The physical reception of the input from suppliers and subsequently issuing it as output to manufacturing and assembly is done by raw material and parts inventory. Although this process may share with finished product inventory and delivery similar problems associated with stock control, the two processes are two different systems functions.

When it comes to considering some of the typical names for the documents, files and screen formats used in practice by the central-purpose input control subsystem, we would expect to find a similar set to those used by the central-purpose output control subsystem, except that now the roles of supplier and customer are reversed.

RQ 7.7 We have mainly interpreted the central-purpose subsystem in terms of a manufacturing organization like Carry-Out Cupboards. What would be the equivalent of:

1 Design and engineering (the goal-setting process of the central-purpose process control subsystem) for MX Marketing?
2 Suppliers (process source) for the Limber Marsh Drainage Consortium?

7.3 THE CENTRAL-PURPOSE SUPPORT SUBSYSTEM

7.3.1 The general model of the financial subsystem

The model of an organization as a system in Figures 7.1 and 7.2 identifies three systems with the role of supporting the needs of the central-purpose system: *human resources*, *facilities* and *financial*. This section will cover these systems in more detail by considering them in terms of the General Model for Organizational Subsystems of Figure 7.5.

The aim of this section, as in the previous one, is to show what is going on in information systems terms behind the physical organizational mask. The distinction between the systems view and the conventional organizational view is particularly important in the area of financial information systems, so we will alter our usual human resources, facilities, financial sequence and consider this system first. Also, as in the previous section we will assume that the term 'system' refers to the whole of the subsystem when we are looking at its own hierarchy, and use 'subsystem' to refer to partial aggregations of its components.

There are three *historical reasons* that the distinction between the systems view and the conventional organizational view is hard to establish as a concept when considering the financial subsystem. I find that I am much more sympathetic with the first two of these reasons than with the third.

The *first* reason for retaining a conventional view of the financial subsystem is accountability. The law, as a major component in the organizational system's environment, affects the financial subsystem much more than the other subsystems. Schedules in the various Companies Acts actually define what things the financial subsystem must do and, to some degree, how it must do them. A production manager who thinks of a new way of processing a product may be rewarded for being original; an accountant who thinks of a new way of keeping the books may end up in prison! The position is further distorted by the fact that some of the financial information processed is *irrelevant to the management and control of the organization*. Thus companies in the UK do not keep Value Added Tax (VAT) recording systems because they help to manage and control their activities; they do it because Customs and Excise requires it. From the systems viewpoint, the company is merely acting as a component of the government revenue-collection system when it does this. The VAT is in fact an *environmental disturbance*, not part of the organization's financial system.

A *second* reason that has a conservative effect on views of the financial subsystem is commercial practice. As we saw when considering typical documentation for the input and output subsystems of the central-purpose system, most organizations act as both customers and suppliers. The physical form of information used within the organization is also used for two-way communication between organizations. It is interesting to note that major changes in the way information and communications technology-based information systems work, like supply chain management, still widely conform to pre-information technology formats.

RQ 7.8   What role in the General Communication System model of Chapter 5 is being referred to here?

It would therefore reduce or even eliminate communication if an organization had a totally different internal format for its information system from that of its customers and suppliers. The most basic example of this is the actual numbers used to represent the sums of money. Conceptually, I and many other people could make a good case for us having a number system based on 12 rather than 10, but practically it is unlikely that any country, let alone any single organization, could survive going it alone on such a system. More widely, if other organizations use such formats as invoices or statements of account, then so must we.

The *third* reason a conservative organizational view of the role of financial information has persisted comes from the way that systems were often computerized. Since the financial functions of organizations were usually the first to be computerized, this precedent made the computer system the possession of the finance department. This factor was reinforced by the fact that most early computers required special housing and conditions, and it was therefore easy for 'the system' to be regarded as a separate physical thing and for the finance department to *own* it.

We discussed in the first section of this chapter why we needed to recognize that this has a much wider application than the particular subsystem with which it is associated. One particular reason we should look critically at the financial subsystem in this respect is that it helps finally bury the view that an information system is a computerization of historical procedures. We shall also see further in Chapter 9 how it helps with critical appraisal of information systems development methodologies.

Figure 7.12 shows the financial subsystem in terms of the General Model for Organizational Subsystems of Figure 7.5. Where the central-purpose subsystem was concerned with the flow of material, the financial subsystem is concerned with the flow of money. It should be noted that we use the word money to represent the *abstract* concept, not just one particular concrete manifestation. This distinction should now be familiar, as it is one we apply to information itself. In the financial context, we can illustrate the principle by noting that money can flow in many other

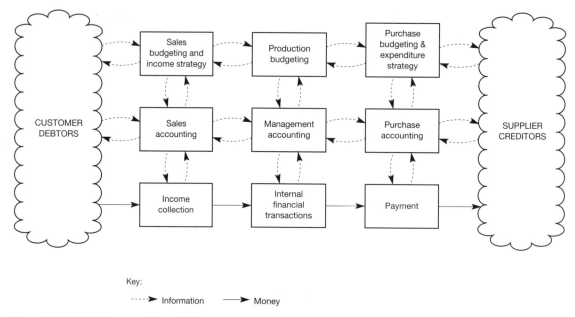

Figure 7.12 An interpretation of the financial subsystem in terms of the GMOS
The description of the various processes is widely applicable. It is important to note that this subsystem is concerned with the support of the central-purpose subsystem. Strategic financial processes will be the concern of the corporate planning and control subsystem.

ways than as actual coins put into the hand or notes paid out by a bank. Very often, a transaction is physically carried out by the alteration of a data in records.

As with the central-purpose subsystem, we shall make the bridge with conventional physical procedures by looking at how some of the systems concepts turn out in practice in the form of documents and files.

The financial input control subsystem

Since this is a component of a system that is supporting the central purpose, the input of money will be governed by the activities of the central-purpose subsystem. So in the case of a marketing- and production-based organization like Carry-Out Cupboards, the financial subsystem is concerned with control of the input, processing and output of money in relation to the manufacture and selling of a product.

Activity by the environment in the form of the customer buying or returning goods will initiate the need to control input in the form of *payment* or *repayment*. Note that this is why the financial flow has been shown in the opposite direction to the central-purpose flow. There are other important money inputs like those in the form of loans from banks or money raised from shareholders, but we saw above that these are the concern of the corporate planning and control subsystem.

The *sales budgeting* and *income strategy* process exerts higher-order control by setting financial sales targets and deciding issues like the *pricing of products*, the *offering of discounts* or the *credit terms* allowed to customers. It should not be surprising that this process occupies the equivalent position in Figure 7.12 to that of marketing in Figure 7.6. While marketing considers the type and quality of product the customer would buy, sales budgeting and income strategy determines the pricing and selling policy that would encourage the customer to buy it. Interactive relationships like this between processes in different subsystems are examples of the general principles shown by Figure 7.2.

Feedback on the success of these goals set by the sales budgeting and income strategy process will come from an analysis of information recorded by *sales accounting*. Sales accounting has the first-order control role over the behaviour of the income collection process by recording the sales of products and the receipt of payment for them. As we saw above, sales accounting and the sales and order processing component of the central purpose are usually mixed together in the physical system. When records kept by these components show that the sales of a product are below target or payment by a customer is consistently behind, higher-order control may come into play in the form of price changes for the product or adjustment to the customer's credit rating.

The close physical inter-relationship of sales accounting and the sales and order processing also means that the documents used by both of them overlap. Reference back to the central-purpose input and output control subsystems shows some typical examples. Also in practice, our conceptual distinction between the income collection process and sales accounting as control is hard to determine: usually one department does both. It is possible, however, to illustrate a physical example of the distinction in the form of debt collectors or bailiffs. Their job is seldom done by accountants or finance clerks.

The financial process control subsystem

This subsystem is concerned with processing and control of the money flows within the organization in response to the behaviour of the central-purpose process control subsystem. For an organization like Carry-Out Cupboards, these financial flows will be governed by the activities that take place when the product is assembled and packed. These will include a wide range of costs, from work done by human resources, to power consumed by plant or paperwork used.

Higher-order control takes the form of *production budgeting*, which sets goals for expenditure on these activities of the central-purpose subsystem. This process of goal setting also requires interaction with other subsystems under the co-ordinating principles laid down by the corporate planning and control subsystem. Thus the amount of time needed by the workforce to assemble a particular product and the materials required will follow from the product design and production procedures determined by design and engineering in the central-purpose subsystem. In co-ordination with this, the pay rate for the job will result from the operation of the human resources subsystem.

Management accounting will attempt to achieve the goals set by production budgeting by the controlled allocation of expenditure to internal financial transactions. The normal business definition of management accounting would cover both these functions, just as sales accounting would cover the income collection process in the financial input control subsystem. We need to use this rather artificial term of internal financial transactions, however, to distinguish the actual process of financial flow from the control functions exerted by management accounting. An example in practice of this distinction would be a typical payroll department. The job of this department is to make or process payment to the workforce according to preset rules, but not to be concerned with the rules themselves.

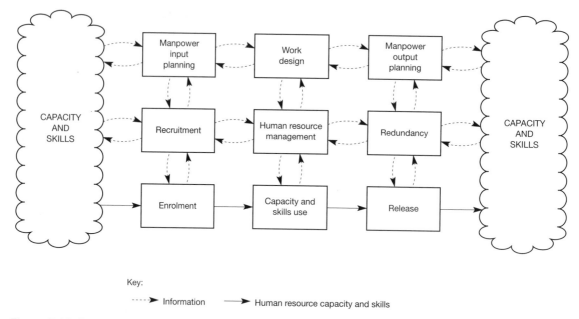

Figure 7.13 An interpretation of the human resource subsystem in terms of the GMOS
Shows the use of human skills and capacity in support of the central-purpose subsystem. The flows controlled are those of the skills and capacity, not the people themselves.

The financial output control subsystem

A financial output to suppliers and other components of the environment will result from their inputs to the central-purpose subsystem. The financial output control subsystem of Carry-Out Cupboards would, for example, pay for the supply of materials, component parts and packaging. As with the financial input control subsystem, we would exclude corporate planning and control operations like transfer of capital.

The *purchase budgeting and expenditure strategy* process sets the goals that *purchase accounting* seeks to meet. These goals define what money has been allocated for the purchase of materials, advertising, leasing etc., as discussed above. Purchase accounting would monitor and control the actual payment process to ensure that these policies were carried out.

The occurrence of these processes at equivalent positions in the General Model for Organizational Subsystems as logistics and supply management and purchasing in the central-purpose subsystem leads us to expect close interaction between them. Typical of the mixing of the two conceptual subsystems in one physical manifestation would occur in activities like vendor rating; determination of the best ordering policies against the costs of storage, ordering and delivery; assessing the benefits of discounts; or deciding the terms of timing and payment to suppliers.

The feedback from purchasing would give information that can be used for the resetting or modification of the above goals. Thus the actual cost performance by suppliers in relation to their quality and delivery might result in vendor rating excluding them as future suppliers, or changes in delivery and storage costs might result in different ordering schedules and quantities.

As with the sales accounting and income collection partnership, the controller and the process controlled are not easily distinguished in practice. Usually a department called 'purchasing' does both and the documents and records used often have several functions, as we saw above. The difference here is that the roles of customer and supplier are reversed.

RQ 7.9   What is the financial subsystem in a bank?

7.3.2 The general model of the human resource subsystem

In the previous subsystems, we considered it was necessary to define what *the flow* through the subsystem was. In the case of the human resource subsystem, is it people? To answer this question we need to go back to two familiar systems principles.

The first is the usual distinction we make between a concept and its concrete manifestation. For people, this often means that we distinguish between the whole person and any one particular systems role they might have. The second is the principle that the boundary of a system is determined by the aims and values of the person whose concept it is. So what are considered to be components of a system depend on why we are looking at it.

Complete people are not just 'human resources' components of a particular organizational system. They do many things and have many qualities that involve them in much wider systems than those concerned with their work. Within the boundary of the human resource subsystem, we only reveal a particular selection of their qualities that are relevant to that subsystem, not whole human beings. Even if we were just to regard people in this restricted way, however, we would still need to be cautious before describing 'people' as the flow through the human resource subsystem. This need for caution comes from our distinction between the roles and the people.

An example might illustrate this point. Suppose Jeff Wilson works as a draughtsman for the surveying department of the Limber Marsh Drainage Consortium. The authority decides to install a computer-aided design system that makes manual draughtsmen redundant. However, Jeff is retrained to operate the new system, so although his old job has disappeared he is not made redundant. Would we say that Jeff himself has 'flowed' through the subsystem, when he hasn't even had to change his office? I think we could see that one job or post has been removed from the subsystem and another has come in its place. In that sense there has been both input and output taking place, but Jeff himself has continued to work without a break. In looking at the human resources subsystem, therefore, we will be looking at the flow of roles or functions in the organization without necessarily implying any one particular physical flow or that people are only what their roles are.

The human resources input control subsystem
The need to recruit skills and roles comes as a result of the activities of the central-purpose subsystem. We therefore show the flow of this supporting subsystem in the same direction as the other central-purpose support subsystems, i.e. in the reverse direction of the product flow that uses it.

The goal-setting process of *manpower input planning* will work in conjunction with the higher-level goal setting of the other subsystems to determine not only the type of skills, but the number required and the cost and timing of their input to the human resources subsystem. In practice, this means that first we need to understand fully the central purpose of the organization itself. For a marketing production organization like Carry-Out Cupboards, this means knowing the kind of product we intend to make and sell, the amount we intend to make, the way we intend to make it, the cost of making it and when we intend making it. This information will, as a result of the activities of the central-purpose subsystem, be co-ordinated with finance and facilities subsystems through corporate planning and control. Once available, it can be used by manpower input planning to decide the skills of the workforce, the number needed, their pay or salary, and when and for how long they would be employed. The process of *manpower input planning* will also need to work in conjunction with manpower output planning to accommodate the human resources subsystem as a whole to environmental disturbances affecting human resource levels, but these are discussed when we cover the output subsystem itself below.

We use the terms *enrolment and recruitment* to describe the input process and its goal-seeking control respectively. In practice, we will find that the physical form of these components of the subsystem are intermingled. Recruitment will be concerned with controlling the input to the process from the environment by publicity and advertisements, responding to direct applications either in person or otherwise. The environment in this context will consist of all those potential employees whose skills might come to fulfil the roles required. They may not, like Jeff Wilson in the example above, necessarily be physically outside the organization. The enrolment process then has the job of the actual mechanics of signing on, making out contracts, briefing etc. In practical terms, the skills and procedures of interviewing, selection and completing contracts between the organization and its new recruits is usually carried out by the same person or team. So the human resources subsystem is normally similar in this respect to other General Model for Organizational Subsystems manifestations of input and output processes and their goal-seeking control.

Higher-order *feedback* on the results of recruitment's control of the *enrolment* process, in terms of its success in achieving goals, will determine the need for further adverts, different ways of recruitment and review of how realistic manpower planning goals turned out to be in the light of experience.

The human resource process control subsystem

The use of skills and roles recruited by the input control subsystem is governed by the process activities of the central-purpose subsystem that it supports. Thus for Carry-Out Cupboards, who does what job in, say, assembly and packing is determined by what jobs there are to be done, what is involved in doing them and by when they have to be done. Design and engineering will have set these goals for the jobs in terms of their design and production method. Production planning and control will be ensuring that they are done correctly and at the right time.

In this context, *work design* attempts to match the human aspects of work with the goals of design and engineering, while human resource management tries to control the human capacity and skills needed to support the implementation of these goals. Work design would look at design and engineering plans to introduce a new process at Carry-Out Cupboards, for example, and decide what skills would be needed for the new process and how the workforce should be organized to meet them. Human resource management would have the everyday task of ensuring that the workforce kept to the procedures. Their degree of success at this would then be the feedback from the skills use process, which determines what modifications should be made to work design.

The human resource output control subsystem

The central-purpose subsystem has to change its behaviour in response to disturbances from the environment. For Carry-Out Cupboards, this will mean altering the design of existing products, developing new ones, and adjusting planned sales levels in response to the demands of the market.

The effect of these changes on the supporting human resource subsystem will be a changes in both the capacity and the skills of human resources required. There will also be direct disturbances of the human resource subsystem as a whole directly from the environment. Some of the most common reasons for reduction in human resource levels of this type would be people leaving for another job and retirements.

Within the human resource output control subsystem itself, the process for which we use the general term 'release' covers any of the particular procedures that result in an intended reduction in the level of personnel employed in a particular role. Most of these procedures are likely to be clerical procedures covering employment contracts, tax and insurance documents, accommodation and equipment. Many will be governed by employment law and will involve co-ordination with the financial and facilities subsystems. We have also seen that the particular person concerned may immediately then appear as input to the subsystem in some different role.

The need and form of the release process will stem from goals originally set by the manpower output planning process. We showed above that manpower input planning was concerned with deciding what capacity and skills were needed by co-ordination with the central-purpose subsystem. In parallel with this, manpower output planning will decide what reductions are needed. In practice, therefore, manpower input and output planning are likely to be carried out by one management function within an organization. Indeed, we will often find that organizations do have a department called 'manpower planning' covering these two processes.

Besides carrying out the goal-setting functions we have described, what is usually called manpower planning also attempts to anticipate and plan for environmental disturbances. The disturbances already considered above were resignations or retirements, and these affected the output from the human resource subsystem. Attempts to accommodate these would come through the actions of the recruitment and enrolment components of the human resource input control subsystem. There are, however, other disturbances to the human resource subsystem from the environment that will affect these inputs. The availability of human resources may be affected by demographic changes or recruitment competition from other firms. What is often described as manpower planning will use a range of quantitative statistical techniques to model processes like ageing, turnover or demographic change. Using these models, it can set goals that try to anticipate the effects of environmental disturbances.

This is an example of the role of forecasting discussed in Chapter 3, and the feedback on the performance of the goal-seeking input and output control subsystems will be important information for use in manpower modelling. Broader policy issues by departments with names like 'manpower planning' are likely to be corporate planning and control subsystem activities, as we shall see below.

RQ 7.10   Is manpower planning for MX Marketing just a question of Ben Lister making sure he has enough administrative and secretarial support?

7.3.3 **The general model of the facilities subsystem**

The particular version of the General Model for Organizational Subsystems for this subsystem is shown in Figure 7.14. The term *facilities* can stand for a very wide range of buildings, plant and equipment used by the organization. For Carry-Out Cupboards, it would include such diverse components of the organizational system as its central packing and assembly factory, the retail outlet buildings, the assembly and packing equipment, the telephones, delivery vans, ventilation system, computers, office desks etc. Some of the support provided to the central-purpose subsystem by the facilities subsystem may seem more direct and specific than others. Thus the assembly and packing equipment or the delivery vans may seem more directly connected with the central-purpose than the ventilation system. But once again, we remember that all the subsystems are systems components that interact with each

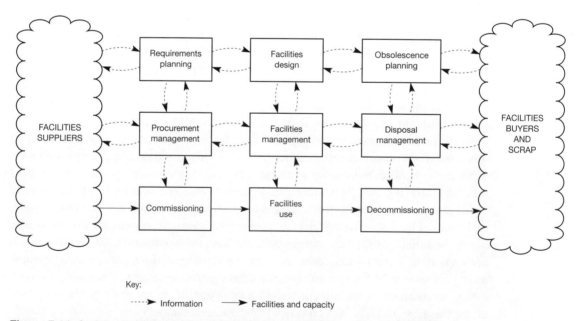

Key:
- - - -▶ Information   ──────▶ Facilities and capacity

Figure 7.14 An interpretation of the facilities subsystem in terms of the GMOS
Shows the control of the acquisition and disposal of the facilities needed. Even in the simplest organization these can be very varied in nature, value and size.

other and are co-ordinated by the corporate planning and control subsystem. For example, if ventilation was removed as a component from the facilities subsystem, the human resource subsystem could not provide its support.

There are two other points applying to this particular subsystem that need to be clarified before we look at it in detail, which I first raised in Harry (1990). First, formal accountancy rules regard facilities as part of the assets of an organization in a way that the skills of human resources, for example, are not. Thus investment in new packing facilities at Carry-Out Cupboards appears in the company balance sheet on the right-hand side under the heading 'assets'. The value of the skills of the workforce that come from investment in training do not appear in the same way.

My aim when I originally made this point was not to launch an attack on accountancy, but to demonstrate once again how a systems view of an organization will give a different, holistic perspective from that of particular management functions. It is interesting to note that as I write this in 2000, there has been an explosion of Internet companies where the major proportion of the assets of a typical 'dot-com' company lie in the skills of its workforce rather than in their often small amount of equipment and facilities.

A second important point about the facilities subsystem is one we touched on earlier in this chapter. It will only carry out the processes of commissioning, using and decommissioning these assets after financial accountancy decisions on the wider issues of investment by the corporate planning and control subsystem.

The facilities input control subsystem

This has a similar job to do in 'recruiting' the right facilities for the central-purpose subsystem as the human resource subsystem has to recruit the right human skills. The higher-order control process of requirements planning will set goals in co-ordination with the needs defined by the design and engineering component of the central-purpose subsystem. If the engineering and design function of Carry-Out Cupboards decides to use a new form of packaging procedure, requirements planning will have to identify potential suppliers of any new equipment needed, and decide what equipment to obtain from what source.

As we saw above, the term 'facilities' covers a very wide range of items. Many of the items that come under this heading will involve more than just a simple commercial purchasing process. Items like large production machinery, specialized buildings or chemical engineering plant are often purpose designed and built for the user. In such cases there has to be close technical co-operation between user and the supplier, which procurement management will have to facilitate. Activities of this kind also involve co-ordinated activity between subsystems of the organization. Here again is an important example of why a systems view, rather than a conventional departmental view, is required; and why information should be seen as a resource in modern database terms and not as a series of 'files'. Thus:

- *The design and engineering* component of the central-purpose subsystem knows what kind of facilities are required.

- The *facilities* subsystem will have technical knowledge and past data about the availability, reliability and performance of facilities.
- The *logistics and supply management* component may also be able to help with supplier performance.
- The *financial* subsystem will have experience and past data on running costs.
- The *corporate planning and control* subsystem will have the data on the availability of funding, discounting and required rates of return on investment.

Once *requirements planning* has defined the plant required in terms of its specification, price, supplier, delivery date etc., *procurement management* will attempt to make sure that the *commissioning* process takes place according to these goals by issuing orders to suppliers and receiving feedback on their performance.

If the new plant is going to require new skills from the user's workforce when it is installed, the supplier may provide the training. In this case, the procurement management will be exchanging information with the human resource subsystem. An example of this would be the training often given by computer suppliers or software houses to their customers.

The performance of the supplier in all these areas will form the higher-order feedback that will be used by requirements planning to judge the selection of future suppliers, learn lessons about forming contracts and build on technical experience in producing specifications.

Environmental disturbances will include most of the familiar reasons for the supply of new plant being late, over budget, not up to specification or some combination of all three. Accidents, bankruptcy, strikes and weather are probably the most obvious examples. From the information standpoint, however, it is often an incomplete or ambiguous specification that can be at fault because supplier and user do not have a rigorous information system to produce it. This issue arises particularly with the commissioning of computerized information system from outside contractors. It particularly involves the process of systems specification, which we will study in the next chapter.

The facilities process control subsystem

The aim of this subsystem is to ensure that facilities are successfully used in support of the central-purpose subsystem. This success will be expressed in terms of goals set by *facilities design*. These goals will be as wide ranging as the facilities themselves. They could cover plant and office layouts, operating procedures for anything from a packing machine at Carry-Out Cupboards to the graph plotter in the surveying department of the Limber Marsh Drainage Consortium, maintenance programmes, or planning the delivery of the central heating fuel for the factory.

The goals set by facilities design could be in terms as wide ranging as the facilities themselves. Examples might include:

- Technical goals, in terms of reliability and quality of performance. Since virtually all facilities require maintenance to keep up their performance and prevent failure, goals will include maintenance programmes.
- Financial goals, mainly concerned with making the plant earn its living in terms of the depreciating tied-up capital it represents. Thus deciding on layout, operating

procedures and the maintenance programmes will not just be done on technical grounds, but by also by taking account of the economics of the decisions made. A good example of this might be deciding the frequency of maintenance given to a particular machine, illustrated by Figure 7.15. The cost of maintenance means that it would be preferable to have very infrequent maintenance checks. However, the costs of failure, in terms of lost production capacity, encourage frequent maintenance. Hence the sum of these two opposing relationships needs to be optimized. Figure 7.15 is therefore yet another example of Figure 4.20.

- Human resource goals relating to the human aspects of facilities design would cover all aspects of operator numbers, skills and the training needed. They would also take into account safety of working practices and industrial relations.

Once goals have been set, they are implemented by facilities management controlling the process of facilities use. Feedback on the success or otherwise of this control will build up experience for future facilities design.

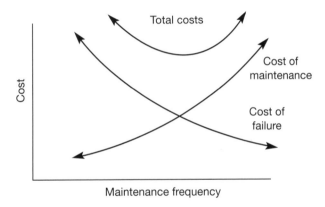

Figure 7.15 Optimizing maintenance frequency
Another example of the 'rubber stamp of operational research' of Figure 4.20.

The facilities output control subsystem

Decommissioning facilities under the control of *disposal* management is carried out according to goals set by a function we could call *obsolescence planning*. At first sight, this might seem to be a relatively crude management system in practice. A machine finally wears out and is not worth repairing, so scrap it. However, in modern organizations the issues involved can be more complex. Environmental concern, rapid technological change and increased social awareness can mean that the environment of the system has a major influence. (Note that again we use the term environment in the systems sense, not the popular 'green' use of the term.)

The conditions we have just outlined are an example of the importance of holistic thinking. Failure or obsolescence are emergent properties resulting from the coming together of several components. Thus a machine may still work well technically, but be too expensive to run compared with more modern equipment or too dangerous or polluting still to be legal. Alternatively, it might be perfect in every way except that we no longer have a use for it because of a change in manufacturing processes or the product made.

This holistic viewpoint extends to the disposal management of the decommissioning process. Besides controlling physical removal of obsolescent plant, through demolition or waste removal, control could be concerned with its sale and financial writing-off and legal negotiations with official bodies. A dramatic example of this might be the decommissioning of a nuclear power plant.

Box 7.2

Football used to be more serious than a matter of life and death: but now, what is football?

M&S strikes deals with football clubs

Patrick Haverson and Susanna Voyle

Marks and Spencer, the high-street retailer struggling to reverse falling sales and profits, has signed deals to sell branded leisure wear for a number of football clubs.

The group has agreed deals with Leeds United and Tottenham Hotspur and is believed to be in talks with other clubs as part of an attempt to tap the £1.4bn-a-year ($2.3bn) sportswear market.

Under the two deals agreed so far, the clothes will be made exclusively for M&S by Coats Viyella, one of its leading suppliers – and will be part of the group's efforts to tailor its offering in different stores, in this case along geographic lines.

M&S, at the centre of bid speculation after underperforming its retail peers, is believed to be seeking a tie-up with at least one football club in each region of the UK.

However, it will not be able to link with Manchester United, the UK's most famous footballing brand, because the club already has a similar agreement with the Debenhams department store group.

Source: Financial Times, 9 February 2000. Reprinted with permission.

Respond to the wave of enthusiasm by applying for our great card today

Designed for supporters of Queens Park Rangers Football Club. Opening an account benefits you and the QPR Youth Academy.

Source: Queens Park Rangers official website, 15 April 2000.

Premier league faces rift over Internet rights

Matthew Garrahan

The Premier League is facing a possible split over the sale of Internet rights to English football when the chairmen of its 20 clubs meet in London on Monday.

The clubs are meeting to examine a tender document assembled by the league that will eventually be sent to media companies interested in bidding for the league's next broadcasting contract, which expires at the end of the 2001–02 season.

It will outline which rights – for example match highlights – are to be unbundled and sold in separate blocks.

The league must appease its biggest clubs – which want online rights to be unbundled so that they can exploit them individually – and also the smaller clubs, which are likely to want the league to retain collective selling.

Big clubs such as Manchester United have much to gain from owning the online rights to their own games. Their website receives 8m hits a month, creating revenue opportunities from gambling and merchandising. Those would be enhanced if it could show video clips of match highlights.

Smaller clubs are likely to be keen for online rights to be sold collectively – as television rights to live games are now – so that they do not miss out. If the Premier League created a website capable of showing clips, revenues generated would be shared by all its clubs, but the big clubs are unlikely to accept such a proposal.

Source: Financial Times, 1 April 2000. Reprinted with permission.

Comment

There's an old joke that says Manchester United is the name of a sportswear shop with a football pitch next door. Commercialism in football seems to be roundly condemned by a spectator market that studiously neglects teams below the Premier League and apparently is happy to pay for satellite TV access.

But is the blame with football clubs, their supporters or the commercial media? Two of our instances above suggest different answers. Manchester United appears to have the whiphand over possible sponsors like Marks and Spencer (M&S), while Queens Park Rangers is apparently courting non-football financial organizations.

Then there is the Internet, which might be making any TV media rights irrelevant.

Any systems approach to all this mess (see Chapter 8 for more about mess) is not about to make us all foot-ball/media millionaires. It does show however that old labels like 'football', 'entertainment' or 'TV' are beginning to be strained. There was a time in the eighteenth century when anyone who was anyone had been beaten at school to make them learn Ancient Greek. When I were a lad, if you couldn't tie a reef knot you were a 'sissy'. Changes in what seems so important a particular time can be a mixture of important losses and important gains. Systems thinking suggests that we:

- keep our eyes on the distinction of whats and hows: it may be described as 'football' but what does it represent?
- recognize that all systems have environments that disturb them: including those that are apparently controlled by international, multimedia tycoons.

7.4 THE CORPORATE PLANNING SYSTEM

7.4.1 The role of the corporate planning and control subsystem in the organizational systems hierarchy

The corporate planning and control subsystem has already been mentioned frequently in the previous sections of this chapter. These mentions occurred when we considered the interaction between any of the four subsystems considered so far. In every case, we were concerned with the issue of individual subsystems having to set goals after taking account of at least one other subsystem, or the interests of the whole organization itself. When we did this, we were implying a *higher level* of control than that exerted by the particular subsystem concerned.

The various roles of the corporate planning and control subsystem in acting as a source of higher-order control can be systemically understood by comparing the General Control Model of Figure 4.10 and the General Model for Organizational Subsystems of Figure 7.5.

The central-purpose subsystem and its three supporting subsystems were individually interpreted in terms of Figure 7.5. This model saw the four subsystems as exclusively concerned with goal-setting and goal-seeking control of their own inputs, processes and outputs. These four instances of the General Model for Organizational Subsystems were therefore particular applications of the General Control Model to their own processes. Where the corporate planning and control subsystem came in was when *methods or procedures of goal setting* were required by *two or more subsystems* to enable them to *co-ordinate* their goal setting. Reference to Figure 4.10 shows that delivering methods or procedures is the actuator or effector of third-order control, which in turn is done using the methodology or policies delivered by fourth-order control to reflect the *world view*, *purpose* or *set of values* of the system's owner/perceiver.

The corporate planning and control subsystem is therefore the system that completes the control hierarchy that any organization must have in order to hold together. As we have emphasized many times, this control is a concept that can occur in many differing concrete forms. There is no automatic implication of a particular management style, formal or otherwise. The fact that a world view is not clearly defined does not mean that it does not exist or cannot have an effect: consider people's subconscious prejudices, for example. The fact that the ways of choosing and delivering methods or policies is not transparent or open does not mean that such processes do not take place: when did you or I have a say in deciding what is socially acceptable behaviour?

As we can see from the last two sentences, the actual operation of the corporate planning and control subsystem is likely to be the most 'political', mysterious or soft of the subsystems we have discussed. This has a strong effect not only on the way it operates, but also on how we might attempt to take account of it when trying to develop systems mainly concerned with lower orders of control. We shall see in the next chapter that the methodology of information systems development has to take account of the higher-order soft, political mess if it is to be managerially realistic.

However, having recognized the often dominant soft nature of the corporate planning and control subsystem, we can still explore what tasks it does and some typical ways as to how the information system can support these tasks.

7.4.2 Processes controlled by the corporate planning and control subsystem

If the role of the corporate planning and control subsystem is to co-ordinate the goal setting of the other four subsystems of the organizational system, we can begin by considering how many types of task this can involve. With four subsystems, there are six possible two-way co-ordinations, four possible three-way co-ordinations, besides the overall co-ordination of the four. Thus we could imagine a minimum of 11 different ways in which the corporate planning and control subsystem could be delivering policies or norms to co-ordinate the goal setting of the other subsystems.

However, this mechanical calculation is an underestimate of the complexity of the corporate planning and control subsystem's role, because there are likely to be many different types of goal setting involved in any one of these 11 inter-relationships. In addition to this, we have not taken account of the rich range of emergent properties resulting from the coming together of component relationships.

Despite these reservations, important clarification of the role of the corporate planning and control subsystem in any organization is possible when we consider examples of each component's elevenfold role as a methodology/policy, method/procedure producer for co-ordinated goal setting. This kind of clarification is essential if we are to break through the existing physical system in order to find out what information is needed and used by the organization as a whole. Without this clarification, any attempt to move to a database, resource view of the information system will be frustrated, since much of this information and the procedures used to produce it will be left chained to a particular 'file' or 'department'. The following list some brief examples for each of the 11 cases in the context of a marketing and production organization such as Carry-Out Cupboards:

1 *Central-purpose–financial subsystems*: co-ordination of the physical systems mix of receiving materials from suppliers, manufacturing a product and delivery to customers, with payment of suppliers and production workers, and receipt of money from customers.

2 *Central-purpose–human resource subsystems*: co-ordinating the technical and skills objectives of production with the 'people management' aspects of fitting the person to the job, training, sickness, motivation, absence, negotiation, discipline, human resources records etc.

3 *Central-purpose–facilities subsystems*: resolving conflicts over maintenance down-time or standardization versus variety of equipment, co-ordinating the specification and selection of new equipment. Establishing a system for recording and analysing machine performance information.

4 *Financial–human resource subsystems*: deciding amounts and methods of payment of employees, relationship between supervision of time keeping and payment. Resolving the confusion of logical human resource information with physical financial records and files.

5 *Financial–facilities subsystems*: co-ordinating procedures for authorization, acquisition and commissioning of equipment with payment for it. Similar co-ordination for subcontracted or bought-in servicing and supplies. Resolution of conflict where computerized information system equipment is seen as the 'possession' of the financial subsystem.

6 *Human resource–facilities subsystems*: modes of operating equipment, safety, ergonomics. Heating, lighting, noise. Status conflicts over furniture, parking spaces. Morale and conditions. Decisions over food or welfare facilities.

7 *Central-purpose–financial–human resources subsystems*: the jungle of pay and conditions, work study and incentive schemes. Redundancy and recruitment.

8 *Central-purpose–financial–facilities subsystems*: conflicts over the cost and timing of maintenance. Allocation of fixed-cost overheads.

9 *Central-purpose–human resource–facilities subsystems*: matching production objectives with skills, working methods and facilities provision. Training and installation of new physical systems, including computerized information systems. The wider concept of 'manpower planning' mentioned in the previous section.

10 *Financial–human resource–facilities subsystems*: controlling the activities of these three subsystems so that they remain as co-ordinated support for the central- purpose subsystem. Preventing the payroll management overpaying itself, the estates department getting the best parking places and human resources having first choice on holiday dates … etc.

11 *Central-purpose–financial–human resource–facilities subsystems*: co-ordinating and resolving conflicts for all of the above. Setting their goals in terms of high-level policies on issues like return on capital, market share, survival, public image, corporate ethics, minimizing risk, growth in assets.

First consideration of these last examples of high-level goals shows that while some of them are clearly soft, like corporate ethics, others, like return on capital, appear to be hard and quantitative. However, if we consider how to formulate return on capital, market share, risk or growth, we find them less clear cut than at first. While they can all be expressed as numbers, the nature of the data collected or the methods used to calculate these numbers can still depend on the policy or motives of those concerned. It might be worth referring back to what we said about probability and utility in Chapter 4, and to Chapter 5 and its lead-in case to revise some of the issues involved. A brief consideration of some of these apparently hard goals should then illustrate the principle that high-level goals usually have soft aspects to them.

Whatever their nature, however, all of the above examples of the corporate planning and control subsystems activities require information in order for them to be carried out. Although this information crosses subsystems boundaries, its physical manifestation is likely to make it the 'possession' of a particular subsystem or one of its components, as we have now seen many times. An analysis based on the systems view of organizations that we have introduced in this chapter will enable us to establish just what *information* resources the organization needs and has. But however it is done, such an analysis will have to precede any technical information systems development in an organization if we are not merely to computerize or modernize the existing problems and limitations.

In the next two chapters, therefore, we shall study the subject of information systems development by setting it in the *management* systems context.

Key words		
Batch ticket	Income collection	Process subsystem
Behaviour	Income strategy	Product file
Central-purpose	Input subsystem	Production budgeting
Central-purpose subsystem	Invoice	Production plan
Central-purpose support	Job ticket	Production planning and
subsystem	Logistics and supply	control
Clock card	Management accounting	Production schedule
Corporate planning and	Manpower planning	Provision/response
control subsystem	Marketing	Purchase budgeting
Customer file	Material and parts	Recruitment
Decommissioning	inventory	Remittance advice
Design and engineering	Needs/request	Role
Destination	Obsolescence planning	Sales accounting
Engineering drawing	Operations sheet	Sales and order processing
Enrolment	Output subsystem	Sales budgeting
Expenditure strategy	Payment	Source
Facilities management	Human resource	Statement
Facilities subsystem	management	Stock record
Financial subsystem	Human resource	Time sheet
Finished product inventory	subsystem	Work design
and delivery		

1 Does size equate with complexity? Take up the issues raised by the following: 'MX Marketing is a complex organization. It does not owe its existence to a range of shareholders like Carry-Out Cupboards, nor to the many people involved in legislation, like the Limber Marsh Drainage Consortium. Instead it is one man, Ben Lister, whose world view ultimately determines the nature of the company and the way it works. I say 'more complex' because Ben's world view, like any individual's, is harder to formalize than Acts of Parliament or corporate company procedures.'

2 We saw in Section 7.2 that the output information from the marketing process would take the form of criteria like 'lots of glass', 'simple geometrical shapes', 'primary colours' or 'economy before elaboration'. How is it possible for surveys to find out about customers' views on very high-level, abstract concepts like this? Do such surveys really work?

3 We emphasized throughout this chapter that conventional commercial documents like invoices or stock records can fulfil more than one conceptual role and contain information used by more than one subsystem. Obtain a copy of such a document and for every data item on it, try to identify its role in terms of the General Model for Organizational Subsystems of Figure 7.5, by asking the following questions:

- What is the information used for?
- Who uses it?
- Where does it come from?

4 In Section 7.2 we considered how people as assets did not appear in a company balance sheet, while things like equipment and facilities did. Is it possible to assess people as assets? Could accountancy be revolutionized to do this?

5 Investigate what facilities are used in an organization to which you have access. How many different departments control their acquisition and disposal? Is there any concept of facilities as a whole, or a common approach to them?

6 Investigate what policy any organization you know about would have towards the expenditure of £500 on:

(a) computer equipment
(b) office furniture.

Do you find that (a) is controlled in a different way and by different people from (b)? If so, why? Given that we are talking of identical sums of money, should there be any distinction?

7 Attempt to interpret:

(a) a service industry
(b) an agency

in terms of the General Model for Organizational Subsystems of Figure 7.5.

8 For a different, and much more widely known, systems approach to organizations from that given in this chapter, consider the trilogy of Beer (1979), Beer (1981) and Beer (1985), plus a supporting reader Espejo and Harnden (1989). What do you see as the principal similarities and differences between the two approaches?

Feedback on review questions

RQ 7.1 For a commercial, profit-based, manufacturing organization like Carry-Out Cupboards, the central purpose will be to discern a potentially profitable market need and produce the product that meets this need.

For a public-service organization like the Limber Marsh Drainage Consortium, the central purpose will be to ensure that it fulfils the statutory obligations as laid down by the legislation that set up the authority and gave it its powers.

MX Marketing is more complex. It does not owe its existence to a range of shareholders like Carry-Out Cupboards, nor to the many people involved in legislation, like the Limber Marsh Drainage Consortium. Instead it is one man, Ben Lister, whose world view ultimately determines the nature of the company and the way it works. I say 'more complex' because Ben's world view or purpose, like any individual's, is harder to formalize than Acts of Parliament or corporate company procedures.

We already looked at and questioned the real purpose of the Child Support Agency in Chapter 2. What we saw there was that its central purpose seemed to be something political like 'to ensure that absent fathers are seen to meet their financial responsibilities'.

RQ 7.2 The way in which a holistic view enables us to answer to these questions comes once again from the distinction between whats and hows, which we said forms the basis of our seeing organizations as systems. What a roof rack producer does is to satisfy a market for roof racks. How it does it can be in various ways, including offering the choice of fitting them. What a hospital does is to provide health care; how it does it can be through a very wide range of curative and preventative medicine.

RQ 7.3 If the central-purpose subsystem is indeed central to what the organization as a system seeks to achieve, then it is its output that is the governor of what the system exists for in the eyes of the systems owner/perceiver, so we start with that concept of overall goals.

RQ 7.4 The equivalent of marketing for the Limber Marsh Drainage Consortium is determining what sort of services it will need to supply in the future. These will range from new 'products' like a new set of drainage channels or provision of new forms of environmental protection, to changes in the level of provision of existing 'products' like regular clearing of drainage channels.

The nature of this market is determined at a high conceptual level by the legislation that established the Authority, but detailed identification is carried out by the members of the Drainage Board.

The equivalents of sales and order processing are the legal processes and clerical procedures the Authority has to go through to get access to the land where the works are carried out, and to be able both technically and legally to do the work.

RQ 7.5 Ben and his staff act personally or over the telephone as sales and order processors. The finished product inventory and delivery process is subcontracted, but is still part of MX Marketing in systems terms, whatever its legal or physical separation.

This example of the role of subcontracting is found quite often in practice. In most cases legal and physical separation does not amount to systems separation.

RQ 7.6 The short answer is no, because the individual 'products' delivered to customers in the form of development schemes and routine services are not charged to the individual. We can see, however, that the drainage rate forms a general revenue-collection process. In this the list of rate payers is the equivalent of a customer file. The individual records of rates charged and their payment fulfil the role of invoices, statements and remittance advice.

RQ 7.7 The equivalent of design and engineering, the goal-setting process of the central-purpose process control subsystem for MX Marketing can be understood if we first recognize what process the central purpose of MX Marketing carries out.

What Ben Lister essentially does is to match markets for products against potential suppliers. We might say that he 'engineers' this connexion in the sense of 'bringing it about'. MX Marketing is thus an example of a wide class of organizations whose central purpose takes some form of agency.

Understanding the equivalent of 'suppliers' or the process source for the Limber Marsh Drainage Consortium is again easier once we recognize the process of its central-purpose subsystem. The Limber Marsh Drainage Consortium takes drainage work that needs doing and then carries it out. The source of what has to be processed is the same as the destination to which it is 'delivered' once processed. Thus the Limber Marsh Drainage Consortium is an example of a wide class of organizations that provide a service.

RQ 7.8 Communication between customers and suppliers on the basis of shared commercial practice represents an example of a shared symbol set.

RQ 7.9 The source of potential confusion here is to fail to make the conceptual distinction between two different forms of money. The central purpose of a bank is concerned with the process of receiving, lending and investing money that does not belong to it. This is the 'material' that the bank 'processes'. The other form of money belongs to the bank and is used to support its operations by doing such things as pay its employees, its electricity bills etc. This latter form of money is the concern of the financial subsystem.

RQ 7.10 Not entirely. Ben also has to consider his own skills and abilities and make provision for them. Very often, 'training' for Ben will take the informal form of talking to people in the know, taking friendly advice, or he may occasionally consider going to an exhibition.

References/bibliography

Beer, S. (1979). *The Heart of Enterprise*. Wiley, New York.

Beer, S. (1981). *The Brain of the Firm*. Wiley, New York.

Beer, S. (1985). *Diagnosing the System*. Wiley, New York.

Espejo, R. and Harnden, R. (1989). *The Viable Systems Model*. Wiley, New York.

Flood, R.L. and Jackson, M.C. (1991). *Creative Problem Solving*. Wiley, New York.

Harry, M.J.S. (1990). *Information and Management Systems*. Pitman Publishing, London.

Morgan, G. (1997). *Images of Organization*. Sage, London.

Stacey, R.D. (1999). *Strategic Management and Organisational Dynamics*. 3rd edn. Financial Times Prentice Hall, Harlow.

CHAPTER 8

Devising and developing information systems

George Michaelson's first night shift

What happened

George Michaelson was lucky to get a job after he graduated with an honours degree in production engineering in the early 1990s. At that time, British manufacturing industry was under a lot of pressure because of a general economic recession, and defence industries in particular were having a bad time as a result of the 'peace dividend' that followed the East–West *détente* of the 1980s.

George joined the international company Technoturbines (TT). TT is a consortium of Anglo-French companies that produces jet engines for aircraft and gas turbines for ships and electrical power generation. The original plan for George and the other graduate trainees was that they would receive a two-week induction course at the company's headquarters in southern France and then be individually allocated to posts in one of the companies of the TT consortium, according to their intended career specialisms.

In fact, nothing like this happened. Towards the end of their induction, all the graduate trainees were told that an emergency had arisen over the implementation of the new computer-based production planning and control system (known as PROPS). It had been introduced to replace the mixed bag of computer and manually based systems used by the members of the consortium with a unified system that would plan and co-ordinate production throughout. The problems encountered with the new system (if any) varied according to which part of the consortium you were looking at.

The directors of TT had decided that all the graduate trainees should join troubleshooting teams that would be sent to any firm in the consortium that was having implementation problems with the new system. The result of this decision was that George and his fellow graduates found themselves sitting in classrooms all day on yet another induction programme, but this time they were mixed in with a wide-ranging group of middle management, computer specialists and representatives of outside computer systems contractors. The idea was to combine specialist systems expertise with management experience. When George asked why new graduates had been included, he was told it was because they had been 'taught to think'.

This second induction was a very intense three-day course. It covered all the main aspects of PROPS. The new recruits to the troubleshooting teams were not expected to become experts in PROPS on the basis of these three days, but it was intended that they should understand the system sufficiently to be able to do the troubleshooting. It was emphasized to the team members that they were not to act as experts or advisers. Instead, each team would interview users of PROPS and record their problems. These would then be passed back to the systems implementation team for follow-up action.

George was allocated to a team that was sent to the Scottish premises of PST, a small company that specialized in the production of shaped sheet metal components for the engines and turbines. He soon learned that the work done at PST was very skilled. The management and workforce he talked to often repeated that they were not involved in crude 'tin bashing', where some common form of steel sheet was used for the mass production of everyday products like trays or metal boxes. At PST they formed precision products from sophisticated and expensive raw materials.

The nature of the product and the materials at PST had an important effect on the production procedures. The bending and pressing processes had to result in a product accurately conforming to very tight design dimensions. 'If it isn't shaped right, it won't have the right shape' was the truism that George found was repeated by several of the management and workforce he talked to. After the formation was complete, the heat treatment of the product had to result in it having very precise qualities in terms of its strength, flexibility, hardness or some other property relevant to its use.

Despite these tough quality standards, production at PST had one feature that made life a little easier. It was often possible to avoid scrapping a product that wasn't right first time. Heat treatment could be used to soften the product so that parts of the forming process could be repeated to correct any wrong dimensions. It was also sometimes possible to repeat the heat treatment processes to rescue the resulting product if it did not have the correct properties of strength, flexibility etc.

These features of PST production processes made it different from many of the other members of the consortium. Most of these other firms made products through processes that involved the removal rather than the shaping of metal. Where a product is made by the removal of metal, there is much less chance of correction once a mistake has been made, and much more chance of it being scrapped. Thus if a hole is drilled too wide or in the wrong position, or if something is cut too short or machined too thin, you can't stick the metal back on. It was these differences between PST and most of the other companies of the TT consortium that led to PST's problems with PROPS, as George found out on the night shift.

When George got to PST he found that he was the only unmarried or unattached member of the troubleshooting team. Whatever the rights and wrongs of the case, he ended up volunteering to cover talking to the night shift. By chance, this turned out to be a lucky break. Most the night shift had been working on nights for years and they were almost like a separate community from the rest of the workforce. When they realized that George was the one member of what they called 'the investigation team' who was 'willing to give up his social evenings to come and talk to them', they became much more friendly and co-operative.

So fortuitously it was George who first discovered the real problem of PROPS as far as production operations at PST were concerned. The initial implementation of PROPS was showing that PST seemed to have incorrect levels of stock and partly finished products, which didn't fit in with the figures for the amount of work being scheduled.

George interviewed people working on production and in inspection. He found that according to the official procedure, every time a component was formed or heat treated, PROPS required that it was 'logged out' of production and 'logged in' to inspection. This was done by the operator keying into a computer terminal. When it happened, PROPS would adjust its files so that there was one less component allocated to production and one more allocated to inspection. Given the nature of production at PST, many of these jobs came back again after inspection for some form of further heat treatment or forming correction, if they weren't right first time. When this happened, the component should have been logged out of inspection and logged back in to production so that the files were again adjusted.

In practice, the skilled operators and inspectors at PST had been used to co-operating with each other without the formality of logging in and logging out. An operator would form the product and then the inspector would then check and explain any corrections needed. The only formal paperwork would be the inspection instructions for correcting the work.

When the new PROPS procedure required the iterations between operation on the product and its inspection to be keyed into the system, many of the operators and inspectors thought this an unnecessary waste of time. The result was that many of the transfers between production and inspection were never keyed in: operators and inspectors kept to the old informal system. This didn't matter when the same thing happened for transfers both ways, but if movements in one direction were not keyed in while movements in the other direction were keyed in, there could be net gains or unrecorded losses in the apparent numbers of components in production or inspection. This error could be aggravated when batches of the same component were split because only some of them passed inspection first time.

George was the first to discover this phenomenon because it was the night shift who was the main source of such errors due to its more informal approach to PROPS. There were many reasons for this, but the main one was that those who originally had the job of installing PROPS and training the users were not too keen on spending a lot of time on the night shift. Once PROPS looked to be going OK on the day shifts, there was a great temptation to assume that the system was up and running.

The night-shift people that George talked to were quite frank about this and they blamed 'the system'. Several felt that they could have designed the procedures much better themselves 'with just someone there who knew about computers to help us sort out the technical bits'. Instead of that, 'there was someone who came on the day shift and drew lots of diagrams. Then they went off and we heard no more about it until the new system came in.'

George realized that he was getting a strongly partisan view from the night shift, but he was in a dilemma when he reported his findings to the troubleshooting team. He did not want his report to result in crude blaming of the night-shift workers who had given him their confidence. Although the workers were technically at fault in not keeping to the new PROPS procedures, the source of the trouble was that these procedures took no account of the special situation at PST. PROPS had been developed as a computerized production planning and control system after very careful consultation with the 'most important companies' of the Technoturbines consortium. As we have seen, PST was very different from most of those other companies in terms of the product, the materials and their effect on the production procedures. The other companies' technology was based on the assumption of removal rather than shaping of metal. This meant that for them it was sensible to make a distinction between production and inspection; for PST it was not.

George was pleased to find that the leader of his troubleshooting team agreed with him. So a report was put in recommending a modification of the system at PST to take account of its particular needs. George was then quite flattered to find that was sent to a consortium meeting of all the troubleshooting groups and the original implementation team to present his report.

When he did his presentation, he found that the contents of his report raised areas of debate that seemed to come up in several of the reports from the other troubleshooting teams. Although all these other teams did not always come down on the same side as George's team, the three issues did seem to dominate the quite heated debate they raised among the systems experts in the implementation team!

The first debate started when George quoted the workers, inspectors and supervisors at PST saying that they could have designed the procedures a lot better themselves 'with just someone there who knew about computers to help us sort out the technical bits'. This led to a long argument about such terms as 'methodology', 'prototyping' and whether 'approaches' should be 'structured'. Although George was not a computer systems man, he recognized all these arguments as just one example of something he had learned as a production engineer. His understanding came from his training in product design and its practical implications for the production process. This had taught him that there was usually a tension between the informal nature of creativity and the need to organize production so that ideas became realities. When computer systems people tried to design and implement a system, they seemed to have the same tension to deal with.

The next big debate came when George made what he thought was the main point of his report. This was that the features of PST's production processes made it different from many of the other members of the consortium, and that PROPS needed to be modified to take account of this. Somebody from one of the other troubleshooting teams at this point muttered, 'So what else is new?' There was then an argument about how far there really were significant differences between the various consortium factories and how far these were only on the surface. People appeared to take sides on this issue purely in terms of self-interest. Most of the systems experts in the implementation team seemed anxious to stress the underlying essential similarities between the different production procedures. George assumed that this was because similarities meant it was easier for them to design one system for the whole consortium with a minimum of irritating special cases. Most of the support for recognizing that there were essential differences came from the troubleshooting teams because they had been focusing on local difficulties. After a lot of argument, it was felt that this issue was so big that it would not be resolved at this meeting. Instead, a full report would be presented to the directors of TT for them to decide the next step.

The third debate seemed to come as an mild afterthought following the previously heated exchanges. When the previous argument had died down, a member of the group of systems experts made a very quiet speech that everybody seemed to ignore at first, but then it heated up the argument all over again. George didn't know the person who made the speech, but everyone who knew him referred to him as MJ. MJ said that they had all been obsessed with their systems in terms of what they did, or didn't, do. He said that the whole focus was on process. 'Would it not be better,' he said, 'to concentrate on what information was needed by the various users in the various factories, and start from there?'

George took time to understand what this argument was about until, he remembered an amusing lecture he had once had as a student on the inter-relationship of design and production methods. The lecturer had pointed out that if your sock was inside your shoe it had implications for which of these you put on first! The desired outcome of a process will determine which choices of method are available. MJ seemed to be saying the same about the design of PROPS: perhaps they had thought too much about the processes and not enough about the desired outcome.

The debate raised by MJ's remark became very high powered and most of the non-experts present felt left out. In the end, it was decided that this meeting was not a place to continue it. George suspected he was witnessing part of something that had been going on between the experts for some time, and that it would continue in the future.

Once the reports had been presented and the debates were concluded, the job of the troubleshooting teams was over. The directors of TT and those concerned permanently with PROPS would now need to take up the findings and decide what systems modifications and developments were needed. For George, it was frustrating to be only temporarily associated with PROPS and not to see the outcome of his work. In fact, he took up a permanent post in production information systems after his training and in later life published a book on the subject.

The issues raised

In the previous chapter, we saw how the systems concepts introduced earlier in this book could enable us to see organizations and businesses as systems. The three main requirements for such a view were:

1 Seeing organizations and businesses in terms of what they consist of and what they do, as opposed to seeing them in terms of how they happen to be physically manifested and labelled.
2 The identification of a central-purpose subsystem with supporting subsystems coordinated by a corporate planning and control subsystem.
3 The use of the hierarchical control model to understand the relationships between the components of the business or organization.

When we look at George's experience as a trainee of Technoturbines, there are several examples illustrating that what was actually going on in the organization did not fit the organizational labels. One example was that George, as a 'mere trainee', was incorporated into a team with middle management, computer specialists and representatives of outside computer systems contractors. Here we can see that what was actually happening at Technoturbines cut across conventional organizational divisions 'once an emergency had arisen', but its systemic function could be easily understood in terms of the hierarchical control model.

PROPS was a computer-based production planning and control system designed to set goals like production targets and stock levels, and to monitor the goal-seeking performance of the system when it attempted to meet these goals. Initial feedback on the poor performance of PROPS suggested that it could be that the implementation was incomplete, that PROPS itself needed modification, or elements of both. Whichever of these reasons we are looking at, they are the concern of a higher level of control than second-order goal setting, since it was PROPS itself that was meant to set goals. The design, modification and implementation of PROPS therefore formed that part of the control hierarchy that determines the method by which the goals are set. In Chapter 4 we called this third-order control.

Setting up the troubleshooting teams was therefore required to ensure that there was the necessary feedback to enable third-order control to design and implement an appropriate method. Since third-order control is a corporate planning and control subsystem function, it is not surprising that it was a directorship decision to set up the troubleshooting teams.

There was another important insight to be gained from George's experience in terms of seeing the organization as a system and applying a hierarchical control model view. When the troubleshooting teams reported back to the consortium meeting, some of the argument was about the method used to develop PROPS and what methods might be used to modify it. This first happened when George quoted the workers, inspectors and supervisors at PST saying that they could have designed the procedures a lot better themselves, as well as in the subsequent argument about such terms as 'methodology', 'prototyping' and whether 'approaches' should be 'structured'. There was also the argument started by MJ that they had thought too much about the processes and not enough about the desired outcome when designing PROPS.

The arguments over deciding the method used to develop PROPS and what methods might be employed to modify it represent an example of controlling the development and use of a method. This is a level of control above the third-order control, which we saw in Chapter 4 was concerned with methodology (in its original sense).

All of the machinations of the PROPS affair, however, confirmed a major aspect of our view of organizations and businesses as systems. This was the concept of a central-purpose subsystem with supporting subsystems co-ordinated by a corporate planning and control subsystem. PROPS was vitally important because it was concerned with the central purpose of Technoturbines, which was the production of jet engines and gas turbines to meet a market need. Any problem with PROPS had an immediate effect on what Technoturbines was there to do as a system.

Finally, our 'organizations and businesses as systems' view of events at Technoturbines brought with it a rich collection of soft issues. These soft issues were mixed with the technical difficulties over PROPS and meant that it was sometimes difficult to know where the problem was. Examples of this confusion included:

- Statements by people at PST that they blamed 'the system' and George's dilemma when he reported his findings to the troubleshooting team.
- Arguments about how far there really were significant differences between the various consortium factories and how far these were only on the surface, with people appearing to take sides on this issue purely in terms of self-interest.

Hence an organizational systems view of Technoturbines raises five issues:

1 What problem features do we have to deal with when attempting to develop an information system?
2 Should the development of an information system be by an unstructured approach, a structured method, or some combination of both?

3 What are the characteristics of the main types of systems development methods and approaches enabling us to make useful distinctions between them?

4 What are the important issues in systems development methodology? ('Methodology' is used to mean the study of method.)

5 How can systems development itself be seen as a system? What are its components and how are they related?

Opportunities for learning

Issue 1 is not a new one, and is illustrated by our closing remarks in the previous section. We have frequently stressed the concept that an information system can be seen as a component of a wider management system. Since management inevitably brings with it the soft issues characteristic of any human activity system, information systems development will take place in a wider context that contains soft issues as well as hard technical problems.

Was the problem that George found on the night shift at PST a management problem or a systems development problem? Was the night shift the main source of errors because its more informal approach to PROPS stemmed from poor management rather than a poor system? Those who originally had the job of installing PROPS and training the users were not too keen on spending a lot of time on the night shift; maybe if they had, there would not have been a problem. After all, PROPS looked to be going OK on the day shifts, and they were working the same system, in the same factory, with the same product and production procedures, so it was a management problem. An alternative view, shared by George, was that good management can make up for a bad system, but it is still a bad system. Strongly active management on the day shift was covering up for a system that was technically inappropriate for the practical situation it was supposed to support, so it was a systems development problem.

Issue 1 therefore recognizes that we need to be able to decide the management problem and its context before we can choose and apply a systems development method.

If we do have a means of resolving issue 1 and we decide that we have a systems development problem, then issue 2 brings up the question of how the development of the information system should be carried out. Should we organize our approach in a structured way, with a clear-cut plan of what has to be done, when, by whom and using what techniques? Or is a more informal unstructured approach appropriate that allows for flexibility and creativity? Or both?

In the Technoturbines case, the argument seemed to depend on whether you were one of the night-shift people at PST that George talked to, or one of the computer specialists and representatives of outside computer systems contractors. The first group thought that the procedure for developing PROPS would have worked a lot better with a heterogeneous collection of themselves and 'someone who knew about computers to help us sort out the technical bits'. The implication here was that the process would be informal and unstructured. The second group, whom we might stereotype as 'the experts', were present at the consortium meeting. They made several differing technical points, but the assumption behind all of their contributions seemed to be that the development of PROPS should be organized and consistently structured throughout the consortium.

Issue 3 comes up if we have a clear information systems development problem and we decide to choose an approach. We have now to decide what the characteristics of the main types of systems development methods are, so that we can make useful distinctions between them and select a suitable one for our needs.

This issue came up at the consortium meeting when MJ said that the whole focus of their view of PROPS was on process. Although much of what was discussed was more technical than George could always understand, he did see that there were different ways you could look at an information system. If you focused on it as something that processed data to produce the required information, then presumably your systems development method would be one that thought about what processes were needed and what data was needed for processing. George also understood from MJ's criticism that perhaps you ought to start by thinking about the kind of information you wanted first, then to think how the data ought to be structured to produce it, and finally to consider the processes needed to produce it. Whatever the various arguments and their merits, George understood enough to see that your view of what an information system was would affect how you carried out systems development (i.e. what method you used).

Issue 4 arises naturally from issue 3. Once we can see that there are different methods with their various characteristics, we next consider what criteria we might use to compare and assess them, so that we can make an informed choice of systems development method. We need a method to study methods themselves, or a methodology. It is interesting to note that George heard a long argument including such terms as 'methodology', but this was often used apparently to mean the same as method. Part of issue 4 is therefore to look at the use of the two terms.

Issue 5 is illustrated by the whole of George's experience on the troubleshooting team. However much the original systems development of PROPS appeared to be a narrow professional activity carried out by computer specialists and representatives of outside computer systems contractors, many other people and things became involved. Expert systems specialists found themselves combined with experienced management and intelligent, but naive, people like George. George, in turn, found himself assessing PROPS with skilled operators and inspectors at PST. Besides this great mix of people, there was the variety of different firms and factories within Technoturbines, and the conflicting views on the analysis of the problems and the methods to be used. In reality, therefore, systems development was not just a process but a system in its own right, whose components and structure also need to be identified and understood.

Our final issue thus comes as a result of resolving all the previous ones. If we have clarified the problems of information systems development (issue 1), used appropriate criteria to select our approach or method according to their qualities (issues 2–4), and considered who and what is involved (issue 5), then we come to the issue that we shall explore in this chapter: what tools are available to support the systems development process?

The learning objectives for this chapter are to:

1 Understand the role of systems development in the wider context of the management system of businesses and organizations.

2 Understand the hard and soft qualities of systems development problems and the implications for systems development methodology.

3 Understand the important features of systems methods and the systems methodology that enables them to be assessed in terms of their successful application to systems development.

4 Understand systems development itself in a management systems context.

8.1 UNDERSTANDING PROBLEMS

The term *problem* can be used in two related but different ways:

1 To imply some rather broad difficulty like a dispute or a doubt, which puts us in a predicament and generally tends to spell trouble, often with emotional overtones.
2 To mean something that is much more clear cut like a question, a puzzle or a riddle, usually seen in intellectual or technical terms.

We shall look further at the implications of these two usages later in this section, but for the moment let us concentrate on what they have in common.

Both of the usages that we noted for the term problem have a common implication that it is something we would like to move on or away from. If it is something vague and broad like a doubt, we would like it to be clarified and cleared up. If it is something quite specific like a puzzle, we would like the solution. Either way, the implication is that things could be *better* if we could find the *right way forward*. This general picture of typical problem situations then leads to the questions of what 'find the right way forward' and 'better' can mean.

The first of these questions assumes that there is a way to be found. We would not waste our time in a management context with problems for which there is no way forward in principle. For example, if a doubt or uncertainty is unresolvable because something like *Ashby's Law* (Chapter 4) or *Heisenberg's Uncertainty Principle* (Chapter 5) applies, then it is a waste of time trying to find any 'way forward' beyond what is theoretically possible. Our view of management, however, is that it is applicable where *meliorism* is an appropriate belief. The 'melior' in meliorism, as we recall from Chapter 4, comes from Latin and means 'better'. So where it is reasonable in principle to try to make things better with an attempt to 'find the right way forward', we see management as being relevant.

If we now want to explore the ideas of *better* or *meliorism*, we should look more closely at the term 'right'. As with the word problem, we find that it has two different but related meanings:

1 We can use the word right to reflect our own opinions about something. Thus what is right in the sense of being ethical, fair, just, or socially proper for you may not be so for me. Or again, something that is just right in terms of taste or aesthetics for me (like I find that the British climate is right for me) may not be the case for you.

2 We can use the word right to mean something that is factually correct in the sense that it can be tested with evidence against agreed standards to determine whether it is accurate or true (like whether Edinburgh is further west than Bristol, which it is).

What therefore follows when we consider the nature of different kinds of problems is that they can have hard and soft properties, just as we found when talking about systems in Chapter 3. In so far as any problem can be seen 'to imply some rather broad difficulty like a dispute or a doubt etc.', we would see it as a soft problem. If it has qualities that mean it can be seen as 'clear cut ... question . . . in intellectual or technical terms', we would see it as a hard problem.

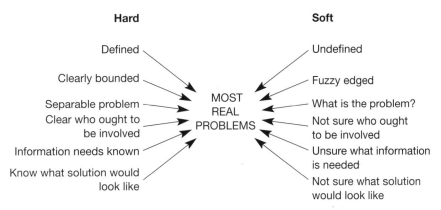

Figure 8.1 Hard problems and soft messes
These should not be seen as mutually exclusive opposites, but rather as extremes on a spectrum that includes most real problems.

Ackoff and Hall (1972) called hard problems and soft problems *messes*. Figure 8.1 shows what we could consider the main criteria distinguishing hard and soft problems in terms of:

- *Definition*: do we know and agree what the problem is? If we do not agree, are there commonly accepted criteria that can be used to resolve the disagreement?
- *Boundary*: does our definition of the problem enable us to clarify what the problem is, and what it is not?
- *Separation*: can we dismiss issues as being not part of the problem as a result of drawing this boundary?
- *Responsibility*: does the definition and separation of the problem make it clear who should be involved in its solution and who not?
- *Information*: if we are clear what the problem is and whose responsibility it is, do we now know what information we need for its solution?
- *Description*: do we now know what a solution would, and would not, look like if all the previous criteria have been satisfied?

If all the answers to these questions are yes, then we have a hard problem. If any of the answers is no, then we could either have a situation of hard uncertainty or a soft problem or mess.

RQ 8.1 How would you see the problems and messes in the Technoturbines case in terms of definition, boundary, separation, responsibility, information and description?

Once we have identified that real-life problems can involve both hard and soft issues, and we aim to 'find the right way forward' to a 'better' situation, the next thing we have to consider is how we can make this change for the 'better'. This then leads us to consider approaches, methods and the study of them both, which can be called methodology.

Box 8.1

Global e-commerce law comes under the spotlight

Patti Waldmeir

Commerce is global. Law, for the most part, is not. That has been mostly true for hundreds of years. But never has that truth caused greater uncertainty than now, as global business clashes with local and national law in the borderless new world of electronic commerce.

'Whose rules govern? Nobody is quite sure,' Mark Radcliffe, an expert on Internet law, told a recent Washington conference on e-commerce law.

All the uncertainty is good for lawyers but not for the growth of e-commerce, says Jay Westermeier, the doyen of Washington Internet lawyers. 'To reap the benefits of e-commerce, an acceptable level of legal certainty and uniformity must be present.'

The threshold question is: whose laws apply? When an American woman slips and falls in a hotel in Italy, can she sue in New Jersey, just because the hotel advertises globally on the Internet? When a Christmas tree catches fire in an American home and causes a fatality, can the store where the tree was purchased sue the Hong Kong manufacturer in a US court, just because the Hong Kong company has a presence in cyberspace?

In both those cases, the US courts said 'no'. But the question of jurisdiction remains unresolved, both internationally and within the US, according to Mr Westermeier. 'What

consumer laws, contract law, privacy laws and other laws apply to e-commerce transactions? Where does a transaction take place? How will conflicts in law be determined?' he asks.

US courts have begun to sketch out a tentative standard for jurisdiction, determined by the degree of interactivity of the website, and especially by whether a sale took place.

So if a Rhode Island company maintains a purely informational website accessed by a resident of Michigan, the company probably cannot be sued in that state. But if the company sells goods directly to the Michigan resident through the web, then his home state's law would probably apply.

The question of foreign jurisdiction is even murkier. According to a draft EU electronic commerce directive, the law of the consumer's home jurisdiction would apply in any case where a purchase was made through a website.

When a Christmas tree catches fire in a US home, can the store where the tree was bought sue the Hong Kong company if it has a presence in cyberspace?

But that raises many problems for US companies, because European privacy and consumer protection laws are much tougher.

Companies are forced either to set up separate websites to comply with local laws, or one

megasite which meets every conceivable national and local legal requirement, says Mr Westermeier. Both options are costly and defeat the supposed efficiency gains of globalized commerce.

A similar collision between the territorial and the global occurs over domain names – those 'com' designations which give an e-commerce company its identity. Identical trademarks can co-exist in different countries, because trademarks are geographically limited. But domain names are global, and must be unique.

Recently, an international body was established – outside the current legal system – to resolve domain name disputes. Icann (Internet Corporation for Assigned Names and Numbers) can apply the law of any jurisdiction which it considers applicable, through a process of mandatory arbitration. Many consider this kind of non-governmental body a model for future internet regulation. 'The whole jurisdictional issue just goes away,' says Susan Crawford, an e-commerce law expert.

But even if Icann can suppress the appetite for litigation over domain names, much work remains for lawyers. Should companies be allowed exclusive rights to a specific way of doing business on the Internet? Amazon.com is suing to defend its patent rights to 'one click' technology, which allows purchases with one click of a mouse. And

Priceline is suing Microsoft for allegedly copying its patented method of 'reverse auctions', which allows buyers to name a price and seek a willing seller.

Companies will still try to shut down so-called 'gripe sites' set up to attack them, such as Delta-sucks.com. But the US constitution largely guarantees such sites as free speech. Many companies choose instead to register a 'sucks' domain name along with their own.

Many other questions remain: can one company use another's name as a 'meta-tag', or invisible label, on their website? One recent case involved a company which embedded a reference to 'Playboy',

so anyone searching for that word would end up at their site. Some companies even use a competitor's name as a meta-tag, as a way to attract the competitor's business.

What about linking, the fundamental comparative advantage of the Internet? How can companies protect themselves against liability for what appears on the linked site? And is it left for companies to 'deep link' to an interior page of the website bypassing advertising on the home page?

The anonymity of the web presents a nightmare for companies. How can US companies avoid contravening export laws by selling to Libyans?

But the thorniest issue of all is probably privacy: how can consumers be protected against e-intrusions, in a world of online profiling, where companies gather information about them without their knowledge? The problem has global dimensions: the US and EU are at loggerheads over an EU privacy directive that could exclude valuable European consumer data from the US, forcing companies to keep separate databases. In the end, it comes back to the same question: how can business be borderless when the law is not? No one yet has the answers.

Source: Financial Times, 23 December 1999. Reprinted with permission.

Comment

What are the boundaries of the problem? This article does a good analysis to show the conflict between legal boundaries and conceptual ones on the Internet. However, the issues are more messy than this. There are fundamental questions about what kind of law, *if any, should apply to what things. Try applying Ackoff's six criteria to this problem, and I suspect you will see it as a mess. Even more challenging might be the Ulrich's 12 heuristic questions of Box 8.3.*

8.2   APPROACHES AND METHODS

The Technoturbines case showed that problems with information systems can often be just part of a wider management system problem within the organization or business system. Part of the problem we may have can be making the distinction between a specific information systems problem and a much wider management systems problem. Later in this chapter we shall look specifically at methods for dealing with this type of situation, but for the moment we shall use the term system in the information systems context, and focus on problems with information systems. We will also introduce the term 'systems development' to generally describe the range of activities associated with creating new systems or improving existing ones.

Many different terms are used when describing or discussing the process of systems development. Often the same thing is described by a different term and the same term can mean different things according to who is using them. Since there is no single consistent way of defining these terms, we will begin by trying to clarify some that are commonly used and come up with working definitions. We will also try to keep these definitions close to a mainstream of systems use by referring to other authors.

Approach, *method*, *methodology*, *technique* and *tools* are all terms often used in the context of systems development. We can begin to make a distinction between these if we compare first the terms *approach* and *method*.

Approach seems to be more often used to mean a much less specific way of doing something than a method. An approach is likely to involve a set of principles or attitudes for performing a task, but is unlikely to go all the way of defining in any detail how it should be done. Consider how we might describe a 'friendly' approach to establishing a relationship with another person. It is unlikely that we would say, 'first, smile; second, say "hello"; third, shake them by the hand; fourth, etc.'. Such a mechanical approach would be more likely to have exactly the opposite effect than that intended. It would be much more useful to give more general advice like 'try to put the person at their ease, show a friendly attitude, be prepared to take an interest and listen, etc.', and leave some flexibility and spontaneity for the relationship to develop naturally.

This last example is not so far removed from systems development as it might first seem. Some of the problems at Technoturbines seemed to arise from too mechanical an approach.

RQ 8.2   What were they?

As we shall see when we cover the subjects of *prototyping* and *object orientation* later in this chapter, an unstructured approach based on a set of guiding principles can have advantages over something more *systematic*.

RQ 8.3   What's the difference between *systemic* and *systematic*?

This last RQ leads us on to saying that a method implies something much more systematic or structured than an approach. We imply this when we use the word methodical to describe a systematic way of doing things. The use of the term *structure* in a systemic context implies the existence of *ordered* components. In a method, these components will be the *steps* or *stages* we proceed through when carrying out the method. Just as defining a system requires us to define its components, so defining a method will require us to define its stages. For the moment we will use the word stages to apply generally to the component steps of a method. As we come to look in more detail in Chapter 9, we shall see that terms like stages, phases and tasks may need to be distinguished.

A method for changing a car wheel would begin 'first, ensure the car is safely anchored; second, release the tension on the wheel nuts; third, jack up the car; fourth, remove nuts etc.'. Notice that in this case the *order* or *sequence* matters: it could be very dangerous to regard the safe anchoring and nut removal as informal principles to be brought in at any time that spontaneity dictated. Just as the structuring of the components in a system affects its emergent properties, so the structuring of the component stages of a method affects its emergent property in terms of the results produced. I always remember the old Victorian cookbook that began a chicken soup recipe with the instructions 'plunge the fowl into boiling water, having first removed the insides and feathers'. It's too bad if you don't read all the instructions before you begin!

Again, the everyday examples we use are not as remote from systems development as they seem. We shall see in the next section that defining the stages of a method and deciding on their sequence is a major issue that ties in with the broader one of classifying and selecting methods.

We shall use the term *technique* to describe the way in which a task is carried out by someone, often with aid of a *tool*. While we would apply a technique to achieve a particular task, a method could involve organizing a whole series of different tasks. Thus one method might use many tools and techniques, and a particular tool or technique might be used by several different methods. If systems development is a holistic procedure, we should not be surprised to find it using tools and techniques from many different areas of management as well as specialist ones.

RQ 8.4   How might the last paragraph be summarized as a diagram?

There is a clear comparison here with the use of tools in other fields than systems development. Mechanics, artists and surgeons all use tools, and each may have a different technique with a particular tool. It is also worth noting that the same tool might be used in a different context. Thus a surgeon's knife may be used by an artist to make lino cuts. We shall find equivalents of this with systems development tools, which may turn up in very different methodologies.

What is sometimes different about information systems developers is that they frequently use logical and abstract tools. These would include the diagramming tools we covered in Chapter 3. Later in this section we shall see how software can be used to support systems development in the form of CASE (computer-aided systems (or software) engineering) tools.

To compare our working definitions of approaches, methods, tools and techniques with those used by other popular systems authors, see Avison and Fitzgerald (1988), Flynn (1992) and Olle *et al.* (1988).

This leaves us with the term *methodology*. In our analysis of the issues in the Technoturbines case, we indicated a reservation about the use of the term when referring to the fact that George heard a long argument in which methodology was often used apparently to mean the same as method. We said that part of issue 4 was therefore to look at the use of the two terms. I think this issue has been correctly summarized by Olle *et al.* (1988) when they say, 'It is recognized that the term methodology should be used to mean "a study of method". However, the common practice over the past decade has been to use "methodology" in place of "method" and this text adopts the line of least resistance by following the current practice.'

For our purposes this lack of distinction will not always matter and we too have to bow to common practice when quoting or referring to other work. Where there appears to be doubt, the best course is to check whether we are talking about one particular method or the study of two or more. It is worth also mentioning that the term meta-methodology is occasionally used to mean methodology in its original sense where the latter term has been downgraded to mean method.

Having raised this caution as to the use of the term methodology, in the next section we will look at systems methodology in its original sense of a study of systems methods.

8.3 METHODOLOGY AND RELATING METHODS TO PROBLEMS

8.3.1 Basic models for methodology

Reference back to the concepts of Chapter 3 will show an important reason that distinguishing method and methodology, as we do in this section, can be important. If a method is a *systematic* way of doing something rather than just a general approach, then in applying a method we are carrying out a process in a way that tries to conform to one or more goals. As we shall see later in this chapter, depending on the method we are looking at, these goals could take various forms. For example, the goals could take the form of a defined sequence of stages each requiring the production of certain deliverables like a flowchart defining what an information system had to do, or a normalized database defining the data that it would use.

By describing method in this way, we present it in terms of the control model of Chapter 4. If we then consider the hierarchical aspect of the control model, there will be a higher-order control that will occur when we modify or choose a new method in the light of experience. It is a form of higher-order control because any modification or choice of method is goal setting. The feedback of our experience of using a particular method can be used as part of a learning process that will enable us to design our method, and hence set goals more effectively in the future. In this sense, we can see that this higher-order control is the 'study of method' or methodology in its original sense.

We can begin our study of method by recalling that meliorism lies behind our view of management: we are trying to make things better and we believe that our actions can have some effect. The actions we are concerned with in this case are those determined by our choice of method. We might summarize such a situation and these assumptions by the simple model of Figure 8.2, which we will call the *meliorist model*.

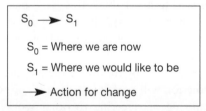

Figure 8.2 The meliorist model
The bare essentials of any situation where we believe that our actions can have some effect on their outcomes. Meliorism is explained in Chapter 4.

The present situation, 'where we are now', we call S_0. There will be all sorts of features of the existing situation that could be described, but for the purposes of methodology we would confine our description to those aspects of the situation that are relevant to the problem in relation to the choice of method. Depending on the nature of the problem, this could be the state of the wider management system or confined to the information system itself. If S_0 is a mess rather than a problem, the boundaries of S_0 may be unclear, and attempting to clarify them could be a methodological issue. We shall say more of this when considering soft systems methodology.

S_1 represents 'where we would like to be'. This will be a better state of the wider management system or the information system aimed for. Whether this state is attainable either fully or in part will depend on our practical success, but S_1 must at least be possible in principle for a meliorist model to be relevant. We might say that however *probable* S_1 is, it must be *possible*. According to our assumptions about how probable the attainment of S_1 is, so our choice of method may be affected.

To move from S_0 to S_1, as shown by the arrow, we need to take some appropriate set of *actions for change* that will be governed by our *method* or *approach*. As we briefly indicated above, the choice of method will be determined by the nature of S_0 and S_1 and, as we shall see, the difference between them.

Obvious and simple as this model may appear, it can take on a number of complications. We can now use an exploration of these complications as a starting point for our 'study of method' or methodology.

8.3.2 The effect of motives on choice of method

We have described S_1 as 'where we would like to be'. In the systems context, this will mean the kind of system we would like to have, and S_0 will be the one we have now. By looking at the different types of reason that would give us a *motive* to want to move from S_0 to S_1, we shall see that systems development methods can be very different in terms of the stages that comprise them and the sequence in which these stages are carried out. The first broad distinction we can make is between:

1 *Failure*-driven motivation.
2 *Aspiration*-driven motivation.

Failure-driven motivation can be understood by considering what S_0, the existing system or situation, might be like. Where we have a situation like that at Technoturbines in which something has failed or is going badly, then we are driven by the existing situation to seek for something better, S_1. Failure-driven motivation starts from the premise that there is an existing system, but it has faults or failures.

When we use the word failure it is important to note that it is an *emergent property*. For a failure to occur, two or more components have to come together. This may seem an odd statement when we first consider it. After all, many common failures seem to be individual events that just happen. If I'm driving along the road and I suddenly get a puncture, where's the emergent property in that? The answer is quite simple:

$$\text{puncture} = \text{pneumatic tyre} + \text{sharp object}$$

or if we become even more analytical:

puncture = pneumatic tyre + sharp object + contact + sufficient penetration force + ... etc.

The serious point to be gained from recognizing failure as an emergent property is an understanding of how it can be removed or avoided. Like any other emergent property, it only happens when all the necessary components come together in a particular structural relationship. The removal of a component or an alteration to the structure will result in something different. This 'something different' could be something better, like the removal of failure and its replacement with something successful; or it could be an alternative equally bad or worse.

The *methodological* implication of this view of failure is that *failure-driven motivation leads to some initial analysis of the existing system, S_0, that will enable us to understand:*

1 The *components* of the existing situation.
2 Their *relationship*.

and hence:

3 The reasons for the failure or shortcomings of the existing system.

Only when we have carried out this analysis will we be in a position to consider what must be done next, and we will pick this point up later.

Aspiration-driven motivation leads us to start from a different position to that adopted by failure-driven motivation. Instead of considering the system S_0 that we have now, we begin by considering what we would like to have, S_1. The most common examples of this occur when there is no existing system, S_0, of any relevance. Just as the first aeroplane was not developed as a result of a detailed analysis of balloons, so we may find that S_1, the system to which we aspire bears little relationship to anything we have at the moment. Aspiration-driven motivation begins, as the term itself makes clear, with our aspirations, our hopes or our desires for the new system we wish to develop. The first stage of any method driven by aspiration is to decide just what it is we require from the new system. Only when this has been clarified can we go ahead with the detailed systems development.

The *methodological* implication of this view of systems development is that *aspiration-driven motivation leads to some initial specification of the desired system, S_1, that will include an analysis of:*

1 The *desired properties* of the proposed system.
2 Its *components* and *structure*.
3 Its *behaviour* and *processes*.

It is important to notice that this stage may also be called *analysis*. The difference between this use and its use in the failure-driven context is that here analysis refers to S_1 and in the latter case to S_0.

We can now take our methodology a stage further by considering, as promised above, what happens as a result of the analysis of a failure. Let's return to the simple example of the puncture. It may be that when we analyse the existing situation, S_0, we find that the removal of the 'sharp object' component and its replacement by a rubber patch will result in a new system, S_1, which removes the failure. It could, however, be that our analysis showed that we got the puncture because we were trying to use the car in unsuitable rough terrain. In this case the desired system, S_1, is not a patched-up car tyre but transfer to horseback or going on foot. Our puncture analogy can go further. It may be that the only reason we got the puncture was because it was sustained as part of a wider car crash. It would hardly be worth mending the puncture if the car is a write-off!

A *failure-driven analysis* may therefore lead to the adoption of an *aspiration-driven* method if the analysis stage reveals that 'repairing' S_0 is impossible or irrelevant. This level of failure is almost always due to major environmental changes to the system rather than faults in the original design. For there to be any existing system at all, it must have been implemented with some success: major failure must therefore have come as a result of subsequent events.

8.3.3 Derivative and innovative analysis methods

Having considered the different *motivations* for systems development, we can now identify the two different types of *method* that can result from this consideration. The two types of method can be distinguished by referring to the two different interpretations of the concept of analysis that we described in the previous section. These differences affect what kind of initial stages the methods have. In this section, we will therefore look at the initial analysis stages of the two types of method and leave the remaining stages of systems development for the next section.

Hence, consideration of motivation enables us to distinguish:

1 Derivative methods.
2 Innovative methods.

Derivative methods will be relevant to situations where:

- we anticipate that our needs are definable in hard terms;
- system S_0 exists which is relevant to our needs;
- there is a shortfall or failure of S_0 in relation to these needs;
- it is possible and reasonable to consider the repair or development of S_0 to meet these needs.

Where such conditions apply, we can see that any new system, S_1, that we develop will have many features of the previous system, S_0, plus others that represent modifications or improvements. Hence our new system can be seen as a *derivative* of the old.

Innovative methods will be needed in situations where:

- we anticipate that our needs are definable in *hard* terms;
- there is *no system* S_0 existing that is sufficiently relevant to our needs, or S_0 is *irreparable*.

Where these conditions apply, the features of the new system, S_1, will derive directly from a definition of our needs, and any S_0 will have been dismissed as irrelevant. ('Irrelevant' refers here to the *initial analysis stages*; we will find when we get into the development of the system that understanding S_0 is an essential precursor to implementation.)

Figure 8.3 shows how our analysis of motivation leads to the choice of a derivative or an innovative method. We can now go on to see how the form of motivation affects what stages are likely to make up the initial phases of the two different types of method.

We saw in the previous section that *failure*-driven motivation focuses on the analysis of the *existing* system. Unless this is abandoned as irrelevant for reasons shown in Figure 8.3, it leads us on to the use of a derivative method. The subsequent stages following identification of the reasons for the failure or shortcomings of the existing system are likely to be some variant of the following sequence:

1 *Record* the existing physical system, i.e. *how* S_0 is implemented.
2 *Define* the logical system behind the existing physical system, i.e. *what* S_0 does.
3 *Define* an improved logical system to meet defined needs, i.e. *what* S_1 *must do*.
4 *Define* a new physical system based on the improved logical system, i.e. how S_1 *should be implemented*.

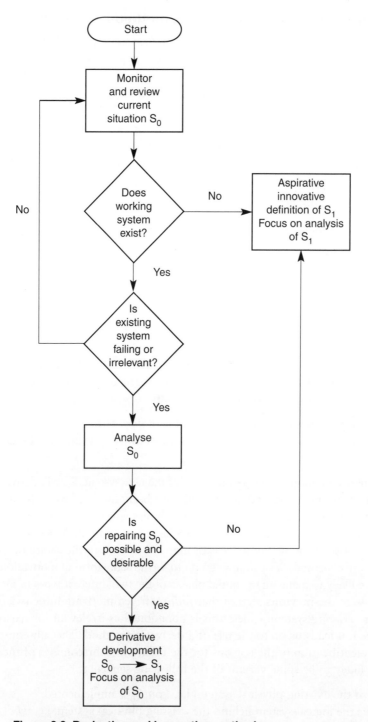

Figure 8.3 Derivative and innovative methods
The terms 'derivative' and 'innovative' can have emotional overtones, with the former implying something undesirable, and the latter presenting a creative image. Here, the terms are
used technically, and any judgement on their desirability is based on their relevance to the
existing situation, S_0.

In derivative methods, Stages 1, 2 and (sometimes) 3 are called *system analysis* and stages 3 and 4 are called *systems design*. It is also common for these methods to precede these stages with an initial stage called a *feasibility study*. The purpose of this is to assess whether the systems analysis and design project is worth bothering about and, if so, what resources can be provisionally assigned to it. (I have strong reservations about the assumptions behind this feasibility study stage, which I will discuss later.)

We can give a specific illustration of a modern and widely used derivative method by referring to one called SSADM, which is an acronym of Structured Systems Analysis and Design Methodology. We shall say more about this method later, but for the moment we can note that SSADM came close to being an official standard in government institutions and with large firms whose systems development activities were required to conform to government requirements. The basis of the analysis stage of this method is shown in Figure 8.4, which is derived from Cutts (1987). Here we can see stages 1 to 3 as the descending vertical sequence, with current system problem and new system requirements inputs. The focus on a current existing system as a starting point clearly makes SSADM a derivative method.

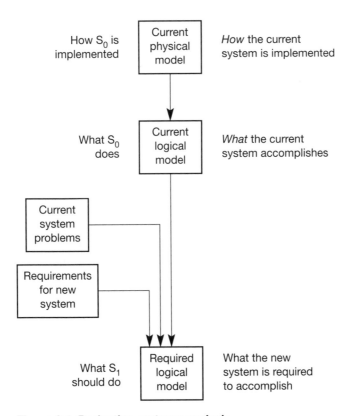

Figure 8.4 Derivative systems analysis
Relevant where it is unlikely that it will be necessary to 'reinvent the wheel' when developing S_1.

The classic examples of the use of derivative methods are to be found in areas where major environmental change has not been likely to make total failures or irrelevancies of existing systems. These would be the wide range of information systems used mainly in the financial subsystem like payroll or company accounts, and conventional central-purpose subsystem functions like order processing or stock control. One of the main reasons that such information systems can be seen as derivative is because the logical, and even sometimes the physical, nature of many of their processes and outputs is defined by law or business practice. As we noted before, people who design original, non-derivative ways of doing company accounts are usually transferred from the information system to the prison system!

However, there are situations where an innovative method may not only be desirable, but in fact the only way forward. This latter situation is illustrated by a problem faced by one of my students who had been set the task of developing a national dog registration system. He decide on his method before looking at the problem, i.e. exactly the opposite to what we are advocating here, and chose SSADM. Once he moved into the analysis along the lines of Figure 8.4 he met up with a problem. The conversation went something like this:

Student: Hey Mike, I've been trying to look at the dog registration system using SSADM.

Me: So what's the problem?

Student: You know in the analysis phase it talks about 'the current system'?

Me: Yes?

Student: Well, there isn't any 'current system' really, is there? I mean, we don't have dog registration at the moment.

Me: No, we don't.

Student: So how can I use SSADM?

Me, musically: Da-da! You can't …

Student: Oh.

Me: … in its standard form.

Having teased the student a little for ignoring my advice and choosing a method before studying the problem, I was able to point out a very simple remedy. If there is no current system to analyse, we just leave references to it out of Figure 8.4. If we do this, we are essentially left with the way innovative methods approach analysis. This involves going directly to determining the 'Requirements for new system' and using these as a high-level specification for the new system, S_1.

Our use of the term high-level here is systemic. We mean high in the sense of defining the boundaries and goals of the system and setting it in the context of the wider management system of which it will be a component. As we shall see in the next section when we list all the stages of systems development, the earlier stages of innovative methods tend to have labels like problem perception, terms of reference and business objectives, strategic requirements planning or simply business analysis, which reflect the wider context of systems strategy.

The result of this approach to analysis is to make methods that use it *top down* in the systems hierarchy sense. We start with the needs of the wider management system and use the analysis of these as a high-level specification for the new system, S_1.

It is worth understanding the reasons for the rise of innovative, top-down methods in recent years. The earliest applications of computerized information systems in the late 1960s and early 1970s were nearly always in the derivative areas we mentioned above like payroll, accounts etc. It is not surprising, therefore, that most methods also contained derivative assumptions; indeed, many of the first computerized information systems were essentially computerized versions of the old manual system.

The big change came in the early 1980s, with the new flexibility brought by the advent of microcomputers. These brought with them more friendly, high-level software like spreadsheets and databases, which reduced the emphasis on programming new applications from scratch. After this, dramatic reductions in the cost of large memory and processing capacity made possible even friendlier sophisticated graphical access through so-called WIMP (window icon menu pointer) user interfaces. The effect of this change was to widen the potential application of computerized information systems to new areas and to make it easier to implement working systems.

Changes like these have had important effects in changing the relative importance of the stages of systems development:

1 A widening of the areas or functions in an organization that may use computer-based information systems has often stimulated a completely fresh look at what the problem is and what the needs are. The move into a computer-based system for the first time in these situations is rather like our earlier analogy of going from balloons to aeroplanes. A derivative method is hardly relevant.
2 Friendlier, easier software has redirected the focus away from programming or systems production problems towards problems of definition of needs and specification of requirements.

The combined effect of points 1 and 2 is that systems development methodology is now seen to raise conceptual as well as technological issues.

8.3.4 The typical stages of systems development

Whatever the differences in assumption and approach between derivative and innovative methods in the initial analysis stages, both types aim to deliver the same result from these stages, albeit in different forms. Analysis should result in a logical specification or definition of what the new system, S_1, must do. Once we know this, the next stages of systems development will be concerned with how it must be done, or design; and finally doing it, or production and implementation.

There are many views of what stages, in what sequence, make up the whole systems development process. We will look at three views and make some comparative and critical comments about them:

1 The traditional systems life cycle view.
2 The information systems life cycle of Olle *et al.* (1988).
3 The b-model of software development of Birrell and Ould (1988).

What is important here is to understand some of the issues the different views raise. Despite the claims of the advocates of different schools of thought, I do not believe there is one exclusively best view, and when we come to look at specific examples of systems development method later in this chapter, we shall find that they are based on very different views of the systems development process.

The *traditional systems life cycle* view is usually defined in terms of six stages:

1 *Feasibility study*, looking at the aims and scope of the new system and its anticipated cost benefits in relation to the existing system.
2 *Systems investigation*, a fact-finding investigation and recording of the existing, often manual procedures.
3 *Systems analysis*, a critical analysis of what the existing system does, as revealed by stage 2, and the derivation of improvements.
4 *Systems design*, the design of output, processes, input and files for the new system defined by stage 3, usually for computerized implementation.
5 *Implementation*, scheduling the run-in of the new system by direct changeover, stepwise introduction or parallel running. File conversion and production of documentation.
6 *Review and maintenance*, monitoring the performance of the new system and repeating the systems analysis and design cycle if the new system has significant faults or omissions.

This is the oldest and most traditional of the three views of systems development that we shall consider. You will still find it referred to in more conservative areas of systems study, such as the manuals issued by some professional societies for the 'computer' or 'information technology' part of their qualification courses. De Marco (1979) and Yourdon and Constantine (1978) quoted versions of the cycle as the context of their methods, and this has been kept up by more subsequent followers, e.g. Page-Jones (1980) or Kendel (1987). So we cannot dismiss this view out of hand and it is worth noting why versions of it still survive.

The first thing we can note is that the view of analysis follows the *derivative sequence* we discussed in the previous section. The systems investigation stage corresponds exactly to the activity 'record the existing physical system', and the systems analysis stage corresponds to the activities 'define the logical system' and 'define an improved logical system'. We have already shown that a widely used, contemporary method like SSADM follows this sequence, so this part of the traditional systems life cycle still survives.

A second thing to note is a point we made earlier, that the first stage is called feasibility study. I promised to be critical of this, so here goes. The feasibility study 'looks at the aims and scope of the new system and its anticipated cost benefits'. *What new system?* Until we come up with at least an outline specification, what are we 'looking at'? The feasibility study seems to be assessing something that isn't even logically defined until the end of stage 3 of the cycle.

I think we can understand how such an apparent contradiction appears in the cycle if we recall what we saw about the classic examples of the use of derivative methods. In those applications the opportunity for major innovation was limited. It was therefore possible to have an initial outline view of what the new system might entail and to come up with 'anticipated' values.

If we return to a modern derivative method like SSADM, we find that it accommodates the 'What new system?' objection by two modifications to the traditional systems life cycle view. Figure 8.5 shows the six stages of this method. First, we can see that the analysis stage is placed before the feasibility study. As Figure 8.4 shows, this stage of SSADM delivers a logical view of S_1 whose qualities can be provisionally 'anticipated'. Secondly, the sequence of stages includes the possibility of a two-pass cycle so that a provisional specification for the logical S_1 can be then analysed in greater depth and modified.

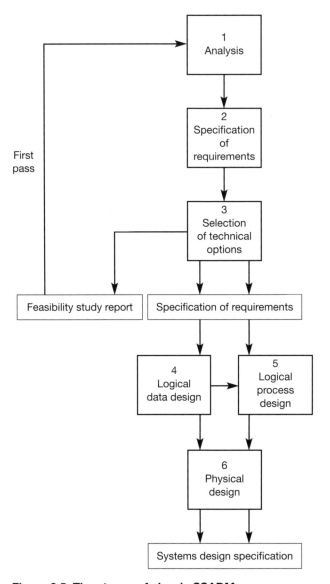

Figure 8.5 The stages of classic SSADM
These are the stages of SSADM as practised into the early 1990s. A more recent version, SSADM Version 4, has some modifications: Weaver (1993). The sequence of feasibility study, requirements analysis, requirements specification and technical systems options still remains as a lead into logical and physical design.

This last feature is an example of the important systems methodology concept of *iteration*. The application of most systems methods is a heuristic process, i.e. one of discovery and learning (see Chapter 3). This means that the implications of what we did in the early stages often only become apparent in the later stages. If we find at these later stages that we made mistakes or left something out in the earlier ones, then we have to go back and repeat them, i.e. iterate.

We took the traditional systems life cycle view as an example of a derivative methodology. A good representative of *innovative* methodology is the information systems life cycle of Olle *et al.* (1988). Their detailed list contains 12 stages:

1 Strategic study.
2 Information systems planning.
3 Business analysis.
4 Systems design.
5 Construction design.
6 Construction and workbench test.
7 Installation.
8 Test of installed system.
9 Operation.
10 Extension and maintenance.
11 Phase out.
12 Post mortem.

These authors regard stages 2–4, and to a lesser extent 5, as the essential framework for their perspective. We will look at their view of these stages in more detail before discussing the whole.

Information systems planning has the purpose of determining the broad nature of the information requirements of the enterprise and its business objectives. It will also check on any existing information system strategy and investigate what objective it has laid down.

Business analysis looks at the business to determine which of its activities may be covered by the information systems development process, what these activities involve, and the properties of any existing information system.

Systems design is the 'prescriptive or definitive activity' that identifies the components of the system to be constructed and describes what they must do.

Construction design involves how the system designed in the previous stage is to be constructed.

This view has an important feature that makes it innovative rather than derivative in its approach. It begins not with detailed analysis of the existing information system, but with the organization or business context and the needs of the enterprise. The authors focus, as we have done, on the crucial criterion of how we interpret the term analysis as being the distinguishing feature between modern and traditional views. They say: 'The term "business analysis" is used to refer to this stage in preference to the widely used term "system analysis". The reason for this choice is to emphasize that the business (or enterprise) is the subject of the analysis and not any kind of "system" (extant or proposed).'

It is interesting to note how the whole sequence of stages as well as this view of analysis reflects a top-down approach to systems development that we have already associated with innovative methods. Any method based on this view would be in line with this concept, because it works top down in stages 1–3 by considering the wider organizational systems context of the potential information system, S_1.

A criticism that might be made of this view, however, is the relative position in the sequence of *information systems planning and business analysis*. The meanings given to these terms seem to suggest the wrong sequence, given the emphasis in this book.

We have conceived of information as a component of control, and of control as a component of management. It is difficult to imagine that planning an information system can precede an analysis of business needs. To be fair, this is not what Olle *et al.* are implying, but their use of terminology is confusing. It comes, I suspect, from the influence of Martin (1984), who saw innovative strategic planning and vigorous use of information systems as a driving force for organizational success. (But as we saw in Chapter 7, the 'driver', the information and control system, is not the central-purpose system 'engine'.)

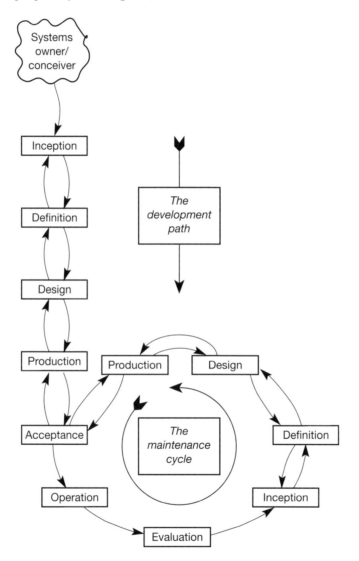

Figure 8.6 The b-model of systems development of Birrell and Ould (1988)
The role of the systems owner/conceiver is not part of the original, but has been added to show the source of any system's *world-view*, *purpose* or *set of values*. Although quite old, I have yet to see a better control systems view of systems development.

We will therefore look at a third view of the stages of systems development that I think best reflects the concepts of information systems in the context of control systems and hierarchy that we have followed in this book. This is the b-model of software development of Birrell and Ould (1988), shown in Figure 8.6.

In order to compare their view with the others we have considered, we should note two ways in which we are going to modify their uses of names:

1 They refer to *software development*, but their detailed review of methods and methodology shows that they are covering the wider field of *information systems development*, which is our concern. From now on we will use the latter term for consistency.

2 They envisage the information systems development life cycle as being made up of phases that can be broken down into stages. Since their phases correspond to what the other views we have looked at call stages, we will use the term stages for consistency.

If we return to Figure 8.6, we can see why Birrell and Ould's view of information systems development fits into the context of control systems and hierarchy. What they call the development path is concerned with deciding what the system must be like, i.e. goal setting. The system is then implemented, i.e. actuation. Having done this, the maintenance cycle assesses the performance of the working system, i.e. feedback. Where the system deviates from the goals laid down for it, maintenance either corrects this, i.e. goal-seeking control, or carries out further development and modification, i.e. goal-setting control.

Birrell and Ould (BO) see seven main stages to systems development. These are listed below together with the pithy descriptions the authors give of what they do:

1 *Project inception*: decide to do something for some reason.
2 *System definition*: agree what is to be done.
3 *System design*: work out how to do it.
4 *System production*: do it.
5 *System acceptance*: have it accepted.
6 *Post-acceptance development*: look after it following delivery.
7 *Project debriefing*: look back on how it all went.

Besides describing the stages in this very effective way, the authors also raise the important issue of how stages can be delineated. How do we decide, for example, what is 'definition' and what is 'design'? We have already seen that in practice systems development includes a heuristic function that results in iteration. This means that the stages can become blurred. We might find, for example, that we get some way through the production stage and then find that there's something missing from the design. At this point we've got to go back to fill in some detail. Are we now 'designing' or 'producing'?

Besides the kind of iteration that involves going back, there is another form that involves looking forward. We don't start out on systems development without having some initial, high-level view that the project is worth attempting. (I find this broader view of what feasibility means more acceptable than the more detailed view we criticized above.) This implies that some thought about design and production will already be taking place at the inception stage.

Given the practical necessity of iteration and the blurring of systems development stages, there are also dangers associated with it:

- It becomes difficult to manage the systems development process through monitoring and control because we are not clear which goals have to be attained.
- Systems development takes place on shifting foundations because the goal setting itself is unclear.

We would see these two points as being a lack of clear goal-seeking and goal-setting control respectively.

There is therefore a need to define each stage and its *boundaries*. The answer to this need is seen by Birrell and Ould in terms of *deliverables*. Each stage has to produce a specified output that in turn forms the input the next stage needs before it can begin. Let's now look at the seven stages in terms of their deliverables or outputs, and the procedures or processes they must carry out to produce them.

Project inception is where we decide to do something for some reason. We have already discussed in detail the motivations based on failure or aspiration providing reasons that make us decide to do something, i.e. move from S_0 to S_1. Our deliverable from this stage will therefore be some clear record or documentation of:

1 *What the decision was.* This will include quite specific details like the name of the systems development project and its aims, as well as an analysis of its business or organizational context. What is it supposed to do? How is it intended to fit in with the wider management system? Answers to these questions will form a deliverable in the form of a requirements specification.
2 *Who authorized the decision.* Besides defining down-to-earth aspects like who will pay for the systems development, this will define the systems owner(s). This more general responsibility is vital if we are to know whose system it is going to be. This knowledge is needed to resolve the soft issues that arise in the early stages of systems development. We shall look further into this in the next section.
3 *The commitment.* This will identify what resources in terms of money, time, personnel and other resources are allocated to the project.

With the previous deliverables, the *system definition* process has to agree what is to be done. Given that we are committed, authorized and resourced to produce a system that will meet the requirements specification, we now need to translate this into:

1 *A functional specification and logical systems model.* These will define what the system must do to be one that meets the specification. In practice, this will be achieved using diagramming and other tools whose particular format will depend on the systems development method being used. The point here is the word 'what'. It must be clear to the systems designer what the system is intended to achieve before it can be decided how it can be done.
2 *A project management plan.* Once we have defined the system in terms of the previous deliverables, we are now in a position to draw up an initial management plan that defines two things. First, if we know what the system is intended to do, we can define quality standards for the system. Secondly, if we know what the system has to consist of, we can produce a scheduled breakdown of what has to be done in the later stages of design and production.

Following the completion of the previous stage, we now have a logical model of S_1. *System design* is the process of converting the logical model into a definition of how the system is constructed, a model of the physical S_1. We therefore see two deliverables from this stage:

1 *A design specification.* The form of this will depend, like the functional specification and logical systems model, on the systems development method. The essential point about any design, however, is that it contains all the information needed by the systems builder to enable them to know how to construct the system.
2 *A refined project management plan.* Having details of how the system is to be constructed, we are now in a position to clarify the project plan in terms of estimating time and other resource requirements. We can also now match the skills of people on the design team to the various construction tasks and get more informed estimates from them of what the job entails.

System production is the construction of the working system corresponding to the design. If we are talking in terms of a mainly computerized information system with supporting manual procedures, then the main construction task is the creation of working software. The main deliverables will therefore be the software itself plus the necessary definition of its complete systems implementation:

1 *Working software.* The computer implementation of the design specification.
2 *Documentation.* Very little working software is entirely self-explanatory. Accompanying documentation will help both the users and new members of the computer systems team to understand it and how it fits into the whole of the new system.
3 *Training schedules.* To support the implementation of the vital human component of the whole system.
4 *Acceptance test description.* To provide an agreed set of procedures that will define that the job of the production team is complete.
5 *Systems conversion schedule.* Once the system has been accepted, the users will need clear instructions for full implementation. The analogy here is with the acceptance of any product from a producer. In these circumstances, you expect an instruction manual, or something similar, to tell you what you have to do and in what order. For information systems, the main issue is usually how the new system is introduced or how the changeover from the old is made.

System acceptance is experiencing the system in action and accepting it. Notice that the implication of this statement is that there is once more a deliverer and a receiver involved, just as there was in the transition between all the previous stages. The important point here is that the deliverer is likely to be a specialist information system team and the receiver is management. When we look at systems development as a system at the end of this chapter, we shall say more about the roles of the people involved. Meanwhile, we can identify the main deliverables as:

1 *A record of acceptance.* Given the important change in the nature of those involved, acceptance is a likely area of political argument and apportionment of 'blame' if the system doesn't deliver. It therefore makes sense to formalize the acceptance that the system fulfils what was laid down by the initial stages of the systems development process.

2 *Monitoring procedures*. The car might be working perfectly well when you drive it out of the dealer's showroom, but what do you do to keep it that way? So with systems acceptance, what are the procedures that enable both the producer and the user to agree what checks should be made to ensure that the system continues to work successfully?

Post-acceptance development is described by Birrell and Ould as 'look after it following delivery'. I think this is where our control systems view would make us modify their description of this stage in relation to the deliverables they define. Their main deliverables from this stage are:

1 *Systems longevity*. The deliverable if, to quote Birrell and Ould, you 'look after' a system should be a system that keeps going, or has longevity, but we would not call this process 'development'. Instead, we are describing the concept of a systems definition (goals) that continues to be implemented in the face of (environmental) disturbances. I think the term 'maintenance' used by Birrell and Ould in Figure 8.6 is more appropriate. It rightly implies the process of trying to ensure that the defined system (goals) is maintained (first-order control).
2 *Record of systems performance*. The implication here is indeed that we will wish to record how well the working information system conformed to the defined system (goals). Why should this be of interest? The answer is easily interpreted in terms of our hierarchical control model: a record of systems performance represents feedback on the implementation of the goals defined for the systems development process, with a view to what the next stage, project debriefing, will require. When we go on to look at what this final stage involves, we shall see that it is concerned with higher-order control: goal setting and the reasoning behind it.

The process of *project debriefing* is described by Birrell and Ould as 'look back on how it all went'. This will mean that we review the experience of the systems development process and analyse the record of systems performance. When we do this, we are not merely involved in a kind of spectator sport where we might say, 'OK, that wasn't too bad' or 'Didn't we do well!' There are deliverables from this process in the form of:

1 *Critical evaluation of method*. We can now make informed comment on the pros and cons of the particular method we chose. This is third-order control feedback, because it is feedback on our goal setting in the form of the defined method.
2 *Critical evaluation of methodology*. Our critical experience also allows us to review the principles we used to choose the particular method that we did. This amounts to the study of method, i.e. methodology. Since we are now reviewing the process of goal setting, we can see this as fourth-order control.

Both of these deliverables can be seen as a form of learning

Given our critical analysis of three representative views of the systems development process, we now need to choose one we can refer to when discussing particular methods. Figure 8.7 represents a view virtually identical to that of Birrell and Ould, but with modifications to emphasize:

- Stage 1 The strategic context of information systems development.
- Stage 2 The role of analysis in defining the logical S_1.
- Stage 6 Concept of control by use of the term maintenance.
- Stage 8 Concept of higher-order control by inclusion of the term methodology.

```
1. Strategy and inception
2. Definition and analysis
3. Design
4. Production
5. Acceptance
6. Maintenance
7. Debriefing, learning and methodology
```

Figure 8.7 The phases of systems development of Harry (1990)
A view that is very close to both Birrell and Ould (1988) and Olle *et al.* (1988). The main feature is the emphasis on setting information systems development is the context of the organizational or business need, rather than reference to existing systems.

The mention of *strategy* leads us naturally to the subject of the next section. When we consider the strategic context of the information system and information systems development, we look at the management system and the whole business and organizational system itself. This will involve us in the soft human and policy components of these systems and the messes at the earliest stage of the systems development process. Since the process will not be able to pass this first stage until these soft aspects are covered, we need to consider how we deal with *messes*.

8.3.5 Dealing with messes

When we considered derivative and innovative methods earlier in this chapter, we found that both were dependent on the condition that 'we anticipate that our needs are definable in hard terms'. We know from our study of systemic properties in Chapter 3 and our consideration of problems and messes earlier in this chapter that this will not be the case for the needs of the wider management system, or the whole business or organizational system itself. Needs at these higher systems levels bring us up against questions of value judgement, policy decision, conflict and other soft issues that make for messes rather than clear-cut technical problems.

Modern views of the methods of systems development based on Figure 8.7 emphasize the strategic context of the information system and information systems development. They involve us in messes at their earliest stage. Failure to recognize that messes cannot be solved by methods intended for hard problems has been a common cause of failure in systems development. An example of how this lesson has been learned can be seen in Figure 8.8, taken from Cutts (1987). If we consider the terms well-structured and ill-structured, we can see that they correspond closely to the properties of a situation that lead us to describe it as a problem or mess respectively. The message of Figure 8.8 is that SSADM is not likely to be successful if applied mechanically to a messy situation for which it is not suitable.

Parameter	Well-structured	Ill-structured
Objectives	Clear	Vague
Problem areas	Known	In dispute
Requirements	Defined	Intuitive
Communication	Reliable	Unreliable
Attitudes	Co-operative	Obstructive

Figure 8.8 Well-structured conditions needed for the appropriate application of SSADM
This derives from an early work by Cutts (1987), but is still relevant comment on the method.

This lesson will apply to any systems development method whose main concern is information systems development. Messes are a wider management systems issue, and need to be sorted out before we start the process of information systems development. If dealing with messes has to take place at the beginning of the strategy and inception stage, and precede any further move with systems development, what can it involve?

We can investigate this issue by returning to the meliorist model of Figure 8.2 and relating it to the criteria of Figure 8.1. We said that these criteria involved agreement as to the boundary, separation, responsibility, information requirements and description of the problem if it was not to be regarded as a mess. Hence the initial stage of systems development requires us to identify where we are now, S_0, and where we would like to be, S_1. The deliverable required by any such systems development method is clarification of S_0 and S_1.

For this reason, when we come to look at information system development methods later in this chapter, we need first to consider what approaches or methods are available to clarify the soft issues involved in any mess before we move on to information systems development itself.

8.3.6 Signposts for a problem–method road map

Our consideration of the terms *problem*, *mess*, *approach*, *method* and *methodology* has now led us to consider how:

- *problems and messes*: concerns with what we have, what we want and the differences between them (S_0 and S_1 in Figure 8.2), can be related to:
- *approaches and methods*: concerns with how we hope to improve our position (the arrow in Figure 8.2).

To understand how such a relationship can be described, it is worth summarizing which attributes of problem, mess, approach, method and methodology we need to take account of.

The differences between problems and messes are summarized in Figure 8.1 and have been discussed in detail above. The essential distinction between them is that problems are seen as hard and messes as soft. Individual problems can be considered to lie somewhere in a range from being exclusively hard at the top end and exclusively soft at the bottom, with most real-life ones being somewhere in between. The vertical axis in Figure 8.9 represents such a range.

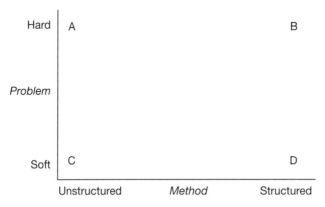

Figure 8.9 Combining problems and methods
Problems can have characteristics that place them on a spectrum of soft to hard. Methods may range from being tightly structured to being open, unstructured approaches. In principle, combinations can occur anywhere in the range shown by the diagram, but the regions A, B, C and D are used to illustrate the main types of combination.

Approaches and methods essentially differ in terms of how formally they are structured. Methods have defined sequences of stages and the deliverables associated with them: they are structured and rational. Approaches use sets of principles to achieve final deliverables, but no fixed sequence of stages or actions is laid down for them. Approaches are therefore unstructured and empirical. In practice, we saw that procedures such as iteration meant that methods were not completely formal in their structure. We can also imagine that an overall informal approach might include the use of some formal methods. For example, an informal talk introducing a new system to users might include a structured run through its main features. So in practice, approaches and methods can be thought to lie on a spectrum ranging from the very informal and unstructured to the very formal and structured. This is the horizontal axis in Figure 8.9.

The whole of Figure 8.9, taken from Harry (1987), shows the range of possibilities that can occur in principle when we match the hard/soft range of possible problems to the structured/unstructured range of possible approaches. On the basis of this relationship, we can recognize four positions, A, B, C and D. These represent the extremes of a range of combinations of problem and approach that we can conceive of as being possible. While it will be rare to find combinations represented exactly by these corner positions in practice, we can use them and the whole of Figure 8.9 as part of a 'road map' to illustrate the features that tend to be shown by particular application of approaches to problems.

Position A represents the situation where an unstructured approach is applied to a hard problem. This means that the problem itself is clearly defined, has objectively measurable criteria for success and all the other hard properties of Figure 8.1. The approach, however, is unstructured and informal. Here we can imagine someone using inspiration, 'feel', guesses, trial and error, and many other unstructured ways of facing hard realities. Sometimes this approach will result in spectacular success, sometimes spectacular failure, and perhaps quite often rather mixed results.

A common example of this combination in the systems development field is the use of *prototyping*. Here the potential user and the systems developer work together in a relaxed and unstructured way to build up a useable system bit by bit. This can be done by using friendly software such as a 4GL (Chapter 6), with possible graphical support like that discussed later in this chapter.

Position B represents the situation where a structured approach or method is applied to a hard problem. This extreme position might be illustrated by the example of a qualified professional applying a body of well-defined techniques in a situation where the problem is clear, and success or failure is clearly defined. An example of this in information systems development might be the normalization of data as part of the application of a tightly structured method like SSADM to an agreed system specification.

Position C represents the situation where an unstructured approach, as in position A, is now applied to a soft problem. Here we envisage a situation where there is dispute about what the problem actually is, conflicting values, and many of the other messy aspects of soft problems. An unstructured approach to such problems amounts to a very open situation. In practice, it could include a very rich range of activities from inspired creation to muddle, or from political in-fighting to enjoying friendly co-operation. The main examples in practice of this position on our road map will come from the human activity component of systems development. We shall say more about this aspect when we look at systems development itself as a system towards the end of this chapter.

Position D is the last of our illustrative positions on the 'road map'. Here we consider the application of a structured approach or method to a soft problem. The situation represented is one where an attempt is made to deal with disputes about the nature of the problem, conflicting values and so on as in Position C, but to approach the mess systematically. The idea of having a structured approach to a mess may seem instinctively wrong. If most messes have their origin in human activity, it seems unlikely that anything as elusive and subtle as a human being can be successfully dealt with like a machine. (I am reminded of a colleague who said that trying to organize academics was rather like trying to herd cats.) In practice, we do use quite formal structures to organize how we deal with soft human issues like taste, opinion etc. Courts, political elections and formal negotiations are all structured approaches to very messy issues.

In the systems development field, we are most likely to be in position D when we are trying to deal with messes at the earlier strategy and inception, and definition and analysis stages of systems development. Here, as we saw in the previous section, we are still likely to be concerned with the wider management system aspects of the problem that have to be clarified before proceeding to systems development.

This last reasoning means that in the next section we shall look at methods for dealing with messes in the management systems context before going on to examples of information systems development methods.

One other important aspect now follows from the important issue of matching methods to problems, which does not appear in Figure 8.9. This is an analysis of what the term 'structured' can mean in the context of systems methodology.

If we look back to see when we have used the word structure so far, there are two principal ways in which we have used the term:

1 The structure of a *system*.
2 The structure of a *method*.

The structure of a system has been used to describe the form of the relationship between the interacting components of a system within the systems hierarchy.

Structure of a method has been used to describe the organization of the actions needed for the process of systems development into the stages making up the method. In this and the previous section, we have been talking about the structure of the method.

If we look at the way in which individual methods are structured, we will find that the structure of a method is often determined by what view is taken of the system being developed. We know from Chapter 3 that there are many aspects of a system that may be important, but the relationship between structure and process is one that can have a major effect on the method of creating or modifying a system, i.e. systems development. We will find that the particular stages occuring in a method, and their sequential order, are influenced by the relative emphasis given to the structure or the processes of a system.

We can illustrate this issue with a simple example. If I look at my 'clothing' system while I am writing this, one of its structural features is the relationship between my socks and my shoes: like most other people, I wear my socks inside my shoes. The fact that such a structural relationship exists also says something about the process of clothing myself. If my socks are inside my shoes, then when I dress in the morning I have to put my socks on before I put on my shoes. I can therefore describe my clothing system in two ways. I can either say, 'I wear my socks inside my shoes', or I can say, 'I put my socks on first and then I put on my shoes'. The first way defines my clothing system in terms of structure, the second in terms of process.

When we consider the structure of many of the methods for information systems development, we find that they tend towards one of two types:

1 Structure-oriented methods.
2 Process-oriented methods.

Structure-oriented methods start from a viewpoint that we first considered in Chapter 2, that information is data organized into a particular structure. When we look at how such methods approach systems development, they take some form of detailing of this data structure as their starting point for describing an existing system or defining a new one. Once these structures have been established, the processes needed for their production can then be derived from them. Once we know that socks lie inside shoes, we can derive the dressing procedure needed to produce such a structure.

Process-oriented methods start from a viewpoint that we also first considered in Chapter 2, that a system does something, and that what an information system does is to take raw data and process it in such a way that it produces the information we want. Methods based on this view take as their starting point a co-ordinated description or definition of what processes the existing system carries out, or what a new system will have to do.

Structure and process are not mutually exclusive, however. Instead, we see them as complementary views that contribute to a holistic view of a system. Similarly, when we talk of a structure- or process-oriented view of methods, we are not pretending that these are mutually exclusive categories. Good systems development methods will have to take account of both structure and process because systems themselves have both these properties. For this reason we use the word 'oriented' to indicate emphasis rather than exclusive classification. When we come to look at examples of certain oriented methods later in the chapter, we shall also explore how strong the particular orientation happens to be. When we do this, we shall find that real methods usually have some features that do not conform to their overall orientation.

If the previous paragraph has led you to look ahead in the chapter, you will see that a third orientation is covered. *Object-oriented* approaches are based on the most recent of the three views we consider. The rise of object-oriented methods is an example of methodology in its true sense of 'the study of method'. As we saw in section 8.3.4, true methodology involves a learning process. What the pioneers of object-oriented methods found was that many of the problems of systems software implementation could be avoided or reduced in seriousness if systems builders learned from their experience. The design and implementation of modern software applications can be complicated enough without those involved reinventing the wheel. The simplification and introduction of consistency into any task, including systems development, make it easier to achieve and less prone to error while it is being carried out.

The important product of the *learning* that comes from an object-oriented approach is the recognition of how concepts of *hierarchy* and *classification* can be used for simplification and the introduction of consistency in systems development. We can return to our sock and shoe example to make the point. My method for dressing needs to cover other articles of clothing apart from my shoes and socks. Thus in the winter I wear a vest next to my skin, a shirt outside that and a sweater on top. We notice that this structure of one item of clothing on top of another is another example of the relationship we've already seen between sock and shoe. It is no surprise therefore that the similarities between sock–shoe structure and the vest–shirt or shirt–sweater structures means that the methods I use to achieve these systems structures are also similar. I can say quite generally that if the structure is:

outer garment
containing
inner garment
containing
body

then the method is:

1 Put inner garment on body.
2 Put outer garment on inner garment.

Once I build up an understanding of structural relationships by using the concepts of hierarchy and classification, these simplify my future systems development and make it less prone to error by enabling me to recognize how I can reuse or adapt features of successful existing systems. If I decide to wear my underpants inside my trousers, I no longer need to develop a management from first principles. If, like a particular popular female singer, I decide to wear a corset on the outside, I only need to recognize it as an outer garment to automatically adapt the dressing method.

We can now see why object orientation is a more recent approach to systems development because it depends on having had some experience to classify.

Two final concepts will help us make sense of the range of systems development methods. These are described by the terms top down and bottom up. The relationship between the concepts of systems hierarchy and emergent property is the key to our understanding of these terms. The words 'top' and 'bottom' refer to the systems hierarchy itself. Thus top-down means looking at the whole system before looking at the components as we descend the systems hierarchy; while bottom up means starting with the lowest elements before looking at rising aggregations through subsystems to the whole system itself.

When systems development methods are referred to as top down, the implication is that the method begins by referring to the characteristics or needs of the whole existing S_0 or desired S_1 system before detailing what these will mean for its components. We can see that a top-down approach is implied by the view of typical stages of systems development that we adopted at the end of section 8.3.4. In that section we noted that a modern view of analysis is that it involves breaking down the high-level, strategic specification for S_1, the desired system, into the implications of that specification for the goals of the systems components. An example of this might be that we would decide that a system for dog registration ought to be difficult to avoid, before we decided how the subsystem file recording dog owners ought to be updated. 'Whats before hows' is the essence of a systemic top-down approach.

At this point in our study of systems methodology, we need to realize that 'top down' is used colloquially to mean something very different. This other use of the term is emotionally pejorative. In everyday life, 'top down' is frequently used to mean that a higher authority imposes its will on those below. 'Top down' might mean, for example, that a local council would exterminate stray dogs whether the majority of its citizens liked it or not. The reason for the difference between our use of the term and the colloquial use is that a systems hierarchy is different from the organizational or political view. As we have emphasized since Chapters 3 and 4, a systems hierarchy is about levels of aggregation, not about 'who is the boss of whom'.

This analysis then leads us to the question of what role the concept of bottom up has in a systemic view of systems development. Given that a system is a holistic concept, trying to describe or define the properties of a system's components before identifying the system itself seems like a contradiction in terms. We don't know whether something is a component until we know what it is supposed to be a component of. For this reason, a bottom-up approach is not normally applied to the initial stages of systems development as defined in Figure 8.8. The strategy and definition stages refer to the whole system, and it would not make sense to try to design the components of a system before having a design for the structure of the whole. Imagine going ahead with the design of an invoice document before even knowing whether the whole system was going to be concerned with order processing in any case!

A bottom-up approach does make sense, however, in the production and later stages of systems development. Systems, like anything else that is constructed, are built by creating and assembling components. The whole can only come into existence after the parts or components, since the whole cannot exist without them. We therefore see that the normal view of systems development is that *we design top down* and *we construct bottom up*.

I have twice used the term 'normal' to describe this view of the two approaches. When we come to look at *Jackson Systems Development* and *prototyping*, we shall see apparently different views, but I hope to show that this difference is only one of emphasis.

Box 8.2

DSS to simplify benefits claims process

FT

Rosemary Bennet

The Department of Social Security is drawing up plans to computerize the applications procedure for benefits and pensions in an attempt to simplify the unwieldy claims process.

Officials are also eager to improve the image of the Benefits Agency, which handles the payment of more than £100bn a year.

'Everybody hates us,' one senior official said. 'We want to do something about that.'

However, the project is inching along slowly, the official added. The department is proceeding cautiously in an attempt to avoid the problems that have bedevilled other government information technology projects.

Angela Eagle, a junior social security minister, is in charge of drawing up the plans, which aim to modernize the 'customer interface' in line with other public services.

The main project will concentrate on the outdated applications procedure that requires claimants to fill in forms running to more than 40 pages.

Ministers want to computerize the system so that once claimants have provided some basic information, the relevant pages of the form would be printed out for completion.

They hope the modernization of the applications procedure will be accompanied by improvements in the provision of information to prospective claimants via a new 'DSS Direct' service, to be run along the lines of NHS Direct and the planned transport hotline.

Computerization of the applications procedure could pave the way for closer relations between the Benefits Agency, Employment Service and local authority staff with the goal of a 'one-stop' shop for the unemployed favoured by many ministers.

After the extensive problems the Department of Social Security experienced over the computerization of payment procedures, Alistair Darling, the social security secretary, has said he wants future information techno-

logy projects to be procured in manageable bits.

Last May the government was forced to abandon part of the £1bn Horizon project run by ICL, the computer services group, to automate Post Office counters and provide anti-fraud benefits swipe cards.

The project cost the government many hundreds of millions of pounds.

Elsewhere in Whitehall, a new computer system conspired with staffing problems and the introduction of children's passports to produce queues and chaos for holidaymakers during the summer rush.

Delays in the delivery of a new national insurance computer system last year resulted in long delays in the payment of benefits and pensions, leaving the government facing claims for compensation.

Source: Financial Times, 23 December 1999. Reprinted with permission.

Comment

Are we learning at last? It does look like the message is getting through that so-called information technology or computer system problems are nearly always management *problems.*

As we see in this in this chapter, systems development itself is a system that has to be controlled. *As we saw in Chapter 4, lags in the control systems reduce its ability to respond to environmental disturbances. We also saw that control systems need* goals. *To develop a system successfully we therefore need:*

- *Clearly defined goals, in the form of a* systems specification. *If management can't sort that out, we can't have control.*
- *The ability to deal with environmental disturbances and/or to limit them. Management should not unnecessarily change the specification and/or should make sure that learning and adaptability is built into the system. One particular way of doing this is to avoid long complex development and keep to 'manageable bits'.*

8.4 METHODOLOGY AND MANAGING SYSTEMS DEVELOPMENT

8.4.1 Systems development as an organizational system that has to be managed

Developing an information or any other kind of system is *an activity aimed at achieving something desirable*. I use italics for this last phrase because it is a direct quote from Section 3.2.1. My aim is to recall the important concept of the relation between *management*, *control* and *information* that we covered in Chapter 3 and that is summarized in Figure 3.4.

We can then relate this to the *meliorist model* of Figure 8.2, by seeing systems development itself as a *system*. Systems development *transforms* any existing situation or system, S_0, into a desired system S_1; as in Figure 8.10. If we are concerned with the *management* of systems development, then this transformation process needs to be *controlled*.

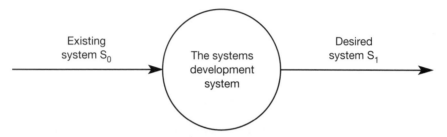

Figure 8.10 Systems development as a transformation process
The aim of systems development is to replace the existing system or situation, S_0, with the desired system, S_1.

So far, our interpretation of the role of control in systems development has focused on the use of methods or approaches to deal with problems or messes. In Section 8.3.1 we introduced the relationship of method to control, and in Section 8.3.4 we went further to show how a model like that of Birrell and Ould in Figure 8.6 spelled out the role of *learning* in the goal-setting process.

If we now go on to consider the wider context of the *management* of systems development, then all our studies so far would tell us that management is more than just method. So what role does method play in management? Once we realize that systems development is itself a system that has to be managed, we can draw some simple analogies with other managed systems to understand the answer to this question. In Carry-Out Cupboards, we would expect there to be methods for assembling the various components of a kit. In MX Marketing, Ben Lister will have an approach to selling his products. What is obvious in these examples is that we would not expect the kits to assemble themselves, or the products to sell themselves. As we saw in Chapter 6, a *systems* view of management recognizes that many different components have to work together in order that management of any organization can pursue its *central purpose*.

As we saw in Section 7.1, a systems view of organizations tells us that the term *organization* does not refer to the name on the company notepaper or on a manager's office door. Organizations as systems are seen in terms of what goes on behind the labels. In the case of systems development, this means that we look at *what* is involved in the transformation process of Figure 8.10, rather than labels like 'IT manager' or 'systems analyst'. Hence the term *organization*, in the context of systems development, refers to the system of components involved in the *central purpose* of transforming the existing system or situation, S_0, into a desired system, S_1. This might be a specialist firm of external consultants, or something more complex like the mixed team of the George Michaelson lead-in case.

Such a view enables us to look at systems development in terms of the information and management systems model of Figures 6.1 and 6.2. If we do this we can distinguish:

1 A *central-purpose subsystem* for systems development that is concerned with the process of transforming S_0 into S_1.
2 *Central-purpose support subsystems* concerned with enabling this transformation process by providing its various needs.

So systems development means much more than method. We know from Chapter 6 that the central-purpose subsystem uses financial, human and facilities components provided by the central-purpose support subsystems, and that all these have to be co-ordinated by the corporate planning and control subsystem. There are therefore many aspects of the systems development process that it will share with other forms of *project management*.

The need for *financial* support will mean that any systems development project will have to be looked at as the allocation of money to an investment from which we expect a return. Standard financial techniques such as investment appraisal using discounted cash flow analysis will be as relevant to the installation of a new information system as they would be to building a new factory. The costs of systems development will need to be budgeted for and controlled just like any other form of management spending. However, systems development does tend to be a project area where lack of promised return and poorly controlled overspending are common. We have already identified that a major reason for this is lack of clear *systems definition and specification*. When we talk of 'poor financial control' in systems development, we are often blaming the financial subsystem for something beyond its boundaries. If we have a poor definition of the system we are trying to develop, it is hardly surprising that we can't determine and control the costs of creating it. The lesson is therefore that clear definition and specification of the central purpose of systems development will be a major influence on the success of its financial control.

The *human* or *personnel* support for systems development will also include most of the activities found in other forms of project management. Issues such as skills, training, motivation, equal opportunities or whatever are as likely to be present in the management of a systems development project as they are in the mounting of a major marketing programme or opening a new pub. What makes systems development different from these examples is the often complex *roles* of those involved. As we shall see in the next section, systems development can be a process in which the marketing manager is also the customer, or the pub drinker has to help brew their own beer.

The *facilities* subsystem will be called on to provide much the same type of resources for systems development as it does for many other forms of project management. Systems development requires desks and chairs for its staff in well-lit, heated and ventilated offices and all the other paraphernalia of twenty-first century organizational life. But the development of *information* systems brings a special feature. In Chapter 6 we saw that a banking system has to distinguish between the money it processes in its central-purpose subsystem and the money provided by its financial subsystem for its own use. Similarly, information systems development needs to distinguish between the information system it uses to help manage its activities and the information that will be used by the developed system, S_1.

If this seems a complex point, consider the example of George Michaelson. He needed all sorts of information in order to understand PROPS. Some of this information was about why PROPS didn't work. This wasn't part of the PROPS system, but it was relevant to the management of its further development. The information George gained about the workings of the relationship between the production and inspection functions at Technoturbines was an example of this kind of information. The other kind of information was that actually used by the information system itself. An example of this would be the information that the inspectors were supposed to key into the computer about the jobs processed in the factory.

As far as the facilities subsystem is concerned, the existence of these two kinds of information can lead to a potential confusion when considering the use of *computers* as a facility provided to support systems development. In this situation, besides being facility, the computer is also a potential *component* of the desired system, S_1. This happens when we use *prototyping* and *CASE* tools. We introduced methods and tools like these at the end of Chapter 5 and we shall say more about them in Chapter 9. They enable the desired system, S_1, to be developed on the computer itself using software designed to help the development process. This can make systems development very quick and easy – and there lies the danger. It is all too easy blindly to accept existing hardware as the basis for the new system, so that the facilities subsystem that is supposed to support the central purpose starts to control it instead. The facilities subsystem tail starts to wag the central-purpose dog.

When considering the role of the *corporate planning and control* subsystem in systems development, I am still surprised how often the subject of project management is not seen as relevant. Final-year and postgraduate students who are also following courses in project management can successfully learn techniques such as PERT or critical path analysis and use computer software for their application. Yet they seem not to realize that these techniques could be used to schedule an information systems development project as well as for a piece of civil engineering. But perhaps the students are not as unthinking as I imply. You notice I used the words *could be used*. The essential ingredient to using PERT or any other scheduling technique is that we have a complete and clear definition of the activities that have to be carried out to complete a project, and we know what sequence or order they can be done in. This is often not the case with information systems development, where the definition and specification of the central purpose form the main problem.

Our analysis of the role of the various central-purpose support subsystems in systems development shows why *method* seems to be such an important issue when we think about managing the process. The main problem we are likely to face in systems development is not that we don't know how to do discounted cash flow calculations, calculate a budget, train people, light a room or draw a critical path network. These are all well-established management activities. But we can only carry out these activities in *support* of the central purpose of systems development if we know what systems development is trying to achieve. In terms of the meliorist model of Figure 8.2: if we don't know what S_1 is, how can we aim the arrow?

If we therefore appear to concentrate on information systems development methodology, rather than the broader issues of the financial, human and facilities components provided by the central-purpose support subsystems, it is not because we are forgetting about holism. Instead, we are trying to focus on those particular issues that often make systems development management particularly complex.

8.4.2 Issues in the relationships between four major components of the systems development process

Figure 8.11 identifies four important components of the systems development process that are involved with the achievement of its central purpose, the production of the desired system, S_1:

1 The client.
2 The systems developer.
3 The problem.
4 The method.

As we saw in the previous section, these four are just a small selection from the range of components involved. They are especially significant, however, in giving the systems development process its particular characteristics.

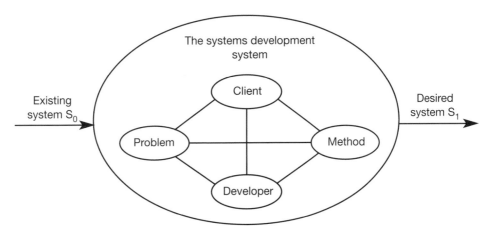

Figure 8.11 Components of the systems development system
The diagram shows roles rather than individuals. Thus one person could play a part as both developer and client. It is also important to note that the the components interact, with effects on each other.

When interpreting Figure 8.11, it is important to note that it is a systems diagram and that it takes a *conceptual* view. Thus, following the approach of Chapter 6, the terms client and developer refer to *roles* rather than names of people or official job descriptions. Likewise, the terms *problem* and *method* reflect the views of problems, messes, approaches and methods found earlier in this chapter.

As components of a *system*, the client, developer, problem and method interact (Section 3.2.6). Looking at the way they interact will help us understand some of the important management issues of systems development.

8.4.3 **Issues of problem–method interaction**

We have already looked at the relationship between problems and methods in Section 8.3.6, but the interaction between these components in systems development raises three further important issues:

1 Are there particular methods that lend themselves to particular types of problem? Thus if we understand a problem, does this automatically mean that we will choose a particular method?
2 Does a bias towards a particular method mean that the problem will be defined in a particular way?
3 After we start to explore and understand a particular problem, are we likely to change the method?

The answer to the first of these questions seems to be yes, if we observe what happens in real life. If my computer software appears to have a bug in it, I am most likely to bring in a software expert who will use some very specific software methods to try to solve my problem. It is not likely that I would apply a method that analysed my whole business system or call in the methods of medical pathology.

Is it necessarily desirable to associate certain kinds of method with certain kinds of problem? Could it be that any association is more to do with laziness or inertia? Flood and Jackson (1991) consider the issue of the relationship between problems and methods when advocating a policy of Total Systems Intervention or TSI. They review six systems methods:

1 System dynamics.
2 Viable system diagnosis.
3 Strategic assumption surfacing and testing.
4 Interactive planning.
5 Soft systems methodology.
6 Critical systems heuristics.

These authors conclude that while particular methods may be associated with 'ideal-type' problem situations, this association depends on the perception of the problems themselves. Since different people may see different problems in the same situation, so different perceptions of an appropriate method are also possible.

While Flood and Jackson are concerned with broad systems methodology rather than specifically information systems development methodology, their conclusions agree with our studies too. In Chapter 3 we made clear the role of the information system as a component of the management system. We established that any system is someone's concept. Any links that are seen between problems and methods are therefore likely to reflect which particular personal concepts of the problem are actually involved. Later in this section we shall see that the client and the developer are likely to be the most important sources of personal concepts of the problem, and we shall study the issues further when covering the problem–client and problem–developer relationships.

Our second question on the problem–method relationship was whether a bias towards a particular method means that the problem will be defined in a particular way. I think the answer to this question is also yes. Just as eyes tell us about light while ears tell us about sound, so particular methods of analysing problems will bring out those features of the problem that the method is best at dealing with. The problem is therefore very likely to reflect the methods applied to it. We shall say more of this when considering the use of the rich picture of the soft systems methodology in Chapter 9.

Our final question was whether, once we start to explore and understand a particular problem, we are likely to change the method as we progress. Here again I think that the answer is yes. The concept of reflective goal setting (Section 3.2.4) tells us that feedback on the success of particular methods can lead to modifications or changes in their use. An example of this is SSADM (Section 8.3.3). Despite being a 'standard' method, it has gone through four major modifications.

8.4.4 Issues of problem–client interaction

The client is a potential source of the values or world view on which the desired system, S_1, is going to be based. To understand the problem–client interaction, we therefore need to answer three important questions about the client:

1 Client *identity*. Who is the client?
2 Client *perception*. What does the client consider the problem to be?
3 Client *motivation*. What does the client want from the solution of the problem?

We begin to answer these questions by reminding ourselves that the term *client* refers to a *role*. Thus when my wife and I first developed a spreadsheet program to do our quarterly VAT accounts for our business, we discussed what sort of information we wanted from the program and how we wanted it presented on the screen. Both of us, as potential users, had inputs into deciding what was wanted from the system, and we were attempting to develop a system for both of us to use. Since the client role involved more than one person, the concept of client perceptions was an *emergent property* that came from the interaction of the individual components of the client role, i.e. my wife and myself.

For a small close partnership like this, and a simple problem like doing VAT on a spreadsheet, the problem–client relationship was pretty easy to deal with; but what of larger, more complex problems? An example of this might be the changes in UK taxation procedures known as 'self-assessment' that came into force in 1996. Potential clients of this system could be the Inland Revenue staff who have to work it, the accountants who may make money out of it, or the taxpayer who has to suffer it. It's hard to imagine them all assembled in Wembley Stadium informally agreeing their perceptions of the problem; both their large number and their different *motivations* would prevent this.

In all situations where small-scale, informal procedures will not answer the questions of client identity, perception and motivation, a more *formal* or *structured* method is needed. This will have to incorporate the following criteria if it is to overcome the *mess* of a complex client role:

1 Clarification of the client role must *precede* definition of the problem.
2 Definition of both client and problem must be a *deliverable* from the *inception* phase of the chosen method.

These criteria raise what are essentially management rather than information systems issues, and many so-called computer or information systems problems stem from failing to meet them. However, the problems of clarifying the client role cannot be dismissed as a problem that has nothing to do with information systems development methodology. As we shall see in Chapter 9 when exploring *soft systems methodology* and *integrated methods*, attempts have been made to recognize the human role in systems development.

8.4.5 **Issues of problem–developer interaction**

The developer role, like the client role, raises questions of subjectivity and values:

1 Can the developer be separated from the problem?
2 Does the developer distort the problem?

If the developer role is a *component* of the systems development *system*, then we know that the answer to the first question is no, and that the answer to the second question is yes.

The assertion that the developer role cannot be separated from the problem is a particular example of the principle that the components of a system *interact*. The developer will interact with other components of the systems development system, including the problem itself. Reference to the George Michaelson lead-in case can be used to illustrate this, since it is based on real experience. The existing system at Technoturbines was itself the product of systems developers. Also, the acceptance that there were problems with the existing system, and the particular view of those problems, were partly the result of the developers' contribution. If George had decided that it was purely a question of forcing production and inspection to keep to the formal system, the view of the problem would have been very different.

In practice, therefore, it is difficult to talk about problems without talking about developers. Developers, like clients, are part of any perception of the problem.

The George Michaelson lead-in case example could also be interpreted to show how developers distort the problem. As we saw, after a few hours on the night shift, George decided that the problem was different from what had originally been alleged. His presence actually *disturbed* the original perception. As we saw in Section 4.3, *measurement*, or any other form of observation, *disturbs*.

8.4.6 **Issues of developer–method interaction**

When considering the interaction of the developer and the method, we could say that the link is true by definition. Whatever actions the developer carries out to develop a system will be a manifestation of the method, however good or bad it is. Similarly, anyone who carries out actions that are part of the systems development is fulfilling the role of developer. Hence the real question is not whether there is much significant connexion between developer and method, but what form this connexion takes. In practical systems development this raises two important questions:

1 What are the motives of the developer when choosing a method?
2 Should the developer change or modify a chosen systems method?

The motives of a developer when choosing a method are not likely to be confined to a straight technical decision about the links between problems and methods that we covered in section 8.4.3. Not only is the perception of the problem influenced by who the developer is, the developer will also have views about choices of method even before knowing about the problem. For example, it isn't hard to imagine that once an organization has invested time, money and human skills to develop a team skilled in particular systems development method, it won't turn to this method first when confronted with a systems development problem.

Having a bias towards certain methods even before we understand the problem may not be as obviously wrong as it seems. If we take a systems view of systems development as in Figure 8.11, the effectiveness of the systems development process is an emergent property coming from the interaction of *all* the components, including the human ones. Thus the ideal method for a particular problem, badly executed, may not give such successful results as a less ideal method carried out well. A good driver in an old van is more likely to be a successful motorist than is a fool in a new BMW.

The danger of sticking to what you are good at, however, is that no *learning* or *adaptation* takes place. Since the control component of management must adapt to environmental disturbances and learn from them, so good systems development methodology includes the ability to change or modify a chosen systems method; thus answering our second question.

8.4.7 Issues of developer–client interaction

We have already touched on one of the main issues of this relationship, that of *roles*.

Developer and client are the names of roles that different people can adopt at different times. Thus in the small-scale example of my wife and I developing a VAT system, sometimes I would make suggestions as to how the spreadsheet could be arranged to meet something my wife wanted, sometimes these roles were exchanged. Who was the developer and who the client? At various times we both played both roles, where one was client and said what they needed, and the other was developer trying to produce systems features to meet these needs. Even in larger organizations with more formal job definitions, this exchange still occurs. The kind of investigating that George Michaelson carried out is similar to what most developers have to do in the early stages of a project, when they try to understand the existing situation, S_0, and its problems. Where the people who are questioned give replies and help out with information, they are contributing to the development process, and it would be a very arrogant and foolish systems professional who didn't recognize this.

The importance of *participation* in the development process is sometimes misinterpreted. Just as the concept of control can be misinterpreted as implying an authoritarian style of management, so participation can be misinterpreted as an assertion of democracy and fair play. In practice, wide participation in the developer role is necessary for two reasons:

1 The knowledge of the existing situation, S_0, which is essential for successful systems development, is likely to be spread well beyond those formally concerned with systems development.
2 Involvement of the client in the development process is a means of ensuring satisfaction, commitment and understanding of the product of systems development.

Recent developments in *prototyping* have helped to blur the client and developer roles further. As we shall see in Chapter 9, the use of *visual programming* enables a non-specialist to explore on a computer screen with the help of the specialist, or even unaided, different possibilities for the outputs from the desired system. Examples of this would include menus, pictorial screen models of how the system would work, or layouts for printed documents. Once decided, the software can automatically develop the programming procedures to produce them. The need for *expertise*, which separated the client and developer roles in the 1970s and early 1980s, is disappearing.

Box 8.3

Critical systems heuristics

Ulrich (1983) believed that many systems failures stemmed from the use made by 'experts' to define *boundaries* of systems and problems in a way that made them look like *hard*, technical *problems*, when they were actually *soft* unresolved *messes*. He devised 12 questions that were aimed at enabling the discovery – hence *heuristics* – of where the boundaries of the system *ought* to be, rather than where a particular boundary is claimed to be by expert exclusion.

His 12 critically heuristic boundary questions in this summary of their combined 'is' and 'ought' forms look like this:

1   Who is and ought to be the actual client of the system's design? Whose purposes are served by it, rather than who does not benefit but may have to bear its costs or other disadvantages?

2   What *is* and *ought to be* the actual purpose of the system's design, in terms of declared intentions, or otherwise, of the involved but in terms of the actual consequences?

3   What is its built-in measure of success judged by the design's consequences?

4   Who *is* and *ought to be* the decision taker? Who can actually change the measure of success?

5   What conditions of successful planning and implementation of the system are actually controlled by the decision taker? What *ought to be*?

6   What conditions are not controlled by the decision taker? What represents the decision taker's environment? What *ought to*?

7   Who *is* actually involved as planner? Who *ought to be*?

8   Who is involved as the expert? What is the expert's expertise and role? What *ought to be* the situation?

9   Where do the involved see the guarantee that their planning will be successful? (For example, in the theoretical competence of experts? In consensus among experts? In the validity of empirical data? In the relevance of mathematical models or computer simulations? In political support on the part of interest groups? In the experience and intuition of the involved?) Can these assumed guarantors secure the design's success, or are they false guarantors? What *ought to be* the situation?

10   Who among the involved witnesses represents the concerns of the affected? Who is or may be affected without being involved? Who *ought to be*?

11   Are the affected given an opportunity to emancipate themselves from the experts and to take their fate into their own hands, or do the experts determine what is right for them, what quality of life means to them etc.? That is to say, are the affected used merely as means for the purposes of others, or are they also treated as 'ends in themselves' (Kant), as belonging to the client? What *ought to be* the case?

12   What world view is actually underlying the design of the system ? Is it the world view of any of the involved or of those affected? What *ought to be* the case?

Flood and Jackson (1991) is a good reference for more examples of applying the heuristics and putting them in a wider systems methodology context.

8.4.8 Issues of client–method interaction

Given the blurring of the client and developer roles, it is worth considering when this is most likely to occur in whatever method is used in the development process.

In small-scale development, like my VAT example, the blurring is likely to occur throughout the systems development process because a small number of people are involved, and they have to play multiple roles most of the time.

For *structured* methods applied to larger-scale projects, like the tax or George Michaelson examples, the client tends to be drawn into systems development at the initial and final stages. Thus in terms of the meliorist model, the client is involved in having to provide information to the developer about the existing situation or system, S_0, as well as what needs and criteria should be applied to the desired system, S_1. Referring to Figure 8.7, this means that the client is involved in Phases 1 and 2. Once the new system has been produced, however, it is the client who has to *accept* it and subsequently use it. Hence phases 5 onwards will involve the client in the method.

But what of the client as a client and nothing else? Suppose the client has no desire at all to be involved in the systems development process? People who buy baked beans or cars don't get involved in their production, so why should the client treat the acquisition of a new system as anything more than a purchasing operation? In situations like these, the client may still be involved with the method in two ways:

1 As purchaser of the method through the choice of systems developer.
2 As quality controller of the method through systems acceptance.

To understand the first of these, consider someone who runs their own business like Ben Lister of MX Marketing. They are unlikely to have either the interest or the time to become involved in systems development. What they are most likely to do is to talk to other business people they know and take recommendations for the choice of a systems developer. This is most likely to be a specialist consultancy company that markets a particular approach or method for systems development. Hence the client chooses the method through the choice of developer, not because the problem itself implies a particular method.

Once a client has chosen a method via the choice of developer, the client is likely to act as a quality controller. Thus it is hard to imagine the Ben Listers of the business world just sitting back and waiting for the system to arrive. They will want to check how well the systems development process is going. The form of the particular method, and especially whether it has clear stages and *deliverables*, will affect the relationship between the client and the method. From the client's viewpoint, a good method is one that allows them to check the progress of the product which they have purchased.

8.4.9 Conclusion

Just as the systems view of organizations shows that *what* happens in an organization is a better guide to the role of information in management than is looking at labels, so regarding systems development as a system reveals a better practical understanding of its complexity. The old labels of 'expert', 'consultant' or 'analyst' hark back to the early days of information technology.

Key words

Analysis	Feasibility study	Problem
Approach	Implementation	Process orientation
Aspiration driven	Innovative method	Project debriefing
Bottom up	Issue	Prototyping
Business analysis	Iteration	Specification
CASE tool	Logical system	SSADM
Deliverable	Maintenance	Structure orientation
Derivative method	Meliorist model	Structured method
Design	Mess	Systems life cycle
Desired system	Method	Technique
Existing system	Methodology	Tool
Failure	Object orientation	Top down
Failure driven	Physical system	WIMP

1 Are *iteration* and *structure* mutually incompatible in systems development methods?

2 Consider the history of the different versions of SSADM. Why were the changes made? Is the concept of a standard method a useful one?

3 What other major components would you have included in Section 8.4 in addition to the client, developer, problem and method?

4 Is the Internet an information system? If so, what management function does it support?

5 Is a specialist profession of systems developer no longer relevant?

6 How does the availability of downloadable software on the Internet affect information systems development?

Feedback on review questions

RQ 8.1 If we look at the question of definition, the problem could be clearly defined in terms of documentary and other errors that could be clearly counted. Also it would take a very academic person to argue that such errors were anything other than undesirable. When it came to the detailed causes of the errors, the problem was much messier. Both poor commitment from those operating the system, and criticism of the system and its implementers, were legitimate possible ingredients to any definition of what the problem was. Deciding on their relative importance was a soft issue, since it depended on individual perceptions rather than an agreed objective way of assessment.

Once we recognize the presence of soft issues in the causes of the problem, then these blur the questions of boundary, since we can't define whether certain issues like operator commitment or modification of the system ought to be included or not. This means that a clear separation of responsibility is unlikely until the definition and boundaries are sorted out. The information needed was obviously not clear because that is why the team was set up, but a description of what a solution would look like was possible in terms of hard, measurable error rates. How such a solution could be carried out was widely disputed and very messy, as the final discussions showed.

RQ 8.2 The assumption that all the factories in the group were sufficiently similar in the way they operated tended towards a standard view of the system, with the implication that implementation could also be according to a formula. It was lack of flexibility that prevented the implementation at PST taking account of local conditions.

RQ 8.3 Systemic, as introduced in Chapter 2, means having the properties of a system or based on systems principles. Any approach or method that recognizes and uses systems principles will be systemic. An example of this would be any approach to developing an information system for an organization that viewed the organization and the role of its information system in terms of the view presented in Chapter 7.

For an approach to be systematic, we imply that it is carried out in an orderly way with definable, logical connexions between the actions carried out. A systematic approach is therefore one we would call a method. If in addition a method was based on a systems view of the problem or used systems principles, then it would also be systemic.

RQ 8.4

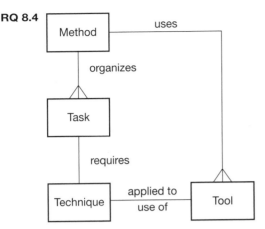

Figure 8.12 A possible relationship between methods, tasks, techniques and tools
This is shown as an entity relationship diagram. The RQ invited you to choose. Other choices may have been digraph or Venn diagrams, or many other ideas I have not listed. The important point is that the choice of the form of diagram should reflect the needed use.

References/bibliography

Ackoff, R. and Hall, J.R. (1972). 'A Systems Approach to the Problems of Solid Waste and Litter'. *Journal of Environmental Systems*. 2: 531–64.

Avison, D.E. and Fitzgerald, G. (1988). *Information Systems Development*. Blackwell Scientific, Oxford.

Birrell, N.D. and Ould, M.A. (1988). *A Practical Handbook for Software Development*. Cambridge University Press, Cambridge.

Cutts, G. (1987). *Structured Systems Analysis and Design Methodology*. Paradigm, London.

Cutts, G. (1991) (2nd edn). *Structured Systems Analysis and Design Methodology*. Blackwell Scientific, Oxford.

de Marco, T. (1979). *Structured Analysis and Systems Specification*. Prentice-Hall, New York.

Flood, R.L. and Jackson, M.C. (1991). *Creative Problem Solving*. Wiley, New York.

Flynn, D.J. (1992). *Information Systems Requirements: Determination and Analysis*. McGraw-Hill, New York.

Gane, C. and Sarson, T. (1979). *Structured Systems Analysis*. Prentice-Hall, New York.

Harry, M.J.S. (1987) *Systems Specification and Design by Emergent Property Analysis*. Paper presented to OR30 Conference, University of Sheffield, England.

Harry, M.J.S. (1990). *Information and Management Systems*. Pitman Publishing, London.

Hoffer, J.A., George, J.F. and Valacich, J.S. (1998). *Modern Systems Analysis and Design*. Addison-Wesley, Reading, MA.

Kendel, P.A. (1987). *Systems Analysis and Design*. Allyn and Bacon, New York.

Martin, J. (1984). *Principles of Database Management*. Prentice-Hall, Englewood Cliffs, NJ.

Olle, T.W., Hagelstein, J., MacDonald, I.G., Rolland, C., Henk, G.S., Van Assche, F.J.M. and Verrijn-Stuart, A.A. (1988). *Information Systems Methodologies*. Addison-Wesley, Reading, MA.

Page-Jones, M. (1980). *The Practical Guide to Structured Systems Design*. Yourdon Press, New York.

Ulrich, W. (1983). *Critical Heuristics of Social Planning*. Haupt, Berne.

Weaver, P.L. (1993) *Practical SSADM 4*. Pitman Publishing, London.

Yourdon, E. and Constantine, L.L. (1978). *Structured Design*. Yourdon Press, New York.

CHAPTER 9

Implementing and maintaining information systems

George Michaelson's first redundancy package

What happened

For George Michaelson at Technoturbines, 1997 began as a very bad year. The SC 322 aeroengine, with which he had been involved for over five years, didn't quite capture the initial orders that a potential world market should have implied. The product was not a failure, but its production seemed to require many fewer skilled people than George had thought when estimating his chances of not being made redundant. So George found himself taking his redundancy money and commencing the various official state procedures that were designed to help people get back to work.

Then one Saturday morning a few weeks later, while George was still unemployed, he got a letter from an old friend from his days at university. Jill Farmer was one of three people he had shared a house with during his last year on the degree course. For some reason that George had never really gone into, Jill had ended up failing her degree in mathematics and serving in a fast-food outlet. He was therefore quite interested to find that she had moved into his local area and had set up a company called Infosure. Both Jill's letter and the name she had chosen for the company sounded more like a public relations handout than a letter from the person George remembered, but he decided to revive the old friendship. A weekend later, he found himself sitting in a restaurant eating chicken dhansak and being subjected to some hard questioning from Jill.

Although George had been mainly concerned with production management during his final time at Technoturbines, Jill was more interested the work he had previously done in production information systems. This had involved him in co-operation with specialist consultants who had used the Structured System Analysis and Design Methodology (SSADM) to develop a new production planning and control system. Jill seemed to be very familiar with the methodology. She explained that before setting up her own company she had worked for a firm of consultants similar to the one with which George had worked. It turned out that Jill herself had been made redundant about a year before George, and it was this that had spurred her into going it alone.

'My first thought, when I was made redundant,' she said, 'was to cash in on my knowledge and experience of structured systems development methods. I soon realized that PCs and networking were outdating many of those large-scale formal systems that you were involved with at Technoturbines. An awful lot of software can be developed into a practical working system without the application of very structured and formal approaches. New visual programming packages mean I can sit down with a user in front of a screen and present them with actual examples of potential outputs right from the start. It cuts out all the formal specification business.'

George wondered exactly what would be designed if people just sat in front of a computer without any specification, formal or otherwise, of what they were aiming at; but he didn't argue, because Jill was clearly warming to her subject. 'People working for organizations these days often find that their children are more in touch with modern software through home computing and the Internet, than the management of the organization they work for.' At this point the arrival of the waiter bringing the coffee interrupted her lecture. By the time they had sorted out who took sugar or didn't take milk, she came to the point of their meeting.

What did George feel about global warming? George was amused. Jill was someone who drove a large, fast car that looked like it was designed to consume all the oil in the world and every other motorist on the road. Was she really a sudden convert to conservation? She ignored his smile. 'The reason I ask is because I am going to make a tender to develop a Water Management Information System for the Limber Marsh Drainage Consortium.' George looked blank, 'What's that, and who are they?'

'That's what I asked myself when I saw the invitation to tender. Apparently nearly a fifth of England is so low lying that it would regularly flood if it were not protected and drained; and that includes a lot of the London area, by the way. The people responsible for flood protection are a collection of drainage boards who cover the various areas. The Limber Marsh Drainage Consortium is one of these. They are inviting tenders to develop a Windows-based system that will analyse data automatically radioed in from pumping stations and present it on screen to the engineers at headquarters. The aim is to give them the information they need to operate the pumping system effectively. Apparently this means preventing flooding while not wasting money on unnecessary pumping. Did you hear about that flood in Holland in 1993? If there really is global warming, we're on to a potential winner with this system.'

'But I don't know anything about water management, let alone Visual Basic,' said George. 'That's not important,' said Jill. 'The main thing is that you understand computer systems and constructing databases; and above all, you have experience of talking to users and finding out their needs. That's the important thing. If I get the contract, will you join us?'

George didn't accept immediately. It seemed like a big step to go from being someone who worked in a large international company to being one of four members of a small business. When he did accept, however, he found that Jill was right. Sitting with her and discussing details of the new system with engineering staff at the Limber Marsh Drainage Consortium did recall the same skills and experience he had used at Technoturbines. He also found that although managing water was very different from managing the production of aeroengines, there were many principles with which he was already familiar. The modelling of the storage and flow of water did link to his own experience of inventory control, and many of the project scheduling techniques used by the authority were familiar to him. Within three months, George felt he was back on course.

The issues raised

In Chapter 8, we noted that the term *methodology* could be used in its original sense of the *study of method*. We found that systems development methods could be understood in terms of:

- their role in the control and management of information systems;
- the types of problem to which they might suitably be applied;
- the motives for choosing them;
- whether they are derivative or innovative in terms of their analytical approach;
- their structure and the role of iteration;
- whether they are process, structure or object oriented.

I chose to continue George Michaelson's story because the history of his career development has paralleled many of the changes that have taken place in the field of information systems development methodology from the late 1980s through to the present. The late 1980s saw highly structured methods like SSADM being widely advocated for the development of systems that were most likely to be implemented on mini-computer systems of the type with which George would have been familiar at Technoturbines. But that was much more the decade in which the personal computer (PC) by-passed many of the older mainframe and mini-computer-based applications. As Jill Farmer said, 'Many people working for organizations these days often find that their children are more in touch.'

Along with this expansion of PC use came a widening of the range of people who used computers. This led to less technical interest in the *hows* of the workings of information technology, like writing programs, and more interest in just making it do *what* the user required. So-called WIMP (Windows, Icons, Menu, Pointer) software was then developed to meet this need. Microsoft Windows is an example of this.

By the mid-1990s, networking software by firms such as Novell and Microsoft had enabled the personal computer expansion of the 1980s to be taken a stage further. There had been a conflict between an individual user's desire for personal computer-based information system on the desktop, and the organization's need for co-ordination and compatibility. Local area networks, using networking software, resolved much of this conflict. A user could still use their machine in their own personal way, but in a software environment that enabled communication and sharing between different users within an organization.

In the early 2000s, the days of systems methodology associated with mainframe and mini-computer systems seem to be over, as Jill Farmer implied.

The issues raised by our final lead-in case should therefore be seen in the methodology context of Chapter 8. In particular:

1 Do recent information systems development innovations, like the networking of personal computer hardware, the emergence of user-friendly visual programming and downloadable Internet software, mean that earlier methods, like structured systems development, are out of date?

2 If some older methods are still relevant, how do we decide which ones to retain?

Opportunities for learning

Issue 1 is best answered by referring yet again to the distinction of *whats* and *hows*. New innovations, of the type quoted above, relate to particular ways of doing things in systems development. They therefore concerned with new *hows* rather than new *whats*. We are still concerned with the same process of moving from S_0 to S_1 that we covered in Chapter 8. New methods should only replace older ones when they represent a better ways of doing this.

Issue 2 then asks us how we decide whether this replacement is needed. I think the answer to this question depends on two important criteria:

1 Do we have a *hard* information systems development problem with S_0 and S_1 clearly defined?
2 Is the *human* context of the systems development process, particularly in terms of the *developer* and *client roles*, small scale and informal?

If the answer to either of these questions is negative, then more recent developments in prototyping and the use of visual programming will either be insufficient or even irrelevant.

The first criterion reminds us that any kind of information systems development, using whatever kind of software, based on whatever kind of information technology, is not much use until we are clear about the problem. Some form of soft systems methodology is therefore as relevant as it was before the 1980s, when its early forms were first developed.

The second criterion leads back to the thought that George had in response to Jill's enthusiasm for cutting out 'all the formal specification business': what would be designed if people just sat in front of the computer without any specification?

The objectives of our final chapter should therefore be to understand enough of applied information systems development methodology to make choices that deal with what we find today, rather than in the past or an imaginary other world.

Learning objectives

The learning objectives for this chapter are to:

1 Understand soft systems methodology and its relevance to information systems development.
2 Understand structure, process and object-oriented information systems development methods.
3 Understand unstructured approaches to information systems development.
4 Understand the study of the human computer interface and human computer interaction as important additions to the subject of information systems development.

Box 9.1

System crash hits share trading

FT

Vincent Boland, James Mackintosh and Aline van Duyn

Trading on the London Stock Exchange was disrupted for nearly eight hours by computer problems yesterday on what should have been one of its busiest days of the year.

The crash of the stock exchange's systems meant trading in UK equities did not start until 3.45pm. That left investors unable to respond to developments overnight in US markets, where a sell-off in technology stocks has shaken confidence.

The tax year expired yesterday and it is usually one of the exchange's heaviest days as thousands of retail investors buy and sell shares for capital gains tax purposes. But the Inland Revenue said it would not extend the tax year by a day to compensate for the exchange's problems.

The exchange stayed open until 8pm yesterday. It normally closes at 4.30pm.

The breakdown coincided with news that the London exchange had re-opened talks with Deutsche Borse, operator of the Frankfurt financial markets, on the possibility of merging their operations.

The Financial Services Authority, which regulates the LSE, launched an investigation into the problem and said it would publish its findings.

'Plainly, as the LSE recognizes, this is a serious matter that requires a very quick response,' it said. 'Lessons need to be learned rapidly and made public, and any necessary systems changes and contingency arrangements need to be made immediately.'

It was the second time that trading on the exchange has been hit. On Monday, technical problems

at Reuters, the financial information company that supplies real-time share price data, were blamed for delays.

Martin Wheatley, director of development at the LSE, said the problems yesterday were caused by unprocessed orders sent by US investors after the close of the London market on Tuesday. Computers interpreted these orders as new transactions when trading was to begin yesterday, putting the exchange's information system out of sequence with its trading system.

'In the overall scheme of things we have a very robust system,' Mr Wheatley said. Other European exchanges had also had recent problems.

Source: Financial Times, 6 April 2000. Reprinted with permission.

Comment

It would be very easy to be a clever outsider and criticize the problems of the LSE system. Instead, I think that the learning, rather than the criticism, that we can derive from this event relates to the concepts of control systems that we covered in Chapter 4.

The environment will always be greater in its power than any system, so success is never guaranteed.

But the implied lessons of this report are about the issues of influencing, anticipating and accommodating the environment that we covered in Chapter 4. These are management issues, not issues of information technology.

9.1 SOFT SYSTEMS ANALYSIS

9.1.1 The role of soft systems analysis in systems development

Before looking any further at methods designed to analyse the soft aspects of problems or messes, we need to answer three questions:

1 Why should consideration of soft issues be relevant to information systems development?

2 What is the relationship between soft systems analysis and information systems development methods?

3 Should methods applied to soft problems be seen as different or separate from those applied to hard problems?

The first of these questions has already been answered in Section 8.3.4, where we saw that the initial strategy and inception stage involved us in looking at both the management system and the whole business or organizational system. We saw that this will involve us in sorting out soft human and policy issues before we can produce the deliverables of decision, authorization and commitment.

Once this question has been answered, it leads naturally to the second question. If we have to sort out the soft issues at the initial stage of systems development and before we can produce the deliverables for that stage, then we would expect soft systems analysis to be carried out right at the beginning of systems development. This seems sensible when we refer back to Figure 8.1. As long as questions of the boundary or separation of the problem are unclear, or we don't know whose responsibility it is, or any of the other feature of a mess exists, we shan't not know just what system it is that we are supposed to be developing.

There is, however, a further answer to the question of how soft systems analysis might fit into the view of systems development presented in Section 8.3.4. In later maintenance and debriefing stages, it is very likely that some of the causes of the need for maintenance and the lessons to be learned at debriefing have messy human origins as well as hard technical ones. In particular, any outright failure of a system is likely to have human implications in terms of motivation, communication or training.

> **RQ 9.1** Is failure therefore a holistic phenomenon?

This leaves the final question of why methods applied to soft problems should be any different in principle from those applied to hard problems. If they are, then we must be accepting that the nature of the problem affects the nature of the method applied to it. This assertion then leads us to question whether all the range of combinations shown in Figure 8.9 are possible. The short answer is that if a problem is mainly a mess, this does imply some differences in the deliverables of the approach compared with those applied to essentially hard problems. These differences, however, do not preclude the relevance of similar concepts such as stages, deliverables, iterations, tools and techniques, like those used by methods on hard problems. The main differences are likely to be that a soft systems method would need to recognize the soft complexity of messes, as shown in Figure 8.1.

We can illustrate these differences in deliverables between methods applied to hard and soft problems by referring to the meliorist model of Figure 8.2. With a soft problem, the conflicts over what the problem is, or what might constitute a solution, mean that S_0 and S_1 are themselves issues of dispute. Any thought about the set of actions needed to move from S_0 to S_1 must therefore be irrelevant until it is clear where the arrow starts from and where it is intended to go. We have seen that the set of actions represented by this arrow will come from the chosen method, but with a very messy soft problem we first need a method to deal with S_0 and S_1 before going on to one dealing with the arrow itself. In the Technoturbines case, for example, until it is decided whether the problem is the behaviour of the workforce, the inadequacies of the system at PST or some messy mixture of both, there is little point in considering what is to be done to clear up the problem.

A soft systems method is therefore likely to have deliverables concerned with trying to define, or at least make more clear, the *nature of the problem itself*, rather than offering solutions. In particular, this will mean trying to get some *clarification* and *agreement* of what constitutes S_0 and S_1. To do this, it will be necessary to distinguish which areas of disagreement come from disputes over soft issues, and which come from disputes over hard fact. If this can be done, then appropriate methods can be applied to each. Disputes about hard facts can be resolved by processes such as measurement, computation, observation or other technical means. Disputes over soft issues will need to be resolved or defused by means like *negotiation*, *persuasion* or *compromise*. In our Technoturbines example, questions about the frequency with which products failed their first inspection are hard ones and can be resolved by reference to recorded data and statistical analysis. Disputes over the relative merits of redesigning the system or imposing greater discipline on the workforce at PST cannot be resolved by reference to some agreed standard, and are therefore soft. Resolution of issues like these will come through negotiation, politics and social action.

The difference between methods focusing on hard and soft problems will not therefore be absolute. Instead, we would expect that methods would tend to vary in their emphasis. Generally, we would expect soft systems analysis methods to put a strong emphasis in their early stages on identifying soft issues and trying to evolve a clarified, shareable view of the problem. Hard aspects of the problem can then be identified for subsequent treatment using the appropriate methods for solving hard problems.

The sequence of considering possible soft aspects of a problem first is a practical one. Any system that is subsequently developed as a result of the definition of the problems associated with S_0, or the requirements of S_1, is a concept reflecting the interests and values of those concerned, and can therefore only be defined after resolving the soft issues.

This necessity of dealing with both hard and soft aspects when trying to create information systems for management has led to attempts at combining aspects of hard and soft methods into integrated methodologies. We shall look further into this below, once we have studied both soft and hard systems methodology. Meanwhile, we will look at the main features of the soft systems method, which has probably held the field above all others for the last 30 years or so. This is the so-called *Soft Systems Methodology* of Checkland (1981), called SSM from now on.

In choosing to cover the SSM first, it is important that I pass on to you warnings I give to my university students when I follow the same sequence in my lectures:

- SSM is a 'methodology that aims to bring about improvement in areas of social concern' (von Bulow, 1989). It is not therefore an information systems development methodology *per se*.
- SSM is not covered first because it is the most important method we consider; but as we saw above, the resolution of messes should logically precede the solving of hard problems.

Given these caveats, we will now look at SSM in more detail.

9.1.2 **The main features of soft systems methodology**

SSM has developed over the years of application that separate Checkland (1981) and Checkland and Scholes (1990). The earlier 'conventional seven-stage' form is represented by Figure 9.1 and the later 'developed form' by Figure 9.2. The reasons given for this development in Checkland and Scholes (1990) will be familiar to us in terms of our study of methods and approaches earlier. They say, 'In the late 1980s the 1975 version seems rather bald, and in any case gives too much an impression that SSM is a seven stage process to be followed in sequence.'

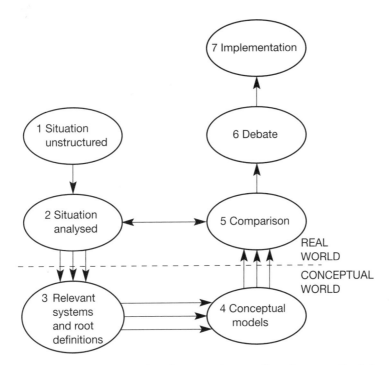

Figure 9.1 The conventional seven-stage soft systems methodology
The essence of the method (see also Figure 9.3) is the comparison of the relevant systems in the conceptual world with the existing analysed situation as means of generating clarification and progress. In terms of Figure 8.2, S_1 is compared with S_0 as a means of specifying action for change.

We should not find it difficult to keep in mind this, and other, reservations of the authors about the mechanistic and undeveloping application of systems methods. Our earlier analysis of messes, the role of structure in methods, and above all the higher-order learning that is true methodology has prepared us for a wide-ranging view of what systems development might involve.

Given this background, we will cover SSM in three stages:

1 We will use the rest of this section to investigate what the authors describe as the 'basic shape' of SSM shown in Figure 9.3, and see how it may be interpreted in terms of our meliorist model of Figure 8.2.

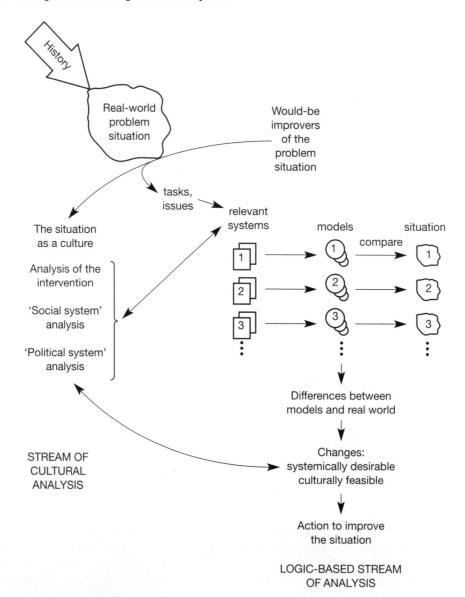

Figure 9.2 Developed SSM
This develops SSM by identifying more clearly the interaction of the cultural aspects of the human situation with the logic-driven seven-stage process.

2 Having got a feel for the methodological principles behind SSM, we will run through the conventional seven-stage form in detail, since this forms the basis of the later developed form.
3 Having acquired a more detailed view of conventional SSM, we can note what developments have been made to it and why.

We will therefore begin with the basic shape of SSM shown in Figure 9.3, before going on to its expression in the more sophisticated terms of the conventional and later models.

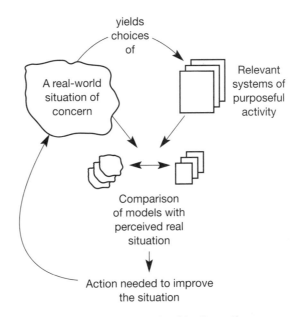

Figure 9.3 The basic shape of SSM as perceived by its authors
Comparison of models with the perceived real situation is the dialectic drive behind the method.

The first feature to note is the 'real-world situation of concern'. This is the S_0 or where we are now of our meliorist model of Figure 8.2. The use of the word 'concern' makes it clear that this situation is not satisfactory and we would therefore like to do something about it.

Since we are considering a mess rather than a clear-cut problem, we would expect the arrow or action for change of the meliorist model to be concerned with clarification or improvement of a mess rather than the solution of a problem. This is represented as 'Action needed to improve the situation' in SSM.

Having found the SSM equivalents of S_0 and the arrow in our meliorist model, we are left with seeing what might be representing S_1, where we would like to be. Answering this question brings in the essential feature of SSM in terms of how its stages fit together and what deliverable we should expect from applying them.

What SSM does is to set a relevant system against any particular aspect of the mess that is giving us concern. This relevant system is a model of the purposeful activity we would like to have, in contrast to the particular feature of the mess we have at the moment. It is this 'purposeful activity we would like to have' that is the SSM equivalent of S_1, where we would like to be.

The important feature we need to remember, however, is that we are dealing with clarification or improvement of a mess rather than the solution of a problem. Hence S_1 represents an aim for which we would like to strive but we may not immediately, if ever, fully achieve. The deliverable from the application of SSM as shown in Figure 9.3 is not therefore S_1, where we would like to be, but the arrow of the meliorist model, i.e. action for change.

The essence of SSM is therefore the comparing of an S_1, the relevant system we would like to have, with S_0, the mess we've got at the moment, to generate, through analysis and debate, the meliorist arrow or action for change.

Two final points: first, we should confirm that the use of the description 'purposeful' implying that we have a purpose or aim, and the belief in action to improve are clear indications that SSM is based on meliorism. Second, the description of SSM as a methodology rather than a method is probably justified in terms of the meanings we established earlier. Since the deliverable of SSM is action, and the form of this action will differ according to the application, we may say that SSM is indeed a methodology whose application delivers a method.

9.1.3 The conventional seven-stage model

We can look at how the basic shape of SSM was first structured and applied. Before we do this, it is important to set out the current context of the seven-stage model.

Although the implication of Checkland and Scholes (1990) is that this version of SSM has been superseded, much of the popular literature and other developments outside the control of its originator have kept it going under its own momentum. When I see this happening, I wonder if Professor Checkland, like Tchaikovsky with his *1812 Overture*, might be a victim of his own success. Patching (1990) is a good example of how someone outside the original school of SSM may take it up successfully for their own purposes, while perhaps not exciting enthusiasm in the hearts of its originators. Whatever the wider arguments about SSM, our attitude is empirical: where it has relevance to the understanding of information systems development methodology, we are interested. If we are to look back to our need to cover messes, or to look ahead to integrated methodologies, we shall find that the seven-stage model is relevant.

The seven stages of the conventional model of SSM are shown in Figure 9.1. To illustrate their application to a messy problem, we will use the dog registration case of Appendix 4.

> **RQ 9.2**   What makes the dog registration case messy in terms of the criteria of Section 8.1?

If the dog registration case is a mess rather than a clear-cut problem, how does the conventional seven-stage model of SSM record the 'Problem situation considered problematic'? The answer to this is the *rich picture* we introduced in Chapter 3. Figure 9.4 is a rich picture of the dog registration case. The important feature of the rich picture is that it prevents a predetermined view of the situation being recorded or being forced into a particular mould.

We can understand why an open, unstructured record like a rich picture is used if we consider what normally happens when we seek to record something about a situation. If we go into a room with a camera, we end up recording what is visible; and if we go in with sound recording equipment, we only record sounds. If our aim, however, is to have a holistic view of what is present in the room, our aims are more complex. We might wish to learn not only about silent, invisible, physical things like smells, but also about abstract or emotional things like the social atmosphere between the people present. No one measuring or recording device or technique will be able to record all this. A rich picture however, is not confined to a limited range of symbols or a definition of what it may include. As a result, it can convey a wide range of hard and soft information, hence the term rich.

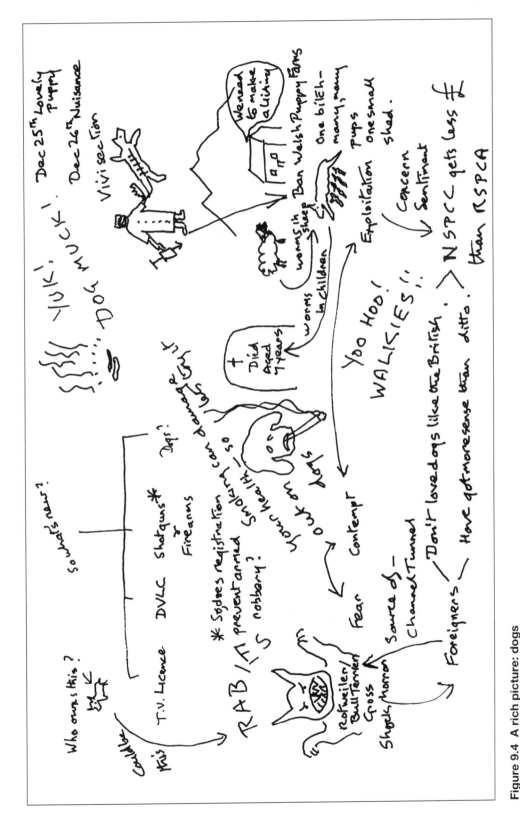

Figure 9.4 A rich picture: dogs

The aim of a rich picture is to capture a holistic view of the existing situation. The open, unstructured nature of this way of diagramming helps prevent the failure to record something just because it won't fit into a particular diagramming convention. Every rich picture will be *someone's* rich picture, rather than *the* rich picture.

Once we have captured our view of the existing situation, we can see what features it includes. Since we are talking about a mess, we are not assuming that there is any particular underlying structure or consistency. Instead, we are concerned to identify *themes* or *issues* in the situation that help us express why we consider the situation to be problematic (see Figure 9.5).

RQ 9.3	Suggest some themes and issues for the dog registration case.

SSM has come to discriminate between those themes that it relates to *primary tasks* and those that are *issues*. This distinction is not meant to be an absolute one, but expresses the extremes of a range. We use an example from Checkland and Scholes (1990) to illustrate the two types. A charity organization set up to relieve hunger is experiencing several committee disputes. Of the themes that come from analysing the situation, some relate to the actual processes directly connected with the activities of money raising and the provision of food. Other themes are more to do with debate or disagreement over the charity's attitudes, policies or philosophy. Primary task themes are those immediately related to the processes for which the organization exists, like a charity's money-raising efforts. Issue-based themes relate to the concerns generated in the wider activities surrounding the primary task, like deciding how open and communicative the committee should be to other members.

Once stage 2 has identified the themes of concern in the existing situation, stage 3 involves conceiving (hence *conceptual* world) a *relevant system* as a model of the purposeful activity we would like to have in relation to each theme. (It should be noted that the sequence of stages we are about to follow from stage 2 through to stage 6 would be carried out in turn for each theme identified at stage 2.)

In our dog registration case we are concerned with several themes, but let us use the example of the issue of identification. In contrast, this particular feature of the mess we have at the moment, the 'purposeful activity we would like to have', would be a dog identification system. It is called a relevant system because it is relevant to one of the themes in the real world identified in stage 2.

Once we have chosen a relevant system, stage 3 requires us to define what properties such a system should have. We say 'should' here because we are talking about a system in the conceptual world that we would like to have, not one we can automatically expect to get. Remember, SSM is looking to deliver improvement or clarification of a mess, not automatic solutions to problems. The role of the relevant system concept is to help with this improvement or clarification. It would be nice to have it, but as we shall see at later stages, it can still play an important role even if we don't.

The root *definition of a relevant system*, which we produce in stage 4, should be a definition of what the relevant system should be in terms of the qualities we would want it to possess. For any relevant system, like our dog identification system, a statement of the root definition should sound like an answer to the question 'What should a dog identification system be?'

Dogs: themes and issues

Danger: Dogs can bite and even kill. Shock pictures in the media of children with severely lacerated faces.

Irresponsible owners: Dogs can be trained and controlled. Problems arise when this is not recognized or acted on. You don't get bad dogs; you only get bad owners.

Identification: If you can't identify a dog, how do you know which dog did it, or even whether it was a dog at all? Even if you know the dog, who is responsible for training, control or restitution for irresponsiblility?

Animal welfare: Exploitation and cruelty to animals. 'A puppy isn't just for Christmas; it's a dog for life.' Breeding dogs for animal experiments.

Health: Dirty dogs fouling pavements and public places leads to concern about effects on human health; e.g. hydatid disease, where dogs act as vehicle for cross-infection by tapeworm that kills seven people annually in England and Wales. Threats of rabies.

Sentimentality/sensitivity/humanity: As the composer Elgar was more concerned about the effects of the First World War on the army horses than on the soldiers, so threats to burn a dog in protest at the Vietnam War almost seemed to raise as many protests as the napalming of human beings. W.C. Fields: 'Anyone who hates animals and children can't be all bad.' Animals' rights. The cruellest animals are human beings.

Figure 9.5 The situation analysed

Themes and issues, that can be identified in the rich picture. There may be others. The iterative nature of SSM will almost certainly mean that these themes would be re-examined, added to and modified.

As an answer we could then say it should be:

'An officially enforced system to identify approved owners of dogs.'

This thus produces a root definition of the relevant system.

It happens that this root definition is not terribly good in terms of being either complete or clear about the qualities of the dog identification system, but how can we know? What makes a good root definition?

The answer to this last question is that SSM considers that six features of the relevant system should either be clearly stated in its root definition, or should sufficiently inferable from it to justify the omission. The six features are called the CATWOE criteria, where CATWOE is an acronym for the six features shown in Figure 9.6. How does our root definition:

'An officially enforced system to identify approved owners of dogs.'

stand up to the CATWOE test? Taking each criterion in turn:

- *Customers*: Presumably meant to be the 'owners' who are identified. Possibly could be whoever is implied by 'officially' or even the dogs? Ambiguous because the root definition does not clearly state who will be the recipients or victims of the relevant system's output. Perhaps if we substituted 'impose identification on approved owners' it might be clearer.

The CATWOE criteria

Customers: Those who would receive the immediate output from the relevant system. Not necessarily the customers of the company, organization etc.

Actors: Those who would be directly involved in making the relevant system work as a *process*.

Transformation process: What the relevant system does in terms of transforming *inputs* into *outputs*. The SSM uses the concept of process in much the same way as we have done in Chapters 2 and 3.

Weltanschauung: German word meaning 'world view' or fundamental set of values and assumptions implicit in the root definition. This is the criterion that newcomers to SSM and all other forms of systemic thinking tend to find difficult because it is seldom explicitly spelled out.

Owner: Person or body ultimately speaking for the nature and purpose of the relevant system based on their potential *control* over its existence or otherwise.

Environment: Defined exactly as we have done in Chapter 2. Those things which strongly affect or disturb the system, but over which the system has only limited influence or control.

Figure 9.6 Criteria for assessing root definitions

CATWOE lists six elements that must either be specified by the root definition of the relevant system, or be clearly deducible from it.

- *Actors*: Not at all clear. If it is 'officially enforced', the implication is that enforcers will decide who should be acting out the system. We really need something in the definition to clarify whether this system is going to be carried out by a national government agency, subcontracted private enterprise or some other agent. In the practical application of SSM, this issue might be separated out, and would lead us back to rethinking the name of our relevant system in stage 3 or redefining our themes at stage 2.
- *Transformation process*: A fairly clear implication that the system will transform unidentified dog owners into identified ones, but is there an implied 'approval' process? This is dangerous, since a root definition should only have one clear transformation process.
- *Weltanschauung*: The phrase 'officially enforced' makes it pretty clear that this relevant system has a strong authoritarian world view. There is nothing much optional or open to discussion about this system.
- *Owner*: If the relevant system is to be 'officially enforced', that is a clear statement that it will be owned by officialdom. Any remaining ambiguity could possibly be removed by using 'legally enforced'.
- *Environment*: The definition is very weak on this point. The 'officially enforced' possibly implies that the relevant system will exist in the context of a defined legal environment, but there is nothing about, for example, the emotive social environment in which this system will have to operate.

The CATWOE criteria show that the root definition of the relevant system needs to be improved. We chose an only moderately successful root definition in order to illustrate the workings of CATWOE. In practice, such an analysis would lead to an iteration back to stage 3 in order to clarify our view of the relevant system and then come up with a new root definition in stage 4. For the purpose of illustrating how a conceptual model follows from a root definition we will take a slightly improved version:

'A legally enforceable agency system to record dog ownership.'

and see what model would follow from this latest definition.

We said that a root definition should define what a relevant system should *be*. Stage 5 of the SSM is concerned to construct a model of what the relevant system *should do to be* the system defined. Doing implies actions or activities. The *conceptual model* is a model that shows the sequence and co-ordination of the activities that must logically be carried out by the relevant system to meet the root definition.

Figure 9.7 shows how such a conceptual model of the relevant system might be diagrammed. Referring back to Chapter 3, we can see that since a conceptual model is concerned with defining what a system does, any diagram of such a model will focus

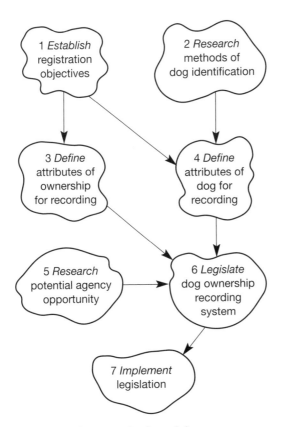

Figure 9.7 A conceptual model
What the relevant system must do to be what the root definition defines. This example would need further detailing of the activities and the addition of some co-ordinating activity of the whole.

on *process*. Its important constituents are therefore activities in a particular sequence. Our understanding of diagramming from Chapter 3 reminds us that any shape of activity 'blob' or form of 'arrow' showing sequence is acceptable provided it is logically correct. Another important aspect that we might find in more detailed studies of SSM is that blobs representing activities can themselves be broken down into more detailed components. For the purposes of explaining SSM at this stage this raises no more issues than those we covered when considering systems hierarchy.

Once the conceptual model of the relevant system has been defined, we have a definition of S_1, the situation we would like to have. In practice, we shall probably be nowhere near this at all, since we are dealing with a mess. Given this situation, the purpose of stage 6 is then to compare:

- what we do have, which is S_0 described by the analysed rich picture of stage 2; with:
- what we would like to have, which is S_1 in the form of the relevant system modelled in stage 5; to produce:
- suggested action for change.

There are several ways of making this comparison and of producing the third bullet, which is the outcome or deliverable from stage 7 of the SSM. Reference to Checkland (1981) Checkland and Scholes (1990) or Patching (1990) will detail what the ways might be. We will choose the one that is probably the most common. This consists of a matrix, as in Figure 9.8, in which each of the activities in the conceptual model is checked to see if it exists in the real-world situation. The results of this check are then used to focus on the question as to what should be done about it. It may be that the absence of an activity is a clear indication that we need to go ahead and try to make it happen. It may be that we can do nothing about the absence of one activity until another is carried out. It may also be that trying to find out whether an activity in the conceptual model is present in the real world merely reveals that we don't yet know. Whatever the outcome of the comparison, its main purpose is to produce an agenda for debate that will lead to action for change.

Figure 9.8 is intended to illustrate how stage 6 leads to stage 7 in the SSM. Our example is only an illustration, however. In practice, stages 3 to 6 would be carried out for all the major themes identified in stage 2. We would also expect much more iteration and refinement than we have shown here.

We warned in the previous sections that SSM should be seen in terms of our previous analysis of the issues involved in information systems development and the context of the meliorist model. We concluded that we would expect the SSM to clarify a way forward from the existing situation, S_0, as represented by the arrow of the meliorist model. Although SSM is not an information systems development method, it might be useful in the initial inception or the later debriefing stages of systems development.

The usefulness of SSM at the inception stage has led to attempts at producing integrated methodologies. These attempt to use elements of the SSM in the initial stage of systems development where the focus is on sorting out messes, and lead through to incorporating tools techniques from hard systems methods in the later stages where the problem has been more clearly defined. We shall look at integrated methodology later in this chapter.

	ACTIVITY	PRESENT	COMMENT
1	Establish registration objectives.	No	Debate already started, so proceed.
2	Research methods of dog identification.	No	Depends on resolution of theme/issue 1. Postpone.
3	Define attributes of ownership for recording.	No	Depends on theme/issue1, but could also affect it. Integrate with 1?
4	Define attributes of dog for recording.	No	Integrate with 3?
5	Research potential agency opportunity.	Yes?	Some existing local authority or other nation's systems. Research further?
6	Legislate dog ownership recording system.	No	Leave until last.
7	Implement legislation.	No	Ditto.

Figure 9.8 An agenda
There are several ways of approaching the comparison stage of SSM, and different forms of the output from it. The device shown here lists every activity in the conceptual model and checks to see how far it may be present in the real-world analysis. Suggestions for action or further analysis emerge from this.

9.1.4 Developed SSM

Having covered the conventional seven-stage model of SSM, we are now in a position to understand its later development as in Checkland and Scholes (1990). We have already noted that although SSM is not specifically an information systems development methodology, we were interested in its possible application in some stages of systems development and its contribution to integrated informations systems development methods. The more recent developments in SSM have a further contribution to make to our understanding of systems development itself as a system, which we shall cover at the end of this chapter. Meanwhile, Figure 9.2 (page 328) shows the more recent form of the process of SSM ('Developed SSM' or DSSM).

The main feature of DSSM is the recognition of two analysis 'streams' in the process. The logic-based analysis stream on the right of Figure 9.2 is the sequence of tasks, issues, relevant systems, root definitions etc. that we find in SSM. The cultural analysis stream, however, recognizes that the process of applying SSM itself becomes part of the existing situation. The analysis process and those who carry it out cannot do anything about the mess without interacting with it. We might draw parallels with what we saw in relation to Heisenberg's Uncertainty Principle in Chapter 4. Measurement or any other intervention in a situation disturbs that situation and makes it different from what it was before. Where intervention has this effect it makes sense to take account of it, rather than to pretend it doesn't exist.

The DSSM cultural analysis stream recognizes three particular areas of the problem situation as a culture:

1 The activity of intervention itself.
2 The 'social system' in the problem situation.
3 The 'political system' in the problem situation

The authors put the terms 'social system' and 'political system' in quotes because they intend them to be used in their everyday, colloquial sense.

The activity of intervention itself is seen in terms of three roles. The authors use the term role in each case to mean a person or persons who may be:

1 The client: whoever caused the study to take place.
2 The would-be problem solver: whoever wishes to do something about the situation in question.
3 The problem owner: no one is intrinsically this. The problem solver should recognize that there will always be several useful sources for perceptions of what is important problematically.

The importance of this first activity of identifying roles should be obvious. If no one (client) has asked nobody (would-be problem solver) to be concerned with nobody's view (problem owner) of a situation, then we are hardly into 'action to improve the situation' as shown in Figure 9.2.

Although I have reservations about the details of these authors' views of the roles in analysis, we can see that a study of similar role relationships would be relevant when considering information systems development. As promised, we will take this up at the end of the chapter.

The 'social system' in the problem situation is seen by the authors in terms of the rich mix of human relationships that we would expect to find in any social situation, including those in organizations. The authors see both formal roles, like 'shop steward', and informal roles, like 'licensed jester', and they recognize the interplay of roles, norms and values. Having recognized right from the beginning of this book that information systems are to be seen as a component of management systems, we see no great surprise in recognizing that all human activities have a human dimension.

Likewise, the 'political system' in the problem situation seems to be no more than a recognition that since Rebekah manoeuvred Isaac's possession of the power of blessing, via her son's use of a gift, to topple the power that Esau possessed on account of his greater age, human society has had in its power possession, exchange, clash and resolution dimensions. Thus in an institution where I recently worked, the system of allocating money for staff development was made completely transparent: everyone could apply for it and everyone knew who got what and why. Needless to say, the system was soon subverted and possessed by a small top management group. The allocation of the money represented power and could be used by its possessors as a lever to their own ends.

So why should the 'political system' in the problem situation be of any more or less interest to information systems development than to any other management activity? The answer to this question is to be found in Chapter 2, where we saw that information itself is a very strong political commodity. This is why information systems development should be seen as a management activity, not just a technical process.

We can conclude that although DSSM does not add anything new to our understanding of human nature, it does re-emphasize the human dimension and keep us on our guard from thinking that information technology is an information system.

9.2 PROCESS-ORIENTED DEVELOPMENT

9.2.1 Traditional process-oriented development

We saw how information systems development methods could be regarded from the different views of process, structure and object orientation in Section 8.3.6.

The process view is the oldest of these three historically, and it dominated information systems development in the 1970s and early 1980s. Classic examples were the structured analysis methods of Gane and Sarson (1979) and de Marco (1979), often coupled with the structured design methods of Yourdon and Constantine (1978).

Combinations like these were traditionally called systems analysis and design, covered in stages 1–4 of our model of systems development in Figure 8.7. They also happened to share some common properties that did not in themselves have any special connexion with the fact that they were process-oriented methods:

1 They were structured, i.e. they had clear stages with deliverables.
2 Their view of analysis was derivative in the sense described in Section 8.3.3.
3 They were top-down methods that recognized the hierarchical view of systems. Their systems development procedures followed the top-down sequence of breaking down high-level specifications of what the system must be, into increasingly detailed logical models of what it should do, finally followed by the detail of how it should be constructed.

None of these three features, as we said, is specifically process oriented. The important criterion of the process view is that an information system is seen as a process that takes components as inputs in the form of raw data, and transforms them into different outputs called information.

This view had a very specific effect on the nature of the tools and techniques that typify these methods and, in particular, the central role of the data flow diagram. We can understand how this came about if we note that the output from any definition and analysis based on a process view is a model of an information system. This being the case, the ways available to us for describing it are the same as those for describing any kind of system.

Thus all the systemic features covered in Chapter 3, and the means of diagrammatically describing them, may be relevant to the analysis and definition stages of such methods. The principal features of any system, including an information system, that need to be defined are:

1 The identity of the system as defined by a structure showing its components, hierarchy, boundary and environment.
2 The behaviour of the system that emerges from transformation processes changing inputs into discernibly different outputs.

We can illustrate how the tools used in process-oriented analysis methods fulfil these requirements by referring to Gane and Sarson (1979) as an example. The tools used are as follows.

A set of *levelled data flow diagrams*, as in Figures 9.9 and 9.10, which cover:

- the components of the system: by identifying the processes, data flows, and data stores;
- the hierarchy of the system: by showing how processes that are components in the higher-level diagram can be seen as subsystems and broken down into lower-level data flow diagrams in their own right;
- the boundary and environment of the system: by identifying external entities that act as sources and destinations of the information system's inputs and outputs, as a result of its behaviour.

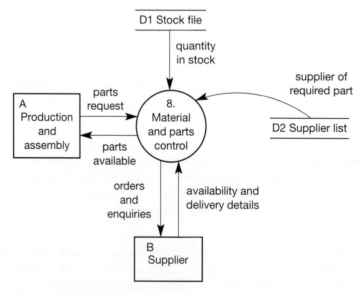

Figure 9.9 Data flow diagram (1)
This shows part of the highest-level diagram of a system.

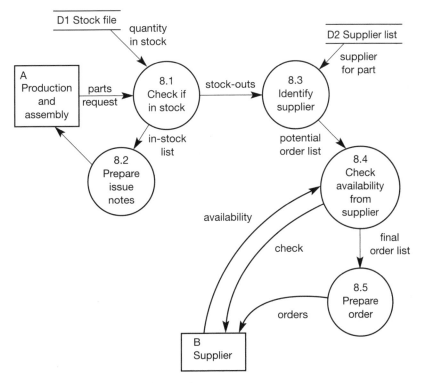

Figure 9.10 Data flow diagram (2)
An explosion of process 8.9 in Figure 9.9 to form a lower diagram detailing the original process as a subsystem. This procedure of exploding processes into lower-level detailed components is called levelling.

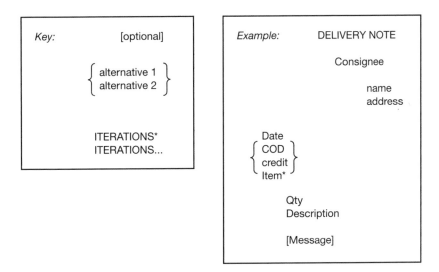

Figure 9.11 Entries in a data dictionary
For traditional process-based information systems development methods, the data dictionary defines structures that either flow through the system as shown in the data flow diagram, or are at rest as stored data in the data stores.

```
Key:

        A = Attribute, e.g. Month
        E = Entity, e.g. Product
        V = Value, e.g. Value of sales

Possible forms of access

        A (E) = ?        Find value of sales for particular product in a particular month.
        A (?) = V        Find which products had certain value of sales in a particular month.
        ? (E) = V        Find which months sales of particular product had given value.
        ? (E) = ?        Find value of sales for all months for specified product.
        A (?) = ?        Find values of sales of all products in a specified month.
        ? (?) = V        Which products in which month had given sales value.
```

Figure 9.12 Data access
Data that is at rest in the data stores has to be accessed by a process. The data dictionary in a traditional process-based information systems development method will define this.

Once the data flow diagrams have been used to define the whole system, its components are detailed using a *data dictionary*, which describes:

- the structure of the data, either at rest in a data store or moving as a data flow, as in Figure 9.11;
- the forms of access required to stored data, based on the principles of Figure 9.12;
- the processes that transform the data into the information required by the wider management system, like some form of process description such as *structured English*, given in Figure 9.13;
- details of the external entities in terms of their own identity and the identity of data flows for which they act as source or destination.

```
IF (KNOWN CUSTOMER)
   THEN IF (IN STOCK)
            THEN (RECORD DETAILS)
         ELSE (NOT IN STOCK)
            SO IF (FILLABLE PART)
                  THEN (RECORD DETAILS)
         ELSE (NO FILLABLE PART)
            SO IF (STOCK ITEM)
                  THEN (RECORD PENDING ORDER)
               ELSE (NOT STOCK ITEM)
                  SO (ACTIVATE REVIEW PROCEDURE)

ELSE (NOT KNOWN CUSTOMER)
   SO (ACCEPTANCE PROCEDURE)
```

Figure 9.13 Structured English
Defines what a process should do in way that can be easily converted into working computer code. There are many minor variants of structured English; this example is based on the convention for conditional used by Gane and Sarson (1979).

A *logical specification* of the desired system, S_1, produced as the result of such analysis methods was then used as the input to a systems design method such as Yourdon and Constantine (1978). A good example of this classic coverage is to be found in Page-Jones (1980), or if you prefer a very elementary introduction, Harry (1990).

We are not going to look at this here for one simple reason. In an article entitled 'Auld Lang Syne', Yourdon (1990) abandoned his earlier position and embraced the new faith of object-oriented analysis and design, which we shall consider in Section 9.7. He said, while dismissing the class of methods we have just considered, 'Object-orientation is the future ... the 1990s are likely to be a period of gradual acceptance of object-orientation ... Meanwhile, just as there will always be a job somewhere on the planet for renegade assembly programmers, there will always be a home for those who want to draw data flow diagrams.'

Although this last quotation is hardly a recommendation for us to study Yourdon's earlier systems design methods, the death of process-oriented methods based on the data flow diagram has been greatly exaggerated. Two developments need to be noted in this respect:

1 Modern methods that inherit the process-oriented tradition have developed to take account of contributions from other methodologies.
2 The advent of CASE tools and automated support (see Section 9.7) has meant that the old view of a data flow diagram as something drawn by hand with a pencil and template is disappearing. Instead, the use of this and other tools can be co-ordinated and integrated to give greater flexibility and adaptability.

We shall now look at a process-oriented method that is very much alive.

9.2.2 Classic SSADM

Before looking in more detail at the method known as SSADM, which we introduced in Section 8.3.3, it is necessary to answer three questions:

1 Why choose SSADM as an example of a process-oriented method?
2 Where and why has SSADM become a widely known and applied method?
3 Why has SSADM become so successful in the organizational context?

The first question that needs to be answered is why SSADM has been chosen for our example of a modern method with a process, rather than some other orientation. As we come to look at the method in more detail, we shall find that it also focuses on such concepts as logical data structure and entity life history. Since these could be taken to imply structure-oriented and object-oriented development respectively, why do we see SSADM as process oriented?

This apparent contradiction can be resolved if we recall two things. The first is our assertion in Section 8.3.6 that we saw the different orientations as complementary views rather than mutually exclusive categories of method. The second is that what determines the orientation is the view that acts as the basis for the method as a whole, and therefore co-ordinates the overall structure of the method. For SSADM the tool used for the overall view of both the existing system, S_0, and the desired system, S_1, is the data flow diagram. The essence of such a diagram is that it sees an information system as something that processes data. What we see before everything else when we look at such a diagram is a model of what happens to the data, i.e. the process.

The second question is one we already began to answer when discussing systems analysis in Section 8.3.3. There we saw that SSADM in its conventional form is based on a derivative view of systems development. Noting this point helps us to understand where and why it has become a popularly applied method. Thus in 1981 it was selected as the mandatory method for UK government projects, and its use by contractors has helped spread it widely in the private sector, as explained in the Preface to Ashworth and Goodland (1990). Again as we discussed in Section 8.3.3, we would expect a derivative method to be popular in government and related organizations, since applications in these areas are likely to have many of their objectives clearly defined by legislation. In such cases the criteria of Figure 8.8 are likely to be applicable.

The third question could be answered by referring to the Preface of Ashworth and Goodland (1990), where they say of SSADM that 'It is a very comprehensive method and, although the techniques do not require a particularly high level of skill to learn, it is often difficult to apply them directly without guidance from an experienced user'. We can understand this *Weltanschauung* or world view in terms of our hierarchical control model of information systems development. We built this up in Section 8.3, and we can now explain it further. If systems development itself is a process that has to be managed, then we can see it as the central purpose of a wider information systems development management system along the lines of the model presented in Chapter 6.

With this view of systems development, we can assess SSADM in terms of the management of information systems development. In this context, there are many reasons that large formal organizations would wish to have a 'very comprehensive method' that would 'not require a particularly high level of skill to learn' but would need 'guidance from an experienced user', because such a method:

1 Minimizes the need to 'reinvent the wheel'. Thus a 'very comprehensive method' means that the expensively disturbing effects of innovative method on large organizations with aims at standardization are reduced.
2 Deskills the human input. Reduces the dependence of the effective implementation of the method on particular individuals because it does 'not require a particularly high level of skill to learn'. Makes individuals more easily replaceable.
3 Strengthens the implementation of the *Weltanschauung* or world view of the organization by ensuring that the method of systems development conforms to the 'guidance from an experienced user'.

This analysis of the role of SSADM in systems development might be used to stereotype it as a 'conservative' or 'reactionary' methodology. Our view of problems, messes and methodology, which we covered in Sections 7.1 and 7.3.2, should prevent this simplification by reasserting the criterion that methods should be judged in terms of their objectives. On this basis, SSADM could be an excellent method to prevent destructive 'innovation' in such areas as democratic government or financial accountability.

Apart from choosing SSADM as an example of a widely applied process-oriented method, we shall also find that it provides a useful link with our other orientations for systems development methods. As we stated at the end of the previous section, SSADM incorporates tools and techniques from these other orientations, such as JSD in Section 9.3.2, and therefore forms a useful lead into the next sections.

With this justification, we can now look at the method in more detail.

9.2.3 **The tools, techniques and structure of SSADM**

The tools used by SSADM (Ashworth and Goodland, 1990), are all ones that have come from existing methodology, since SSADM itself is at the end of a line of methodological development, rather than being a new, innovative method. This is not necessarily a criticism of the method itself; instead, it shows its potential strength in using tested technical resources. The chief tools used by the method are:

1 Data flow diagrams (DFDs), which show the data flows, data stores and processes used by the information system, together with the external entities that act as sources and destinations for data outside the system (Figure 9.14).
2 Logical data structures (LDS), which show how data is brought together to form the emergent property of information.
3 Entity life histories (ELH), which show how information is changed during its life-time in relation to the entity to which it refers (Figure 9.15).

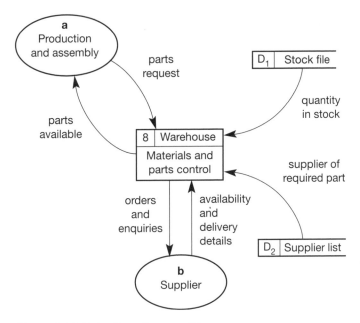

Figure 9.14 Data flow diagram (3)
An SSADM version of Figure 9.9.

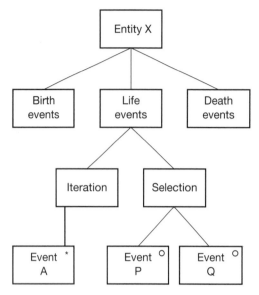

Figure 9.15 Entity life history
However portrayed, this must show the event that results in the birth of an entity into the system, those events that happen to it during its life in the system, and the event that results in its removal from the system. Entity life histories in SSADM are portrayed in a similar manner to that used in the JSD method (see Section 9.3). This is because SSADM has inherited certain aspects of methodology from JSD, and is an example of how process and structure orientations interact.

To understand the structure of SSADM as a method, it is worth referring to:

1 The stages of SSADM as shown in Figure 8.5.
2 The inputs and outputs of these stages as shown in Figure 9.16.

We can note that the use of defined inputs and outputs for each stage of Figure 8.5 is close to that of our general model of the deliverables of the stages of systems development presented in Figure 8.7 and discussed in Section 8.3.4.

It is also important to note that in the detailed application of SSADM, each *stage* is broken down into *steps*, which define the *tasks* needed to *transform* defined *inputs* into defined *outputs*. All the terms in the previous sentence that I have put into italics are those defined by the method itself, except the term transform. This latter term is one I have deliberately chosen to show how the stages of the method can be viewed as component processes of systems development seen as a system itself, as in Section 8.4.

Our aim in subsequent sections is now to understand what these stages of SSADM seek to achieve. In doing so, we shall look at the main tasks, tools and techniques that are used. Our approach will concentrate on seeing how the workings of the method relate to the systems and information concepts we developed in earlier chapters and the view of systems development methodology found earlier in this chapter. Since there are over 50 tasks and subtasks in fully detailed SSADM, Cutts (1991) or Ashworth and Goodland (1990) should be referred to for a fully detailed run through a case study.

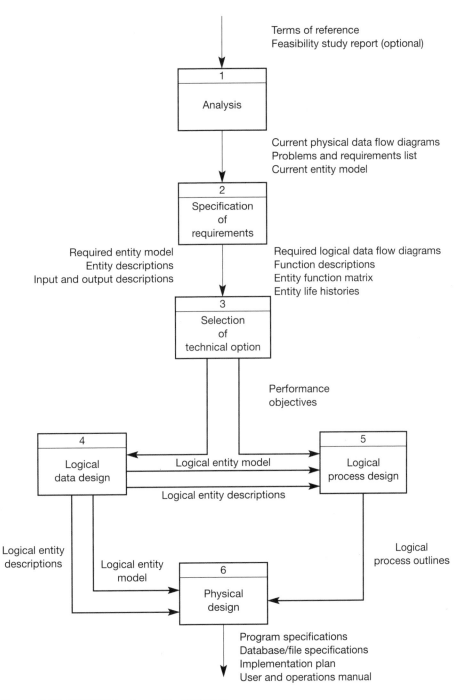

Terms of reference
Feasibility study report (optional)

Current physical data flow diagrams
Problems and requirements list
Current entity model

Required entity model · · · · · Required logical data flow diagrams
Entity descriptions · · · · · · · Function descriptions
Input and output descriptions · · Entity function matrix
· · · · · · · · · · · · · · · · · Entity life histories

Performance
objectives

Logical entity model

Logical entity descriptions

Logical entity
descriptions

Logical entity
model

Logical
process outlines

Program specifications
Database/file specifications
Implementation plan
User and operations manual

Figure 9.16 SSADM tools and techniques
The diagram shows how these are used in relation to the various stages of the method.
Although this shows a particular sequence of stages for a particular method, the link between
the tools and the techniques and the methodological processes is much wider. Thus, for
example, data flow diagrams are used to record or define physical and logical systems in
many methods.

9.2.4 **Analysis**

Stage 1: analysis will take as its starting point the terms of reference for the whole project and, possibly, a feasibility study report. The need for terms of reference clearly puts SSADM into the category of a top-down approach, which sees the information system in the role of meeting the needs of a wider management system of an organization. The Cutts (1991) criteria of Figure 8.8 make it clear that any soft, messy issues need to be sorted out before moving into a problem area with a clearly structured hard systems method like SSADM. In particular, the ownership of the system must be clear, otherwise we don't know whose view of S1 we are trying to fulfil. (This concept too will be developed in Section 7.11.)

The feasibility study report is an optional requirement for stage 1. As we saw in Figure 8.5, the first three stages of SSADM may be repeated in an attempt to gain an initial view of the potential system or choice of systems. Where this happens, the second pass through the analysis stage will include the input of the feasibility study output from stage 3.

Where SSADM is being applied in an innovative situation, in the sense discussed in Section 8.3.3, the analysis stage will essentially consist of documenting the new system requirements list alone. More typically, however, the method will be used for derivative systems development. In this case, analysis (cf. Figure 8.4) will consist of gaining a thorough understanding of:

1 The current system and how it works.
2 What problems are associated with the current system.
3 What additional requirements we have for the new system.

The outputs from this process will be:

1 Data flow diagrams of the current physical system (cf. Section 8.3.3) and an entity model showing its LDS (cf. Section 5.1), to cover 1 above.
2 A problems and requirements list to cover 2 and 3 above.

9.2.5 **Specification of requirements**

Although the detailed input to this stage can be listed as current system physical DFDs, LDS and a problems and requirements list, what the analysis stage must essentially deliver, as the result of producing all these, is the potential for understanding the current system. This understanding enables those concerned with the systems development to see what is wrong with the present system, S_0, and what any new system, S_1, should deliver.

If this understanding has come from analysis, then it makes possible the main tasks in the detailed operation of *stage 2: specification of requirements*. These involve extracting and defining the logic lying behind the existing physical system and setting this against the problems and requirements list. As a result of this comparison, business system options (BSOs) are identified that would represent improvements to the logic of the existing system that would meet user requirements. We would see this as analysing the shortcomings or failures of the logical S_0 and identifying possible candidates for a logical S_1.

Once a preferred BSO has been selected, the 'specification' referred to in the stage's title is that of the logical S_1. Hence the outputs from stage 2, shown in Figure 9.16, are all essentially concerned with defining a logical view of the required system.

9.2.6 **Selection of technical options**

The first five stages of SSADM place the emphasis on logical analysis and design, and they follow the classic sequence of Section 8.3.3 for a failure-driven, derivative method. The intrusion of *stage 3: selection of technical options* seems at first like a regression to a bottom-up 'I've got a computer; what shall I do with it?' type of approach.

In fact, there is good reason for the inclusion of a preliminary consideration of the potential physical implementation before the completion of the detailed logical design. Subsequent choices of physical implementation can actually affect the range of logical choices open to the systems developers in stages 4 and 5. Thus, for example, the logical design of the processes in stage 5: logical process design can be affected by the envisaged processing power and storage capacity of the computer system. A specific instance of this would be the dependence of the logical choices available on the decision to have real-time rather than batch processing procedures. The choice of a logical system that assumes real-time processing of files will normally imply large-scale processing power and data storage.

Stage 3 is not therefore concerned with detailed physical design choices, since these can only follow the complete logical data and process design of stages 4 and 5, but it does detail those physical aspects necessary to refine the specification of requirements sufficiently to allow detailed logical systems design to go ahead.

9.2.7 **Logical data design and logical process design**

We shall consider these two stages together. If we look at Figure 8.5, or its equivalent in any other specialist presentation of SSADM, we can see that stages 4 and 5 are seen as parallel, or at least complementary. We can understand the reasoning behind this if we recall the complementary nature of structure and process views of a system that we discussed in Section 8.3.6. It is also important to recall that we said in Section 8.5.2 that SSADM is a latter-day process-oriented method that has taken on board elements of structure and object-oriented methods. The way that SSADM regards the inter-relationship of stages 4 and 5 is an illustration of this point.

Stages 4 and 5 are concerned with the detailed logical design of the requirements of S_1, as specified in stage 2 and developed further in terms of the choice of expected technical implementation decided on in stage 3. The complementary nature of these two stages of systems development in SSADM can be illustrated by the example of data access first discussed in Chapter 5. Defining the way we access data, which is about process, will depend on how that data is arranged, which is about structure. Hence the detailed tasks of stage 4, which include creating a detailed logical data design, can be seen to be intimately involved with stage 5 tasks such as defining logical enquiry processing.

Both stages of the method need to be complete before any unambiguous physical system can be developed in stage 6. We can interpret this criterion in terms of the model of systems development that we put forward in Section 8.3.4. We saw there that a design must essentially consist of all the information that the systems builder needs to create a system conforming to the specified needs of its users.

9.2.8 **Physical design**

Stage 6: physical design is concerned with how logical views of the desired system, S_1, can be implemented into a physical working system conforming to the logical design of S_1 delivered by the previous stages. Our use of the word 'implemented' reveals the need for a third type of model that can make the link between a very abstract, logical view of the data and processes, and the way in which these are physically done.

What is this link? SSADM does not see it as an automatic or standard move from a preceding stage of the method to the next. This is because the move forward from the definition stages 4 and 5 to producing the deliverables of stage 6: physical design depends on the implementation medium. The details of implementation will therefore depend on the type of systems software to be used in the practical application. Reference to Chapter 5 shows how this bridge between logical and physical views of the treatment of data, which makes up information, should be dealt with using a systemic view.

A final note should be made about SSADM as a very tightly structured, hard information systems development method in the wider context of this book. SSADM can be, and in my experience of talking to users is, sometimes blindly applied to soft, messy situations in the hope that technical expertise will roll like a juggernaut over the soft mess. In practice, this results in either:

- truculent acceptance by potential actors, using this word in the sense of Section 8.4.3; or
- naive acceptance by systems owners, also in the sense of Section 8.4.3, that if SSADM is 'official' it must be OK.

Either of these views detracts from the way in which SSADM can accommodate a wider, holistic view of systems development. If we look at the details of the structure of the method in terms of its stages, stages 3, 4 and 5 are all defined as contributing to the final stage of physical design. Our systems view of systems development should help us see that SSADM need not be 'derivative' or 'process oriented' in any colloquial, pejorative sense. Indeed, the concept that the final implementation in stage 6: physical design takes account of technical options, logical data and process views of the desired system, S_1, makes it more holistic than either its supporters or opponents may realize.

9.3 STRUCTURE-ORIENTED DEVELOPMENT

9.3.1 **The main features of structure orientation**

We saw in Section 8.3.6 that *structure-oriented methods* use the view that information is data organized into a particular *structure* as their starting point. Once this structure has been established, the processes needed for its production can then be derived from the structure itself. Typically, the tasks performed when developing a system using a structure-oriented method are:

1 Identify the data structures that make up the information that the system must process.
2 Analyse the relationship between the components of the data structures in terms of sequence, conditionals and iteration.

3 Define the processes that will produce the components of the data structure.

4 Map the structural relationship of the data into a control hierarchy for the processes.

We can illustrate these general principles of structure-oriented methods by choosing the specific example of the method known as *Jackson Structured Programming* (JSP); see Jackson (1975). We choose this particular method because, although it is a software programming method rather than a systems development method, it fulfils two of our requirements at the same time. Besides illustrating structure orientation, it also provides the background to a later systems development method that Jackson also developed. This latter method is known as Jackson System Development (JSD) – see Jackson (1983) – which we shall study in detail in the next sections.

The stages of JSP require the following:

1 Analyse the data structure.
2 Convert the data structure to a program structure.
3 Define the program operations.
4 Insert the program operations into the data structure.
5 Convert the structured program operations into pseudo-code.

Comparison of the first four stages of JSP with our principles for determining what constitutes a structure-oriented method shows that JSP conforms closely to the principle of making the data structure the basis for determining the organization or structuring of the process.

We can now look at a simple example to illustrate JSP. Suppose we wish to develop a program that has to produce a monthly statement of account for a customer. The account statement has to show what they have bought on credit during the month and how much they owe at the end of the month. The logical structure of such an account can be illustrated with a diagram such as Figure 9.17. This is called a data structure diagram, and resembles many other similar forms of diagram used to show hierarchical structure.

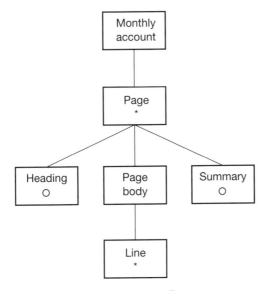

Figure 9.17 Data structure diagram
By defining the logical structure of the data, it also defines the processes that have to be carried out to produce its physical representation.

Sequence in such a diagram depends on the convention of reading from left to right, iteration by the use of an asterisk symbol for those components that may iterate, and an *o* character for conditional components whose occurrence depends on a particular condition being true.

Hence we see that the monthly account will consist of:

- one or more (i.e. iteration of) pages;
- pages that may be (i.e. conditional) first, intermediate or last;
- one or more (i.e. iteration of) lines.

Presenting the logical structure of the monthly account in this way will fulfil the first stage of JSP: analyse the data structure, and conforms to what we said any structure-oriented method would do in terms of analysing the relationship between the components of the data structures in terms of sequence, conditionals and iteration.

The second stage of JSP requires us to convert the data structure to a program structure. This is very easy. Once we have decided in what physical form the logical structure has to be manifested, we just have to put the appropriate verb or imperative action in front of each component. So, if we wanted the monthly account to be printed, we would put 'print monthly account', 'print page' etc. in front of each component in the structure diagram.

Stages 3 to 5 require us to define the program operations, to insert the program operations into the data structure, and to convert the structured program operations into pseudo-code. Figure 9.18 shows what the results of these three stages might look like in terms of our monthly account example. The sequence of operations is reflected by our movement down the listing. Iterations ('do while') and conditionals (true/false or 'not') are expressed in terms of 'do while'/'do while not' type statements, which we can find in any modern processing software.

```
open files
while not end of Monthly Account
do

        write page heading
        initialize line count
        while not end of page
        do

                write line
                increment line count
        end while
write summary line
end while
close files
```

Figure 9.18 Pseudo-code
For it to be unambiguously converted into working software, cf. Figure 9.13.

The important feature that comes from this brief study of JSP is that specification of what the software should do, i.e. process, derives directly from the structure of the information it is intended to produce. In developing his systems development method

JSD, Jackson applied the same principle. JSD builds a model of the desired system, and uses the structure of this model to derive specifications of what processes the software must carry out.

9.3.2 Introduction to JSD

We will try to justify our choice of Jackson System Development (JSD) as an example of structure-oriented development by asking some initial questions, as we did when justifying the choice of SSADM:

1 Is JSD a structure-oriented method?
2 How does JSD fit into our view of methodology developed in Section 8.3.6?
3 Are there any additional reasons to choose JSD?

The first question has already been partially answered in the previous section. Since JSD was developed after JSP by the same person and using a common *Weltanschauung*, it would not be surprising to find similarities of approach. Indeed, Jackson himself (1983) regards a system as a 'large program' and JSP as an extension of JSD. As we go further into JSD, I think we shall see that its initial emphasis on the structural make-up of entities and the relationship between them gives the method a strong structure orientation.

Other authors come close to our view. Pressman (1987) describes JSD as 'data structure oriented' rather than 'data flow oriented' or 'object oriented'. Booch (1991) categorizes JSD as 'data driven' rather than 'top-down structured', i.e. design methods linked with data flow orientation, or 'object oriented'. Sutcliffe (1988) says, 'JSD guides the analyst to model the systems *basic structure* rather than some of its more obvious manifestations as *functions* ... Most of JSD's rivals fall into the functional school of methods which concentrate on the process communication model.' (The emphases in the quotations are mine.)

Having shown why I think JSD can be described as structure oriented, we shall also see that, as with SSADM or any other method, the orientation is not exclusive. The concept of making the system model entities in the real world gives it certain characteristics that link it to object-oriented methods, as we shall see below.

In answering our first question above we have already run naturally into the second question: how does JSD look in relation to our view of methodology developed in Section 8.3? We have already seen it as a structure-oriented method, but what of the methodological questions of:

- approaches and methods;
- the stages of systems development;
- top-down and bottom-up approaches?

The answers to these methodological questions show JSD to be a very individualistic method, so we shall look at them each in turn.

JSD is certainly a structured method rather than an unstructured approach, because its earlier and later versions are structured in the sense that they have steps and stages respectively. Figure 9.19 shows the steps of the earlier version of JSD, to be found in Jackson (1983), and the stages of the more recent version in Sutcliffe (1988). It also shows how the stages of the more recent version represent a partial amalgamation of the earlier steps.

Harry (1990)	Jackson (1983)	Sutcliffe (1988)
Definition and analysis	Entity/action	Modelling
	Entity/structure	
	Initial model	Network
Design	Function	
	Systems timing	
Production	Implementation	Implementation

Figure 9.19 Steps and stages
The table shows the approximate correspondence between the steps of the original form of JSD with the stages of the later form. These are both related to the overall methodological view of the stages of systems development given in Figure 8.7.

The next methodological question is how JSD compares with the view of the stages of systems development that we set out in Section 8.3.4. But if we look at this question, reference to Jackson (1983) shows that it cannot be separated from the third question of top-down and bottom-up approaches.

Jackson sees JSD as a bottom-up approach that ignores the conventional view of 'the systems life cycle' or 'analysis' followed by 'design'. His explicit statement in Jackson (1983) that his method is bottom up thus appears to reject the top-down view implicit in Birrell and Ould (1985) that we developed in Section 8.3.4. His reasoning is that high-level decisions about what S_1 should be are decided 'at the time of greatest ignorance', i.e. when we begin the systems development process.

However, I think that we can see that JSD does have features that follow our view of the top-down nature of systems development. First, we notice that the implementation follows those stages concerned with modelling the system. Hence 'whats' come before 'hows'. Secondly, no attempt to model a system can proceed without some concept of the whole that enables us to decide what is and what is not part of the system to be modelled. When JSD refers to a 'model', we only have to ask 'model of what?' to realize that somewhere a high-level concept has already been decided on, even if not made explicit by the method, which is being realized top down as we build the model up. Figure 9.19 therefore shows how the steps or stages of JSD correspond to our methodological view.

Finally, it is worth noting that several authors, like Avison and Fitzgerald (1988), point out that JSD is not a complete method. While its activities run right through to systems implementation, it omits detailed guidance on such topics as database design.

Having set JSD in its context, we will now look at its main features. To do this we will go through the sequence of steps to be found in the earlier version, but set them in the combinations that make up the stages of the later version, as in Figure 9.19.

9.3.3 **The modelling stage**

The concept of a model plays a central role in JSD. We introduced the concept in Chapter 3, where we saw that the purpose of a model was to represent something. That 'something' could be an existing physical, concrete system or an abstract concept.

The particular concept of modelling used in JSD fits our general view. In this case, what is being modelled is what goes on in the real world. A strong emphasis is placed on the correct modelling of the way things change over time in the real world so that the information system we develop will accurately reflect the dynamics of the real-world system it seeks to control.

We also need to note the concept we introduced in the previous section. JSD uses a bottom-up approach in much of its detailed application.

With these two fundamentals of the JSD approach to modelling, we are ready to understand the first, entity–action, step of the method. As its name implies, this step is concerned with identifying entities and actions in the real world that are relevant to the information system that JSD seeks to develop. Once identified, these entities will be used to build a model of the real world.

Identifying entities is not an automatic procedure. It requires skill and judgement. The most commonly recommended way of doing it is to identify the nouns in any description of the real-world situation that we seek to model. If we take the example of Carry-Out Cupboards, we find the following entities mentioned or implied:

- customer
- supplier
- supplier list
- order
- stock record
- cupboard.

Not all of these are entities in the JSD sense. The use of the term 'entity' in JSD is not the same as the one we described in Chapter 6. Entities as defined there could include entities that were part of the computerized information system, such as a supplier list or a stock record. JSD would not include these as entities in the entity–action step because they are part of the way in which the existing information system describes the real world rather than being part of it.

Sutcliffe (1988) says that 'discovering entities within a system is one of the more difficult tasks in JSD'. I think that our control systems view of businesses and organizations that we established in Chapter 4 and developed in Chapter 7 makes this task easier. We saw that a control system sought to control a process, with its inputs and outputs, by means of an information system, which provided the sensor, feedback etc. JSD is concerned with developing a new information system that will control the processes of a business or organization. Any entities that are part of that existing information system are not part of the real-world process that JSD seeks to model and control. Hence entities within the existing information system, or outputs from it, are not included in the entity–action step.

Entities that are included must be uniquely named and must retain their individuality or type throughout their life. A specifically important property relevant to this step of JSD is that they perform actions, or have actions performed on them ('suffer' actions), in a set order. Actions must:

1 take place at a point in time. Actions are not continuous. Thus 'selling' would not be an action in JSD, since it is a continuous activity; but 'concluding a sale' would be, because it occurs as an event at a point in time.

2 take place in the real world. This requirement is a repetition of the need that we identified above to distinguish between the real-world system and the information system that seeks to control it. Thus 'print supplier list' is not an action but 'engage supplier' is.

Having identified the relevant entities of the real-world system and the actions they perform or suffer, we are ready for the next step, entity structure. This seeks to establish the structural relationship between an entity and its associated actions. The tool used for this can either be a structure diagram or a structure text.

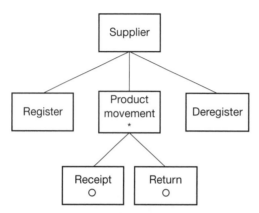

Figure 9.20 JSD: Entity life history
The similarity to Figure 9.15 comes from the inheritance of the tool by SSADM.

Figure 9.20 shows a structure diagram, sometimes called a process structure diagram (PSD), for the entity 'supplier' as it might be for Carry-Out Cupboards. Notice that the diagramming convention is identical to that for the structure diagrams used in JSP, Figure 9.17. Structure text in JSD also follows on from the principles established in JSP. JSD structure text is very similar to the pseudo-code of JSP, with conventions for showing sequence, iteration and conditionals.

9.3.4 The network stage

The conclusion of the modelling stage has left us with a detailed structured view of individual real-world entities and their actions, which concern us as systems developers. We now seek to specify an information system that will enable us to model, and by means of this model, control these real-world entities and their actions.

This talk of 'models' and 'modelling' may seem confusing. Haven't we just been 'modelling' in the previous stage? What 'model' are we talking about now? Answering these questions leads us naturally into the first, initial model step of the network stage.

In the previous stage we were concerned with identifying and describing the entities and their actions that we wished to model. We need therefore to distinguish between the real-world entities themselves that we have identified, and the description of them that we wish to use in our model of the real world.

JSD recognizes the need for this distinction and has a convention to deal with it. When representing any entity, it uses a suffix to the name of the entity to distinguish the real-world entity itself from its representation in the model. The suffix '-0' is placed after the name of a real-world entity, and the suffix '-1' after the process we use to represent it and its actions in the model. Thus Supplier-0 refers to an actual supplier to, say, Carry-Out Cupboards, while Supplier-1 refers to a process in the model that specifies the information system.

At this point we should note two things. First, the 0 and 1 in the suffixes have nothing to do with our use of them in S_0 and S_1. Secondly, our use of the word 'process' in the previous paragraph requires further explanation.

The aim of the initial model step is to begin the specification of the information system. It does this using a systems specification diagram (SSD), which acts as a simulation model (see Chapter 3) of what happens in the real world. Since the model simulates the real world, every entity in the real world will be represented by a process in the SSD. Thus the SSD shown in Figure 9.21 includes the entity Supplier-0 and the model process Supplier-1. What each process does will be defined by the structure text that we developed for the corresponding entity at the previous entity structure step.

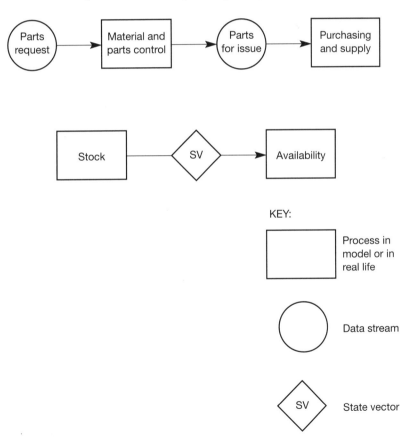

Figure 9.21 JSD: System specification diagrams
These are used to form the initial model before merging into the network stage. The diagram shows the two forms of process connexion used in the modelling.

The representation of real-world entities as processes in a model was already prepared for by the previous step of JSD. If the SSD is to be a simulation model of a system, however, we now need to consider how these potential *components* are *connected* into a *whole*. (The use of italics here is aimed to point us back to the important properties of any system, as per Chapter 3.)

Reference to the diagramming components of Figure 9.21 shows how systemic connexion can be made. JSD SSDs represent the connexions both between model processes, and between them and the corresponding real-world entities, by defining how they communicate. JSD distinguishes two kinds of communication:

1 A *data stream connexion* is one which where a stream of sequential messages, such as text being keyed into a microcomputer, connects two processes, as between material and parts control, and purchasing and supply, shown in Figure 9.21.
2 A *state vector connexion* represents the situation where one process inspects the state of another process at a particular point in time, like the checking of stock availability shown in Figure 9.21.

The deliverable of the initial model step gives a simulation model of the real world that the information system is designed to control. This model still lacks a description of how it will be in communication with this real-world system. Since the model needs to communicate in order to function, the next step of the network stage that defines this communication is called the function step. It covers the omission of communication in the SSD by adding a specification of the function processes that produce the required outputs and those that receive defined inputs. These processes will be defined by structure text and connected through data streams or state vectors like other model processes. Since JSD is a structure-oriented method, the definition of these function processes will derive directly from the structure of the data involved, as for JSP in Section 9.3.1.

At the end of the function step we have a SSD showing:

• All the model and function processes.
• The connexion of all processes to each other and the real world via data streams and state vectors.
• Structure text reflecting the structure of a modelled entity for model processes.
• The structure of input or output data for function processes.

Although the function step leaves us with a complete logical model in terms of connexion, we still have not considered when information is needed and therefore when processes should run. This is very much in line with what Jackson considers to be a bottom-up approach, which avoids unnecessarily early decisions made at a time of ignorance. The systems timing step continues with this philosophy. It only builds timing constraints into the SSD where these are needed to define a process itself. Thus if a vendor rating system for Carry-Out Cupboards required a regular print-out of supplier performance, the timing or frequency of this process would only be settled in the SSD if it had been specifically defined to produce an output, such as a 'monthly average', whose actual nature has a specific timing implication. Where the SSD is not affected, the timing constraints are left until the final implementation stage.

9.3.5 The implementation stage

The implementation step of the earlier JSD and the later version's implementation stage are the same. The aim is to convert the system specified by the SSD into working software. Given the tight nature of structure code and its virtual similarity with many high-level programming languages, this conversion could be virtually automatic. As Birrell and Ould (1988) amusingly point out, we could allocate a separate microprocessor to each process and use shared memory for communication between them; a logically possible but hardly efficient implementation!

The final stage of JSD is therefore concerned with deciding how to:

1 Share processors among processes.
2 Schedule processes.
3 Share memory among parts of processes.

However, making these decisions is essentially one of allocation and arrangement. The essence of JSD is that the code is seen as a semi-automatic derivative from the SSD and its structure text. Code is never written directly or changed: it is only generated from higher-level descriptions.

(We might note finally that the use of the term 'higher-level' in the previous paragraph means that we are right to have reservations about Jackson's 'bottom-up' assertions for JSD.)

9.4 OBJECT-ORIENTED DEVELOPMENT

9.4.1 The main features of object orientation

Object orientation is the most recent of our views of systems development. Placing it last in our study of systems development methodology is not just a question of historical sequence. Given our earlier distinction of method and methodology in Section 8.2, it makes sense that our study or learning about method, i.e. methodology, should place object orientation last. This is because object orientation is a view that comes as the result of experience and learning in systems development, as we shall see later. Meanwhile, it is worth referring to some of the initial concepts relating to object orientation that we covered in Chapters 3–5, in particular hierarchy, classification and object-oriented databases.

To begin understanding object-oriented systems development, we need to answer similar questions about object orientation to those we asked about process- and structure-oriented methods. Important questions we should answer are:

1 Is object orientation actually a systems development method?
2 How does object orientation fit into our view of methodology developed in Section 8.3.6?
3 What is the relationship between object orientation, other orientations we have studied and systems thinking?
4 Why does object orientation appear to be a present fashion or vogue in the field of information systems and computing?

I think the answer to our first question is likely to be very messy. To explain this opinion further, we need to recall that in Section 8.3.6 we distinguished between structured methods and unstructured approaches. Methods we saw as having a clear-cut, definable sequence of stages, each with its specific deliverables. Approaches we saw as less structured but still based on a clear set of principles. We can find references to 'method', 'milestones' and 'products' in major authors like Booch (1991). This sequence of terms sounds suspiciously like methods, stages and deliverables respectively; but I think we should treat this similarity with caution. Booch himself emphasizes the strongly iterative nature of object-oriented design, and many practitioners of object orientation advocate that one of its main advantages is that it is not tied to a rigid development sequence. (At a recent major conference on object-oriented design, I heard one very experienced delegate maintain that anyone offering object-oriented methods would, by definition, not know what object orientation was actually about!) We shall say more about this issue when considering prototyping below.

Meanwhile, a clue to how I do think object orientation ought to be viewed comes from the devious way I switched from object oriented to object orientation earlier in this section. I think that what we are considering in this section is object-oriented approaches or an object orientation in our view of systems development, rather than a structured method. As we shall see, an object-oriented approach brings very specific definitions, procedures and deliverables with it; but it does not bring anything as detailed as the stages we find in SSADM or even JSD.

Answering this first question then leads naturally to an answer for the second. If object-oriented systems development is an approach rather than a method, but it involves specific definitions, procedures and deliverables, then we can see it as unstructured but hard. We would place it more towards region A of Figure 8.9 rather than region B.

What of the other methods we have considered? What is the relationship between object orientation and other method orientations we have studied? This is the third question we raised above.

We can use JSD as the link here that helps our understanding of the answers to these questions. JSD saw modelling of real-world entities as a central task. The model that was then developed was used to inform us of the state of the real world, so that we could make decisions as to how to control it.

Examples of this method of control are very common outside the field of business or organizational information systems. Thus a modern railway signal box has an electronic screen diagramming the track layout and the position and movement of trains. Changes in the real-world situation are reflected by changes in what is shown on the screen. Thus as a train moves along the track, so a light representing the train moves along the diagram of the track on the screen.

RQ 9.4 What difference would you see between the railway model and those used in systems development?

Object orientation uses modelling in a similar way. It also creates a systemic software model of the real-world situation we wish to control, but this model is made up of objects. The concept of an object was first used in the Simula programming language. In that and subsequent object-oriented applications, objects existed in programs to simulate some aspect of real-life. Thus the components of an object-oriented model will include clusters of program language code that enable to do this.

Thus far, we can see a close similarity with JSD. We are concerned with simulating some particular thing that exists in the real world and we can apparently call either an entity or an object. However, real-world entities are not the only objects that an object-oriented approach will consider in developing the software that implements the information system through the model. An object can be any concrete or abstract identifiable element or component of what Booch (1991) calls 'the problem domain'.

We can further develop the concept of an object in systems terms by quoting Halbert and O'Brian (1988), as edited by Booch (1991): 'Other important kinds of objects are inventions of the design process whose collaborations with other objects serve as mechanisms that provide some higher level behavior.'

There are three important phrases or words used here, which will enable us to understand how an object-oriented approach can be seen in systems terms:

- The use of the word 'invention'.
- The phrase '*process* (my italics) whose collaborations'.
- The term 'higher level behavior'.

We will now look at each of these in turn to see how an object-oriented approach to information systems development relates to the other orientations we have presented.

The use of the word 'invention' implies that an object is someone's concept: inventions do not come into being without the existence of inventors. The quotation describes objects as inventions of 'the design process', but any implication that this is an abstract, impersonal procedure is nonsense. People make design processes work and they set the *Weltanschauung* for them. The false implication that objects are somehow objective is something we shall look at more deeply later in this chapter.

Process and collaboration have strong systemic implications. Together, these words not only imply that objects do something, but that they do it in a ordered and connected way. Thus the systemic concepts of process, connexion and structure are clearly present when modelling the world in object terms.

Behaviour is a holistic concept of an emergent property that the definition places in the context of hierarchy by its use of the term 'higher level'.

Given this set of systems concepts and the systems thinking behind the definition, is object orientation no different from the kind of systems view we have considered so far? I think the answer to this question is best understood if we begin by rejecting the false implication that a systems view and object orientation are somehow opposites or alternatives between which we have to choose. An object-oriented model of real life, with its components, connexion, interaction, structure, hierarchy etc., can easily be seen as systemic. What gives it an object orientation, rather any other orientation, is the particular way it views:

- the components (i.e. the objects) and their interactions through the passing of messages;
- the nature of hierarchy and how types of hierarchy can be classified.

In formal terms, the essential concepts that give object orientation this view are:

- abstraction
- encapsulation
- modularity
- hierarchy.

Abstraction focuses on the essential characteristics of an object that clearly define it relative to the perspective of the viewer. Thus in Carry-Out Cupboards, someone interested in order processing would see a cupboard as a sales item in terms of characteristics like sales to date or stock levels, while someone interested in assembly and packing might see a cupboard as a physical product in terms of its components and their structural relationship within the finally assembly.

We are very familiar with this concept as a result of our study of systems. What a system is and is not seen to be will depend on whose values and purposes we are referring to. Similarly, 'the essential characteristics' of an object will depend on whose 'perspective' we are taking. The concept of abstraction is particularly important in developing the further concept of hierarchy, which we discuss below.

Encapsulation is not something we have explicitly met with before, but I think it is not entirely new to us. It is the process of specifying what essential characteristics an object has, while 'hiding' how it produces them. I think that the concept of a black box (Chapter 3) is similar to encapsulation. In both cases we know what kinds of input will produce what outputs, but we don't know what goes on to produce them. The difference between the two concepts is that encapsulation involves deliberately hiding how an object carries out operations or methods. This is done to protect the object from unnecessary modification or interference during systems development, implementation and use.

Understanding encapsulation is an important prerequisite to the understanding of the concepts of message passing between objects and their behaviour, which we study later. For the moment, we should note that the concept of encapsulation enables us to see objects as 'an encapsulation of a set of operations or methods which can be invoked externally and of a state which remembers the effects of the methods' (Blair *et al.*, 1991). We might illustrate this by considering an object like a packing machine in the central assembly and packing facility of Carry-Out Cupboards. Such a machine can assemble and pack a specified quantity of one of the cupboards in response to 'requests' from another object, like a production scheduler.

Modularity 'packages abstractions into discrete units' (Booch, 1991) or 'with the introduction of objects, a system has a natural modular *structure* (my emphasis) consisting of a number of objects interacting (my emphasis again) via message passing'. We can therefore see the object model as showing the same characteristics we have always emphasized for any system. It just happens to be a particular form of system where the components are exclusively objects, where the structure is expressed as modularity, and in which interaction between components takes the form of passing messages.

Object orientation uses the term *hierarchy* in both the 'kind of' and 'part of' senses that we introduced in Chapter 3. For most of this book our control model view of management has led us to emphasize the aggregation or 'part of' view. In object orientation the classification or 'kind of' view gets much more attention. It enables us to classify objects according to shared characteristics, at increasing levels of abstraction. This in turn enables the reuse of implemented software for commonly shared characteristics. We will now say more about this while answering our final question.

The final question we posed at the beginning of this section was why object orientation appears to be so dominant. My approach to answering this comes from the view of systems development presented in Section 8.3.4, where we saw methodology in its true sense as involving learning in the context of higher-order control. We have now had several decades during which computer-based information and other systems have been developed, used, modified and discarded. We have gained a large amount of experience, including the kind of which Oscar Wilde said, 'Experience is the name we give to our mistakes.'

A major feature of object orientation is that the emphasis on hierarchy and classification we introduced above enables us to build on our existing experience. In systems development terms, object orientation enables us to avoid having to re-invent the wheel, if all we want is a new wheel with a different diameter. But to pursue this analogy further, object-orientation enables us to cash in on the fact that a wheel is a circular object, to avoid the need for designing a manhole cover from scratch. In the software context, this principle leads to the feature of 'reusable code' as an important product of an object oriented approach. It means that once a particular software need is seen as an instance of a wider category of application for which we already have working software, the new software is generated from what exists, rather than being built from scratch.

This important feature then brings others with it. Reusable software, or even whole designs, reduces the risks that come from starting with something completely new and untried. It also allows for evolutionary systems development based on learning.

Given this 'plug' for object-oriented systems development, let us now look at some of its main principles in more detail.

9.4.2 Objects and their properties

An object has three important properties that we need to understand:

1 State.
2 Behaviour.
3 Identity.

When considering these for more than one object, we can develop the further concept of:

4 Class.

Booch (1991) says that the state of an object encompasses 'all of the (usually static) properties of the object plus the current (usually dynamic) values of each of these properties'.

We can explore this view of the state of an object by developing the example of one specific cupboard from the Carry-Out Cupboards range. One of the properties of such a cupboard is the total quantity sold. This property is static because it is unlikely to be changed to anything else, like the total quantity bought. As long as Carry-Out Cupboards is in the business of selling cupboards, this property will be one of continued interest. The value of the property is dynamic, however, because the total quantity sold will take up different values through time.

Although properties and values are referred to as being 'usually' static and dynamic respectively, they can be otherwise. The value for the property surface finish will be static, since it will remain unchanged as long as the cupboard exists as part of the Carry-Out Cupboards range. The property of VAT code is likely to be fixed for the commercial life of the cupboard, but it is not impossible that VAT could be changed or abolished.

The value of a property can denote another object rather than a simple quantity. Thus the state of a Carry-Out Cupboards retail outlet will include references to individual cupboards stocked.

Like many other concepts in object orientation, the concept of the state of an object is not as new or as unusual as may sometimes be claimed. Just one example of what we are already familiar with is that of an attribute of an entity taking on a particular value. This will not seem terribly different from the concept that a property of an object will take on a particular value. A difference does begin to appear when we go on to consider the additional concepts that can be applied to thinking about objects. When we have considered them, we shall find that an object is a richer concept than that of an entity in terms of how it is applied.

The *behaviour of an object* is described in terms of the changes of state it undergoes as the result of passing and receiving messages to and from other objects.

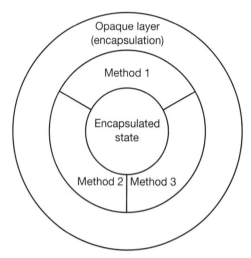

Figure 9.22 Object orientation: an encapsulated object
An object is an encapsulation of a set of operations or methods that can be invoked externally, and of a state that remembers the effect of the methods.

The concept of message passing was introduced in the previous section. We can now see an object (Figure 9.22) as being an encapsulation of:

1 A set of operations or methods that can be invoked by a message from another object. (Since a message is an operation that one object performs on another, the terms are 'two sides of the same coin'.)
2 A state that remembers the effect of the methods.

Behaviour is therefore an emergent property describing the whole of what an object suffers and does as a component with these properties.

Recalling the concept of emergent property is also a useful way of understanding *object identity*. A mistake that is easily made is to confuse the name of an object and the object itself. As long as we recall the holistic thinking behind the concept of emergent property, then we can see that the identity of an object is not just a name or a label, but the emergent whole of the properties that make the object what it is.

This view of identity goes beyond the use of keys, labels or variable names, and an object keeps its identity even when its state is completely changed.

Once we have the concepts of state, behaviour and identity to help us understand the nature of individual objects, we can then move on to understand something of the *relationships* between them. We can use this understanding to build an object-oriented model of the real-life situation we seek to control.

Object-oriented approaches describe the forms of such relationships in terms of the concept of *class*. These relationships can be:

1 Using relationships.
2 Containing relationships.

Using relationships are those where objects are principally seen in terms of how they affect one another. We could see, for example in Figure 9.23, that any object that had a control function might send a message to another object in order to check on some value of its state in order to receive feedback information from that object.

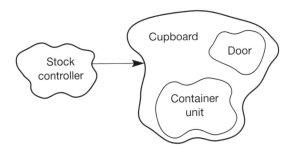

Figure 9.23 Object orientation: using and containing relationships
The stock controller *uses* the object cupboard when it sends a message in order to
check its availability. The cupboard itself has a *containing* relationship with its hierarchical
components, container unit and door.

Containing relationships are those that we can see in terms of our view of the aggregation of components within a systemic hierarchy, as in Chapter 3. In the Carry-Out Cupboards case, we would therefore see a cupboard as consisting of components like container unit, doors etc., as in Figure 9.23.

I think that our systems view would interpret these two forms of object-oriented relationship in terms of the process and structure contributions that each makes to the object-oriented model. Thus:

• Using relationships are principally concerned with *process*.
• Containing relationships are principally concerned with *structure*.

We can now consider how the concept of class enables us to understand how an object-oriented approach goes beyond the view of objects and their properties as the same as that of entities and attributes. We said that a difference would appear when we considered additional concepts that can be applied to our thinking about objects. Class and class hierarchy are the additional concepts that enable us to see that an object is a richer concept than an entity.

9.4.3 **Class and class hierarchies**

To understand how object orientation sees the concept of a class, we need to look back to the important role of modelling in an object-oriented approach. We said above that an object in our object-oriented model represents 'any concrete or abstract identifiable element or component ... of the problem domain'. The concept of class then leads us to seeing how a set of objects can share a common structure and a common behaviour. When we do this, we see a class as an abstraction of the properties that enable us to relate and distinguish objects in terms of their characteristics.

Four kinds of class hierarchy relationships can be found in object orientation:

1 Inheritance.
2 Using.
3 Instantiation.
4 Meta-class relationships.

We can explore the idea of class and class relationships by referring to a usefully stupid question that I know was once set in an IQ test:

> *Which of the following three things is the odd one out:*
> *a dog, a cat, or a television set?*

The question was set at a time when both dogs and televisions required licences and a cat didn't, so the official answer was that a cat was the odd one out. Presumably that meant that people like me, who thought a television was the odd one out because it wasn't an animal, had a low IQ! Anyway, when I learned the answer to this, I sarcastically suggested that a dog was the odd one out because a cat and a television are both working components of the Harry family dogless household. However, we are indebted to whoever set this question for simply illustrating some important points.

The first point is about classification itself. Although the 'obvious' answer to the IQ question may have been to see a television as the odd one out, in practice it would depend on what purpose we had in attempting to classify the three types of objects. Thus the viewpoint of a vet would be different from that of an object-oriented systems developer trying to create a national system for licensing televisions, dogs, shotguns etc. An object, we saw earlier, is someone's concept; and this concept is in turn dependent on the standpoint and aims of the person whose concept it is.

An important practical systems development point follows from this. Although it is likely that the implementation of object-oriented systems development will lie in the hands of a systems programmer, the *Weltanschauung* or world view built into the system by the assumptions behind any classification should reflect the management perspective. We again see the importance of systems specification, as in Section 8.3.4.

Once we do decide on a form of classification, we find that the four types of relationship listed above are possible between classes.

Inheritance relationships are those where one class shares the structure or behaviour defined in one (single inheritance) or more (multiple inheritance) other classes (superclasses). Inheritance comes from 'kind of' relationships.

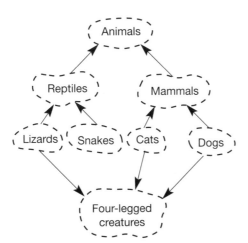

Figure 9.24 Object orientation: inheritance relationships
Classes inherit behaviour from superclasses. Thus mammals inherit behaviour from the fact they are animals. Multiple inheritance occurs where a class inherits from more than one superclass. Thus lizards inherit some behaviour from the fact they are reptiles, and other behaviour from being four legged.

Figure 9.24 illustrates these concepts. Both dogs and cats inherit behaviour, like suckling their young, from being members of the mammal superclass. This is an example of single inheritance because the behaviour of suckling the young derives from that defined by the one superclass. However, there are many other ways in which we might classify animals. To classify in terms of how many legs divides animals in a different way. Hence the structure and behaviour of being a four-legged animal that suckles its young form a multiple inheritance.

| RQ 9.5 | Suggest some examples of inheritance shown by the Carry-Out Cupboards range of products. |

When we saw dogs and cats as different from television in our IQ question above, we were using the concept of inheritance as the basis of our classification. *Using relationships* arise when we classify in terms of aggregation. Using relationships are 'part of' relationships. Thus cats and televisions are classes of objects are part of the superclass 'used by the Harry household', while dogs are not.

The concept of a using relationship can be extended to build on the idea of the *instantiation* of any set of relationships. Thus the 'instantiation of licensable household objects' (according to 1960s UK laws) would include dogs and televisions, but not cats.

Understanding *meta-class relationships* follows from realizing that classes themselves may be regarded as objects. We can then see that we may have classes of classes. To understand the way in which classes may be classified we can then use the same criteria of inheritance, using and instantiation as before.

This concept of *meta-class* relationships leads to two other important points that we can consider as being important for an object-oriented approach:

1 Understanding that classes are objects but objects are not classes.
2 Clarifying the possible confusion of objects and classes.

Our systems view of hierarchy helps us with understanding the first point. We understand how a system can be a component (or subsystem) of a wider system. Thus a system can have components and also be a component itself. We used the term 'element' to distinguish the lowest level of component in the systems hierarchy. What this level would be would depend on our view of the system. Thus in a retailing operation, an individual television might be seen as an element of a stock control system. To a television technician, however, the television itself might be seen as a system of electronic components.

The relationship between classes and objects has similarities to our systems hierarchy view. We have already seen that what constitutes an object depends on our motives for modelling a system. Thus whether we saw a particular dog as an object or a class would be different if we were designing a dog licensing system (individual dog is object) to when we were modelling canine physiology (dog is using class of body-part objects).

Although this comparison with our systems hierarchy view is a help, we need also to clarify the possible confusion of objects and classes. In its common generic use, 'dog' means a kind of animal, not one particular animal. In this sense, dog is a class. If by 'a dog' we mean one particular instance of a dog, then we are referring to an object. So if we are thinking of dog licensing, 'dog' is a class and Fido or Rover are the values of the property name of individual instances of objects in that class.

When building an object-oriented software model, we normally see classes as static, with their form and relationships fixed before execution of the model. Objects, however, are created and destroyed during the lifetime of the model's application. Thus the class 'dog' remains throughout the life of our licensing system, but individual objects like 'Fido' or 'Rover' come and go.

9.4.4 Developing an object-oriented model

We saw in Section 8.7.1 that an object-oriented model will take the form of computer code able to represent the real world we seek to control in terms of objects interacting by the passing of messages. Now we understand some of the basic object-oriented concepts like object, class, inheritance and instantiation, we can look further into the tasks, tools and deliverables involved in developing such an object-oriented model. To do this we will consider three things:

1 The processes involved in object-oriented systems development and their deliverables.
2 Possible roles for diagramming.
3 Object-oriented software.

We introduced the issue of whether object-oriented systems development was a method or an approach in Section 9.4.1. We decided that the issue was a messy one. We found references to 'method', 'milestones' and 'products' in major authors like Booch (1991); but we also saw that claims to see object orientation as a method can be dismissed by statements like 'object-oriented design may seem to be a terribly unconstrained and fuzzy process'.

The information systems methodology that we introduced in Section 8.3.6 should not give us any problems with these supposed contradictions. We see object-oriented systems development as an approach with clear concepts that have to be delivered, but that are not tied to a rigid development sequence. In this context we can consider four tasks:

1 *Identifying classes and objects.* What we see in the problem situation as objects and classes will depend on the purpose of our systems development, so no structured or systematic method is generally available here. What may be useful as a general guide is the recognition that names of things or nouns in any description of the problem situation could be indicators for object or classes of interest.

2 *Defining the semantics of classes and objects.* Here we seek to establish the activities and behaviour of the classes and objects so that we know exactly what they are (and are not). Again, no rigid method is available, but consideration of the verbs in any description of the problem situation could be a good indicator of behaviour. Life cycles can be constructed for objects as a heuristic method assembling all they do and suffer (cf. JSD, Section 9.3.3).

3 *Identifying relationships between classes and objects.* Once our definitions have made clear the nature of the classes and objects themselves, we can then try to clarify how things interact within the system. For classes this means identifying inheritance, using and other relationships. For objects it means establishing their static and dynamic properties.

4 *Implementing the classes and objects.* This involves creating the object-oriented software model itself. Besides the software implementation of classes and objects, it will involve their allocation to modules within the program, and the allocation of programs to processors.

Consideration of these tasks shows why object-oriented systems development is unlikely to be a structured method. Identification of classes and objects can easily come after observing behaviour. Identifying class relationships can often be mixed with identifying classes themselves. In these and other ways, we can see that a set sequence of task 1 to task 4 is unlikely in practice.

Tasks 1–3 above imply that we will have some means of exploring, recording and defining various characteristics of classes, objects and their relationships and behaviour. This leads naturally to our second subject of possible roles for diagramming.

The need for diagramming is not so obvious in object-oriented systems development as in other methods, for two reasons.

First, object orientation aims to model the world directly. There is a close correspondence between model objects and the real-world items they represent. In this situation there is much less of a clear division between the logical model and the physical model than in other methods. In these methods a detailed system in terms of data flow diagrams, logical data structures etc. is converted into working software at the systems production stage. In object-oriented systems development the modelling is the production.

Secondly, even where some documentation is needed as a prelude to software implementation, diagrams are not necessarily the best choice. Much of the definition of behaviour and relationships for classes and objects is better done using templates or formal tables. These can list their properties and values, message synchronization etc.

Booch (1991) does detail a number of object-oriented diagram types. The four most important are shown in Figures 9.25 to 9.28. These are:

1 *Class diagrams* (Figure 9.25). To specify what classes exist and how are they are related. Their symbols are chosen to reflect forms of class relationships and cardinality.
2 *Object diagrams* (Figure 9.26). To specify what mechanisms are used to regulate how objects collaborate. These have symbols for objects and messages and message synchronization.
3 *State transition diagrams* (Figure 9.27). To specify how the time ordering of external events can affect the state of each instance of the class. These have symbols for start state, state, stop state, events and actions.
4 *Module diagrams* (Figure 9.28, often called Booch diagrams by other authors). These illustrate the physical packaging of classes and objects into software modules.

Diagram types 1–3 might be used throughout tasks 1–3 above. Module diagrams, however, apply to task 4.

Our final subject is object-oriented software. Theoretically, we could adapt or bend most kinds of programming language to be object oriented, since object orientation is a principle not a method. However, in practice computer programming languages need to deal conveniently with the main object orientation concepts of abstraction, encapsulation, modularity and hierarchy that we introduced in Section 9.4.1.

Five principal languages do this:

1 Object-oriented forms of Pascal, e.g. Turbo Pascal (Borland).
2 C++, an object-oriented development of the C language.
3 CLOS (Common Lisp Object System), an object-oriented development of the LISP language.

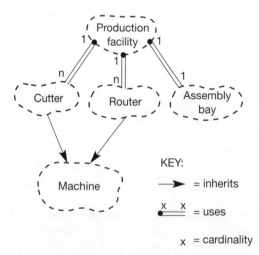

Figure 9.25 Object orientation: class diagram
These specify what classes exist and how they are related. The symbols used are a selection from Booch (1991). Thus one production facility uses many (=*n*) cutters. Both cutters and router inherit behaviour from being machines.

4 Smalltalk, e.g. Smalltalk V or Smalltalk 80. Unlike the previous examples, this was created as an object-oriented language from the beginning.

5 Eiffel, another specifically created object-oriented language.

A detailed comparison of these and other languages is in Booch (1991). For the other references try Schmucker (1986), Faison (1991), Keene (1989), Muevel and Gueguen (1987) and Meyer (1988).

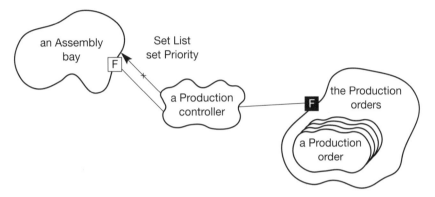

Figure 9.26 Object orientation: object diagrams
These specify what mechanisms are used to regulate how objects collaborate. The symbols are again from Booch (1991).

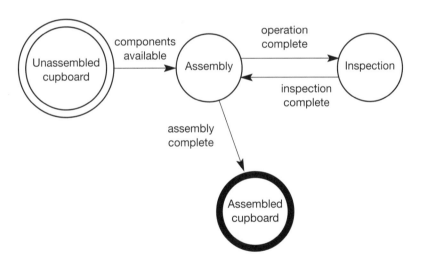

Figure 9.27 Object-orientation: state transition diagrams
These specify how the time ordering of external events can affect the state of each instance of the class. The symbols are again from Booch (1991). Here: unassembled cupboard is a start state, assembly and inspection are states, and assembled cupboard is a stop state. Labels for events and actions are added to the linking arrows.

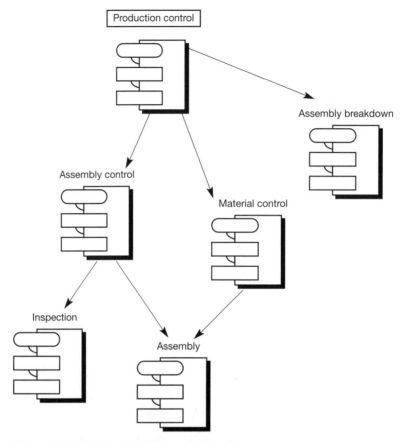

Figure 9.28 Object orientation: module diagrams
The symbols are again from Booch (1991). The relationship between the object and its software representation bears a close conceptual relationship to the way real-life entities are represented by models in JSD. Thus, just as process-oriented methods like SSADM incorporate structure-oriented concepts like entity life histories (see caption for Figure 9.15), so the concepts of object-oriented methods have links with structure-oriented methods.

9.5 PROTOTYPING

The concept of a prototype is probably familiar from its use in manufacturing and engineering. It is normally used to mean the first of a model to be produced, like a prototype car or aircraft, which is then utilized for further research and development. The common assumption is that the prototype will probably be modified as the result of testing, before the model goes into final production.

Prototyping has a similar meaning in systems development, except that instead of being the first of many copies, a prototype is more likely to be either:

- the first version of a complete system that will be modified after testing; or
- a component of a system whose creation may subsequently act as a guide to the creation of others in the complete system.

Another slight difference between the engineering and systems uses of the word lies in the form of the development and testing. Testing a prototype engineering product like an aircraft usually takes place with the finished product and focuses on physical performance. With systems prototyping, testing is likely to be a continuous process as the system is built up, and is usually done in co-operation with the user. Much of the testing of a systems prototype is concerned not so much with 'Does it work?', but with 'Does it work the way you (the user) want it to?' Prototyping is the term then used to describe the whole process of building bottom up, bit by bit, and continually consulting with the user in the process.

Prototyping is the other side of the argument that led to the need for structured methods. When systems development gets into a mess because objectives are not agreed or are changed, or people join and leave the development team and continuity is lost, or there is no definition of what should be delivered at various stages of development, we feel the need for order. This is when we call for clearly structured methods with defined stages and deliverables. But structured methods also have their disadvantages. Rules and structure can be suppressive of imagination and creative activity. Furthermore, the frequent use of iteration in structured methods in practice shows that systems development is not a serial activity. It does not consist of separate individual activities that follow one another a step at a time. Human creativity is a rich, holistic activity that cannot be done to a formula, so where creativity is required in systems development, structure can be a disadvantage.

In total, however, systems development is no different from any other practically applied creative processes, in that it requires the freedom that stimulates imagination and the order that leads to deliverable results. To understand the role of prototyping, we therefore need to identify its relationship with structured systems development, rather than seeing the two approaches as mutually exclusive. Prototyping is most likely to be appropriate:

1 For small intimate systems that can be developed informally by a small intimate band of analysts and potential users.
2 For clearly identifiable components of a wider system where it is possible to delegate detailed development without conflicting with the whole.

A house-building analogy can help us here. We could hardly prototype a house in the systems development sense. Imagine standing around throwing out ideas about the materials to be used, the location of the building, the numbers of the rooms etc., and then frequently changing our minds so that part-built structures were demolished and rebuilt. The only practical way to co-ordinate such a project is to agree the design with the architect before we start. As we have seen above, the systems design stage of systems development produces much the same deliverable for the systems builder of the production stage as the architect does for the house builder. All but the smallest systems, like all but the smallest buildings, need a structured approach to development.

We can take our analogy further, however. Although we would want the architect to design the house, I doubt if we would need their services to help us with arranging the pictures on the walls or deciding where to put the television. Most people decide such details by trial and error. So even if a structured method has been used to design a system, it is possible to see prototyping as an excellent way of designing such intimate things as screen presentations and sequences for users, or formats for print-outs.

Note, however, that just as our choice about the television is limited by where the architect put the electricity points, so our choice of systems details will be determined by the overall systems design. For a detailed account of incorporating prototyping within structured systems development, see Crinnion (1991).

However, even if the context of prototyping has been fixed within a wider plan, there are other reasons that it may not be appropriate. In our house-building analogy, we considered a house dictated by one client. In all but the smallest organizations, the client is more likely to be a client set. In these circumstances, the idea of having two or more people all shouting instructions to the house builder would be a recipe for chaos. This might be overcome by co-ordinating the demands of the various prototypers, but if we do this we are back to forming some agreed model of the overall system that is being aimed at. This then implies the potential for a more formal approach.

Another restriction on prototyping comes when the costs of trial and error become high. If the client is in need of large amounts of time and support in order to make the prototyping software effective, then its cost could be much more than handing over a larger proportion of the systems development process to a professional.

Finally, prototyping may be so client centred that its results can be very conservative and colloquial. This can occur because attempts to talk about the new system often relate its development to the existing physical one. The use of analogies can then carry through bad features of the old system into the new. This is especially the case where some form of computerized graphical user interface is used as a systems development tool, since these often interpret systems concepts in terms of older physical analogies by showing files as filing cabinets or inputs and outputs as particular documents etc.

However, given these cautions, prototyping is a vigorous and often swiftly effective way to sweep aside red tape and get a working system.

Having set a context for prototyping, it is worth noting two main ways in which it has been implemented:

1 The use of fourth-generation programming languages (4GLs) for prototyping.
2 Prototyping using object-oriented programming languages.

4GLs, as we saw in Chapter 6, are declarative languages. Users state what they want from, say, a database, rather than having to specify how the software should obtain it. As we also saw in Chapter 6, these languages use English-like statement whose meaning is easy to understand.

A further step forward in making software easy to use has been the advent of graphical user interfaces, with pull-down menus, icons, use of the mouse and the overall removal of the need to know a programming language. It is now possible for users to develop personal systems by showing what they want rather than telling the computer how to do it.

Object-oriented systems development lends itself to a prototyping approach because of its iterative, building block approach, as we saw in Section 9.3.4. Direct prototyping with object-oriented languages is an expert's job, however. While most people would find little difficulty with a 4GL, C++ code looks much less friendly. It is worth noting that object orientation does lie behind the development of many of the user-friendly graphical interfaces (including most video games) used by the non-expert.

The power that prototyping places in the hands of the non-expert developer raises one vital issue of systems development. If it is now increasingly 'possible for users to develop personal systems by showing what they want rather than telling the computer how to do it', this throws a strong emphasis on to knowing what you want. For management of business or organizations, this leads to the central theme of this book, that information systems should be seen in the context of management systems.

9.6   INTEGRATED METHODS

We have now almost completed our survey of information systems methodology, or study of method. We began this chapter by emphasizing that information systems development can only hope to be successful once we have sorted out the messes in the wider management system.

We justified our study of soft systems methodology (SSM) in Section 9.1 as a way of coping with messes. We also saw in Section 8.3 that the initial strategy and inception stages of information systems development involved us in looking at both the management system and the whole business or organizational system. This involvement required sorting out the soft human and policy issues before the deliverables of decision, authorization and commitment could be produced.

The need for that 'sorting out' explains why an integrated methodology of information systems development has begun to appear since the mid-1980s. Our previous studies show that we can identify a soft systems methodology that will deal with the messes of the wider management system. We have also studied specialist information systems methodology that will deliver working information systems in response to a defined problem. We can now ask if these two components can be brought together to produce ideas about how we can have an integrated information systems methodology combining the functions of soft and hard systems methods.

The publication of details of the Multiview (MV) method of Wood-Harper *et al.* (1985) was the first attempt that I have identified of this synthesis. Avison and Harper (1990) is a more recent reference.

The Multiview synthesis envisages five stages:

1 Analysis of human activity systems.
2 Analysis of entities, functions and events.
3 Analysis and design of sociotechnical systems.
4 Design of human–computer interface.
5 Design of technical subsystems.

Figure 9.29 shows the details of the method.

Analysis of human activity systems essentially involves the SSM we covered in Section 9.1, in the conventional seven-stage model of Section 9.1.3. The stages used by Multiview go as far as stage 4 of SSM, specification of the conceptual model. As we saw, this model defines what the system that we would like to have, S_1, should do to be the desired system. In terms of our model of systems development in Section 8.3.4, this produces the conceptual model as a high-level form of the eventual deliverable from the definition and analysis stage of systems development.

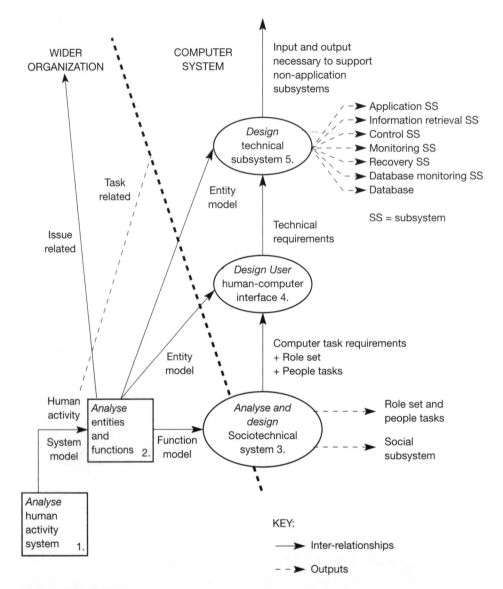

Figure 9.29 Multiview
This has probably been the leader in integrating hard and soft methodology.

Analysis of entities, functions and events takes the high-level definition of S$_1$ in the form of the conceptual model and models the detailed breakdown of the desired information system. The terms entity, function and event are used in the conventional ways that you will find earlier in this chapter and in Chapter 6. This stage is sometimes called information systems modelling, to reflect that it follows mainstream information systems development components and process in this field.

Analysis and design of sociotechnical systems recognizes that 'all change involves conflict of interest' (Mumford, 1983). This is a reference to a *Weltanschauung* of a systems development method that assumes that working information systems are 'both technically efficient and have social characteristics that lead to high job satisfaction'. The implication of this *Weltanschauung* is that there is a need for:

- A knowledge fit because employees (would we call them actors in the SSM context?) should believe that their skills and worth are being adequately used.
- A psychological fit that conforms to the employee's view of their aspirations.
- An efficiency fit that covers the balancing of financial rewards to employees against the requirements of the employer in terms of job performance.
- A task structure fit that reflects the success in making the job appropriately demanding and fulfilling for the employee.
- An ethical fit between the values of the employee and the employer.

Design of human–computer interface takes a holistic view of the design process by looking at the design of how human and computers may work together before detailing the final stage: design of technical subsystems. Thus if we have different technical alternatives like choices of hardware and software, these are detailed after consultation and consideration as to how they would work in the wider human–computer system context. (One way of doing this could be the use of prototyping.)

Although Multiview is the only major attempt at integrated information systems development of which I am aware, I think that our view of management systems would lead us to expect continued attempts at developing some form of integrated approach. Real-life management systems always have their hard, technical components interacting with soft, human ones. Practical information systems development will therefore need to take account of this holistic situation.

9.7 AUTOMATED SUPPORT FOR SYSTEMS DEVELOPMENT – DIAGRAMMING AND CASE TOOLS

Most modern information systems development is carried out knowing that a computer system is likely to be a major component of the information system being developed. It would be very strange if the process of information systems development were then to ignore the existence of the computer as a tool for its own use.

The potential for using the computer in systems development has been increased since the late 1980s by two important and related developments:

1 The proliferation of personal computers with internal memory in megabytes, advanced processors, SVGA monitors and very high-capacity hard disk storage.
2 A parallel development of sophisticated graphical user interface software that can support diagramming, data modelling, object hierarchy and classification, and many other activities and tools of systems development.

As a result of these technical advances, we can now find three types of software to support the systems developer:

1 Diagramming tools.
2 Visual programming.
3 CASE tools and Workbenches.

The need for diagramming tools comes from the fact that many of the methods covered in this chapter, and individual tasks and techniques used in previous ones (such as Chapter 6), use diagrams for the reasons we discussed in Chapter 3. Diagramming is therefore an important systems tool, although drawing by hand is not only labour intensive but also repetitive. Conceiving what must be included in a data flow diagram requires great skill, but drawing the same symbols with a pencil and template is very tedious. We take the term diagramming tool to mean software that enables us to draw diagrams, and nothing more than that. Diagramming tools designed specifically to draw data flow diagrams, structure charts and other diagrams used in information systems development are sometimes called CASE tools. If all they do is draw diagrams, this is a false description. We shall see below that a CASE tool does more than just draw diagrams.

Visual programming uses graphical devices like easy-to-recognize symbols called (upsettingly for some of us) icons, tabular structures or preset document formats. These enable the less specialist systems developer to define the high-level procedures carried out by the desired system, S_1. This use of a visual programming 'language' compares with the way in which 4GLs have made programming easier for the less expert by the use of English-like language.

Some of the different ways in which this kind of visual support can be given are:

1 Graphical environment to assist in:
   - visualization of information about data;
   - visualization of programs and execution;
   - visualization of software design;
   - general visual coaching.

2 Symbol languages for:
   - handling visual information;
   - supporting visual interactions;
   - programming with visual expressions;
   - diagrammatic systems;
   - iconic systems;
   - form systems.

This classification is close to Shu (1988).

When discussing diagramming above, we contrasted the skill needed to decide a diagram's contents with the routine process of drawing from a small set of symbols. If we are designing a whole system, even with the support of a diagramming tool, other routine tasks remain that can make the process tiresome and therefore open to errors and inconsistencies.

Thus if we considered developing a system using a process-oriented method, typical tools might include data flow diagrams, data modelling, structured English and entity life histories. Using these tools would involve the analyst in some quite laborious paperwork. It would involve drawing data flow diagrams by hand, with carefully and systematically numbered processes, data stores, external entities etc. Details of all these features would then have to be recorded in some form. Again, consider the procedure when using a diagram for modelling entities, attributes and relationships. Deciding what the entity is, and what form of data should be used for the attributes, is only one of the tasks. It is also necessary to check that a particular name for an entity has not been used before and, if so, where it occurs in data stores. For these actions we again require some record to back up the diagramming.

Unless the analyst were superhuman, there would be much redrawing and modification involved in the diagrams, which in turn would require renumbering of entities and changes to whatever record is kept of them. A good deal of time would be spent erasing and copying. The situation would be further complicated by the fact that several members of the team would be working on the project, so that co-ordination and consistency would be needed to prevent conflicting versions of the system appearing.

It would be beneficial to have a tool that would help not only with the diagramming, but also with recording and checking these routine cross-references across the various diagrams. Such an overall record (usually called a data dictionary or encyclopaedia) would keep track of the processes, entities, attributes, structural relationships etc. used in developing an information system.

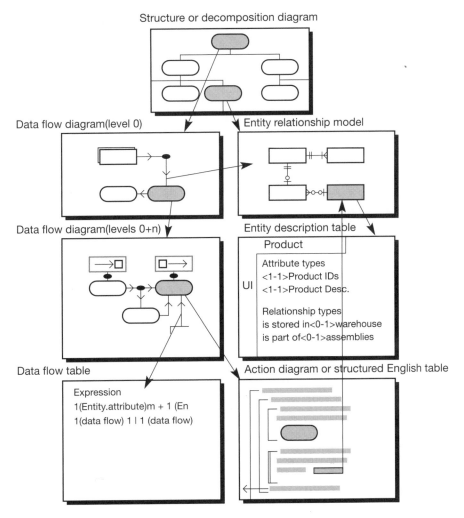

Figure 9.30 CASE (computer-aided systems or software engineering) tools and techniques
CASE tools are not just diagramming tools: they co-ordinate both the tools and techniques used and the users themselves.

Tools like these are usually called CASE tools or Workbenches. CASE is an acronym for computer-aided systems (or sometimes software) engineering. A CASE tool makes it possible to avoid many of the problems of carrying and co-ordinating the systems development process. Typical CASE tools enable diagrams to be drawn on a computer screen using a mouse and a menu of diagram symbols. When additions are made to the diagram, an entry is automatically opened for it in the data dictionary. The CASE tool will check the naming and numbering of entities to avoid duplication and omission, and to keep the entries in the data dictionary in line with the diagram and vice versa. CASE tools are also able to check the logic of diagrams. All these facilities are combined with the more general ones associated with wordprocessing and graphics editing.

The typical diagramming components of a CASE tool are shown in Figure 9.30. The actual components in any particular CASE tool will depend on the method with which it is intended to work. This particular example illustrates a Workbench designed to support systems development for a process-oriented method. Its main components are *six types of diagram or tabular representations*:

1 Data flow diagram. Conventional data flow diagramming with choice of symbol conventions for process, data flow, external entity and data store.
2 Structure or decomposition diagram. Hierarchical diagram using diagraph (see Chapter 3) convention to show relationship between system, subsystem and components.
3 Entity relationship diagram or model. To show entities and their inter-relationship, including cardinalities.
4 Action diagram or structured English table. Diagrammatic or verbal definition of processes in terms of sequence, conditionals and iterations.
5 Entity description table. Defining the attributes of the entities and their relationship type.
6 Data flow table. Identifies data flows and details the data structures that make them up.

A further component consists of *encyclopaedia reports for*:

1 Lists of objects and their properties. Enable us to list all the processes, entities or any other object recorded anywhere by the CASE tool for the project.
2 Consistency and propriety. Enable us to check for omissions or inconsistencies in the record at any stage of development, e.g. processes with no output or data that gets 'lost'. Generally a good CASE tool will prevent illogical entries or omissions from being made. Thus you cannot enter a data flow without its having both a source and a destination, or you may not give two different data flows the same name.

The properties of a typical CASE tool described so far are mainly designed to support the analysis and design stages of systems development. However, modern tools can support a much greater range of the stages of systems development. More recent CASE tools are making links between the definition, design and production phases by incorporating program generators. These are able to take the process specifications and turn them into working programs. A set of such tools are available to work with ORACLE (see Chapter 6). With facilities like these, it is not surprising that at least one famous British brewery is retraining its programmers as analysts to avoid them being made redundant.

The availability of such tools leads to an important management lesson. Since a CASE tool aims to automate most of the later stages from analysis through to production, it places even more emphasis on the importance of resolving initial soft issues and the high-level systems definition stage. Otherwise, we are using a powerful tool to automate conflict and ambiguity. The emphasis of the future is likely to move away from the mechanics of software towards the management and strategic issues of systems development.

Box 9.2

Whitehall pins IT hopes on partnership

FT

Meg Carter

Concern over how public money is being spent on private sector consultancy for major government information technology projects has highlighted the need for greater professionalism in project management.

Last week's report by the Commons Public Accounts Select Committee urged government to act swiftly to prevent further 'fiascos' stemming from basic project errors. It identified a possible need for greater central coordination and monitoring across all Whitehall departments – a suggestion many civil servants and consultants believe is long overdue.

The government's recent track record in project management has been, to say the least, poor. Last November, the Home Office admitted that 13 of its 17 IT projects were behind schedule or over budget.

Other problems have included those at the Passport Agency, where delays in issuing passports caused major problems last summer. Siemens Business Services, which provided the systems under the government's private finance initiative, is not expected to complete a computer and printing system at the agency's six offices until February 2001, almost two years late.

A project to install a new generation of national insurance computers, undertaken by Andersen Consulting, is having to deal with a backlog of contributions more than two years after the system was meant to be installed. And ICL's Horizon project to automate Post Office Counters and provide a fraud-resistant benefit payment card was three years late by the time it was partially abandoned in May.

Civil servants have blamed computer companies and IT specialists for these delays. In a written explanation, Home Office officials referred to 'revised consultancy costs and staffing levels' delaying a project to upgrade prison phone systems.

The committee has high-lighted problems with government IT projects on 25 occasions during the 1990s, including 14 since Labour came to power in 1997. It claims such failures could jeopardize Labour's 'modernizing government initiative' which aims to make 25 per cent of the public's interaction with government achievable by electronic means by 2002.

Government spending on IT in 1998–99 reached £7bn, with contracts ranging widely in scale and complexity. In view of the huge sums involved and potential disruption to public services, government bodies have been urged to make greater efforts to secure unambiguous contracts with private sector suppliers.

Some consultants have taken advantage of public sector imprecision in commissioning projects, observers admit. While leading firms insist they share common best practice standards, many have distinct ways of doing business. Although top consultancies pride themselves on their expertise and internal systems, not all firms are as efficient as they might be...

'The problems in Whitehall's approach to some of our projects is well-known: poor project definitions, poor project management, poor contract management and poor management of suppliers,' says Mr Timms.

Source: Financial Times, 13 January 2000. Reprinted with permission.

Comment

I couldn't bring myself to go any further with this article from the Financial Times. It contains the same issues that I would have put into the first edition of this book, which appeared in 1994. Given that that edition was based on fairly ordinary experience that dated back to the 1960s, what is still going wrong?

The methodology of Chapter 9 contains a summary of the 1960s to 1900s period of rational thinking about systems development. I would suggest that Ashby's Law, which we covered in Chapter 4, tells us a different story.

Attempts to reduce the complexity of the holistic variety of the systems development process have more to do with reassuring ideas of strategic management control than recognizing that learning and acceptance of uncertainty are part of control.

The retention of traditional information systems development methodology in this chapter is a recognition of what is still believed in by, and is still relevant to, many systems developers, but I suspect that the networked world we explored in Chapters 3 and 5 is the immediate future.

9.8 | **HUMAN–COMPUTER INTERACTION AND THE HUMAN–COMPUTER INTERFACE**

9.8.1 The changing role of the human–computer relationship in information systems development

If we stand back from the details of the various information systems development methods in this chapter to consider a general picture, it is possible to discern a historical theme. Thus process-oriented methods were the earliest to be developed and object-oriented are the most recent. We then dealt with prototyping, CASE tools and visual programming as some of the latest tools to arrive in the late 1980s.

The important factor that lies behind this historical sequence is the change in the role of the computer. The early forms of process-oriented systems development like de Marco (1979) made clear distinctions between the *logical* and *physical* systems in analysis and design (Section 8.3.3). This was because design and implementation could be quite clearly distinguished as stages in systems development. The design was something specified *separately* from the computer using such tools as diagrams on paper. In the mid-1970s, much programming still took the form of handwritten documents that were later encoded.

The main change that has taken place in the last ten years is the involvement of the computer as *facility* for systems development (Section 7.4.2), not just a potential component of the system once it has been implemented. The idea of using CASE tools to automate the development process was the first step forward. Instead of drawing diagrams on paper or working out data models by filling out forms, this could now be done on the computer. The advantage was not just replacing paper with computer screens or filing cabinets with disks; a CASE tool could also check for consistency and co-ordinate the various components of the development process. But notice that this improvement still left design and implementation as two separate things: the computer was helping the human to produce a design, not actually to implement the new system. The next stage was therefore to produce programs that could convert the design produced by the CASE tool into a working software implementation.

It was at this point that an important change took place in the nature of the human–computer relationship. Why use a computer to help develop a separate design which the computer then has to implement? This may have been logical in the days when the user knew little about computers. At that time it was sensible for the systems developer to help the user to define their needs away from the computer. Once agreed, a design that met these needs could then be implemented by the specialists. But if the user could actually try out ideas directly on the computer system, using easily understood graphics instead of complex computer code, there would be less need for a systems developer to help translate the user's ideas into practice.

It was the advent of *visual programming* linked to *object orientation* and *prototyping* that brought about this final change. Software such as Microsoft Visual Basic makes it possible for the potential user to be directly involved in the *creation*, not just the design, of such outputs as screen presentations, menus or print-outs directly in the Windows environment in which they will be used. In such a situation, there is a blurring of the logical and physical requirement concepts, as well as of the developer–client roles (Section 7.4). Essentially *sequential* models of systems development like Figure 8.6 are not the best way of describing what goes on in such circumstances. Instead, an interactive model like Figure 8.4 is more appropriate. Here we see the same type of activities as before, but a much less of a sequence. The model in Figure 8.4 could be seen as Figure 8.6 in conditions where a high degree of *iteration* has finally removed any significant degree of sequence.

This new relationship brings out the importance of the *interface* between the computer and the human users. Human users can *interact* with the computer through such means as:

- entering commands and responding to dialogues;
- navigating menus;
- adopting ready-made templates, spreadsheets and form layouts;
- manipulation of graphical, and other toolbox components.

These examples all refer to visual, screen-based communication between human and computer via keyboard and mouse, but speech and other media are already becoming available. The central issue, however, is that success in information systems development is depending more and more on successful direct interaction between human and computer through the human–computer interface. The acronym *HCI* is frequently used to refer to *human–computer interaction* through the human–computer interface.

9.8.2 Human aspects of HCI

When we use the term 'human' in the context of HCI, we are referring a rich range of situations. One way of making sense of the different forms of human activity involved in HCI is that of Preece (1994). She identifies:

- cognitive psychology
- social knowledge
- organizational knowledge

as sources of understanding how human beings interact with computers.

Cognitive psychology can help us to improve the workings of the human–computer interface in three particular ways:

1 By correctly *assessing* what humans can, and cannot, be expected to do.
2 By giving a greater *understanding* of why humans fail to deal with some kinds of problem.
3 By supplying models, methods and tools that *enable* human beings through appropriately built interfaces.

Assessing what humans can do first requires us to identify what sorts of activity the word 'do' refers to. In the HCI context the most important of these are:

- perception, especially visual perception, of what is represented by the computer system;
- attention to, and memory of, what is presented;
- understanding and knowledge of what is presented, by the use of model and metaphor.

The identification of *social knowledge* as an aspect of HCI recognizes that human beings interact with computers as groups as well as at an individual level. This will include group interaction with a computer system, like a team using a common piece of software, or individuals becoming a group through their interaction via the software. A popular example of the latter would be discussion groups on the Internet.

The questions we need to answer in order to promote social knowledge are:

1 What is the social context?
2 How do people work together?

Organizational knowledge refers to the formal conditions in which individual human beings come together as a social group. The rules, job titles, responsibilities and other aspects of being an employee, member or other component of a formal system will affect what kind of human–computer interface we have to deal with.

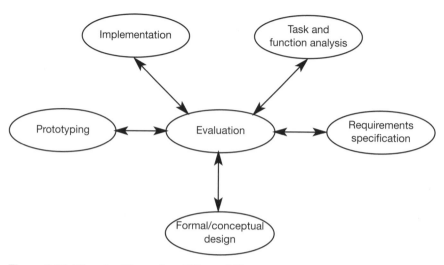

Figure 9.31 The star life cycle of Hix and Hartson
The central role of evaluation shows the heuristic and empirical nature of this approach.
Source: Hix, D. and Hartston, H.R. (1985) *Developing User Interfaces: Ensuring Usability through Product and Process*, Wiley, New York.

Key words

Abstraction	Existing system	Physical system
Action diagram	Failure	Primary task
Analysis	Failure driven	Problem
Approach	Feasibility study	Process orientation
Aspiration driven	HCI, human–computer	Project debriefing
Bottom-up	interaction	Prototyping
Business analysis	Implementation	Pseudo-code
C++	Inheritance	Relevant system
Case tool	Innovative method	Rich picture
CATWOE	Instantiation	Root definition
Class	Issue	Sociotechnical system
CLOS	Iteration	Soft systems methodology
Conceptual model	JSD, Jackson systems	Specification
Conceptual world	development	SSADM
Containing relationship	JSP, Jackson structured	State vector
Data dictionary	programming	Structure orientation
Data flow diagram	LISP	Structured English
Data stream	Logical system	Structured method
Data structure diagram	Maintenance	Systems life cycle
Decomposition diagram	Meliorist model	Technique
Deliverable	Mess	Tool
Derivative method	Meta-class	Top down
Design	Method	Using hierarchy
Desired system	Methodology	Using relationship
Encapsulation	Modularity	WIMP
Entity life history	Object	
Entity–action step	Object orientation	

1 We saw in Section 9.1 that SSM is a broad systems method applicable to a wider field than information systems development. What other broad systems methodologies are available? How might they be classified? Can they be used in conjunction with specific information systems methods? Try Flood & Jackson (1991), Wilson (1990), Wolstenholme (1990) and Roberts et al. (1983), as references.

2 Are all systems-based methods coercive? Try Flood and Jackson (1991).

3 In Section 9.3 we used the analogy of building a house to explain the stages of information systems development. In RQ 9.5 we drew an analogy between object-oriented approaches to information systems development and the use of hierarchical classification of products for manufacture. Is systems development just a particular form of a manufacturing or production system? What differentiates systems development from any other form of development? Can other analogies be used to enrich development methodology?

4 I gave some students the task of developing a registration system for a specialist sheep breed society. Students soon realized that any such system could then be adapted for any breed of sheep with hardly any modifications. Small modifications could then extend it for any farm animal, racehorse, pedigree dogs, etc. Choose an established and apparently specialist system such as car registration and consider how it might be broadened in its application with minimum modification. (You may choose to use the principles of object orientation.)

5 I stated in Section 8.5 that SSADM was at the end of an established line of methodological development. What are the origins and ancestry of SSADM? What changes have been made to it?

6 'All professions are conspiracies against the laity' (George Bernard Shaw, *The Doctor's Dilemma*). Can this be asserted about professionals in the field of computerized information systems development? Is it a big issue? What remedies are available?

7 Can the analogy of systems development with product manufacture tells us what changes are likely to occur in systems development methods? Will there be a 'Henry Ford' for systems development? Will an appropriate/intermediate information technology movement arise? Will there be a violent information systems Luddite movement?

8 Is there a case for an official standard for graphical user interface iconic symbols? What principles would you use to devise such a system?

9 'Computer programmers are a dying breed.' Discuss.

10 What are the arguments for and against modifying or redesigning business processes in order to exploit information and communications technology systems?

Feedback on review questions

RQ 9.1 We first recall from Chapter 3 that it is not the presence of human components that makes something holistic. Rather it is the presence of emergent properties that show the whole to be more than the sum of its parts. To say that failure is 'therefore' holistic just because humans are involved is incorrect.

However, I think that failure is a holistic phenomenon in its true sense, since failure itself is an emergent property. If we think of any failure, it is inevitably the result of at least two contributory components coming together. The failure of the system at Technoturbines came about not only because of the workforce were lazy about making the correct entries, but also because supervision allowed them to get away with it. In control systems terms, environmental disturbances alone do not make failures. This also requires the absence of effective feedback and corrective actuation or knowledge of goals. In the Technoturbines case, these would be represented by poor supervision and poor training respectively.

RQ 9.2 There is no clear definition of the problem. Is it a dog problem or an owner problem? Is there any problem at all, or is it a media invention?

The question of boundary and separation is then blurred by these soft issues. If there is a health problem, then the vets ought to be involved. If it involves money, then we perhaps we are into local government finance. Questions like these raise issues of responsibility.

As to information, until we can decide on such questions as whether it is owners or dogs, health, danger or media hype, the information we ought to be seeking is also debatable.

What would a solution look like? If we could agree what the problem was, or whether there is a problem, we might be able to answer that, but for the moment any description eludes us.

RQ 9.3 There are both high-level themes and more specific issues. We can see general themes like fear, hysteria and sentimentality, as well as more specific issues like fouling footpaths, attacks by dogs, incidence of various diseases or the number and identity of dogs.

Since we are concerned with a soft, messy problem, it is not surprising that there is no 'correct' list of themes.

RQ 9.4 In terms of Section 3.4, many practically applied models like the signalling example make use of iconic and analogue modelling. Systems development symbolic models, and particularly diagrams, tend to dominate. Note that, as we saw in Section 3.4 also, many so-called icons used in graphical user interfaces are symbolic models.

RQ 9.5 All cupboards (as opposed to some other class of furniture) inherit the property of having a container unit. Within the class of cupboards, members of the subclass of standing cupboards inherit the property of having four feet, and so on.

Note that the production system of Carry-Out Cupboards is using the concepts of classification to simplify its production of cupboards for the same reasons of principle that object orientation uses them to simplify information systems development.

References/bibliography

Ashworth, C. and Goodland, M. (1990). *SSADM: A Practical Approach*. McGraw-Hill, New York.

Avison, D.E. and Fitzgerald, G. (1988). *Information Systems Development*. Blackwell Scientific, Oxford.

Avison, D.E. and Harper, T.W. (1990). *Multiview*. Blackwell Scientific, Oxford.

Birrell, N.D. and Ould, M.A. (1988). *A Practical Handbook for Software Development*. Cambridge University Press, Cambridge.

Blair, G. Gallagher, J., Hutchison, D. and Shepherd, D. (1991). *Object-oriented Languages, Systems and Applications*. Halsted Press, New York.

Booch, G. (1991). *Object Oriented Design*. Benjamin/Cummings, Redwood, CA.

Bulow, I. von. (1989). 'The Bounding of a Problem Situation and the Concept of a System's Boundary in Soft Systems Methodology.' *Journal of Applied Systems Analysis*. 16, 35–41.

Checkland, P.B. (1981). *Systems Thinking, Systems Practice*. Wiley, New York.

Checkland, P.B. and Scholes, J. (1990). *Soft Systems Methodology in Action*. Wiley, New York.

Crinnion, J. (1991). *Evolutionary Systems Development*. Pitman Publishing, London.

Cutts, G. (1987). *Structured Systems Analysis and Design Methodology*. Paradigm, London.

Cutts, G. (1991). *Structured Systems Analysis and Design Methodology*. Blackwell Scientific, Oxford.

de Marco, T. (1979). *Structured Analysis and Systems Specification*. Prentice-Hall, New York.

Faison, T. (1991) *Borland C++ Object-Oriented Programming*. SAMS, Carmel, IN.

Flood, R.L. and Jackson, M.C. (1991). *Creative Problem Solving*. Wiley, New York.

Flynn, D.J. (1992). *Information Systems Requirements: Determination and Analysis*. McGraw-Hill, New York.

Gane, C. and Sarson, T. (1979). *Structured Systems Analysis*. Prentice-Hall, New York.

Halbert, D. and O'Brian, P. (1988). 'Using Types and Inheritance in Object-Oriented Programming.' *IEEE Software*. 4, 73.

Harry, M.J.S. (1990). *Information and Management Systems*. Pitman Publishing, London.

Jackson, M. (1975). *Principles of Program Design*. Academic Press, London.

Jackson, M. (1983). *System Development*. Prentice-Hall International, New York.

Keene, S.E. (1989). *Object-Orientated Programming in Common LISP*. Addison-Wesley, Reading, MA.

Meyer, B. (1988). *Object-Orientated Software Construction*. Prentice-Hall, New York.

Muevel, A. and Gueguen, T. (1987). *Smalltalk-80*. Macmillan Education, New York.

Mumford, E. (1983). *Designing Participatively*. Manchester Business School.

Page-Jones, M. (1980). *The Practical Guide to Structured Systems Design*. Yourdon Press, New York.

Patching, D. (1990). *Practical Soft Systems Analysis*. Pitman Publishing, London.

Preece, J. (1994) *Human–Computer Interaction*. Addison-Wesley, Wokingham.

Pressman, R.S. (1987). *Software Engineering*. McGraw-Hill, New York.

Roberts, N., Andersen, D.F., Deal, R.M., Garet, M.S. and Schaffer, W.A. (1983). *Introduction to Computer Simulation.* Addison-Wesley, Reading, MA.

Schmucker, K. (1986) *Object-Oriented Programming for the Macintosh.* Hayden, New York.

Shu, N.C. (1988). *Visual Programming.* Van Nostrand Rheinhold, New York.

Sutcliffe, A. (1988). *Jackson System Development.* Prentice-Hall International, New York.

Warnier, J.D. (1974). *Logical Construction of Programs.* Van Nostrand Rheinhold, New York.

Wilson, B. (1990). *Systems: Concepts, Methodologies, and Applications.* Wiley, New York.

Wolstenholme, E.F. (1990). *System Enquiry.* Wiley, New York.

Wood-Harper, A.T., Antill, L. and Avison, D.E. (1985). *Information Systems Definition: The Multiview Approach.* Blackwell Scientific, Oxford.

Yourdon, E. (1990). 'Auld Lang Syne.' *Byte,* 15 (10).

Yourdon, E. and Constantine, L.L. (1978). *Structured Design.* Yourdon Press, New York.

Carry-Out Cupboards

1 Company and product outline

Carry-Out Cupboards designs its products for those who require variety in their choice of cupboards and some related household furniture such as tables, chairs and worktops, but at a reasonable price. Instead of being sold as expensive completed products ready for use, each Carry-Out Cupboards product is sold as a packed kit that can be easily assembled by the customer. The only skill needed is to clip and screw things together according to the instructions supplied.

Carry-Out Cupboards sells its products through a chain of retail outlets (RO). All of these retail outlets are supplied with kits by the central assembly and packing facility (CP) of Carry-Out Cupboards. The CP mainly uses materials and components bought from a range of suppliers to produce the kits, and uses only limited production processing like cutting and finishing off of materials.

When customers come to a retail outlet, they can see catalogues and assembled examples of the products on display. Customers may then buy their own choice of product in kit form to take home and assemble.

At any one, time Carry-Out Cupboards sells up to 12 different surface finish designs. This is done by keeping the basic structure of units and parts the same, but making the products from chipboard 'veneered' with a glue-bonded surface design. (A 'veneer' is a thin skin of wood or other substance with a decorative appearance.) The surface design, colour and other minor details of the product can thus be changed without major production or overall structural upsets.

A particular kit is usually an assembly made up of one or more parts. Each kit is used to make up a particular product like a cupboard, but the products themselves can be variations on a basic idea. Thus cupboards may:

- be freestanding with worktops or hung on the wall;
- have swing or sliding doors;
- have internal shelves or drawers;

or various combinations of these possibilities can make up the different assemblies forming the product range. Figure A1.1 gives an example of how differing combinations and selections of common components can produce six different cupboard types. Combined with six different surface designs, for example, there is the possibility of 36 different cupboards for a range of applications from kitchen to bedroom.

Since Carry-Out Cupboards performs relatively few manufacturing processes of its own, much of the activity at the CP is concerned with assembly and packing of components. All of these components, plus the small proportion of raw materials used in manufacturing processes, have to be ordered from a range of outside suppliers. This situation means that the cost of components represents a relatively high proportion of the final product. Carry-Out Cupboards therefore ensures competitive pricing and reliability of supply by usually

| KITCHEN UNIT TYPES | COMPONENT QUANTITIES | | | | | | | | | | |
	Unit container	Feet	Wall fittings	Single worktops	Door	Full drawers	Half drawers	Slide guides	Hinges	Handles	Inside shelves
STANDING UNIT											
Single –sliding door	1	4	0	1	2	0	0	4	0	2	2
–hinged door	1	4	0	1	2	0	0	0	4	2	2
–two drawer	1	4	0	1	0	1	1	4	0	2	0
–three drawer	1	4	0	1	0	0	3	6	0	3	0
HANGING UNIT											
Single –sliding door	1	0	4	0	2	0	0	4	0	2	2
–hinged door	1	0	4	0	2	0	0	0	4	2	2

Figure A1.1 Details of the breakdown of some Carry-Out Cupboards products
The thinking behind this structure of permutations of common components is explained in the text.

having more than one supplier for each component. The performance of suppliers, in terms of product quality and delivery, is regularly reviewed.

The ROs depend on being able to offer the customer kits off the shelf. They therefore aim to have all kits in the range available from stock, and to be able to obtain easy replenishment from the CP.

The context in which both the CP and the ROs operate means that they are very concerned with various forms of *stock control* as a major subsystem of their central-purpose operations. We saw in Chapter 4, holding stocks is necessary when we wish to *buffer* different patterns of supply and demand or, more generally, *inputs* and *outputs* to a *transformation process*. There are many examples of this in Carry-Out Cupboards, because it makes sense in terms of processing and organization (first and higher-order control) for the following to occur:

- Suppliers deliver their products in particular numbers that reflect the sizes of such things as containers and lorryloads.
- Manufacturing, assembly and packing at the CP do so in batch sizes that reflect the set-up costs to perform a particular operation against the holding costs resulting from long runs of that operation in terms of stock levels.
- Retailers at the ROs hold stocks of all the product range because they cannot control or accurately predict when customers will come to buy which product.

2 Designing stock control systems

There are many different forms of detailed working stock control systems in organizations and business practice, but all of them are based on attempting to answer two questions:

1 *How much* should the actuator make the input to the transformation process to achieve the desired output? For a stock control system, this means 'How much should we order?'
2 *When* should we implement the value of the input to allow for the time taken by the transformation process to achieve the desired outputs? For a stock control system, this means 'When should we place an order?'

These two questions are not independent of each other. Although the purpose of holding stock is to enable different *patterns* of input and output to be co-ordinated, the total inputs and outputs have to be equal in the long-term if they are to balance.

Without such a long-term balance, stock would either eventually run out for good or grow without limit, depending on whether the long-term output exceeded the long-term input or vice versa.

In practice, therefore, the average input, or deliveries, must equal the average output, use or sales. If the average sales of a particular cupboard are 10 per week, then the average delivery rate must be the same. An answer to question 1 above that decided to order in quantities of 20 at a time would therefore lead to delivery orders being placed every two weeks on average. Thus a decision that 'how much' should be 20 would automatically result in 'when' being every two weeks in order that the average demand be met. Similarly, a decision in answer to question 2 above, to order on a regular four weekly basis would require an order size of 40 if the average demand were to be met. In this case, a decision to make the 'when' four weekly automatically resulted in a 'how much' of 40.

Although any stock control has to answer both the questions above, in a situation of a known average demand answering one of the questions automatically answers the other. In practice, therefore, individual stock control systems tend to work on the basis of dealing with one of the two questions above. They focus either on quantity or how much as the criterion for reordering, or else on timing or when to reorder. Figures A1.2 and A1.3 show examples of each approach.

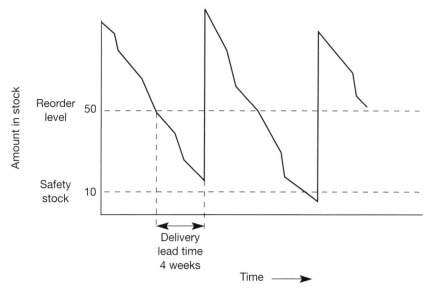

Figure A1.2 Stock control (1): An ROL system
When to reorder is determined by *how much* is in stock.

Figure A1.2 shows the behaviour of a *reorder level* (ROL) system. The amount in stock is shown following a typical 'saw-tooth' shape. The down slopes of the shape show demand depleting the stock. The particular form I have shown in the figure is the situation for stocks of finished products being sold to the customer. Here the curve falls irregularly, reflecting the variation of individual customer demand around the long-term average. For stocks of parts or materials used in production, the down slope would consist of clearer steps, as individual set batch sizes were issued into the manufacturing and assembly process.

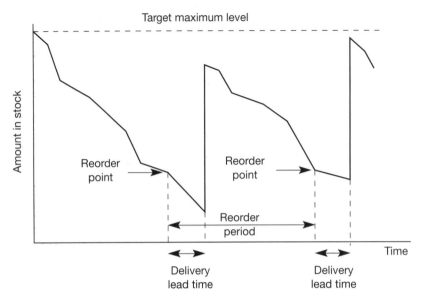

Figure A1.3 Stock control (2): An ROP system
How much to reorder is determined by *when* the order is placed.

Whatever the pattern of stock depletion, this system uses a particular level of stock, called a *reorder level*, as a trigger for reordering. When stock reaches this level, a replenishment order is placed. In all real business situations, it will take time for the order to be processed and the new stock to be delivered, so the reorder level must leave enough in stock to cover the demand for the product over this *lead time*. Since demand for stock will be a *stochastic* (see Chapter 4) figure, the demand used to determine the reorder level will be an estimate of the maximum with which the system wishes to cope.

In the example of Figure 3.2, a lead time of four weeks and a reorder level of 50 implies that Carry-Out Cupboards doesn't think it is worth trying to cope with a demand in excess of an average of 12.5 packs per week at a particular RO.

Most of the time, however, the reordering of stock has only to cope with a demand closer to the average. The *mininum* or *buffer* level shown in Figure 3.2 and A1.2 represents the lowest level that the stock would be expected to reach on average. Any occasion when the stock fell below this level could indicate an above-average demand or exceptional circumstances such as delayed delivery. Whatever the reason, depletion below this level usually calls for additional action to ensure that restocking takes place before stocks run out altogether.

The characteristics of a *reorder period* (ROP) system are illustrated by Figure A1.3. Again, we see the saw-toothed shape of stock levels as they deplete and are then replenished. The difference here is that the reordering takes place on a regular, periodic basis. The quantity ordered is whatever is needed to 'top up' stocks to a *maximum* level. This is calculated as the level needed to cover the maximum demand expected over the reorder period.

The ROP system makes sense where it is more economic or convenient to have regular deliveries, rather than the irregular pattern generated by an ROL system. This regularity may work in well with batch processing in the information system. If, for example, we carry out stock level checking in co-ordination with doing such things as calculating and updating financial accounts, this may be a convenient time to generate and send off a replenishment order to a supplier. An ROP system makes particular sense where the *cost of checking* is high, since we do not need to keep a *real-time* record of stocks. We can therefore see that the reasons for preferring ROL or ROP systems are example of the issues covering control frequency, which we discussed in Section 4.2.

3 Unstable behaviour in complex stock control systems

Everything we have discussed so far applies to the control of stock at one particular point in the sequence from supplier, through manufacturing and assembly, to retail outlet and sales to customers. Extra issues of *systems behaviour* come into play when designing the co-ordination of the stock held at different points along the sequence.

The old way of ordering and stock control at Carry-Out Cupboards is shown in Figure A1.4. The retail outlets each sent a weekly order to the CP, which took a week to process and deliver to the ROs. Thus each retail outlet expected its orders to arrive the week after they had been ordered.

The CP also worked on a weekly basis, both for sending replenishement orders to the ROs and for placing its own orders on its various suppliers of materials and components. The turnround time from suppliers, however, was four weeks, because these were usually manufacturing components, not just assembling and packing like most of the Carry-Out Cupboards operations.

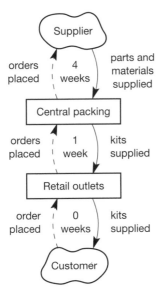

Figure A1.4 A sequential reordering system for Carry-Out Cupboards
Each component of the system operates a need/request and provision/response sequence as in Figure 4.18.

Such a sequential system of processing and stock control systems was inherently unstable. Figure A1.5 gives an example of how such instability could arise. The figures are deliberately simplistic to keep the illustration easy, but the principles they illustrate are important and realistic.

	Retail outlet (RO)				Central packing (CP)			
Week	Demand	Supply	Ordered	Deviation from desired stock level	Demand	Supply	Ordered	Deviation from desired stock level
1	10	10	10	nil	100	100	100	nil
2	11	10	12	−1	120	100	200	−20
3	11	12	11	nil	110	100	70	−30
4	11	11	11	nil	110	100	110	−40
5					110	100	110	−50
6					110	200	110	+40
7					110	70	110	nil
8					110	110	110	nil

Figure A1.5 The effects of a simple disturbance on the system of Figure A1.4
The form of the disturbance and the associated data are simple, but the results illustrate important principles covered in the text.

We start by considering the decision facing an RO manager who has regularly dealt with a demand of 10 for a particular cupboard. When a demand of 11 occurs in week 2, he might carry out one of three actions depending on different assumptions about the significance of the increase in demand:

1 Ignore the rise in demand on the assumption that it is a 'one-off' exception, and continue to reorder 10 per week as in the past. Such an action would leave his stock permanently depleted by one unit. If further increased demands were experienced, this policy would eventually exhaust the stock and make it impossible to fulfil the demand. So this action will only work in a long-term stable market.

2 Reorder 11 on the assumption that the average demand was still 10 but an extra 1 was needed to replenish the stock level. This is acceptable for RO stock control, but does not alter the principles that we will establish on the basis of any assumption of increased orders on the CP, as in action 3.

3 Reorder 12 on the assumption that the average demand has risen to 11. Hence a reorder figure of 12 would be made up of 11 for the anticipated next week's demand, plus 1 to replenish the stock.

Given the danger that action 1 postpones the potential problems associated with eventual changes in the demand, we will consider the effects of taking action 3. As we shall see, any assumption of increased demand will have the same effects in principle as action 3, so action 2 can be seen as being similar but less intensive in its effects.

The CP management has to deal with the orders from all the ROs. If we consider the effect of 10 ROs taking action 3, the CP will find itself faced with a demand that moves from 100 to 120. In real life such exact figures would be unlikely, since different ROs would experience different increases in a rising market, but we can take some particular figures to illustrate the principle of the effects of increased demand.

The CP management is therefore faced with a similar set of potential actions as that of an RO manager. The only difference is that the CP management has to interpret an apparent increase from 100 to 120, rather than an increase from 10 to 11. The logic, however, is the same. If a demand of 100 has gone to 120, with a lead time of four weeks, CP management has to reorder 200. This figure is made up of the old order of 100, plus the 20 increase, and the other four lots of 20 increases that have to be covered until the new order arrives in four weeks' time.

In week 3, however, the total orders received by the CP management drop back to 110. Using the same logic as before, the CP management now finds itself faced with an order that appears excessive in terms of the new assumption of a demand of 110. Allowing for the potential depletion and refurbishment of stock that is 'in the pipeline', an order of 70 should eventually put stock levels back to where they were before the changes in demand.

At this point, Figure A1.5 stops. It has illustrated with simple data the effects of a simple change in the inputs to a sequential stock control system like that of Figure A1.4. These effects are illustrated by Figure A1.6. The important principles that this analysis establishes are:

1 Any complex stock control system in which the components' feedback loops interact sequentially on a demand–response basis is potentially unstable when disturbed.
2 The effects of the disturbance are increased by increased lags in the demand–response between components.
3 Both the complexity and the amplitude of the disturbances increase with increasing numbers of components in the sequence.

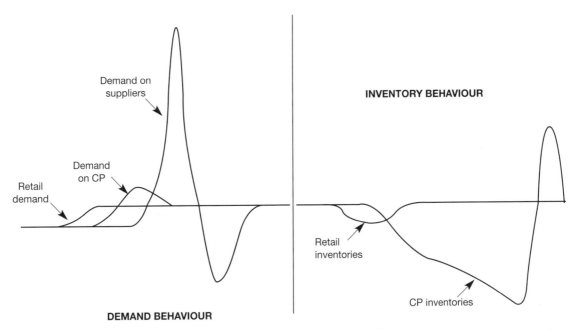

Figure A1.6 Examples of the reaction of the old system of reordering and stock control at Carry-Out Cupboards to a disturbance
An apparently theoretical illustration of a principle that has been further illustrated by a wide range of actual examples in the text. It illustrates we need *supply chain management*.

4 A potential stabilizing role for information systems

We have illustrated some principles that explain potential instability in stock control systems. In fact, any system whose components are individual control systems responding to each other in this sequential way, with lags, is potentially unstable. As we saw in Chapter 4, since all real-life processes take time, lags are inevitable in practice. This means that any real-life system with a demand–response sequence of this type will exhibit the instability features illustrated by our Carry-Out Cupboards example. Since, in turn, virtually all real-life systems will have such a feature in some form, the principles of instability we have just explored are nearly universally applicable.

The key to removing such instability is to remove or at least reduce the lags. A very effective way of doing this is to enable all the component control systems to have access to information at the same time. Thus in our Carry-Out Cupboards example, we would attempt to give the CP and the suppliers direct access to the latest figures on RO demand, without waiting for it to be fed sequentially through the system. The effect of this would be to remove the guesswork in interpreting fluctuating demand figures like the 100–120–110 for the CP, or the horrendous 100–200–70–110 sequence sent to the supplier.

The principle that would enable common and virtually simultaneous access to important information, like that of RO demand in the Carry-Out Cupboards case, is that of information as a common organizational resource. The concept that can deliver this resource to management is that of a database. If, instead of the individual control systems running their own separate systems of physical files and data processing, the whole organization can integrate its information system through a database, great improvements in stability are possible.

Supply chain management software has developed to cope with this problem. Products like those produced by SAP (try www.sap.com) are designed to cover the overall integration of:

● tendering
● procurement
● inventory
● distribution and logistics
● delivery fleet management.

Without the *imposition* of such products, systems thinking also tells us that are strong human reasons for individual RO managers at Carry-Out Cupboards not having any strong wish to share their data with others. Systems like those of SAP bring different problems, however. As in the lead-in case for Chapter 8, there is a conflict between the *variety* and flexibility of local human management dealing with its own special problems, and the benefits of integration. I suspect that you will find that successful implementations of supply chain management are for *low-variety* management systems.

5 Central-purpose subsystem information flows for Carry-Out Cupboards

Customers–marketing

Information to establish what kind of product Carry-Out Cupboards can sell to what kind of customer, where and when. For the product, defined in terms such as function (type of cupboard and components), appearance, finish, quality and price. For the customer, defined in terms like income/social class, sex, age and geography. Trends and forecasts.

Most likely to occur in the form of a professional market research report carried out by the marketing department of Carry-Out Cupboards or from a professional agency.

Marketing–customers

Investigations and requests to potential customers as part of the market research activity. Projecting information of existing products and Carry-Out Cupboards' image.

Verbal interview questions, questionnaires, media stimulation inviting potential customers to communicate their needs and ideas. Example: Competition in DIY magazine to choose 'my idea of a favourite cupboard'. Image through advertising media and actual view of Carry-Out Cupboards given by premises and personnel.

Marketing–sales and order processing

Details of the current product range: what kits are currently being offered, official description, code numbers, price etc. Advanced notice of modifications, deletions and additions. Possible help with sales targets and forecasts.

Catalogues: printed. Product lists: either printed or on computer file. Notification of changes: either a document or could be e-mail.

Sales and order processing–marketing

Sales statistics to enable marketing to monitor and modify its evaluation of the market for the various products offered by Carry-Out Cupboards.

It would most likely be marketing's job to acquire the data and analyse it. In a manual system this would involve a very tiresome physical sifting through documents containing sales data, recording them, and performing the necessary statistical analysis. In a computerized system, programs could be included that would automatically update a file of sales data and provide marketing with a sales analysis, either periodically or on demand. (A statistical package like Minitab could do this.)

Customers–sales and order processing

Orders or enquiries from customers, concerning type, quantity, price, availability, quality and sales conditions.

For Carry-Out Cupboards these will be mostly verbal, as customers place orders in retail outlets. If Carry-Out Cupboards offers a credit card service, the orders could be by phone, e-mail or over a website.

Sales and order processing–customers

Informing the customer whether their order can be fulfilled, with or without modification, or whether it has to be delayed or rejected as confirmation of acceptance or notification of delivery. Also stimulating sales talk.

Since most Carry-Out Cupboards customers come personally to the retail outlets, this is likely initially to be verbal communication, but confirmation of the order as recorded on an order form will either be given to the customer or sent as a delivery note with the goods. A receipt, although mainly a financial document, could fulfil this role in confirming physical collection by customer at RO.

Sales and order processing–finished product inventory

Either enquiries as to product availability or instructions as to the delivery of the order. As far as most customer orders are concerned, these go to those who get the stuff off the shelf and hump it to the customer's car! Where an order is delivered to the customer's address, the information would go on from the lifters and carriers to the van driver.

Sales staff enquiries would probably involve quizzing a printed or screen-based stock record. If stock was available, sales staff at the retail outlets would pass on a filled-in copy of the standard order form, sometimes called a picking list, which would tell helpers or deliverers what to load.

Finished product inventory–sales and order processing

Information about what stocks are available or have been dispatched. The former in response to the customer's original order the latter in response to subsequent enquiry, nagging and complaint both received by finished product inventory via sales and order processing.

The medium for this information flow is likely to be the same as the previous flow. Thus if this flow were a picking list, it could be the same document with the items ticked off or signed. If it involved someone at a Carry-Out Cupboards retail outlet looking at what is physically in stock or at a record (manual or computer) in response to a request, the return of this information would be the flow.

Marketing–design and engineering

A specification of what qualities the product should possess in the context of market research. This could be the results of the market research interpreted by marketing in terms of appearance, finish, quality, price etc. and passed to the design people as a set of detailed instructions. Alternatively, it could be in the form of higher-level concepts like 'convenience' or 'hygenic appearance', which the designers would creatively realize in the form of their own product design. Which it was would depend on whether Carry-Out Cupboards saw marketing as serving design, or the other way around.

Since this flow would probably combine iteratively with the next flow, I suspect it would initially be mainly verbal leading to a final product specification document. The discussions would probably be carefully minuted and would finally centre around detailed concepts revealed next.

Design and engineering–marketing

Proposals by design and engineering to meet the requirements of the previous flow, plus information on Carry-Out Cupboards' productive capability and capacity to produce the concept. Design and engineering may also initiatate proposals for product modification based on production experience.

Verbal feedback as part of the previous iterative discussion. May be a formal minuting if there is distrust between engineering design and marketing, accompanied by designs or prototype/mockup/model. CAD/CAM helps here too.

Design and engineering–production planning and control

All the details of the design of the various cupboard kits produced by Carry-Out Cupboards that are necesssary to enable the kits to be assembled and packed correctly. This will include information on components, methods and machinery used.

Design drawings, parts/component breakdowns, lists of assembly operations. Can be screen or paper based.

Production planning and control–design and engineering

Information on the feasibility and success of working to the instructions issued by design and engineering, as in production to purchasing. This would also include details of quality performance. Design and engineering would use this to build up their experience in judging what could be achieved by production planning and control.

Documented data, manually or computer collected, probably used in connexion with meetings held to discuss strategic production plans.

Sales and order processing–production planning and control

Total orders for each item in the product range over the order period used by Carry-Out Cupboards. Could also include forecasted orders, if Carry-Out Cupboards has learned the lesson of the effect of lags in a process on the control system. Could be a standard reorder quantity if the retail outlets use an ROL stock control system.

Either standard paperwork or electronic data communications, depending on what degree of computerization is at work in Carry-Out Cupboards. The paperwork or order screen used will probably consist of a product table or list, with details of scheduled times and quantities for the kits.

Production planning and control–sales and order processing

Information on the estimated ability, in advance of actual production, to meet the scheduled needs transmitted in the previous flow, or the actual performance of production planning and control in trying to meet the order needs.

For a manual/paperwork system, this could be the original or a duplicate of the product table or list mentioned above, with the extra performance information added. For electronic data communications, the order screen could be added to in a similar fashion. If production was falling behind, both this and the previous flow could take the form of some lively verbal exchanges!

Production planning and control–manufacturing and assembly

A schedule detailing how many of each kit must be assembled and packed by various target dates, plus instructions on assembly and packing methods.

Both manual and computerized systems would normally produce the schedule as a document, although in a computerized system this would also be available on screen. The schedule could be broken down into individual tasks or collections of tasks defined by a job ticket issued to the worker or section of the workforce responsible for its execution, or a separate operations sheet or list is sometimes used in conjunction with the job ticket.

Manufacturing and assembly–production planning and control
Details of actual production performance against the schedule. These would include quantities and dates of completion for the various kits scheduled, plus excuses for failure.

Most likely to be recorded as entries on the original schedule document/screen. Excuses formally encapsulated in quality control reports.

Design and engineering–logistics and supply management
Parts and materials requirements and specification, which includes details of quality standards and also possibly how manufactured. Example: design details of the hinges used in Carry-Out Cupboards' cupboards.

Almost certainly a documented record with drawings and a detailed quality specification, so that standards are clear and can be monitored. Modern CAD/CAM packages could integrate drawings and assembly breakdowns with quality specs.

Logistics and supply management–design and engineering
Details of the availability of products and materials from suppliers, including the quality and delivery performance of suppliers. Could include suggestions for alternatives and new products.

Logistics and supply management will almost certainly have a formal hard-copy/computer file record of these details for existing suppliers, of which design and engineering can be given copies. There are also trade reference books listing suppliers in a particular field. Look in the reference section of a library.

Logistics and supply management–purchasing
Details of suppliers of materials and parts, which materials and parts inventory needs to know about when ordering supplies. Besides details like their addresses and whom to contact, information would also include specifications of what is supplied, order quantities and procedures.

Specification of the product supplied is likely to be held as a document agreed with the supplier, of which both parties have a copy. Details of supply, like reorder quantity or supplier's address, could be on a supplier's file and/or on a stock record. Both of the latter could be screens and print-out for a computer-based system, or paper records for a manual system.

Purchasing–logistics and supply management
Analysis of supplier performance in terms of quality, quantities, costs and lead times.

Sometimes called 'vendor rating', for Carry-Out Cupboards it is most likely to be a combination of informal verbal feedback by purchasing management and an analysis of data extracted from stock and financial records of delivery, quality conformance and payment. These will subsequently be combined in a report with a summary of supplier performance statistics by logistics and supply management.

Production planning and control–purchasing
Similar to flow between sales and order processing and production planning and control, this could be a list of total quantities of material and parts needed to make up the kits actually ordered by the retail outlets, or a list of total quantities of material and parts needed to meet the forecast requirements of the retail outlets.

If the purchasing function in Carry-Out Cupboards is physically separate from production planning and control, the latter would break down quantities of kits (ordered or forecasted) into quantities of material and parts. These would be forwarded as paperwork or via a computer system order screen, and purchasing would use these to generate orders to suppliers.

Purchasing–production planning and control

Notification of the supply of parts and materials against the order schedule generated by the previous flow.

If the purchasing function in Carry-Out Cupboards is physically separate from production planning and control, the latter would inform about the quantities of material and parts delivered and provided (or not!). These would be provided as an updated paperwork list or via a computer system on screen, supplemented by more informal verbal communication at times of crisis.

Purchasing–materials and parts inventory

Enquiries about stock availability. Instructions to purchase (for a reorder level type of stock control system) or purchasing schedules.

This information flow is likely to involve someone at Carry-Out Cupboards wanting to know the contents of a stock record (manual or computer), so the information flow is likely to be some form of manual/electronic/verbal communication.

Materials and parts inventory–purchasing

What is in stock, has been supplied, or details of delivery time and quality conformance.

Since this information flow is likely to involve someone at Carry-Out Cupboards looking at a stock record (manual or computer), the information flow is the visual/verbal communication. However, if instructions are sent for someone else to do it, the medium for the flow of these instructions is likely to be a physical copy or extract from the stock record.

Logistics and supply management–suppliers

For new parts and materials, this could be both invitations to tender to new suppliers and notification of needs to existing suppliers. In either case, requirements specifications, including details of quality standards and also possible methods of manufacture, might be incorporated in the information sent.

Although initial enquiries might be verbal, the contractual nature of the eventual request implies that this would be a formal document, possibly with drawings attached, copies of which would be held by both parties.

Suppliers–logistics and supply management

Tenders, directly communicated information on products, information gained from adverts and other indirect communication.

Tenders and directly communicated information on products are most likely to come from suppliers in written form, possibly fax or e-mail. Information gained from adverts is likely to come via trade magazines or directories. Personal contact through sales reps or visits could result in the use of samples and other forms of visual communication of product qualities.

Purchasing–suppliers

Individual orders for materials and parts sent to the appropriate supplier, giving details of identity, quantity and delivery.

The order might begin as an informal telephone or personal enquiry, but an order form generated by Carry-Out Cupboards would be needed to confirm it.

Suppliers–purchasing

Confirmation of orders placed and/or notification of delivery.

Notice of supply, delivery notes or goods received notes (GRNs) are typical examples.

Limber Marsh Drainage Consortium

1 Introduction

The Limber Marsh Drainage Consortium is a fictitious body, but its background, duties, operations and problems are similar to those of real 'drainage boards' operating under the 1995 Land Drainage Act.

2 Historical background

Much of the land on the East Coast of England from London to East Yorkshire is flat. Until the seventeenth century, most of this flat land was a mixture of wild marsh and slow-flowing rivers. Any agriculture was mainly confined to the grazing of sheep and cattle on the marshes during the summer months when water levels fell and the grass grew.

From the end of the seventeenth century onwards however, various drainage schemes were carried out. Many of these were instigated by the large landowners who sought the profits that came from the major improvements in British agriculture during the eighteenth century. The work was often done by Dutch engineers or used skills acquired from them.

By the late nineteenth century most of this East Coast land was as it is today: fully drained by a complex network of drainage channels (known as dykes) and rerouted rivers. What has changed, however, is the kind of farming carried out. British food needs during the Second World War, developments in agricultural technology, and the effects of British membership of the European Union, have transformed this land into areas of large-scale arable farming.

In the last ten years, the results of another trend have started to appear. The growth in large-scale, capitally intensive arable farming has had a depopulating effect, but this has been counteracted by other factors. Increased British ties with Europe have pushed the 'centre of gravity' of the UK eastwards, with an expansionary effect on ports and the location of industries. The decay of some inner cities has also pushed population out into the countryside. Hence many of the towns and areas of the East Coast have grown in population and wealth. As we shall see below, all these changes have affected the workings of the drainage boards, including the Limber Marsh Drainage Consortium.

3 Contemporary context

The result of the various drainage schemes described above has been to leave much East Coast agriculture, industry and habitation dependent on successful drainage. Yet the word 'drainage' has often been associated with the mundane and amusing. It has overtones associated with sewerage, and popular phrases like 'down the drain', which have nothing to do with the activities of the drainage boards.

Recent developments are removing such ignorant prejudice. Increase in the interest in 'green issues' and publicity on the potential effects of global warming are drawing attention to the possibility of increased risks of flooding for low-lying areas like the East Coast. This concern has revived accounts of 1953, when a combination of wind and tide led to serious flooding in the area, with dramatic damage and death. Serious flooding in the Netherlands in the 1990s, in which people died, reinforced such fears. Then over Easter 1998, the town of Northampton and many areas around it suffered 'the worst floods in 50 years' (*The Times*, 11 April 1998). By September of that year, residents from the Northampton area were demonstrating against the Environment Agency in King's Lynn, Norfolk.

Another green issue has been the kind of agriculture that drainage has encouraged and its effect on wildlife. Before the seventeenth century, the East Coast marshes were a rich environment of birds, fish and flora. Now only the dykes remain as limited habitats for fish and hunting grounds for water birds, in areas dominated by the results of modern arable farming.

Various ecologically conscious political groups are now in place criticizing this situation, with farmers and politicians increasingly sensitive to the criticism.

4 Statutory duties

The Land Drainage Acts of 1991 and 1995 were an attempt to consolidate previous legislation governing the operation of land drainage. They focus on the operational need to avoid the dangers of flooding by containing sections on 'control of watercourses' or 'restoration and improvement of ditches', ditches being the official term for dykes. They also recognize the wider environmental role of drainage by referring to 'duties with respect to the environment and recreation'.

A view of a wider system, of which the drainage boards form a component, would recognize the role of the Environment Agency (EA) and local councils. The EA is concerned with the issues of drainage, pollution and ecology associated with natural rivers, and has powers to intervene in drainage board affairs. The local councils are not only represented on drainage boards, but may also be assigned powers by the EA.

Within this context, however, a drainage board has to carry out the operational and environmental duties above in the area over which it has been granted statutory powers. For the Limber Marsh Drainage Consortium, this area is the Limber marsh itself.

5 Technology

The technology used by drainage boards falls into four general categories:

1 Civil engineering equipment used to create drainage systems and ensure that they work. This would include machines for excavation, clearing out dykes, pumping etc.
2 Surveying and planning equipment used to draw up plans and maintain records. Historically this would be equipment such as theodolites, measuring lines and paper maps. Modern surveying now also uses electronic devices that can accurately locate positions using satellites and computer-aided design (CAD) software that can automatically produce maps and from surveyor's measurements.

3 Conventional business computer systems for maintaining accounts and payment of employees.

4 A computerized *telemetry* system, which enables remote monitoring of water levels and control of pumping. This is done using radio communication and control software, which runs within a Windows environment.

All the information technology systems run on a network, but the telemetry system can also be accessed by senior engineering staff from their laptops.

The Limber Marsh Drainage Consortium is thus well equipped with modern forms of information and communications technology.

6 Finance

Drainage boards are financed by a 'drainage rate' levied on all property in their area. Properties are valued by an official body that is independent of the boards. The boards then set a 'rate', which is a fixed charge for every £'s worth of the property's value:

$$total\ drainage\ charge = property\ value \times drainage\ rate$$

For agricultural land, the charge is collected directly from individual land owners by the board. For residential property, the local council is charged a single sum by the board for the combined value of all the residential properties in its area. The council then recovers this money from individual residential property owners as part of the local Council Tax.

7 Politics

Politics comes into the Limber Marsh Drainage Consortium with both a big and a small *p*. Each kind of politics stems from the way the authority is governed. This is done by a board of elected and nominated members designed to reflect the interests of those who finance its operations. Thus the agricultural landowners are entitled to elect members directly to the board, and the local council may nominate members to represent the domestic and industrial property owners, who in turn elect the council.

The membership of the board brings in 'small *p*' politics through members directly elected to the board by agricultural landowners. The voting system laid down by the statutory legislation gives power to electors roughly in proportion to the amount of land that they own, but this is only approximate. At a detailed level, owners of small areas of land are disproportionately more powerful. This means that if such owners are determined enough, they can outvote the large 'agribusiness' farmers hectare for hectare.

The membership of the board brings in 'big *p*' party politics through the members nominated by the local council. Where one form of party politics dominates the local council, then the members nominated to the board reflect this party political bias.

In the past, both forms of politics have been low key. Most agricultural landowners have been content to allow well-known figures in the agricultural community to be elected to the board, sometimes unopposed. The local council, in turn, has mainly consisted of independent members with no official party allegiance, so that nominated members were an individualistic, heterogeneous group. However, in the early 1990s the situation began to change.

First, educated middle-class people who moved into the area from the towns and cities began to occupy some of the smaller agricultural holdings. Their views of agriculture were often less commercial than those of the large agribusiness farmers, with more emphasis on opposing high-tech farming and concern for 'the environment'; by which they usually meant more consideration for natural vegetation and wildlife.

Second, many of both the previous and the new population who were hit by the recession and unemployment of the late 1980s and early 1990s began to question both the political and economic effects of the Limber Marsh Drainage Consortium's policies on development and growth. There was an element of 'a plague on both your houses' from some council members, who felt that the agribusiness and the ecological influences on the board were enemies to industrial development.

A particular butt of such criticism was a local ecology group. The group consisted mainly of educated middle-class people. It was set up in 1987 in response to concerns about the effects of modern agriculture on the environment and a belief that the Limber Marsh Drainage Consortium was essentially a tool of the large farmers. Whether they were incoming smallholders, young idealists or retired people, the members of this group were all concerned about pollution or the protection of wildlife. The group has the intention of fielding candidates in board elections.

Another political factor that seemed to creep into the public debate was the concept of privatization. Since so many services provided by official and local government authorities had been put out to contracting private enterprise, the feeling throughout the members of the governing board was that the Limber Marsh Drainage Consortium itself might soon become essentially a subcontracting organization rather than a direct operator in the drainage of East Farthing.

Some thought that the fashion for privatization could work the other way, with the Limber Marsh Drainage Consortium becoming the Limber Marsh Drainage Company, with an obligation to earn more of its income from bidding for private work that would use its special skills and equipment.

A major catalyst for a debate of all these issues was the Cross-link Channel Scheme. This was a proposal to build a new drainage dyke that would connect two of the main channels leading to the sea. As a result, one of the existing main channels would become redundant, and this would leave the beautiful conservation area of South Limber free from the kind of regular maintenance operations that the Limber Marsh Conservation Group considered a threat to wildlife. The agribusiness element was concerned that this would imply that the area was no longer of major agricultural importance, and that conventional farming might eventually be made impossible by the increasing imposition of conservation-based restrictions. The supporters of industrial development were not sure if this meant a victory for the 'no development' conservationists or an opportunity for development.

The main result of the proposal seems to be that drainage is no longer an obscure subject on the Limber Marsh.

MX Marketing

Ben Lister's first encounter with information technology was in 1988, when he met information systems students from a local university. Both he and they attended an introductory talk and demonstration to some local business people in their area. It covered the main features of a typical office microcomputer-based system and included some simple demonstrations of database, wordprocessing and spreadsheet software. An important aspect of the presentation was to caution against the automatic assumption that 'computers were a good thing', regardless of situation or need. The systems students took the initiative to suggest that they were available as a group for more detailed investigations of potential office systems computer applications. They explained that this would be on the basis that they could make tentative recommendations in exchange for an opportunity to apply their skills to a practical problem.

They were subsequently approached by Ben Lister who was present at the demonstration. Ben owned a small merchandising business, which he ran from an office attached to his home and of which he and his wife were the owning partners.

The students made the following notes from initial conversations with Ben:

1 Civic/rural/farm products selling organization, essentially one man (the owner) travelling, exhibiting, visiting and selling.
2 Small office block (extension to private residence) with secretarial support consisting of wife (his business partner) plus temporary, part-time secretary. Use of 24-hour answering machine.
3 Rented storage for products 20 miles away from office. Subcontracted delivery by transport company owner of rented storage.
4 Five categories of product:
   ● GRP/cement containers, troughs, storage tanks.
   ● Drainage materials.
   ● Plastic storage bags, nets etc.
   ● Farm animal feed supplements.
   ● Crop storage additives.
5 Customers in the hundreds.
6 Turnover in five figures.
7 Cautious about computers: seen too many dusty machines in farm offices.
8 Main attractions towards computers are wordprocessing and data retrieval for correspondence and ability to produce selected customer lists. Overdue need to produce computerized accounts.

As a result of the report that the students produced, Ben felt confident enough to go ahead with a conventional PC-based office system that served him well until the mid-1990s. By that time, he wanted to update the storage capacity and speed of the equipment, so that he could run more modern accountancy software and improve his printing and scanning abilities.

By 1998, MX Marketing was well set up with a stand-alone system, but Ben began to find that e-mail and access to the Internet could no longer be ignored. Perhaps it was time to go to another business demonstration and find some co-operative university students. After all, Ben couldn't afford consultants, and he knew about salespeople.

Dog registration

Until the late 1980s, I suspect that most people in the UK had not heard of a breed of dog known as a rottweiler. Now, following some highly publicized attacks on children, the name has entered colloquial language to express the concept of aggression and danger.

A recent addition to the gallery of dogs reputed to share these characteristics has been the pit bull terrier. Adverse publicity about this dog in the UK led to the introduction of measures of ownership control and the culling of dangerous or unregistered dogs of the breed. Many dog owners and sympathizers feel that this attitude is not only exaggerated and misleading, but also results in the culling of harmless dogs due to hysterical over-reaction.

These reservations about current legislation on dangerous dogs does not mean that all dog sympathizers are against the concept of registration. Many organizations and individuals who support the interests and welfare of dogs favour the idea of compulsory registration of dog ownership. Their view is that bad dog behaviour is the result of irresponsible owners, and that compulsory registration would help to control ownership and enable convicted irresponsible owners to be banned from keeping dogs at all.

People and organizations holding this opinion cite many examples of how registration of ownership would protect dogs. Breeders of dogs above a certain quantity already have to be registered, but there are some small breeders who exploit bitches by keeping them and their offspring in dirty conditions and do the bare minimum to keep them alive until they become a marketable product. An important example of this market is the breeding of dogs for medical research.

During the economic recession in European agriculture at the end of the 1980s and into the early 1990s, some farmers in Wales identified an opportunty for using their buildings and facilities profitably, by breeding dogs for medical experiments.

Pet shops and dealers have often been too eager to concentrate on the sale of a lovable puppy, without drawing the buyer's attention to the assertion that 'a dog is not just for Christmas: it's for life'.

Professional and official bodies also have views on the issues. Besides the question of welfare, vets are concerned about animal health. Loose or stray dogs represent a potential health threat to both themselves and to humans. Increased international travel and the opening up of free-trade areas have exacerbated this problem. At a more local level, some councils are concerned at the health and safety aspects of footpath fouling and the danger of stray dogs in traffic.

A less common view among official bodies is that if dogs are a popular commodity, they represent a potential source of tax revenue. Registration could bring in income for either local or central government.

Many politicians, knowing dogs to be an emotive issue, wish to avoid the subject of dog registration altogether.

Index